Modern Technology in Foreign Language Education:
Applications and Projects

Edited by Wm. Flint Smith

In Conjunction with the American Council on the Teaching of Foreign Languages

D1417067

National Textbook Company
a division of *NTC Publishing Group* • Lincolnwood, Illinois USA

1991 Printing

Contents

Contributors

Part I: CHAPTER AUTHORS

Introduction

Wm. Flint Smith *(Ph.D., Purdue University)* is Professor of Spanish and Coordinator of the Beginning Spanish Curriculum at Purdue. Editor of *Modern Media in Foreign Language Education: Theory and Implementation* (Lincolnwood, IL: National Textbook Company, 1987), he is a member of ACTFL, AATSP, IALL (International Association of Learning Laboratories), and IFLTA (Indiana).

Chapter 1

Sue E. K. Otto *(Ph.D., University of Iowa)* is Adjunct Assistant Professor in the Department of Spanish and Portuguese and Director of the Language Media Center at the University of Iowa, where she teaches foreign language CAI and directs all of the Center's computer-mediated activities. She is also Technical Coordinator and Spanish Series Editor of PICS (Project for International Communication Studies), for which she develops foreign language video resources and interactive video software, and 1987-89 President of IALL (International Association of Learning Laboratories). Her professional affiliations include AATSP, CALICO, and IALL.

Chapter 2

Charles P. Richardson *(M.A., Ohio University)* is Director of the Language Laboratory and the Language Computer Lab at Ohio University, where he is also Lecturer in Modern Languages and consultant to campuswide media projects. Former Editor for *NALLD Journal,* he is Executive Director of IALL (International Association of Learning Laboratories), and a member of AATG, ACTFL, CALICO, and OFLA (Ohio Foreign Language Association).

Sharon Guinn Scinicariello *(Ph.D., University of North Carolina)* is the Director of Foreign Language Studies at Case Western University in Cleveland, Ohio, and has given numerous workshops on the use of the language laboratory and associated media. She is chairman of the Publications Committee for IALL (International Association of Learning Laboratories) and a member of ACTFL, AATF, MLA, The

Medieval Academy of America, and OFLA (Ohio Foreign Language Association), where she serves on the Committee for Teacher Education and Certification.

Chapter 3

Michael D. Bush, *Maj. U.S. Air Force (Ph.D. in Foreign Language Education and Computer Science, The Ohio State University)* is Deputy for Research and Tenure Associate Professor of French at the U.S. Air Force Academy, Colorado. Former Director of Research in the Department of Foreign Languages at USAFA, he is a member of CALICO and Phi Delta Kappa.

Jill Crotty, *Maj. U.S. Air Force (Ph.D. in Curriculum and Instruction, University of Kansas)* is Director of the Language Learning Center and Tenure Associate Professor of French at the U.S. Air Force Academy. She is also a member of the Interactive Video Special Interest Group for CALICO.

Chapter 4

Janet H. Murray *(Ph.D., Harvard)* is Principal Research Scientist in the Department of Humanities and Director of the Athena Language Learning Project at Massachusetts Institute of Technology (MIT). She is a member of MLA and ACH (Association for Computers and Humanities).

Douglas Morgenstern *(ABD in Hispanic American Literature at Stanford)* is Lecturer in Spanish in the Department of Foreign Languages and Literatures at MIT and principal designer of the Spanish courseware No Recuerdo for the Athena Language Learning Project. His professional affiliations include AATSP and CAAL (Canadian Association of Applied Linguistics).

Gilberte Furstenberg *(Agrégée, University of Lille, France)* is Lecturer in French in the Department of Foreign Languages and Literatures at MIT and pedagogical designer for the French videodisc Direction Paris. She is a member of AATF, CALICO, and MAFLA (Massachusetts Foreign Language Association).

Chapter 5

Gail L. Robinson *(Ph.D., Stanford)* is Executive Director of the Center for Language and Crosscultural Skills (CLCCS) in San Francisco, California, and frequently keynote speaker at conferences around the world, including the 1987 International Conference on Computers in Post-Secondary Learning, Calgary, Canada. Author of books on language learning, she has taught at universities in this country and abroad and was Language Research Specialist for Sony Language Laboratory in Japan in charge of media applications and Senior Research Officer for the New South Wales Department of Education (Australia). Her professional affiliations include ACTFL, CALICO, TESOL, AERA, MLA, and ALA (American Linguistics Association).

Chapter 6

James E. Becker *(M.A., University of Paris, La Sorbonne)* is Associate Professor in the Department of Teaching, Chair of the Modern Language Department in the Malcolm Price Laboratory School at the University of Northern Iowa, and a doctoral candidate in Foreign Language Education, at the Ohio State University. Recipient of a Rockefeller Fellowship and the 1986 IFLA (Iowa Foreign Language Association) Award for Outstanding Foreign Language Educator, he has given many workshops on using CALL and CALL materials. He is also editor of the *Chapter Bulletin* for AATF in Iowa and Associate Editor of the *IFLA Bulletin,* and he serves on the Executive Council for ACTFL and IFLA and the Advisory Council for the Central States Conference.

Chapter 7

Graham D. Davies *(M.A., Queen Mary College, University of London)* is Project Leader of the National Center for Computer-Assisted Language Learning (NCCALL), based in the School of Language Studies at Ealing College of Higher Education, London. Author of CALL software and consultant to numerous projects related to computers in education, he is also Assistant Editor of *ALLC Journal* for the Association for Literary and Linguistic Computing and Editor of *CALLboard,* a newsletter on computer-assisted language learning published by NCCALL.

Part II: (PROJECT AUTHORS)

Project 1

Rick Altman *(Ph.D., Yale University)* is Professor of French and Communication Studies and Co-director and French Series Editor of the Project for International Communication Studies (PICS) at the University of Iowa, Iowa City.

Project 2

Lois Vines *(Ph.D., Georgetown University)* is Associate Professor of French and Graduate Chair of Modern Langauges at Ohio University, Athens.

Project 3

Harry S. Wohlert *(Ph.D., Oklahoma State University)* is Professor and Coordinator of German in the Department of Foreign Languages and Literatures at Oklahoma State University in Stillwater, where he is also Noble Professor for Technology-Enhanced Distance Learning.

Project 4

Beverly D. Eddy *(Ph.D., Indiana University)* is Associate Professor of German and coordinator for the use of telecommunication in language teaching at Dickinson College, Carlisle, Pennsylvania.

Project 5

Randall L. Jones *(Ph.D., Princeton University)* is Professor of German and Director of the Humanities Research Center at Brigham Young University, Provo, Utah.

Project 6

George M. Henry *(M.S., Northern Illinois University)* is a doctoral candidate in Instructional Technology and an Instructor in Computer Science at Northern Illinois University, Dekalb.

John F. Hartmann *(Ph.D., University of Michigan)* is Associate Professor of Foreign Languages and Literature (Thai) at Northern Illinois University, Dekalb.

Patricia B. Henry *(Ph.D., University of Michigan)* is Assistant Professor of Foreign Languages and Literature (Indonesian) at Northern Illinois University, Dekalb.

Project 7

Larrie E. Gale *(Ph.D., University of Utah)* is Associate Professor of Communications and former Director of Research in the David O. McKay Institute at Brigham Young University, Provo, Utah.

Project 8

Miguel Verano, *Maj. U.S. Air Force (Ph.D. in Foreign Language Education, University of Texas)* is Associate Professor of Spanish, Director for Courseware Development, and Chief of the Educational Technology Division for Foreign Languages at the U.S. Air Force Academy.

Project 9

Gladys M. Rivera-La Scala *(Ph.D., University of Pennsylvania)* is Associate Professor of Spanish and French and former Director of the Interactive Video Project at the U.S. Naval Academy, Annapolis, Maryland.

Project 10

Frederick Jensen *(Ph.D., University of Wisconsin)* is Assistant Professor of Spanish and Coordinator of the Spanish Section in the Department of Foreign Languages and Literatures at the University of Idaho, Moscow.

Mary Ann Lyman, *(Ph.D., University of Idaho)* is Assistant Professor and Director of the Five Colleges Foreign Language Resource Center at the University of Massachusetts, Amherst.

Project 11

Joan Rubin *(Ph.D., Yale University),* President of Joan Rubin Associates, Berkeley, California, has taught at the universities of North Carolina, Hawaii, Georgetown, and Tulane.

Project 12

Jerry W. Larson *(Ph.D., University of Minnesota)* is Associate Professor of Spanish and Director of the Humanities Learning Resource Center and Foreign Language Testing at Brigham Young University, Provo, Utah.

Project 13

Patricia Dandonoli *(A.B., Clark University)* is Development and Special Projects Consultant at ACTFL Headquarters, Hastings-on-Hudson, New York.

Project 14

Robert S. Hart *(Ph.D., University of Illinois)* is Assistant Professor of Humanities and Associate Director of the Language Learning Laboratory at the University of Illinois.

Project 15

Robert S. Balas *(Ph.D., University of Wisconsin)* is Professor of French and Coordinator of the Computer Laboratory at Western Washington University, Bellingham.

Project 16

Frank Domínguez *(Ph.D., University of Michigan)* is Associate Professor of Romance Languages and Literatures (Spanish) and Director of the Language Laboratory at the University of North Carolina, Chapel Hill.

Project 17

Dana Paramskas *(Ph.D., Laval University)* is Associate Professor of French and Director of French Studies at the University of Guelph, Guelph, Ontario.

Project 18

Stephen Harroff *(Ph.D., Indiana University)* is Associate Professor of German and former Chair of the Department of Modern Foreign Languages at Indiana University-Purdue University at Fort Wayne, Fort Wayne.

Foreword

Modern Technology in Foreign Language Education is the second of two volumes in the ACTFL Foreign Language Education series devoted exclusively to media. The writings represent a broad spectrum of topics related to educational technology in second-language teaching and research.

In contrast to its companion volume, *Modern Media in Foreign Language Education: Theory and Implementations, Modern Technology* is subtitled "Applications and Projects" and is divided into two principal sections. Part I, Applications, contains chapter-length essays on the language laboratory, television, interactive video, the Athena Language Learning Project, pedagogical research using the computer, popular software for language teaching in the American high school, and an overview of computer-assisted language learning (CALL) in the United Kingdom. Part II, Projects, holds a collection of reports on developmental efforts and comparative studies and on experimental algorithms or prototypical courseware in which a variety of hardware and software are used in second-language teaching and learning.

The reports chosen for *Modern Technology* were selected from many submitted in abstract at the editor's invitation. Their election to this volume is based on contemporaneity and innovation, representativeness of media application, accessibility, and significant impact on the reader. Many other projects undoubtedly would have merited reporting had they come to the attention of the editor or his advisers in time to be considered for the book.

The breadth of languages mentioned in this volume (Chinese, English, French, German, Indonesian, Italian, Japanese, Korean, Latin, Portuguese, Russian, Spanish, Swahili, and Thai) is as varied as the technology described (interactive audio and video, computer-assisted instruction, satellite TV, and distance learning via television and telephone). Equally broad is their range of purpose (drill and practice, games, tutorials, simulations, interactive fiction, sheltered subject-matter teaching, testing, authoring, and text analysis). Noteworthy too is the variety of learning environments represented (from children and adults under teacher supervision to individualized learning at work stations where the software is both teacher and monitor).

Modern Technology is the result of the collective efforts of many individuals, in addition to the authors and contributors. The Advisory Board to the editor (Robert Ariew, University of Arizona; Col. Ruben Cubero, U.S. Air Force Academy; Glyn Holmes, University of Western Ontario; Sue E. K. Otto and James P. Pusack, University of Iowa; Charles P. Richardson, Ohio University; C. Edward Scebold, ACTFL; David Weible, University of Illinois at Chicago) provided invaluable guidance. Grateful appreciation for their support is also accorded the departments of foreign languages at the U.S. Air Force Academy and at Purdue University. Trevor Crain, Carol Gog, Terri Hope, Carolyn Horrall, and Rhonda Woods (Purdue) and Carolyn McDonald (USAFA) helped with the extensive typing and word processing. Berthold Geiss and Capt. Arthur Edmonds (USAFA) provided technical advice. The index was prepared with the help of Kuan-Yi Rose Chang (Purdue).

Modern Technology in Foreign Language Education: A Synopsis

Wm. Flint Smith
Purdue University

The term *technology* means the application of knowledge for practical purposes. The authors in *Modern Technology* present various operations and strategies for language teachers to that end. These ideas and products do not promise better results than teaching languages without technological aids. Rather, the value of their example is in the alternatives they suggest to help teachers and students reach common goals. These strategies and products give teachers yet another set of options to supplement the textbook, workbook, or standard realia. Investigators profit as well from carefully constructed routines that incorporate detailed record-keeping on how students learn a second language. Taken together, the writings in *Modern Technology* provide compelling evidence that the combination of media, materials, and their creative use is a significant force in understanding the language-learning process, and for teaching foreign languages.

Part I: Applications

The expanded role of the language laboratory is the focus of Chapter 1 by Sue Otto, who notes that a new generation of hardware, improved materials, and a new confidence among teachers in media for language teaching have helped to redefine the lab's purpose and function. No longer limited to language teaching, nor to mechanical drills or lock-step exercises, the language laboratory has evolved into a multimedia learning center that can deliver a wide range of audio programs, television materials, and computer coursewear in many disciplines. Moreover, although audio and video

1

software—and especially foreign language television via satellite—and computer-assisted language learning currently hold center stage, the administrative uses of the computer in the language laboratory also play an increasingly important role, especially in the formulation of databases for the management of library holdings and other recordkeeping tasks. Three decades of experience have substantiated the value of the language lab as a practice medium. Otto underscores nevertheless that its success in the computer age depends more than ever on the creative use of appropriate materials, modern and reliable equipment, and on dynamic leadership.

Television in language teaching is the subject of Chapter 2 by Richardson and Scinicariello who relate how TV, like the language laboratory, was introduced into education with expectancies not realized in practice for some time thereafter. Both technologies underwent a lengthy period of experimentation before being accepted as positive adjuncts to the teaching/ learning process. Now, television is more popular than computers in the classroom. Richardson and Scinicariello describe the various standards, formats, and equipment that define television technology (VCR, videodisc, monitors, cameras, satellite systems), paying specific attention to decisions that should affect the selection of materials and their integration into classroom instruction (within the bounds of sound pedagogy and fair use and copyright restrictions). Television, like the language learning laboratory, is here to stay. Teachers and students are comfortable with the medium and understand its use. The opportunities to use television in teaching increase each day thanks to the technology that brings us videos, cable TV, and satellite programming from abroad. The challenge is for the teacher to know the medium and its limitations and to use it intelligently (and legally).

Combining the strengths of the computer and the videodisc (an optical storage environment) is the subject of Chapter 3 by Bush and Crotty. Interactive videodisc (IAV) materials and strategies are relatively new in language teaching, and the medium is still largely experimental. IAV uses the computer's data-processing capabilities to guide and evaluate the student's learning and to generate learner profiles based upon individual responses to CALL lessons. These profiles, in turn, can be used to branch the learner automatically within an IAV lesson in accordance with predetermined performance objectives. The videodisc component of the system (mediated by the computer) is the repository for an enormous number of still or motion graphics (54,000 frames) and audio of all types. The CALL/IAV system demonstrates the expanding role of synthetic video in teaching. Using CALL/ IAV, authors will be able to develop exercises that can be based in a variety of ways upon what the program comes to "know" about each learner. Bush and Crotty offer several suggestions to aid the course writer develop CALL/ IAV lessons in accordance with the tenets of second-language acquisition theory. The authors note the importance of comprehensible input, meaningfulness, etc., but caution that research is still needed to find which activities are profitably accomplished by the interactive system and which can best be left to the teacher. The authors also mention several current projects in which this research is underway.

Design issues and decisions that derive from the use of CALL and CALL/IAV in communication-based language learning are described in Chapter 4 by Murray, Morgenstern, and Furstenberg of the Athena Language Learning Project (ALLP) at MIT. ALLP is developing communication-based exercises and strategies under the rubric LINCS (Language Instruction through Computer-based Software) to shape a new work station medium and learning environment that combines the pseudo-intelligence techniques and knowledge-representation capabilities of the computer with the optical storage capacity of the videodisc. Added to this combination are cleverly designed exercises called "structured conversations" that engage the learner in problem solving both through natural language processing and through the tracking of discourse functions in accordance with the knowledge representation for a specific conversational purpose and setting. At the work stations, students practice listening and reading while interacting with the CALL/IAV materials in simulation. The production side of language is practiced through (1) input that the student types at the keyboard and (2) in conversation with peers that accrues at the work station in cooperative learning and class recitation. One category of prototypical exercise engages the student in conversations with the personae of the computer in order to manipulate objects in a defined space; another inserts the student as the principal protagonist in an interactive narrative whose fiction develops on the basis of progressive learner intervention. In both cases, the exercises are predicated on strategies that effectively engage the learner in practicing the functional aspects of language through creative problem solving. The ALLP initiatives are sure to have a far-reaching influence on technology-aided second-language learning in the decade ahead with respect to the form and function of an integrated work station environment, the development of other examples of innovative, "third-wave" software, and the collection and analysis of data—especially error histories—toward a better understanding of the second language learning process.

The computer as a medium to compare the effectiveness of a variety of pedagogical principles for the presentation and management of instructional materials is one of the topics that Robinson of the Center for Language and Crosscultural Skills (CLCCS) treats in the investigation reported in Chapter 5; the impact of different answer-judging strategies for error feedback is another. This short-term study was designed to isolate factors related to meaningfulness versus form and to compare their contribution to achievement in a highly controlled environment among junior high students of Spanish. The results suggest important guidelines for textbook and CALL courseware authors; they also demonstrate that the cumulative effect of CALL can be significant if the lessons are episodic, personally appealing, and reflect the student's world knowledge, and if the learner can select their thematic content out of personal interest. The study further confirms that effective CALL error feedback guides the student to discovery and problem solving via hints that highlight mistakes rather than through explicit correction. Finally, Robinson counsels that a balance in the degree of student versus computer control in this process is as important as the way these factors are combined with the human element in the classroom. The real challenge is to integrate all of these insights into the total course of instruction.

An overview of the computer and foreign language software in secondary education in the United States is the focus of Chapter 6 by Becker, who reports that despite a proliferation of equipment in high schools and the efforts of a few teachers, CALL has not made significant inroads in high school language teaching. The reasons are familiar—lack of time and shallow interest to become computer literate, insufficient equipment and materials, and lack of training in the pedagogical uses of CALL. Becker presents some first areas of concern for the novice—hardware considerations, criteria for courseware evaluation, and a brief sketch of the five most common types of software and their purpose. The majority of Becker's remarks, however, are given to an overview of a wide range of representative CALL materials— stand-alone, textbook, and course-related software in five languages—and their sources. Equally informative are the word-processing and popular generic software that Becker discusses for creating materials and for record keeping.

In Chapter 7, Davies describes the evolution of CALL in the United Kingdom where software has turned heavily to materials that incorporate graphics and increasingly emphasize group activities over individualized use. Drill programs continue to be popular, but more and more of the software in the UK, judging by the numerous examples Davies offers, require learners to work out individual learning strategies through games and simulations. These programs hold a variety of CALL-controlled activities and are task-rather than form-oriented. Some of them focus on specific structures and vocabulary, but the majority require the learner to develop and apply a range of problem-solving skills. Davies also notes advances in authoring packages for the teacher, and experimentation in the use of word processing to teach writing. Some work is also underway with CALL-integrated speech and interactive video. Davies notes that efforts in all of these areas have been influenced by changes in the public examination system, which have brought about a new concern for the role of the computer in teaching and testing language performance. This concern, in turn, has led to the establishment of a National Center for Computer Assisted Language Learning (NCCALL) in the UK. NCCALL like its U.S. counterpart CALICO (Brigham Young University) serves as a resource center and clearinghouse for CALL materials, produces and evaluates software, and actively engages in courseware applications. NCCALL also publishes a newsletter, *Callboard,* and trains teachers through workshops and seminars.

Part II: Projects

Television and Distance Learning

Foreign language video and programming on satellite television is revolutionizing language teaching. Materials that were once available only on film, slide, or filmstrip are commonplace on videotape and can be used easily in the classroom or language laboratory. The largest challenge for the teacher is locating sources to rent or purchase them and knowing how to exploit them pedagogically to enhance student achievement and attitudes.

PICS (Project for International Communication Studies) at the University of Iowa (Report 1 by Altman) has become the clearinghouse in foreign languages for television standards conversion, subtitling, and production and manipulation of video formats for distribution (by subscription) throughout the United States. A challenging role for PICS is the direction of a consortium of individuals, still in its formative stages, to elaborate these materials for classroom use. In the meantime, PICS represents an important, easily accessible, and inexpensive source of video in several foreign languages.

Media courses taught in French and Spanish for journalism and communications majors at the Ohio University (Report 2 by Vines) draw heavily on video materials from PICS along with foreign television broadcasts intended for native speakers. (Other materials are received directly via satellite or reflect "canned" materials from publishers.) The purpose of these courses is to motivate students to acquire second-language skills that will help them professionally. The six-quarter experience, capped with a practicum—the production of a French language news program recorded on video—has been instrumental in retaining journalism and communications students in foreign language classes beyond the language requirement.

Distance learning is the linking of learners and teachers, in real time, by telephone and telecast via satellite. *German by Satellite* (Report 3 by Wohlert), which emanates from Oklahoma State University, uses live talk-back TV classes taught by an expert for schools whose enrollments are too small to justify hiring a full-time language teacher. The telecasts are supplemented with CALL software that students can use *in situ* to enhance the telecast lessons. Participation requires a subscription fee but is not limited to schools in Oklahoma; rather, any school in the continental United States and Hawaii with a dish antenna can access the beginning German course on Weststar IV Satellite.

Annual, live interactive video telecasts and enhanced audio telecasting between Dickinson University and The University of Bremen (Germany) are yet another example of how technology can bring language students and the target culture together even across continents in real time (Report 4 by Eddy). An important corollary in both the Dickinson and the Oklahoma State projects is the impact these creative uses of technology have had on the learner's attitude toward language study. Students uniformly assert that they learn quickly the real value of studying a second language is crosscultural communication, and this awareness motivates them to try to learn the second language well.

Interactive Audio

Interative audio (IA) has run a somewhat parallel course of development with interactive video, although the technology garners much less attention. Nevertheless, IA can play a useful role in the presentation of comprehension exercises and is an equally strong medium to practice interactive speaking. Moreover, the hardware (and software) to execute IA is considerably less costly than an interactive video system.

Interactive audio can be added to CALL at any time to overcome some of the limitations a standard computer presents with typical foreign language courseware (Report 5 by Jones) but several criteria, including quality of speech needed, speed of access, cost, and flexibility of use, must be kept in mind. A range of equipment choices (from the standard playback cassette recorder with interface to a specially designed random-access tape recorder) await the consumer depending upon the degree of interactivity needed, frequency of use, and budget.

FLIS, The Northern Illinois University Foreign Language Instruction Station for random-access interactive audio (Report 6 by Henry et al.) is a lesson authoring and presentation system that can interface with computer-displayed text and graphics. Using FLIS, any audio segment can be accessed instantly and manipulated (repeated, slowed, etc.) on demand. Henry et al. have used FLIS to author interesting types of interactive lessons, including some called "interactive story" and "hyper-speech" for the teaching of Indonesian and Thai.

Interactive Video

Interactive video (IAV) is a powerful instructional tool because of the density the medium can offer in materials storage and presentation. An interactive video system (with audio) weds the videodisc's enormous capacity for visual display with the microcomputer's vast capability to guide its use. The result is a learning environment that multiplies substantially the number of interactions with lesson materials that can be experienced in a teacher-guided classroom setting.

Two project reports demonstrate the power of interactive video in comparative instructional settings. The first (Report 7 by Gale) traces three phases in the development of IAV materials at Brigham Young University, then offers evidence from a study with high school students of beginning Spanish that supports using personalized interactive video (PIV) or class interactive video (CIV), in that order, over the traditional teacher-directed textbook lesson. In the second report (Report 8 by Verano), lesson content on videodisc was presented in three different formats—linear, segmented (questions introduced between predetermined portions of the text), and in an interactive manner—with achievement and retention favoring U.S. Air Force Academy students who worked with the materials for beginning Spanish in the fullest interactive mode. Interestingly, Gale found that the best students under the traditional mode achieved only as well as the average learner in the interactive mode. Verano also noted that interactive video apparently increased the students' concentration and attention to task. Both investigators reported that learners who used IAV were favorable in their comments about the experience and the medium.

Finding materials for IAV is a major undertaking. PICS has resolved that problem to some degree for video, but the recording and preparing of instructional materials for videodisc is a significant problem and requires a large amount of time and money. As of this writing, videodiscs can only be "read from" but not "written to" or changed once they have been mastered. On the other hand, the computer software that mediates how the materials on the disc are displayed (or how other ancillaries are interfaced—glossaries or other tutorials held on audiocassette or compact disc, for example) is much more amenable to revision, thanks to efficient authorizing systems like CALIS (Duke University Humanities Computing Facility), Delta (University of Pennsylvania, Language Analysis Project), Genesis (Interactive Technologies Corporation), and Quest (Allen Communication) for orthographies, and IconAuthor (AIMTECH Corporation), a unique iconographic authoring environment that allows the coursewriter to (re)program the videodisc for a variety of instructional purposes with relative ease.

The Annapolis Interactive Video Project (Report 9 by Rivera-La Scala) describes efforts to identify and organize visuals for interactive videodisc programming and to integrate them into the language curriculum. Similar efforts are underway at the U.S. Air Force Academy (Part I, Chapter 3, in this volume).

Interactive video with videotape is an alternative to videodisc technology, although the storage capacity and retrieval time of its subsegments are greatly reduced. Nevertheless, materials are plentiful in a videotape format and usually require no change for use in educational programming (within copyright restrictions); all admit some degree of computer mediation. One example for language teaching is described in Survival Spanish Interactive© (Report 10 by Jensen and Lyman) where the way CALL/video materials are integrated into a course of study is revealed to be as important a factor in successfully influencing student attitude and achievement as the scope and content of the software itself.

The Language Learning Disc (Report 11 by Rubin) represents a creative extension of the interactive videodisc medium to learning how to learn a second language. Unique in content and purpose, the LLD and associated software provide the learner insights into the language-learning process, then demonstrate cognitive and sociolinguistic strategies the learner can employ to improve memory and to listen, read, and converse with confidence in another tongue. LLD users can choose a wealth of interactive exercises in as many as twenty languages for practice.

Tests

Using the computer to ascertain a student's level of previous language experience for placement into a parallel curriculum is the subject of S-CAPE: A Computerized Adaptive Placement Exam (Report 12 by Larson). S-CAPE, an individualized test developed and validated at Brigham Young University, is a test bank holding a large number of items previously determined to describe expected learner behavior at levels that reflect the scope and content of the lower division Spanish curriculum at BYU. S-CAPE progressively probes the learner's ability, offering a more difficult item after ones answered correctly and simpler ones after incorrect responses, until a level of constant performance is reached, whereupon the test ceases and the student is "placed" in a remedial, parallel, or continuation course. Larson reports a considerable savings in time (and personnel) using S-CAPE, in addition to reliable and valid placement.

The ACTFL Computerized Adaptive Test of Reading Proficiency (Report 13 by Dandonoli) emulates the ACTFL/ILR Oral Proficiency Interview (OPI) to assign a proficiency rating, but uses the computer as the delivery medium to probe the test taker's ability to read authentic texts. Pilot research with the adaptive testing concept is being done in French, but computerized adaptive tests will be written in other languages too on the basis of templates created for the French version, and as a result of experience gained in its field test.

Teacher Education

CALLIOPE (Computer Assisted Language Learning and Instruction Outreach Project for Education) at the University of Illinois-Urbana (Report 14 by Hart) is designed to teach elementary and high school foreign language teachers to use computer technology for testing or instruction through a series of correlated workshops, intensive summer institutes, and an internship program. Participants in CALLIOPE learn about hardware and software and examine a variety of publisher's programs for the microcomputer; they also receive some training in the use of instructional management courseware and word processing and explore pedagogical applications that touch a wide range of media.

Software

More and more good instructional software packages for language teaching are becoming available as course writers gain sophistication with interactive media and the authoring languages and systems that can guide their use. The reports listed under this heading complement the range of prototypical or experimental courseware mentioned elsewhere (see Becker, Chapter 6, and Davies, Chapter 7, in Part I of this volume).

WestCenter (Report 15 by Balas) at Western Washington University demonstrates the value of a team approach to writing foreign language software. The eleven programs described briefly therein encompass a range of lesson types and purposes for practice in grammar, vocabulary, listening, reading, and problem solving. The software is designed to integrate with class and lab work without being textbook-dependent. Especially noteworthy are the creative integration of sound and images and the use of context within materials organized by semantic fields. The software, which can be used for many languages, also has open architecture for ease of editing in the authoring mode.

Other examples of large-scale team efforts include Spanish MicroTutor (Report 16 by Domínguez) and particularly CLEF (Chapter 17 by Paramskas). Both of these initiatives produced course-length drill and tutorial software that encompass a range of grammar topics, respectively, for Spanish and for French; Both are intended for out-of-class use, thereby freeing class time for the development of communicative skills. The lessons are creative, self-contained, and textbook-independent, and they can be used in any course in which the knowledge of grammar is important. Varied exercise formats, self-tests, feedback, and display of the materials on the screen plus vocabulary organized thematically with on-line glossaries make these tutorials interesting and useful supplements (or alternatives) to the standard textbook.

LITLAB (Report 18 by Harroff), a computer-mediated approach to teaching about literature, demonstrates how an expert (the literary critic) might read and analyze a literary text. The software, designed for a first course in methods of research and literary criticism, uses color-coded steps to lead the student to practice one approach to reading and marking a test. Aside from the instructional purpose of the software, LITLAB also contains several subprograms in the form of note-taking processors to help students gather, record, organize, and report their findings using the same medium.

Conclusion

Technologies change and media evolve; progress is constant. Examples of both in the late 1980s are numerous and compelling: The language laboratory has matured and joined the computer age; the use of video and television in language teaching has become commonplace, and computer-assisted language learning is no longer a curiosity. While the computer is recognized as a valid medium for the presentation and management of courseware as well as a powerful research tool, interactive video and other optical storage media (the most recent technology to attract the attention of both teacher and researcher) add to that power a richness of a wide range of audiovisual stimuli whose application for teaching all aspects of language is limited only by the course writer's imagination. In short, the essays and project reports in *Modern Technology in Foreign Language Education* underscore that modern media have the potential to enrich the learning environment substantially and significantly; the writings further hold many instructional models to emulate, strategies to refine, and a host of materials and media applications worthy of consideration.

PART I
Applications

1

The Language Laboratory in the Computer Age

Sue E. K. Otto
University of Iowa

Introduction

Twenty-five years ago the term "language laboratory" referred to a room equipped with audio recording machines and headsets. In those media-naïve times, the laboratory was acclaimed as the "magic wand" that would revolutionize language learning. Experience has altered this perspective greatly, however, and we now admit that "Le laboratoire de langues n'est plus l'instrument-miracle et unique." (Richterich, 28, p. 18) Nevertheless, through improvements in recorded materials and refinements in the techniques of using audio, the lab has earned a permanent role in foreign language education. At the same time, new technologies have emerged that can support language instruction. For this reason, audio is no longer considered to be the sole component of an effective language-learning laboratory. Many institutions have transformed the traditional audio laboratories into foreign-language-learning centers that offer a variety of international media resources—audio, computer, and video—and assist learners at many levels and in many disciplines. While the term "language laboratory" is still used to refer specifically to audio classroom equipment, in the pages that follow it should be read with a broader definition in mind. Except when modified by the words "audio" or "traditional," which are meant to specify the narrow interpretation (audiotape machines, headphones, teacher console), the denomination "language laboratory" is not distinguished from other terms such as "language resource center," all of which are used interchangeably to designate the multi-media facilities that have evolved to meet the demands of contemporary language teaching and learning. This chapter (1) offers a brief review of the insights gained from early experiences with audio labs, then (2) examines in detail the changing face of the language

13

laboratory in the computer age—its expanded instructional role, its current and emerging technologies, and its personnel.

Reflections on the Past

The generalized use of audio equipment began in the post-Sputnik era; subsequent funding provided by the National Defense Education Act bought many language laboratory installations for colleges and high schools. Conventional language laboratories had a teacher console linked to student booths that were equipped with audiotape machines specially designed for working with recorded materials. Professionals touted the combination of this hardware and the audiolingual method as the solution to the foreign language deficiency in American education (Brooks, 2; Gionet, 7). But the results of using the new audio equipment fell far short of expectations; the machines produced minimal gains for the learner and frustration for uninitiated teachers. It was unrealistic to expect dramatic success instantly; it takes time for materials, techniques, and strategies to evolve around any technology (Capretz, 3).

Unfortunately, language lab technology became associated in the minds of many language teachers with the most mechanical aspects of the audiolingual method. For those practicing ALM, the goal of laboratory work was to provide students with models of native voices and drills in order to internalize pattern structures and foster the ability to respond automatically. The taped materials devised for this purpose centered upon exercises that were passive intellectually, uncontextualized, and boring in format and content. It was actually possible to respond to the drills without thinking or without understanding what was being said. Students and teachers viewed the lab as a place devoted to creating linguistic automatons. The unpleasantness of lab usage via the audiolingual approach was compounded by the drawbacks of a technology in its early stages of development—clumsy tape decks and consoles, uncomfortable headsets, and frequent mechanical breakdowns. As the popularity of ALM waned, so did the use of the language laboratory.

Language learning during the 50s and 60s is frequently remembered in grim scenarios of students herded into rooms, deposited into impersonal niches and turned into parrots, yawning or doodling in boredom, ultimately incapable of producing spontaneous utterances. By the 70s many labs had fallen into disrepair and disuse, apparently doomed like the dinosaurs to fail the test of time. Since then, critics of technology for language learning have admonished us to avoid the mistakes of wasting money on costly equipment when the key to effective language instruction lies in good teachers using better methods toward clear goals (Grittner, 8). The lab was the convenient scapegoat in explaining why, even with a large infusion of money for equipment, desired results were not achieved. Problems that rightfully should have been attributed to deficiencies of the approach or the materials and their underlying theory were blamed primarily on the hardware (Davies, 5, p. 6).

Yet, despite an inauspicious beginning, the language lab has survived, and the experiences of the first decades of language lab use have yielded a number of important insights. High-quality materials that engage the student's mind are essential. As Rivers (29) observes, "Technological wonders cannot assist learning without... a carefully designed and executed language sequence that provides authentic language materials which are interesting enough to retain the student's attention and encourage perseverance" (p. 5). Production of such courseware requires time, resources, imagination, and thoughtful application of pedagogical principles to media.

Expectations concerning the role of the technology must be realistic; tools are used only if they are used approrpiately. Machines do not replace the teacher; they are generally incapable of providing a "complete" language experience because the true give-and-take spontaneity of conversational interaction cannot take place between a person and a machine. Technology does offer, however, real advantages of other kinds. As Dodge (6) notes, technology can increase efficiency in teaching large numbers of students, provide greater diversification of learning activities, and effectively motivate students who live in a technologically developed society (p. 102).

Certain long-standing convictions about valid reasons for using technology in the language laboratory have been sustained, regardless of changes in methodology: it is still important to be exposed individually to a variety of native voices speaking, to practice on pronunciation and listening comprehension skills, and to work in privacy with the best possible acoustic control (Hocking, 13, pp. 13-14).

Current Trends

This chapter contains no blueprints for the ideal language lab in the computer age. Decisions about what to include in an effective lab for any given institution are contingent on a number of factors: (1) the teaching methods the faculty subscribe to, (2) the number of students to be served, (3) the size of the institution, (4) the general availability of resources from other units (computer center, library, video center), and (5) the administration's philosophy on technology and education. However, there are several discernable trends in the kinds of facilities and services that modern language laboratories typically offer.

The traditional audio lab primarily served language students in first- and second-year courses and pronunciation classes. Students were expected to outgrow it, advancing into literature studies and composition and conversation courses that focused on activities outside the lab. As resources broadened to include computers for foreign languages, video, and periodicals, the lab has come to provide more relevant services to language students in upper-level and special-purpose courses. Intensive and extensive work with authentic video documents, for example, can be integrated at many levels of instruction, but it is particularly suitable for meeting the demands of advanced learners. Translation and business language students benefit by using computers because they can work more efficiently on assignments and projects; in addition, they gain experience with computer tools used by professional translators and business people.

The recent hypotheses and movements that have made an impact on current methods of foreign language instruction include Krashen's Second Language Acquisition Theory, Asher's Total Physical Response, the Communicative Approach, the Natural Approach, and the proficiency movement and communicative competence (Oller and Richard-Amato, 23). While some language professionals devote themselves exclusively to the techniques of a single theory or movement, the majority develop an eclectic approach, adopting aspects that suit their pedagogical convictions and teaching styles. In general, collective wisdom dictates eliminating mechanical grammar-oriented practice from the classroom and concentrating on more meaningful activities that can occur only through student-teacher interactions (Blair, 1, p. 7; Hammerly, 10, p. 585). In addition, current theories emphasize development of the receptive skills—particularly listening comprehension—before requiring extensive performance in the productive skills (Winitz, 31). These trends translate into increased reliance on media to support individual learning activities. For teachers who have not totally rejected any kind of repetitive practice of grammar structures and pronunciation, the lab with audio and computer resources remains the ideal setting for drill and practice. Even those who do not believe in the efficacy of mechanical drills support the notion that the lab can provide important sources of listening comprehension materials. For example, Krashen (16) remarks that "Comprehensible books and tapes are the components of the language lab of the future" (p. 21). He notes further, "The language lab should be a place where students can go to get a healthy dose of comprehensible input on topics of their choosing. They should be able to select from a variety of topics and hear and read input at their own levels of competency" (p. 21).

The emergence of programs that cut across curricula has created some significant changes in the use of campus resources. A case in point is the proliferation of international studies curricula that have brought together faculty from a number of disciplines while diversifying the language lab clientele. Names like "international media center" and "humanities resource center" replace the standard "language laboratory" designator to reflect the expanded role of international media in the liberal arts. These centers serve faculty and students from communication studies, journalism, history, political science, and foreign studies programs in addition to language departments. More than ever before, building an archive of varied and easily accessible materials constitutes an important mission for the lab. Foreign media—video, audio, and print—can enhance many areas of study, although each area's intended goals for the same material might be quite different from the other areas'. For example, a German student might work intensively with a news broadcast to understand the language, while a journalism student might well be focused on the style of the broadcast proper. (See Vines, Part II, Report 2, pp. 179-86.)

The metamorphosis of the one-technology language laboratory into a multimedia language-learning center implies a greatly enhanced capability to serve the needs of the independent learner. It seems perfectly feasible to expect, as does Davies (5), that the laboratory should support self-instructional language programs (especially for less commonly taught languages) and that a highly motivated learner can achieve a basic communicative competence through a program of self-study supported by a textbook, audio and video tapes, and the computer (p. 8).

Self-instructional curricula suit the purposes of a number of learners in special circumstances: the professor who is going abroad and wants to acquire some language skills before leaving; the student who comes to the university with a skill level that does not mesh with the courses offered and who needs some remediation or additional work to fit into the program; the person who has taken formal coursework in the distant past and wants to get back in touch with the language.

Finally, self-contained courses aside, a language center with a good media library will naturally attract a number of browsers, who come in to use audio, video, computer, or printed materials for pleasure and enrichment. This kind of informal use convincingly demonstrates the power of media to engage our attention; similarly, it serves to corroborate the belief that media-based instruction can significantly motivate and sustain interest in learning.

Audio Technology

The audio equipment found typically in the language laboratory of the 1980s ranges from regular consumer machines (radios, record players, and tape recorders) to hardware specifically designed to meet the particular needs of language instruction. The shortwave radio, a technology not originally designed for purposes of language instruction, has many advantages as a language-learning tool. It is cheap, portable, and reliable and provides access to an abundance of authentic listening comprehension materials in a variety of languages (Wood, 32). Nevertheless, radio stands as an excellent example of a technology that has not attracted a large following of language teachers. Random exposure to language via any medium is not efficient; it takes a great deal of time and effort to cull out suitable material from the air waves, especially if scheduling is not obtainable. Further time is required to produce support materials and integrate the finished product into the course syllabus. Many labs no doubt provide radios for evening and weekend use by learners eager to get as much exposure as possible to live language. While there is much to be said about the applications and benefits of having these generic audio tools available in the lab, the major focus in this section will be the current state of specialized language laboratory equipment.

Audiotape technology has changed radically since the early days of language laboratories. Reel-to-reel decks with control knobs that clack loudly when rotated, dial-access systems with multiple banks of playback machines, and endless-loop tape cartridges have joined the ranks of wire recorders and record player/headset configurations in the museum of obsolete language laboratory tools. In his monograph on language laboratories, Hocking (13) offered an interesting and detailed account of the evolution of language laboratory technology, describing equipment and applications used in language teaching from the turn of the century through the middle 60s. Two decades later we find language laboratory technology heavily influenced by the computer revolution with its silicon chips and microprocessor-driven functions.

Language Laboratory Consoles

In particular, the teacher consoles available for modern classroom laboratories reflect the impact of microchip technology on lab design. A console with the familiar function of old-style models can be produced as a portable unit about the size of a briefcase. Essentially a control center wired to a number of student booths, the compact console allows the instructor to monitor and communicate with individual students, address the whole class or some portion of it as a group, broadcast programs to all or part of the class, record student responses, and pair students so that they can converse with each other and work together. Typical features of other state-of-the-art consoles are control over automatic high-speed duplication of tapes at student carrels, full remote control of student decks, flexible random pairing or grouping of students, and the capacity to manage simultaneously inputs from as many as sixty-four stations.

Although most consoles bear a definite resemblance to their 60s predecessors, a few models integrate radically different technologies. For example, one manufacturer (Sony) has produced a multi-media system incorporating a microcomputer with a CRT display (a small TV-like screen). Instead of pushing buttons or flipping switches on a panel, the instructor makes selections and controls activities by simply touching one of the choices printed out on the CRT. This system features the capability to (1) sense student responses keyed in on a number pad (suitable for multiple choice, true/false, discrimination tests, etc.), (2) score, record and analyze them, and (3) print out results on a built-in printer. A video projection unit that combines the capabilities of opaque, slide, and overhead projectors can be purchased as an accessory. The student tape deck can be tied to a microcomputer for interactive audio programming. The price tag, even without the projector and interactive audio components, is probably more than most institutions can currently handle. Furthermore, the skeptical consumer of language lab equipment might dismiss a system combining computer, audio, and video as "technical overkill." Yet this multi-media concept represents a real effort on the part of industry to respond to the laboratory needs arising from current methodologies and new perspectives on what functions the lab performs best.

It is now the exception, rather than the rule, that instructors take their classes to the lab and spend the whole period working with taped drills, as was common practice in earlier times. Class time is simply too precious to waste on mechanical tasks that can be done almost as well individually, outside of class with mediated courseware. The perception of valid group use of the lab has shifted toward activities that require close one-on-one interaction with the instructor or that benefit from a controlled environment with greater security, improved audio quality, and flexible grouping of students. Included in these activities are intensive work on improving pronunciation, small group work with dialogues, skits, and question/answer exercises, and testing of listening comprehension and speaking skills. Often these are not and should not be hour-long activities. Multi-media consoles and lab classrooms enable the teacher to move easily from audio-based activities to others focused on video or person-to-person communication without changes in location.

Student Audio Decks

The look, feel, and functions of student tape decks have also changed dramatically in the past twenty years. The old reel-to-reel machines have been replaced by fast, quiet, compact, microprocessor-controlled cassette decks with light-touch controls. Unlike their predecessors, these new machines are reliable and easy to use; and their accompanying headsets are reasonably lightweight and comfortable. Standard features allow moving from function to function with the press of a single button, automatic sentence repetition (quick scanning for the pause before the sentence), the capability of rewinding a short distance corresponding to the length of time a button is pressed (skip-back), automatic resumption of the play mode following skip-back, and function displays that provide graphic confirmation of current machine mode or activity. In addition, manufacturers are developing a variety of innovative options for their decks. One good example is the "visual text" feature (P/H), which provides a way to display text for the student as the tape is playing.

The recording mechanism of a student deck determines how it records the student voice. Decks are available in either half-track or quarter-track format, both of which use regular audiocassettes. Half-track, the standard for many yerars, uses half of the tape surface for the master program and the other half for the student recording. Because the half-track format uses the whole width of the tape during playback of the master program and recording of the student voice, a ninety-minute cassette can accommodate only forty-five minutes of program. When the tape is turned over and played in record mode, the student recording is played backward and the master program gets erased. Since students naturally turn the tape over to work with side 2, accidental obliteration of the master program is a frequent occurrence and is, therefore, one of its major drawbacks. Furthermore, a student recording made in the lab on half-track equipment can be played back only on lab equipment, so teachers who wish to evaluate recordings made by students during practice sessions or tests must come to the lab to do it (lacking half-track playback machines in their homes or offices).

Quarter-track format makes it possible to record master programs on both sides of a cassette, using two tracks for the master program and the remaining two tracks for student recording. Student tapes recorded on quarter-track can be played back on standard equipment outside the lab. But the major advantage of quarter-track technology from the lab's point of view is the considerable savings in the number of cassettes purchased and in the amount of space needed to store them. Many commercially recorded lessons are longer than 45 minutes; therefore, the format can mean storing and handling only one cassette rather than two. Some audio quality is sacrificed in quarter-track format because a narrower track means lower fidelity. But because of continued improvement of the quarter-track technology, the relatively minor loss in audio quality is far outweighed by factors of convenience and practicality.

Portable Labs

For those instructors who do not require that student responses be recorded onto tape, a portable laboratory configuration consisting of a teacher console and headsets for students is a more suitable alternative than a full-function laboratory classroom. If the lab is used only to administer listening comprehension tests to which students respond on paper or to define groups of students working together on oral activities, then expensive recording decks are a waste of money. Portable labs are less expensive than their permanent counterparts by a factor of 4 or 5; they also make it unnecessary to displace the class to the language lab for audio-based work and, thus, may encourage the routine use of audio materials to enhance in-class activities. Portable labs are categorized as wireless or hard-wired. Wireless systems employ headsets that allow communication with the console through a built-in receiver/transmitter; hard-wired systems rely on cabling to connect headphones to the console.

Portable labs have suffered from bad press in the past because of a number of technical problems that persist in many models: size is a problem with some; they are portable in the same sense that a refrigerator is portable. The real interpretation of the term "portablility" is that components are not built into the room. Headsets for wireless models tend to be heavy, can pick up extraneous signals, or suffer from inferior audio fidelity. On the other hand, the hard-wired approach lends itself to spaghetti-like entanglements of cables and cords. Nevertheless, many of these difficulties are being solved by advances in technology. For example, one portable unit on the market (Tandberg) has a briefcase-size console that weighs less than 20 pounds. A series of junction boxes is wired to the console, into which students plug headsets.

The problem of tangled wires can be solved by combining installed components with portable equipment. When junction boxes are installed permanently in the classroom, all the instructor must do is bring in the console and headsets, which can fit on a cart or in a carrying case. The instructor connects the console to the installed wiring with a simple cable and students plug their headsets into the junction boxes to become linked to the console. A combined system like the one described above would be improved greatly by replacing the wired components with lightweight, high-fidelity, wireless headsets. Infrared technology shows promise in meeting these requirements and will perhaps find its way into language laboratories when it becomes less expensive and if sufficient channel separation can be achieved to provide two-way communication with individual students (Moseby, 19).

Individual Audio Carrels

In building a modern installation with audio workstations, few institutions can afford the luxury of spacious private listening rooms for individual audio practice, although they do exist in some laboratories. The cost of equipping an audio carrel with a recording deck and headphones ranges from three hundred to several hundreds of dollars. The costs of each station in the carrels vary similarly, and depend on material and relationship to other carrels (how many shared partitions there are). According to Ramsay (26), a specialist in media systems, facilities, ergonomics, and communications, the optimal size of a work station for individual study has a work surface that is 42" wide and 24" deep. Ramsay comments that narrower carrels do not provide enough room for the student and that wider carrels waste space. Although traditional audio language laboratories and listening rooms were configured with straight rows of carrels saturating the space, modern designs give a higher priority to less confining layouts and more appropriate furnishings to produce a better, more inviting place to work. The layout of the listening facility and any other group of individual lab areas should take into account the special needs of users in wheelchairs. Extra aisle space and an increased work-surface height (31-32" rather than the standard 29") must be planned to accommodate a wheelchair for at least one station. New arrangements of four or six carrels (Figure 1) lessen students' feelings that they have been pigeonholed in long rows. Stations can be constructed to curve around the student to improve privacy. Completed with a comfortable chair, the station provides a pleasant environment for undistracted individual study.

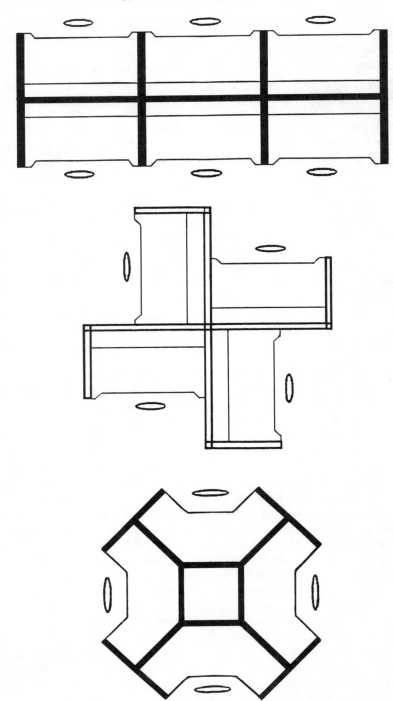

Figure 1. Carrel Configurations.

Whether arranged in clusters or other, more traditional linear patterns, the overall sense of spaciousness—of not crowding listeners together—will dictate the number of work stations a given area will hold. Building many small carrels close together may seem a more efficient use of space; but if students do not have work room for arms, books, and papers and are constantly distracted by traffic and nearby users, they will not feel encouraged to use the lab.

The "Walkman Phenomenon"

On campuses these days, belts and backpacks abound with cassette players connected to students by the ubiquitous earphone. These student-owned machines can be exploited as portable audio labs. Language learners can be released from the bonds of language lab carrels by learning centers or libraries that provide copies of audio programs for use on personal tape players in a variety of disciplines. The advantages of this alternative greatly outweight the disadvantages. For many learners it is psychologically uncomfortable to sit in a carrel. They prefer the flexibility of working where and when they wish or spreading out tasks over a convenient number of short sessions. Some of them are therefore more motivated to listen to the materials repeatedly. Students avoid having to schedule themselves into the open hours of the lab, which is sometimes difficult for those with a heavy course load during the day. Moreover, they do not have to compete with other students for use of laboratory equipment. When students are first assigned to do lab work at the beginning of fall semester, long lines at the listening center typically frustrate a significant number to such a degree that they simply refuse to subject themselves to the experience again.

In an experiment conducted at Harvard (Mueller et al., 20), fifteen students from three parallel sections of beginning French were provided cassette materials for a semester to use at will where and when they chose. Students filed weekly reports on the length and location of their listening sessions and submitted an evaluation of their experiences. The response to the "Walkman Operation" was generally very favorable; four out of five preferred the advantages of the portable alternative—particularly the flexibility of time and place.

Personal players, which are essentially passive, obviously do not constitute the most effective technology for some kinds of language practice where there is an advantage to recording responses and comparing them with the prerecorded native voice, as with phonetic and intonation drills. But it is a well-observed fact that otherwise students seldom take the time to record, play back, and compare their responses with those on the tape, nor are they particularly good at self-correction (Higgins, 12). Many laboratory activities require no more than a playback system: cloze exercises, dictations, multiple-choice comprehension questions, sound-discrimination exercises, and playing texts and dialogues to strengthen listening comprehension skills.

One can debate whether the totally unstructured "Walkman approach" is the best. The distractions of the free environment are likely to be much more disruptive than those encountered in the laboratory. Just being in a laboratory environment where all activities focus on language practice may make it easier for less disciplined learners to stay on task. In addition, some students find that the extra functions on laboratory decks, such as automatic sentence repeat, make listening work easier and more effective.

With few exceptions the lab remains the place where lesson tapes are duplicated. One model for distributing materials is the tape exchange, a program for providing copies of lessons to students for home use. Typically, two blank tapes are needed for each student. Students begin with a copy of the current lesson. When finished, they exchange it for a tape recorded with the next one. The first tape in the meantime is re-recorded with the lesson after that. Such a system can be implemented with a small amount of high-speed cassette duplication equipment (or perhaps in a laboratory classroom with high-speed duplication capability) and unskilled student labor. If the number of students and the financial situation of the lab warrant, an enrollment fee might be charged to defray costs.

A second model is defined by the inexpensive packaged sets of textbook tapes that publishers have produced on cassettes for sale in bookstores. This is an attractive alternative for students who want the flexibility of owning a complete set of tapes. Students can keep or resell them at the end of the course.

Publisher-Produced Audio Materials

The textbook and related materials adopted by a language teacher usually serve as the centerpiece of class instruction, providing most of the exercises and activities for the course. What comes from the publishers has an enormous impact on what is taught and how. For years, textbooks have been sold with at least two standard ancillaries: a workbook of written exercises and a language laboratory program consisting of a set of audiotapes and a student lab manual. One would be hard pressed to find a first- or second-year language textbook published in the last two decades that does not have accompanying taped materials for language laboratory work. Countless hours of inappropriate and uninspired audio exercises derive from the fact that tapes have been viewed as an obligatory supplement to language textbooks, regardless of the book's methodological orientation or the author's interest in and ability to create valid audio materials. A particularly unfortunate case in point was a German grammar review book published with an audio program consisting entirely of translation exercises. The cues were rather lengthy English sentences, and the student was to respond spontaneously during the pause with a translation. Fortunately, such flagrant disregard for methods and media is not characteristic of recent audio programming.

Publishers, realizing that no single approach has won the hearts and minds of the profession, have compensated by offering a variety of texts, all targeting specific groups (e.g., third-year college Spanish, first-year high school French). Some materials reflect a strong focus on a specific approach or theory currently in vogue; others are best described as "eclectic," incorporating the elements from methods that show the most promise for a given topic or activity.

Houghton Mifflin's new German textbook, *Deutsch Natürlich! A Communication-Oriented First Course* (Clausing and Rings, 4), provides an excellent example of one effort to respond to a specific philosophy of language instruction—communicative competence. Special emphasis has been placed on authenticity of language, on contextualization, and on complete integration into the course of all skill-building activities, including the tape-based ones. This orientation has resulted in a tape program with some very interesting differences. The audio activities have not been packaged as a separate program; rather, the main textbook refers directly to them and they, in turn, are made to form the basis for a number of in-class and individual activities. The tapes comprise a series of prose texts, dialogues, listening comprehension exercises, and songs—all of which were recorded in Germany by a variety of native speakers from different regions. No grammar drills have been included. Some of the dialogues are recordings of genuine, unrehearsed conversations taped on the scene and include all the interruptions, pauses, and repetitions common in conversational speech. Other dialogues were produced from unaltered transcriptions of real conversations between native speakers, re-enacted with realistic sound effects and background noise. Whether or not one agrees with this innovative approach, the *Deutsch Natürlich!* audio program represents a healthy trend for language laboratory tapes. In short, materials have been carefully planned and professionally produced; special emphasis has been placed on interest, authenticity, and effectiveness in building communicative skills; and the audio materials have been completely integrated with other components as an essential aspect of the instructional concept.

A cross-section of beginning language textbooks from major publishers reveals several additional discernible trends, regardless of the methodological orientation. Most textbooks and their supplementary programs attempt to cover all the bases in some sense by including more traditional grammar-related structural exercises as well as those associated with the current emphasis on proficiency in communication. Lab activities are frequently combined with workbook exercises under soft cover to afford a system of management for individual work outside of class. There is a greater variety of activities that deal with language in a context, especially those that relate to practicing and testing listening comprehension: cloze exercises, dictations, presentation of a text or dialogue followed by true/false, logical/illogical, multiple-choice, or short-answer comprehension questions. Pronunciation practice still follows familiar formats—dialogue repetition and sound-discrimination exercises. Traditional oral grammar drills (substitution, transformation, etc.) have not disappeared from the program nor have they been improved substantially. Nevertheless, their continued presence is evidence that some still view them as an effective way to provide the repetitive practice necessary to internalize the forms of the language toward automaticity.

Major publishers of language textbooks, responding to the interest in new forms of media, have begun to add computer and video software to the repertoire of materials. Although it is too early to predict the extent of their success, major publishing houses have an important edge over the independent computer and video software vendor since adjunct courseware has been planned with a specific textbook in mind and, thus, comes with recommendations for integrating texts and software into the course curriculum.

Locally Produced Materials

Although production of programs to support a given text has been largely the province of the author and publisher, some language teachers prefer to write courseware themselves. Disappointed by the quality or scope of the commercial product, they consider it a worthy effort to invest time and energy in producing materials that are more interesting and more consistent with their program goals. In a recent project at Ball State University (Indiana), for example, faculty took up the challenge of applying some "first aid" to the lab program in German by reworking commercial language tape programs and producing activities of their own (Johnson and Dvorscak, 15). In an effort to generate a program that was more "interactive, communicative, and true-to-life," the authors streamlined pattern drills to eliminate predictability, alternated between written and oral activities, made extensive use of songs, created new exercises with game and story formats, and experimented with nonstandard cues such as sound effects and pictures to evoke student responses. Not surprisingly, students reacted well to the improvements.

Overhauling an audio program cannot be accomplished in an afternoon, however. The team of Ball State faculty and technicians spent twelve months producing the tapes and accompanying worksheets; but their considerable investment of time and work to plan, develop, and produce the materials resulted in an audio program that suited their needs and objectives precisely.

Special projects like the Ball State initiative need special support both from the administration in the form of faculty release time and from funding of programs to promote research and development. The language laboratory must also be in a position to supply assistance in instructional design as well as technicians, equipment, and the leadership to coordinate a major effort in materials production.

Video Technology

If one technology currently dominates the media spotlight in language instruction, it is video. The language laboratory is faced with the challenge of adapting to the demands that accrue from video-based activities. The use of foreign video in language teaching provokes a number of different responses. Some find video frivolous, pointing out that study is "hard work that should be done with sweat and tears. Education is not a show. If they want a show, let them go to the cinema" (Odum, 21, p. 80). But others feel that video can enhance language learning in a significant way. As Davies (5) comments, "nothing makes a situation as real as seeing it, and television can contextualize language in a way no textbook or even audio tape ever can" (p. 9). (Chapter 2, this volume, and the project reports on television and distance learning, pp. 171-203, offer further information on this topic.)

Most labs have had at least some video equipment for years, used almost exclusively in the classroom as a more flexible version of the film projector. Video cameras for taping class skits and other kinds of presentations have traditionally formed the other facet of video for language learning. In-class video is still a common lab-supported service provided by video equipment on carts or by large-screen projection systems, but this is not the only way the lab can give learners access to video. Teachers have broadened the use of video documents for intensive study by assigning students video-based tasks to be completed outside class.

Video Viewing Stations

Individual study with video can be done in a carrel with the same dimensions as a generous-sized audio booth. Although a video workstation can be equipped for about the same cost as an audio workstation, some aspects of a video operation are considerably more expensive for the lab. For example, playback machines are more complex and more costly to maintain. Commercial video software is much more expensive than audio materials, and videocassettes needed for check-out copies cost more. Duplication costs are higher because more staff hours are required for copying, which is done at normal playing speed, rather than at the high speeds possible in duplicating audio recordings.

Working in a carrel with a headset, video player, and small monitor, the student can watch and repeat segments of the tape at will in a private environment. Facilities for small-group video viewing are also important. A typical group video facility should be configured as a separate room so that students can confer and converse without being constrained by headphones and without bothering other listeners. The small-group viewing room must be large enough to accommodate the video player, a large monitor and seating for up to six students. A small group of students (2-6) watching a videotape can work together to understand and interpret the content. Often students helping each other and discussing what they are viewing produce better results than individuals working alone.

Satellite dishes and cable TV have become common installations on campuses, providing access to video programming in an increasing number of foreign languages. Through subscription fees (for cable) or simple permission arrangements, many cable and satellite broadcasts can be viewed legally from laboratory video carrels and viewing rooms. Considering copyright restrictions, this resource should not be abused in an attempt to build a video archive. Nevertheless, it is an excellent way for students to be exposed to significant amounts of authentic language through video that has not been watered down or tampered with to suit an educational situation. Access to foreign language video programming is probably the best service a lab can offer the advanced student, whose greatest need is to learn to cope with authentic models of real-life speech.

Foreign Television Standards

It is a well-known fact that video suffers from problems of machine-software incompatibility (see also Part I, Chapter 2, this volume). Just when we had VHS, Beta, and U-matic figured out, we are confronted with NTSC (National Television Standards Committee), PAL (Phase Alternation by Line), and SECAM (Séquence de couleurs avec mémoire). NTSC, PAL, and SECAM refer to the major standards or systems used to generate color TV signals; they were developed by the United States, West Germany, and France, respectively. A confusing number of variations of these three systems exist in different countries around the world (Shubin, 30). Frustration joins confusion when it becomes clear that tapes from most foreign countries will not play on American equipment. Incompatibility of standards has victimized many unsuspecting language teachers, who have brought videotapes back from their travels, planning to use them in their language classes. Equipment for conversion of standards costs a great deal of money and commercial conversion fees are high. Therefore, the most direct and most economic approach to software with different standards is to purchase multistandard VCRs and monitors. No self-respecting language laboratory should be without at least one player/monitor combination that handles NTSC, PAL, and SECAM.

Copyright

One of the most confusing and emotional issues facing language laboratories is copyright. Copyright is the legal right to duplicate, distribute, perform, and modify a work such as a book, composition, or film or videotape (Reed and Stanek, 27). Interpretation of the laws and guidelines available for observance of copyright is often clouded by certain dispensations granted to educators for nonprofit instructional use of materials. There is a wide range of opinion regarding what is legal and what is not. What follows is an attempt to comment on and clarify some of the issues involving copyright and the use of copyrighted materials in the language lab. No claims or statements made here should be used to judge the legality of specific practices. Consulting a lawyer is the best way to make sound decisions about copyright matters.

Software (audio, video, and computer) purchased through regular commercial channels almost always carries a clear statement of what restrictions exist in regard to the right to make and distribute copies. Copyright permissions may state that the user has no right to make any copies, the right to make one backup copy, license to make as many copies as necessary for a given site, or rights to make unlimited copies, normally with a stipulation that credit be properly attributed to the originators of the material. In most cases there is little doubt about the copyright restrictions on a given product, at least as far as the private consumer is concerned. The same applies to products sold to institutions by vendors of educational media; agreements and restrictions that accompany these materials are written clearly to address the specific situation of schools and media centers and the way they serve patrons. However, many products marketed for home use are bought by educational institutions, which use and circulate them in ways not covered specifically by the restrictions stated on the copyright notice that accompanies the product. The two options in these cases are to negotiate agreements with the company and to observe fair-use guidelines.

Obtaining permission to duplicate and distribute commercial audio materials, such as textbook series, is a long-standing and familiar practice. Similarly, licensing of computer software is also a reasonably straightforward procedure. It is in the realm of video that many questionable practices arise, specifically in the legal retention of off-air recordings and the circumstances under which copyrighted materials can be used by individuals and groups on media center equipment.

The proliferation of VCRs and satellite dishes has contributed heavily to the temptation to keep videotape copies of off-air programs; there are no labels on blank cassettes warning of possible prosecution for copyright infringement and it is legal to own a satellite dish and watch the signals that it receives. By and large, most of what comes through the air waves, foreign or not, is copyrighted. In some cases copyright clearance for keeping and using copies of broadcasts can be obtained easily—sometimes for no charge, usually for a fee. But even in cases where copyright has not been or cannot be obtained, some allowances have been made for educational use of off-air recordings. In 1981, the "Guidelines for Off-Air Recording of Broadcast Programming for Educational Purposes," written by a committee consisting of representatives of the television industry, performers' unions, and educational organizations, were presented to Congress by Representative Robert W. Kastenmeier (Wisconsin) and published in the *Congressional Record* (9). Generally, these guidelines allow nonprofit educational institutions to record programming to be used in the classroom for ten days; the tape may be kept for a maximum of forty-five days but may be used only for teaching evaluation (to make a decision about the program's value and whether to pursue copyright permission) and not for student use after the first ten days. There are other restrictions regarding how many times the recording can be screened, how many copies can be made, how far in advance the request is made for recording the program, alteration of content, and inclusion of copyright notice. For exact details of these guidelines, as well as ones for the copying and use of books, periodicals, music, and computer software for multiple stations, consult *The Official Fair-Use Guidelines* (22) compiled and published by Copyright Information Services.

Given the effort required to develop supporting instructional materials for video programming, most teachers will be unwilling to invest the time to produce even one vocabulary list or worksheet exercise from a program that will have to be erased after forty-five days. The answer to this lies in buying materials for which copyright clearances have been negotiated and in using off-air sources for extensive listening comprehension practice or foreign-language entertainment rather than for intensive work requiring development of support materials. In cases when off-air recordings are deemed indispensible, copyright clearance should be negotiated.

Legitimacy of the copy aside, there are questions about the showing (performance) of copyrighted materials. Public performance of copyrighted videos requires that a performance license be secured. There are, however, exemptions for educational situations. In his discussion of the Copyright Revision Act of 1976, Miller (18), an expert on copyright issues, outlines the conditions under which educators can fairly use copyrighted videos intended for home use in the course of face-to-face teaching activities. Miller's interpretation of the definitions and provisions of these rights holds that it is legal for a student or group of students to come to a library or media center to view video materials if the performance of the video forms part of the instructional activities of a course. Under these circumstances, the media specialist is considered to be part of the teaching team. Miller suggests, however, that it is an infringement of copyright for libraries (and media centers) to check out videos to individuals to watch at their own initiative on library equipment, citing that this is public performance and is not sheltered by the educators' exemption. Not all copyright experts are as conservative on this issue. The general disagreement on the definition of the term "public" has led some to classify viewing a video by one person or one family at a time as a "private performance" and, therefore, a legal library service (Reed and Stanek, 26). Clearly, the legality of this service needs to be more precisely defined.

Many teachers (and technicians) in foreign languages fail to observe copyright restrictions that involve off-air recording, since ignoring them saves money and time. Experience has taught, albeit erroneously, that the chances of prosecution are rather slim. No lab or media center, however, should be asked to take the risks of performing illegal services.

In the final analysis, everyone's best interests are served when acquisition and copying of language archive materials are handled legally. If educators ever expect to negotiate with producers of materials for agreements that meet their needs and financial resources and if they hope to be able to exchange video-based instructional materials with colleagues, then copyright laws must be respected scrupulously.

Computer Technology

Computers are present in more and more aspects of modern life; the language lab is certainly no exception, taking advantage of instructional as well as administrative applications of computer technology. Many have viewed with dread the addition of computers and computer-assisted instruction to the lab, for the spectre of past "failures" of the language lab cautions them not to embrace computers too optimistically. Some teachers fear that the computer will "replace the language lab of the 60s with the same utopian expectations and probably the same dismal results arising from a lack of interesting [language lab] programs." (Park, 24, p. 54) But any new technology with some promise of application to language learning must go through a period of experimentation, of elaborating methods, materials, and protocols. The best use of the technology is not always intuitively obvious; advantages and limitations can be discovered and proven only with time and testing.

Laboratory Support for Instructional Computing

Computer-assisted language learning (CALL) has been a part of the educational scene now for some time. Computers were hailed as the ideal, endlessly patient drill master (and, therefore, a perfect tool for language study): capable of true individualized programmed instruction with performance-sensitive branching and remediation, able to provide instant diagnostic feedback for student responses (Higgins and Johns, 11; Hope, Taylor, and Pusack, 14). In a frightening rush to repeat the pedagogical mistakes of audio history, early forays into CALL produced programs that suffered from many of the same problems and drawbacks as early taped materials: they were boring, not highly contextualized, not well integrated into the curriculum, and not designed to strengthen any real practical communicative aspect of language—productive or receptive. Everything software authors knew about language pedagogy took a back seat to their view of the machine's strengths and to their level of programming sophistication. (The use of CALL and its place in the foreign language curriculum are topics of Chapters 3-6, and of a majority of the reports in Part II in this book). The following paragraphs will explore the support needed to deliver computer-based materials and the lab's potential role in the development of CALL.

The inclusion of computing (in the form of terminals or microcomputers) in the language laboratory setting is consonant with the traditional view of the lab as a place for individual machine-supported study. Computing equipment does not mix well with other media in laboratory carrels. Audio patrons are bothered by keyboard and printer noise and by the distraction of computer users consulting among themselves. Audio patrons' voices and the noise of their decks starting and stopping, in turn, interfere with the concentration of students doing CALL. Computer work demands a self-contained environment.

Probably the most common configuration of computing facilities in the lab is a designated computing room with terminals or micros arranged on tables. A common rule of thumb is that each station requires a minimum of 25-26 square feet. Sufficient space beside the machines is needed for users to arrange materials they might require for reference during the work session. The computer room should be monitored by staff who can troubleshoot basic equipment problems, answer questions about use of the machines and software, and guard against abuse or theft.

A microcomputer facility has some additional concerns beyond those of a special area equipped with standard terminals. Micros are more complicated than the average terminal, so staff and users need more training to understand the computer's operating system, to care for and handle diskettes, and to troubleshoot problems with multiple components. The software library can either be a collection of diskettes checked out to users or, budget permitting, held within a hard-disk system networked to the computers. Allowing students to check out diskettes is feasible when the software holdings and the number of stations are fairly limited, but shuffling hundreds of diskettes in a facility with many computers is not an effective approach. Easy access to a large program library can be accomplished with a hard disk-drive connected to the micros via a networking system, a configuration which provides as well the only viable avenue for comprehensive recordkeeping for a large number of students. Some programs cannot be transferred to a hard disk because of licensing restrictions or copy-protection; therefore, a diskette checkout system must still be maintained even if the investment in a hard disk and network is made.

Complete, clear instructions ("documentation") for use of the systems and software should be available on site to users. Good documentation will include instructions for operating the equipment, the procedure for using the program, a synopsis of the special commands used by the program, and an index of lessons or exercises. If students are to use micros or computer terminals outside the lab, documentation should be provided in handout form.

Despite the popularly held impression that today's students have a great deal of computer savvy, the chances are remote that they know what CALL is and how it might benefit them in their studies. For this reason, hands-on demonstrations of procedures and materials to students are important, particularly if program use is voluntary. A brief demonstration during the class period will succeed in breaking through barriers of apathy or anxiety, where a thousand words of explanation and encouragement will fail. In any case, not all students instantly love the computer; it strikes some as being too dehumanized and others as too much like "Big Brother." Surprisingly, these people are not always the same ones who criticize the udio lab as being too sterile and mechanical.

Even the most conservative evaluators of CALL will agree that a well-designed computer program with a variety of exercise materials, good error feedback, and student recordkeeping makes the traditional paper-and-pencil workbook obsolete. In light of this, the language lab in the computer age offers a valuable and popular service to students and teachers in the form of the electronic workbook. (See Domínguez and Paramskas, Reports 16 and 17 in Part II of this volume.) In language teaching nothing is less rewarding than evenings spent marking student workbook exercises, knowing that the delay in providing corrective feedback keeps the assignment from really helping the learner. At the University of Iowa, some students in the first-year courses of several foreign language departments use electronic workbooks for assigned homework in lieu of standard paper-and-pencil exercises from the workbook. The computer keeps a complete record of each student's session, including the specific exercises done, the student's scores based on correct responses in one and two attempts, the amount of time spent in completing each exercise, and the date and length of the session. Lab personnel generate weekly reports for individual instructors. Most students (and all instructors) are pleased with this arrangement. It would not work, however, if students did not have good access to the computer program. Besides the computer facility or cluster in the language lab, there are twenty satellite clusters in other campus locations, including the main library and several dormitories. The homework exercises are accessible from any of these clusters.

The development of personnel with special computer expertise is a necessary step in establishing a working computer operation in the lab. The basic responsibilities associated with the routine administration of a computing facility include (1) hiring, training, and supervising monitors; (2) conducting demonstration and orientation sessions for students and faculty; (3) overseeing maintenance of equipment: (4) providing documentation for software and its use; and (5) maintaining and managing the software library.

Computer-Managed Media Libraries

The role of computers in the lab extends beyond instructional applications into important administrative activities. Many standard computer tools can simplify and expedite administrative tasks—word processing, budget management, compiling and representing usage statistics, and scheduling. These tasks alone justify placing computer equipment on the desks of laboratory staff. However, a somewhat more specialized application of computing has far-reaching implications for the language lab, namely, library management by means of computer databases—the electronic files that store a vast amount of information that may be managed and manipulated by a computer program. One can request that the program search for and retrieve quickly and easily specific information from a database. In the past, when the laboratory library consisted primarily of commercial tape series, miscellaneous tapes and records (mostly music), and a few slide and filmstrip packages, the catalog of materials often resided comfortably in the minds of laboratory staff. Potential users of the collection found out what was in the library by personal interrogation: "What do you have in Spanish music?" As language laboratories evolve into language resource or learning centers and the building of significant collections of material becomes a high priority, effective systems to catalog and retrieve information about media holdings become a critical need.

In a library of printed materials, it is still common practice for patrons to peruse the card catalog briefly, go to a particular area in the stacks, and browse through the books to find what specifically suits them. This is not a productive strategy for the nonprint media that fill the libraries of language laboratories, especially if the collection is very large. The computer-managed catalog provides the best option currently available to solve the problem of adequate access to resources. More than just an alphabetized inventory of holdings, the catalog functions as a flexible resource that potentially meets both the needs of the laboratory and the demands of teachers, researchers, or casual browsers. A database catalog can quickly find and display all the catalog entries for German videotapes of news broadcasts, for second-year French pronunciation audio tapes, or for materials in any format pertaining to Spanish music.

Formulating the database is straightforward. The same information that is put on cards is entered into the computer using a database management program: ID number, title, author/artist, technical data (format, length, etc.), production information, subject and genre classification, language, level, contents, and miscellaneous comments. Once keyed into the computer, the information becomes more than a mere replacement of the standard drawers full of catalog cards. A catalog in database form provides multiple benefits: fast, thorough, efficient searches of entries to find materials that suit specific needs; easy generation of printed catalogs designed specifically for individuals or departments; automatic label printing; a management system for check-out materials; and remote access to media library information (if the computer on which the database resides is configured to communicate with terminals or other computers).

Computer-Controlled Media

Audio and video have been familiar language-learning tools for a long time. The search for effective uses of computers in language instruction has engendered a number of hybrid systems that deliver computer-controlled ("interactive") audio and video. Their natural habitat, like other forms of intensive individual work with language materials, is the language laboratory. Their proliferation in modern facilities is no doubt just a matter of time. (See chapter 3 of this volume and reports 5 through 11 on interactive audio and video, Part II, pp. 205-61.)

These hybrids are very much in the experimental stages and are fraught with all the accompanying difficulties that restrict the impact of any new technology. The hardware is expensive and complicated, support staff often lacks sufficient expertise to work with it, and there is a dearth of software for the computer and recordings for the associated audio or video machine. Nevertheless, these realities have not appreciably dampened enthusiasm for the concept of computer-controlled media.

Interactive video has particularly attractive possibilities, even for those who reject other forms of CALL as being mechanical or ineffective. Video— generally accepted as an effective medium for exposing students to authentic, contextualized language experience—can be enhanced significantly when linked to the computer. Among the features provided by the computer are precise, flexible control in playing and replaying any portion of the program, built-in help utilities (glossaries, hints, transcriptions, critical commentaries, etc.), comprehension-checking mechanisms, and usage and performance recordkeeping facilities. In short, computer-controlled video is a very efficient way for a student to work intensively with a video document.

An interactive audio system linking an audio player/recorder to a computer offers many of the same benefits as interactive video: precise control of playing and replaying, on-line help utilities, comprehension-checking, and usage and performance records. It can also add an audio dimension to standard computerized drill and testing applications, thus satisfying those critics who object to the silence of the computer. Voice-recognition devices and speech synthesizers constitute an additional dimension. By the start of the next millenium, students may be able to speak with a computer just like the ones seen in the movies. Considering what real progress has been made in teaching computers to interpret and respond to natural human language, however, conversation with a computer seems very unlikely.

Compared to interactive video, which has captured the imagination of many language professionals, there is little progress being made toward real implementation of interactive audio for language learning purposes. One system (EIS), which has been on the market for nearly a decade, utilizes a 15″ floppy disk with a storage capacity of approximately 23 minutes of audio (either program recordings or student responses). The device provides extremely accurate, flexible random access of recorded material and can respond in less than half a second to instructions to play or record any segment. Although high-priced, the unit is far superior technically to the computer-controllable cassette decks now offered for sale at about half the cost by established manufacturers of language laboratory equipment (Sony; Tandberg). Interactive audio tape decks cannot offer the precise accuracy of the floppy disk system and demonstrate long access times owing to the linear format of materials stored on cassette. Even though advertisements highlight the use of standard audiocassettes, the recording must have significant pauses between segments (one system requires four seconds) to be able to find and play them accurately. This precludes direct use of most commercial tapes, which would have to be edited extensively to include pauses long enough to satisfy the specifications of the system. One of the most serious drawbacks to any of the interactive audio machines is the lack of good attendant computer software—the perennial problems of all computer-based applications. Authoring programs are being developed for interactive audio CALL (see Henry et al., Report 6 in Part II), but this takes time, and the technology has not evolved or stabilized enough to make development of software tools a good risk for major software developers.

Forecasting what kinds of interactive media labs will be using a decade from now would be foolhardy. The appearance of compact disks on the market has prompted many to speculate about their educational potential. The CD-ROM (compact disk read-only memory) has been joined by the CD-I (compact disk interactive), and CD-V (compact disk video) all of which have amazing capacity for information storage and retrieval. The compact disk is a flat, silvery disk that measures about 5″ in diameter and stores up to 540 megabytes (540 million characters) of information (Miller, 17, p. 21). It is hard not to be stunned by the capacity of CD-ROM, especially when those megabytes are described in understandable terms. Pournelle (25), a computer columnist, describes CD-ROM as the medium that has made the Library of the Month Club a potential reality and provides us with these elucidating equivalencies: "Nearly 100 million English words. A quarter of a million pages. A thousand average-sized books. All that on a nearly indestructible disk you can carry in your coat pocket and produce for under $2." The CD-I format offers the same enormous capacity to store digitally encoded data with the additional benefits of built-in programming to retrieve and use the information. While the attributes and advantages of this new tool will probably inspire significant interactive educational projects, it is too early to predict how the technology will evolve or what impact it will ultimately have on language instruction.

Personnel for Operations, Research, and Development ____

Although a great deal of money was invested in equipment in the early days of language laboratories, not much was invested in staff to operate the lab or to provide vigorous leadership for its use. The lab director was usually a language department faculty member who was assigned responsibility for the lab in addition to other duties. The support staff, if there was any at all, consisted of student monitors and a part-time technician to fix the equipment. The primary goal of laboratory personnel was to keep the facilities working and available.

Today's laboratory has a twofold mission: to support routine operations and to engage in research and development. No longer can a draftee with minimal technological expertise and a full teaching load be expected to direct the lab effectively. Neither can the director be a media technician with no background in language instruction. Such an individual is invariably dismissed by faculty members as a "technician that has encroached upon the academic field." (Gionet, 7) The director must be a language professional with significant technical experience, a person who can form strong bonds of collegiality with faculty members in exploring applications of technology to language instruction, and who can effectively administer the laboratory.

Sustaining an effective and vigorous program of operational support for a facility that includes audio, video, and computing equipment and programming can be more than a full-time job. Typical responsibilities include the following: (1) planning the facilities, (2) orienting students and faculty in the use of equipment and programs, (3) training and supervising students who will monitor work areas and check out materials, (4) scheduling equipment and laboratory classrooms, (5) maintaining and replacing the equipment, (6) managing the collection in the media library, (7) providing faculty and students with working copies of materials, and (8) generating documentation to help users operate equipment and access materials. Because continuity is essential to smooth operation, these support services cannot be provided by transient student workers, but rather require a permanent staff with a commitment to the important role of media in language instruction.

As technologies become more varied and complex, lab personnel must assume a more active role in instructing and advising faculty in the use and potential of the new tools at their disposal and in fostering research and development projects that involve media. To do this, the lab staff must be a team of professionals who keep up to date with technological advances, are expert in language instruction, and are in tune with current directions in language teaching methodologies. The director plays a pivotal role, taking the lead in establishing programs to educate faculty, building and shaping the media collection, evaluating new technologies, and initiating pilot projects to develop staff expertise and illustrate possibilities to faculty.

The lab staff must be prepared to reach out to other faculty, who are not inclined or equipped to explore new technologies alone. Offering demonstrations, workshops, and short courses is a good way to encourage faculty interest in media and to develop their knowledge enough to become working partners in using and generating effective media-based instructional materials. The lab must follow through by providing consultation in instructional design, help in selecting and acquiring equipment and materials, a work environment for project participants, assistance in technical areas (e.g., computer programming, recording, and editing), help in piloting the new materials with students, and support in conducting evaluation.

Many projects are strengthened if they are undertaken by a team of faculty members; such teamwork takes advantage of common interests and goals, of complementary backgrounds and expertise that cross narrow departmental boundaries. A busy faculty member, reluctant to direct a large project alone, may be willing to take part in a team endeavor. Laboratory personnel have a unique vantage point because they have contact with members of many departments, and often they are in the best position to help colleagues discover each other and form productive alliances.

Actively promoting research and development activities leads ultimately to participation in writing grant proposals and supporting grant-funded projects that involve media and language instruction. Grants serve to create a framework for production that could not otherwise be carried out, given the ordinary constraints of the academic environment. Development of valid materials takes time—a commodity most faculty do not have in sufficient quantity to devote to large-scale projects. Through grants, faculty members can negotiate release time for sustained intensive work. The language lab benefits through gains in both technology and personnel. Although most grants do not provide for massive purchases of equipment, receiving a grant is an effective means of persuading administrators to spend institutional funds to buy needed project-related equipment. Project experience builds staff expertise, boosting the scope and caliber of their work. Staff may be strengthened in numbers, too, when the demands of grant activities cannot be handled sufficiently by existing personnel. Above all, grants stimulate the growth and improvement of media-based materials that ensure the continued vitality of the language laboratory.

Conclusion

In the mid-80s, language laboratories have been redefined as multi-media learning centers that deliver computer and video services to faculty and students in addition to familiar audio resources. These expanded laboratories provide a variety of services to a broader segment of the academic community, including foreign language departments, international studies programs, and independent learners.

Audio has retained an important role in language learning, although it is no longer the only laboratory medium. Equipment has improved dramatically, as have techniques for using audio programming. Experience with audio has revealed that new technologies must be regarded realistically and given time to evolve. Furthermore, success with hardware is contingent primarily on the development of effective software, a time- and resource-consuming process. In both commercial and locally produced audiotape programs, traditional structural drills have been complemented, if not replaced, by a variety of listening-comprehension and contextualized language activities that are designed to be interesting and challenging for the student. Although learning centers will continue to have permanent full-audio classrooms and individual carrels, portable classroom-labs and programs that provide students with lesson tapes for use on personally owned equipment promote audio work outside the laboratory setting and reduce the number of classrooms and workstations the lab must provide.

The interest in video—particularly foreign TV materials—for language instruction has grown rapidly. Video has wide applications in many levels of language learning and attracts more advanced learners to the laboratory. The laboratory supports video-based learning by providing facilities for individual, small-group, and classroom work as well as access to broadcast programming (via satellite and cable) and prerecorded tapes. Problems of incompatibility with foreign television standards and with copyright matters are solvable and do not significantly hinder progress in using video in the classroom or the lab.

The computer is a powerful tool for the language laboratory. Computer-assisted language learning fits naturally into the language lab, which delivers other kinds of media for individual study as well. Laboratory support for CALL includes maintaining computer workstations, providing program documentation, and introducing students to the machines and materials. Computer-controlled audio and video show great promise for enhancing the effectiveness of these media for intensive language work. Computers can also benefit the laboratory operation in management of the collection and routine administrative tasks.

New technologies have placed new demands on language laboratory personnel. Directing the operations and development of a multi-media center requires a professional staff with expertise in both language pedagogy and the technical aspects of the equipment. They, in turn, must collaborate closely with faculty members in exploring promising new instructional technologies and developing media-based materials vital in building strong laboratory programs. In taking an aggressive role in research and development, language laboratory personnel will ultimately fulfill their potential to become important and respected partners in foreign language instruction.

References, The Language Laboratory in the Computer Age

1. Blair, Robert W. *Innovative Approaches to Language Teaching.* Rowley, MA: Newbury House, 1982.

2. Brooks, Nelson. *Language and Language Learning.* New York: Harcourt, Brace & World, 1960.

3. Capretz, Pierre. "The Language Laboratory: A Relic of the Past or the Solution to the Future?" *NALLD Journal* 4, 1 (1969):32-42.

4. Clausing, Gerhard, and Lana Rings. *Deutsch Natürlich! A Communication-Oriented First Course.* Boston: Houghton Mifflin, 1986.

5. Davies, Norman F. "Foreign/Second Language Education and Technology in the Future." *NALLD Journal* 16, 3/4 (1982):5-14.

6. Dodge, James W. "Educational Technology," pp. 99-119 in Thomas H. Geno, ed., *Our Profession: Present Status and Future Directions.* Report of the Northeast Conference on the Teaching of Foreign Languages. Middlebury, VT: The Northeast Conference, 1980.

7. Gionet, Arthur J. "A Challenge to Language Learning Directors." *NALLD Journal* 9, 3 (1975):8-13.

8. Grittner, Frank. *Teaching Foreign Languages.* Second edition. New York: Harper & Row, 1977.

9. "Guidelines for Off-Air Recording of Broadcast Programming for Educational Purposes." Presented to Congress with additional comments, background information, and letters by Representative Robert W. Kastenmeier and recorded in the *Congressional Record* October 14, 1981: E4750-E4752.

10. Hammerly, Hector M. *Synthesis in Second Language Teaching.* Blaine, WA: Second Language Publications, 1982.

11. Higgins, John, and Tim Johns. *Computers in Language Learning.* Copublished by London: Collins ELT; Reading, MA: Addison-Wesley, 1984.

12. _____. "Problems of Self-Correction in the Language Laboratory." *System* 3, 3 (1975):145-56.

13. Hocking, Elton. *Language Laboratory and Language Learning.* Second edition. Washington, DC: Department of Audiovisual Instruction, National Education Association of the United States, 1967.

14. Hope, Geoffrey R., Heimy F. Taylor, and James P. Pusack. *Using Computers in Teaching Foreign Languages.* Orlando, FL: Harcourt Brace Jovanovich, 1984.

15. Johnson, Lathrop P., and Andrea Dvorscak. "Is There a Doctor in the Language Lab? or: First Aid for Lab Programs." *Unterrichtspraxis* 17, 1 (1984):28-32.

16. Krashen, Stephen D. *Inquiries and Insights.* Hayward, CA: Alemany, 1986.

17. Miller, David C. "Finally It Works: Now It Must 'Play in Peoria.' " pp. 21-35 in William H. Gates, ed., *CD ROM, The New Papyrus.* Redmond, WA: Microsoft Press, 1986.

18. Miller, Jerome K. *Using Copyrighted Videocassettes in Classrooms and Libraries.* Friday Harbor, WA: Copyright Information Services, 1984.

19. Moseby, Erik (Product Manager, Tandberg of America, Inc.). Telephone conversation.

20. Mueller, Marlies, Garth McCavana, Maureen Ramsden, and Sharon Shelly. "Language Learning Laboratories: The End of a Lukewarm Affair?" *Northeast Conference Newsletter* 17 (1985):22, 26, 28.

21. Odum, William. "The Use of Videotape in Foreign Language Instruction: A Survey." *NALLD Journal* 10, 3/4 (1976):73-81.

22. *The Official Fair-Use Guidelines.* Friday Harbor, WA: Copyright Information Services, 1985.

23. Oller, John W., and Patricia A. Richard-Amato. *Methods That Work: A Smorgasbord of Ideas for Language Teachers.* Rowley, MA: Newbury House, 1983.

24. Park, William M. "Computer-Assisted Instruction: The View from the Language Lab." *Unterrichtspraxis* 17, 1 (1984):53-55.

25. Pournelle, Jerry. "CD-ROMs Are Facing a Limited Life Span." *Infoworld* 8, 11 (March 17, 1986): 21.

26. Ramsay, George (President of Instruction Systems Associates). Personal telephone conversation, 1986.

27. Reed, Mary Hutchings, and Debra Stanek. "Library and Classroom Use of Copyrighted Videotapes and Computer Software." *American Libraries* 17, 2 (February, 1986):A-D.

28. Richterich, René. "Laboratoire de langues et didactique des langues secondes (notes)." *Bulletin CILA* 40 (1984):9-19.

29. Rivers, Wilga M. "Understanding the Learner in the Language Laboratory." *NALLD Journal* 16, 2 (1981):5-13.

30. Shubin, Mark. "Bon Video Voyage, 7 Myths about Foreign TV." *Video Review* 4, 6 (September 1983):44-46.

31. Winitz, Harris, ed. *The Comprehensive Approach to Foreign Language Instruction.* Rowley, MA: Newbury House, 1981.

32. Wood, Richard E. "Off the Air." *NALLD Journal* 16, 3/4 (1982):35-37.

Television Technology in the Foreign Language Classroom

Charles P. Richardson
Ohio University

Sharon Guinn Scinicariello
Case Western Reserve University

Introduction

Television for foreign languages once conjured up an image of students sitting before a monitor while a "talking face" taught them French, Spanish, or German. The classroom teacher, who frequently did not know the language, assumed an equally passive role. It is no wonder that experiments with educational television in the sixties were often unsuccessful. Two other factors that contributed to the lack of success were limited broadcast range—so that communities in outlying regions could not pick up the signal—and an absence of technology to record it—so that teachers (and students) might use the program at a time other than when the programs were scheduled for broadcast. Although televised films were available occasionally, they were too expensive for many school systems as well as being difficult to use. The few successful uses of television were in spite of, not because of, the technology.

Many of the technical difficulties that beset the early use of television teaching have now been overcome and video software is clearly superior to early attempts to exploit the medium. A recent report (26) indicates that more teachers use instructional television than use computers. Satellite reception systems allow schools and colleges even in remote areas to receive broadcasts in French, Spanish, Russian, and several other languages. Moderately priced videocassette recorders are widely available; some models can play and record tapes in any of the television standards used by other

43

countries. Two-way interactive television permits teachers and students in different locations to see and hear each other, thus overcoming one of the major drawbacks of early televised teaching. Video materials, including feature films and tapes of broadcast television in many languages, are readily available at prices generally lower than the cost of renting a film.

Throughout this chapter the terms *television* and *video* are used interchangeably to refer to a technology. How the foreign language teacher can use this technology effectively, what its implications are beyond the classroom, and what future technological developments will be particularly important for the foreign language teacher are some of the concepts addressed below. (See Part II, pp. 171-203, this volume, for other reports on television in language teaching.)

Why Use Foreign Language Television

The arguments for using television technology in the classroom are so convincing that perhaps those not using it should be asked why they have neglected this important aid to second language learning. Students of today are truly a television generation, accustomed to gaining knowledge about the world from the TV screen instead of from newspapers and magazines (Lee, 39). Schultz (57) reports that newscasters, for example, have more credibility than newspaper reporters; because the audience has "eye contact" with the former, they seem more "real." Although the printed word cannot be neglected as a means of communication, it is useful to take advantage of the students' natural predilection for visual learning by using video materials.

Beeching (7), Jensen and Venther (32), and Lynch (44, 45) stress the role of authentic examples for language learning. In contrast to much of the artificial language in classroom and lab, video materials provide a readily accessible source of language in context as used by native speakers. Because printed texts cannot keep pace with linguistic change, television is often the best source of current vocabulary, pronunciation, and idioms. Video materials also provide the visual and paralinguistic clues—proxemics (distance), kinesics (body language), and vocalization—that must be included in language instruction if students are to learn to communicate in a second language (Pennycook, 51).

The speaking skill is promoted through viewing interesting materials; discussion is stimulated when the students ask questions based on a desire to know facts about the program's content. Some video programs present native speakers modeling pronunciation so that students may see how words are articulated and then attempt to emulate them. Others show native speakers with different regional accents, providing students with a range of "real world" speech. Finally, students will speak, too, when directed to produce their own television programs, an activity that produces a high degree of enthusiasm and real language practice.

Programs from target countries provide a rich source of information about civilization and culture. Television "simplifies and clarifies foreign conditions, and it overcomes differences of time and space" (Svensson and Borgarskola, 62, p. 149). Both Tamarkin (64) and Skirble (59) emphasize the importance of pointing out the similarities as well as differences between cultures. Skirble believes that a benefit of the visual element in language learning is the elimination of false or negative stereotypes. Moreover, students' view of their own culture can come under as close a scrutiny as their view of the outside world. Students have been shown to take a closer look at their own environment as a result of video pen pal programs (1; 71)—as they seek to explain it to students abroad.

Lastly, there are persuasive practical reasons for the increased popularity of video over film as a means of presenting visual materials. A television program can be viewed in any type of light and with the total absence of equipment noise. In addition, the teacher can freeze a frame of action for discussion, fast forward to another, or repeat a scene several times for reemphasis. In stark contrast to film, videotape is normally good for at least a hundred plays without deterioration of the image or the sound. In the case of videocassette recorders (VCRs) with dual sound tracks, two different levels of language (dialog and narration, for example) can be used with the same images. Perhaps even more important, video equipment is extremely reliable; problems are the exception instead of the rule. There are no broken sprockets or burned-out bulbs to contend with as when using film.

The Technology of Television Video

Today's generation of teachers and students is increasingly familiar with the use of television equipment and generally has some knowledge of how to operate it; however, it is important to know more than simply how to turn equipment on and off (Utz, 69). Choosing equipment that meets classroom needs requires some basic technical knowledge. In the foreign language classroom, it is especially important to understand fundamental differences in video formats and television standards.

Television Standards and Video Formats

Television Standards. Three basic standards define how programs are recorded and/or broadcast in the world of television: NTSC (National Television Systems Committee) is found in the United States, Canada, Mexico, Japan, a number of other countries in the Americas, and in the Far East; SECAM (Sequential Color and Memory) is the standard for France, the Middle East, Russia, and many countries of eastern Europe and Africa; PAL (Phase Alternate by Line) is used in the Federal Republic of Germany, England, Spain, and other countries in Western Europe. To complicate matters, there are at least seventeen variations on these three standards worldwide (Wilson, 77; Jeppson, 33). Furthermore, programs or videotapes recorded in PAL or SECAM cannot be played on an NTSC standard videocassette recorder or vice versa, even though the cassette may fit the machine. Viewing programs broadcast or recorded abroad requires multi-standard playback equipment, including both recorder and monitor. Fortunately, these systems, although still expensive, are becoming more readily available. A device called a standards converter is yet another solution to video tapes not recorded in NTSC but is generally too expensive for the average educational user. Commercial conversion is also prohibitively expensive.

Cross-country differences in voltage and in cycles per second present another problem to teachers or students who want to record programs while abroad; a VCR made to run at 110 volts and 60 cycles (the U.S. standard) will run more slowly on the 50-cycle electricity found in Europe and Latin America. Teachers who would record abroad will need to use battery-powered equipment in order to avoid equipment damage and fluctuations in recording speed.

Video Formats. In addition to the different broadcast standards, another source of difficulty confronts the user: three video formats now exist, and another (8mm) is gaining popularity. The 3/4″ U-Matic format was the first to be used widely but is being replaced gradually by VHS and Beta, both of which have excellent audio and video quality as well as ease of handling and storage. Although VHS and Beta both use a half-inch standard, they are incompatible, because the cassettes are physically distinct and their playback equipment is configured differently. Beta is considered to have better picture quality, but VHS provides more hours of recording time (up to 8 hours) on each cassette. VHS has surpassed Beta in sales and has become the standard machine in many school systems in the United States.

Equipment

The Videocassette Recorder. In addition to the Beta and VHS formats mentioned above, the buyer is faced with a bewildering array of features including programmability, number of heads, choice of recording speeds, stereo/high fidelity, digital, and wireless remote control. Of particular interest to the language teacher are machines that have a second track for audio recording. The second audio track can be used to record student-produced soundtracks or a second track that differs from the original in its linguistic level or function (Allan, 2). Digital VCRs are becoming generally available and offer a "freeze frame" function that allows the teacher to hold a picture (either from broadcast TV or from the VCR) so that it may be talked about at length (Kenny, 38; Vizard, 72). In general, however, choice of equipment should be determined by the features the teacher will actually use, the availability of programs in the format chosen, the access to professional routine maintenance, and, above all, ease of operation. Portable VCRs are particularly useful because they can be transported easily and used in areas lacking usable electrical outlets. Available recording time of the battery pack equipment, however, is usually limited to an hour or less. Assistance in choosing equipment should be sought from someone (not a dealer) who has experience in this field. In addition, there are several magazines that publish yearly buying guides for video equipment that provide a good overview of the market (*Video Review, Video, Consumer Reports*).

Whatever equipment is chosen, a good preventive maintenance program is essential. The most common problem faced by users of VCRs is dirty recording and playback heads, which should be cleaned whenever the quality of the picture deteriorates (all abrasive materials—chalk dust, for example—should be excluded from the VCR environment). Cleaning is accomplished with a special, nonabrasive head-cleaning cassette.

Videodisc. The interactive use of videodiscs is dealt with in Chapter 3 (and on pp. 221-61, Part II) in this book. This medium can be used in the classroom in the same way as a VCR. The cost of a laser videodisc player has decreased to about the price of a color monitor and is now more accessible to the average school, but only a limited number of programs in foreign languages are available. These programs are recorded using two different formats: (1) CAV discs—continuous angular velocity—offer special effects such as freeze frame, instant access to individual frames, and the possibility of a second audio track; (2) CLV discs—continuous linear velocity—do not provide these special effects, but can hold more material on each side. Some foreign language feature films, programs on art, and operas are less expensive on videodisc than on videocassette. The videodisc is a superior medium for classroom use because of its relative indestructibility, ease of handling, and quick access to any part of the program. The videodisc player is almost certain to replace the VCR when and if suitable programming is made available.

Display Devices. Televised materials are displayed on various devices—the standard TV set, video monitor/receiver, and video projector. The type chosen for the classroom depends upon planned use and budget, and the buyer must also consider ease of operation and the size of speaker and screen (in the absence of a clear white surface). Allan (2) notes that the screen should be minimally 24″ (measured diagonally) for a class of twenty-five.

A standard television receiver does not reproduce the same picture quality from a VCR or videodisc player as does a TV monitor and will not be usable with these devices unless they have an RF (radio frequency) output—the type of signal received by standard cable or through a TV antenna—because they have no input jacks for video and audio signals.

A monitor can receive direct video and audio signals but lacks the tuner of a TV set and cannot receive broadcast signals unless connected to a tuner-equipped VCR. The picture quality of a monitor is superior to a TV set because, in addition to holding more lines of resolution, the video and audio signals do not pass through the tuner stage. A monitor/receiver is slightly more expensive but combines the capabilities of the TV set with that of the monitor.

Video projection systems that duplicate the role of the monitor cost several thousand dollars but are an absolute necessity when showing programs to a large audience, since they enlarge the TV picture considerably. Early models required a special screen for viewing and a very dark room. Moreover, the field of vision of the audience was limited so that viewers seated at the sides of the room could not see the picture well. Newer devices, many available in multistandard formats, project a picture approaching the quality of 16mm film and can be seen in brighter light on any white surface and from almost any angle. Although the large screen helps to hold attention and heighten interest in the programs being used (Brooks, 12) classroom use of a projection system is hindered by its lack of mobility; most projectors are bulky and have to be refocused each time they are moved.

Video Cameras. Choosing a video camera is difficult because of the many options available and because it is more complicated to operate than a video recorder. Desirable camera features include a built-in monitor, zoom lens, both automatic and manual iris control, and the ability to record good images with a limited light source. A tripod provides a stable platform for the camera and relieves the operator of the weight of the camera. A power supply/ signal amplifier is required to use the camera with a VCR that has no camera input jack.

Camcorders (portable and compact camera/recorders) that combine the functions of the VCR and camera in one unit, are now available in three formats: 8mm, VHS, and Beta. A camcorder that is compatible with the VCRs owned by a school is usually a sine qua non; tapes made on the camcorder can then be played back on any available equipment. In most

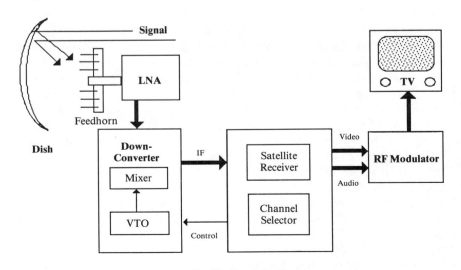

Figure 1. Satellite Reception System.

cases, the recording time of the camcorder is limited by the battery's endurance and by the size of the cassette.

Satellite Systems. Although films and prerecorded cassettes of foreign language programs and films are available in considerable quantity (see Appendix of this article), a rich source of broadcast programming exists 22,000 miles above the earth—the communications satellites in geosynchronous orbit, which provide programs for network affiliates, cable systems, and others with satellite receiving systems. The cost of a satellite reception system has dropped from tens of thousands of dollars to less than half the cost of a small car (Meigs, 48); many of these systems have been purchased by an increasing number of schools, colleges, and private individuals. A variety of foreign language programming is available in French, Spanish, German, Japanese, Italian, and Russian.

A satellite reception system consists of a dish (often mistakenly referred to as a "disk"), a Low Noise Amplifier (LNA) that boosts the weak signal received by the dish, a down-converter that changes the frequency to match the receiver, and a receiver/tuner (Figure 1). The dish is usually constructed of fiberglass, aluminum, or a metallic mesh (Long and Keating, 42). At the present time, two frequency bands contain most of the foreign language programming: the C-band (3.7-4.2 GHz) and the KU-band (11.7-12.7 GHz). The diameter of the dish required to receive signals from the C-band (the seat of most satellite signals) is between 9 and 15 feet, while the KU-band may be received with a dish only 3 feet in diameter. Dishes designed for the C-band can be converted to receive the KU band signals if they are made from a solid material: the extremely short wavelength signals of the KU band pass through the mesh dishes as though they were invisible. The KU-band presently holds a small number of foreign language programs, but there is every indication that the number of foreign language programs will increase in the future.

The installation and setting of the satellite dish are very important. Trees and buildings in the line of sight will interfere with signal reception. If the dish itself is not made of solid material, the bracing of its segments will have to be very rigid or its shape will be distorted in strong winds—with subsequent loss of signal quality (Aulestia, 4, 5; Banning and Yerrick, 6). The antenna must be mounted so that it can "see" the range of satellites that carry foreign language programs, most of which orbit above the equator at a speed that matches the rotation of the earth exactly so that they seem to remain stationary in relation to any point on the ground. Once a dish is pointed at a given satellite, it will not need to be moved until a different satellite is sought. A motorized actuator can be purchased to facilitate this adjustment. Television from the USSR is available only from satellites that are not stationary in this way. The only practical way to obtain programming broadcast from the USSR is to purchase a system that includes a computer programmed to track nongeostationary satellites.

There are several magazines that show typical satellite "footprints" (the area in which the signals of a given satellite can be received) and provide program schedules; among them, *On-Sat, Satellite World,* and *Orbit.*

Satellite reception of foreign programs does not eliminate the differences among the TV standards mentioned above. To watch Russian programs via satellite requires SECAM equipment. Areas of the east coast that are in the footprint of European broadcasting must use special receivers to pick up broadcasts in PAL and SECAM, and must acquire multistandard monitors to view them.

Copyright, Fair Use, and Other Legalities

Broadcast television is only one of many sources of foreign language video materials; however, the use of all programming is subject to the restrictions of copyright law. Although the "fair use" guidelines for off-air taping do not have the force of law (Sinofsky, 58) they appear to be a valid statement of educators' rights and are included in the Appendix of this article. Slightly different legal restrictions apply to videocassettes of films and other video materials purchased by a school system. A nonprofit educational institution has the right to show videos in its classrooms for teaching purposes even though those videocassettes may be labeled "For Home Use Only"—however, copying these tapes for any reason is illegal (16).

More recently, questions have been raised about the legality of receiving unscrambled satellite transmissions. The reception of signals from satellites is governed by various laws, both domestic and international. With regard to the reception of foreign satellite signals, Rothblatt and Samara (56) conclude:

> The various legitimate concerns of broadcasters of program-carrying signals have been abated by both international and domestic law. The Brussels Accord, to which many countries are party, prohibits the unauthorized interception of program-carrying signals and makes each signatory ensure that its domestic law will enforce the Accord. U.S. domestic law ensures that its nationals adhere to the Accord through two or more laws.

The guidelines that pertain to off-air copying of American broadcasts therefore apply to international transmissions.

A different sort of legal problem has arisen with regard to telecourses broadcast across state lines by satellite or some other means. Jaschik (31) reports that "State officials are uncertain of their ability to license or regulate such programs" (p. 13). Since state regulations apply to those organizations that have a "physical presence" in the state, courses offered through telecommunications seem not to be covered. Distance learning of this type is becoming more common (see Part II, Report 3-4, pp. 187-203, this volume) and additional legal problems are bound to occur.

Television in the Language Curriculum

The advantages of foreign language video are many, but they can be negated unless care is taken in the use of this technology. Even advanced students are frustrated in watching programs for which they have not been prepared. "Authentic" materials—those intended for native speakers of the language—present a variety of problems to the student accustomed to the caretaker speech of classroom or lab: the rapidity of the speech (particularly in news broadcasts), differences in accent, and background noise. Visual cues that should aid comprehension may only serve to overload the student's receptive system (Ur, 68, p. 21).

Fortunately, the effective use of television technology does not require a totally new methodology. Many classroom exercises customarily used with print or audio texts can be adapted for visual ones. Above all, video in the classroom must be used to stimulate and not discourage student responses. The activities used in connection with video must be designed to overcome the passive viewing habits students have acquired watching TV at home.

Choosing Appropriate Video Materials

Effective use of video requires the careful matching of video segments to course objectives, student ability levels and interests, and classroom activities. Video is a particularly valuable tool in the teaching of listening comprehension, vocabulary, and culture, and it can help as well to elicit discussion and creative speech. Although the best video segments teach language and foreign culture together, programs dubbed into another language, silent programs, and programs in the students' native tongue can all be used successfully.

Commercial, Broadcast, or Self-Produced? A distinction can be made between materials meant to be broadcast and those intended to be viewed on videotape. A more important distinction for the classroom teacher separates programs into three categories: (1) video materials intended to be used in the foreign language classroom; (2) video materials intended for native speakers, including feature films and broadcast television; and (3) video materials produced by the teacher. Each has its own virtues and disadvantages. Classroom materials are usually made in appropriately short segments and come with supporting materials but often model language and contexts that are artificial. "Authentic" materials can offer a greater variety of language—regional accents, specialized vocabulary—but tend to overwhelm all but the most advanced language students. Producing one's own videos can ensure that they meet specific goals, but production requires time, planning, and technical skill. Expense is also a factor; professional equipment and help may be needed to achieve the desired quality.

Teachers choosing between pedagogical and "authentic" materials should base their selections on instructional objectives. Where video is used to model spoken language in context, it may be useful to distinguish between "authenticity" and "genuineness" (Jensen and Venther, 32). Spoken language is "genuine" when it is produced spontaneously. "Authentic" language may not be spontaneous: most television programming, for example, is scripted, and the language often does not have the redundancy and filler words of spontaneous speech. On the other hand, classroom video may be "genuine" but not "authentic," since it is produced to teach language. For example, students at the University of Illinois at Urbana-Champaign watch videotapes of native speakers playing roles in a number of common situations. Both the language and paralinguistic cues are natural and "genuine" because the conversations are unscripted, but the instructional objectives—sometimes even specific structures and vocabulary to be included—have been established in advance (Omaggio, 50).

Teachers with access to live foreign language television may want to use this resource. Live programs offer the thrill of immediacy—"l'étudiant peut s'adonner à l'illusion de se comporter comme un natif" (Bufe, 14, p. 88). Simply turning the television on as students enter the classroom can help the teacher create a "cultural island." Regularly scheduled programs may be used as the basis for language activities; a teacher whose class meets every day at the same time a soap opera is broadcast can use it as the basis for exercises in plot summary and projection. Of course, the teacher has no control over program content and no way to eliminate what is inappropriate in the classroom. In general, taped programs are more flexible because they can be previewed by the teacher, activities can be designed to maximize student learning, and they can be used over an extended period of time with classes that meet at different hours.

Student Interests, Student Abilities. Student interests are an important factor in the selection of video programs. A hockey game narrated in French may not be received well in a Sunbelt classroom; a program on fashion, no matter how extensive the use of vocabulary, may not be the best choice for a class that is predominantly male, particularly if the students are very young. Adult learners will probably not want to watch children's programming. What interests teachers may not appeal to their students, and students who are not interested in the material will not spend the time necessary to overcome any difficulties in comprehension.

The level of the students is also extremely important. Novices, as defined by the ACTFL Proficiency Guidelines, have a particularly hard time understanding authentic language. They need very short (1-2 minutes) action-oriented segments in which there is visual support of the meaning to the extent that comprehension is possible without the soundtrack. Subject matter should be limited to everyday needs and vocabulary. At the Intermediate level, segments may be slightly longer, but they should still be short enough to allow for repeated viewings interspersed with classroom activities. Intermediate students are not yet ready for abstraction, so the best choices remain action-oriented segments about everyday events and programs about topics of personal interest, e.g., sports and music. Advanced students, with some preparation, are ready for "real world" language and are often stunned to discover that they can understand a foreign language delivered at a native level in an audiovisual medium. Advanced students can comprehend longer programs that contain more talk than action if the subject is already familiar. Talk shows and documentaries about art, literature, and history will interest them. Visual support need not be as obvious as at lower levels, but students can be led into misunderstanding when picture and sound contrast (von Faber, 74). As the learners progress from the Advanced to the Superior level, the teacher can choose materials containing a broad range of accents and levels of speech. At these levels students have the ability to understand some verbal humor, so situation comedies are useful programs for them to experience.

Commercials. Commercials are especially valuable for the foreign language learner because they are short and contain a great deal of redundancy, a factor that aids comprehension of the message (Campana, 15). Beginners can usually answer successfully the questions "What is being sold? To whom does it appeal?" They can also fill in the blanks of a cloze exercise that eliminates a few key words of the message (Lee, 39). More advanced students can analyze the imagery or supply their own narration for a commercial that is played without a sound track. Students can also practice pronunciation by repeating jingles. Some commercials can be used as a basis for storytelling because they offer a complete text in and of themselves (Lynch, 44, 45). Many commercials are minidramas in which meaning is conveyed through body language and facial expressions, and other nonverbal cues that students can draw upon (and imitate) to increase their understanding. Students also acquire knowledge of the target culture when the commercial reflects customs specific to the target culture (e.g., the bringing of a gift when one is invited to a German home).

Film. Most films are now available on videocassette and, consequently, movie projectors are gradually disappearing from classrooms. Language teachers, who often use films to motivate students and show aspects of everyday culture, can use movies on tape to good advantage. It is important to remember, however, that feature films are works of art intended to be seen on large screens in one sitting. Teachers interested in the interpretation of cinematic texts need to be concerned with the change in the medium that occurs when transferred to tape; the smaller screen and lack of definition may affect the director's original artistic intent. When classroom activities are based on short segments of a film, students should also be given the opportunity to appreciate it as an artistic whole.

Using Video

In Class, In the Lab, or at Home? Video materials can be used very successfully as a basis for classroom activities, but watching television for more than several minutes is undoubtedly not a good use of limited classroom time.

Extensive viewing is therefore best accomplished in the language lab, media center, or at home. Although the restrictions of copyright law will limit some of this activity, video materials can be placed in the language lab for independent viewing, lent to students, or broadcast over a campus TV system. Particularly at the more advanced levels, it is valuable for students to watch foreign language video materials of their own choosing and at their leisure. Advanced students "hear" more like native speakers as they listen with interest (Bufe, 14). Novice and intermediate students will find extensive viewing of most programs frustrating, but they can enjoy cartoons and sports because the action defines the context of the language. This kind of viewing helps students grow accustomed to the sounds and rhythm of the target language.

Whether programs are viewed in the classroom or independently, the same preparatory and followup activities can be used. In the classroom, teachers must prepare students for what they will see—with vocabulary lists or drills and a preliminary discussion of the theme. Special preparation can be minimized if the teacher chooses video segments that use vocabulary, structures, or themes that are being emphasized in other activities. For example, a segment of a World Cup soccer match might be used while students in a conversation class complete a unit on sports that includes soccer vocabulary.

The preliminary discussion or preparation may be supplemented profitably by a "viewing checklist"—a short series of objective questions that can (1) focus attention on key points of the segment, and (2) give the student a sense of having watched a program successfully (Steele, 61). Because the questions are intended to help the student comprehend, these guides should not require extensive reading and writing—tasks that would take the student's attention from the screen. For example, beginning students watching a weather report can be asked to match pictures of the sun, clouds, rain, and snow to the cities mentioned in the broadcast. They can check their answers by replaying the tape. Slightly more advanced students can be asked to choose a synonym that best suits the context of the segment or fill in a form based on information in a dialogue. Groups of students can watch the same segment with different tasks in hand: one student can note, for example, expressions of emotion, while another focuses on conventional gestures, and a third follows uses of a grammatical structure. In this way, one segment can be used to explore many aspects of language (Lonergan, 41).

Followup activities are intended to ensure the students' comprehension of the segment and to use what has been learned to extend their linguistic and cultural knowledge. The type of activity will depend upon the teacher's goal in choosing the segment. Short segments can be watched in class and difficulties explained. New vocabulary and structures can be repeated and then practiced in different contexts. Intermediate and advanced students can prepare oral and written summaries of longer programs. Video segments can be used as models for role playing. It is particularly effective to ask each student to prepare a dialogue based on a video segment and then to pair students at random. The first student leads the conversation according to his or her own "script" while the second has to respond spontaneously. Teachers may also prepare audiotapes of the soundtracks and incorporate worksheets and exercises for student use in the language lab to reinforce what has been heard.

Different Activities for Different Goals

Video for Listening Comprehension. Television can be used very effectively to teach listening comprehension at all levels of instruction. The novice learner may simply understand the words that have been spoken or the statement made at a very literal level, but an advanced student is learning to grasp much implied information and to infer, for example, the age and social status of the speaker, the age and status of the listener compared to the speaker, the place the language is being spoken, and the implications of tone of voice and type of speech. Since the context of the conversation determines the listener's expectations, this sociolinguistic information is very important; it is also very easily conveyed by the visual aspect of television.

An activity that focuses on listening comprehension is the cloze exercise. The teacher writes the text of a commercial, news item, or other short segment on a worksheet or transparency, leaving blanks for certain key words. The students fill in the missing words while watching the videotape. This exercise works particularly well for novice language learners who can only be expected to comprehend a few known words. Students can be led to a more global understanding once they have grasped several words or phrases. Weissenrieder (76) examines how this can be done for students listening to news broadcasts. Once students have grasped a few key words (airplane, military, crash), they can base their guesses of what the item is about on knowledge of what makes news. They can listen again and attempt to find words and phrases to confirm or refute their assumptions. This cycle is repeated until the desired level of comprehension is reached. This technique works equally well with commercials and other segments that deal with familiar concepts.

Teaching students to notice prosodic information is more difficult. Programs dubbed from the students' native language to the target language (e.g., *Dallas* in French) can be useful in helping them think about the information conveyed by the voice because they are already familiar with the social status, background, and original voices of the characters they see. By comparing the original and the dubbed voices, they can begin to generalize about different expectations of pitch and volume in the target language. Later they can listen to a sound track, describe their impressions of the speech, and then compare them to the image on the videotape (Smith, 60).

Video for Vocabulary. Video can be an effective teacher of vocabulary. Broadcast television is an excellent source of current words not often found in textbooks. It is also a valuable resource for teachers who learn new terms through print media and may be unsure of the pronunciation of words that have entered the target language recently. Technical terms are often illustrated in news programs and talk shows; since these same terms carry over to print discussions of the news, the audiovisual context becomes an efficient means of introducing vocabulary as an advance organizer for reading. Students can verify their learning in a followup exercise in which they match terms to pictures after viewing an appropriate video segment. Unfamiliar vocabulary can be introduced very simply; as a segment is played, the teacher can use the freeze-frame feature to focus on and label an object (Longeran, 41).

Video for Speaking and Writing. The objective of most language classes is the production of spoken langauge. Questions about what has been seen, drills using the vocabulary and structures of the programs, discussions of themes and content all serve this purpose. Television then can play a major role in eliciting more creative speech. While watching a silent cartoon (either intended to be silent or viewed with the sound off), students can provide narration, explain the characters' motivations, and consider what might happen next (Bragger, 11). They can create dialogue and then compare how closely their creation matches the script. Soap operas, among other programs, often show one-sided telephone conversations. After viewing such a segment, the students can invent the other side.

Video has also been used for improving pronunciation (Ecklund and Wiese, 20). The technique consists of videotaping initial readings by students, critiquing their pronunciation, and using the videotape to show how their mouth movements affected the pronunciation. Ecklund and Wiese also develop the students' ability to critique their classmates' performance to increase their awareness of the errors. Tapes made at the beginning and ending of the class allow students to see how much improvement they made.

An extremely motivating activity for students is to produce video programs themselves. Students can learn to use the video equipment easily and, because mistakes can be corrected almost immediately, typically approach performing with confidence (Phillips, 52). Students who dislike being in front of a camera may prefer to use puppets as characters. Puppet plays are ideal for amateur video production because they require minimal space, little scenery, and few changes in camera position thanks to zoom lenses (Reimers, 54). When students are expected to prepare the script, this activity has the added advantage of giving them the motivation to write in the target language.

Video for Teaching Writing. At a time when foreign video was less accessible than it is now, Berwald (9, 10) successfully used American commercial television to stimulate student writing in French. Students watched a live program segment in English five to ten minutes long, taking notes in French. After they had expanded their notes to composition form, teachers and students worked together to produce a "stylistically sound finished product"

(9, p. 222). The same procedure could be used with segments in a target language rather than in English. Berwald also experimented with adding foreign soundtracks to American television programs. His report mentions that, since the dubbed material need not be related to the action on the screen, this activity also stimulates student creativity.

Video for Culture. Bufe (14) calls foreign language television "un pont audio-visuel entre le pays cible et le pays de l'apprenant" (p. 87). Students who see a variety of programs can generalize about (1) what native speakers of the language like (both in TV programs and products), (2) how they act in various circumstances, (3) what physical appearance is prized or disliked, (4) how native speakers use body language, (5) how they look at other areas of the world, (6) how different groups of native speakers differ from each other in accent and vocabulary, (7) how informal and formal language is used, (8) what daily life is like and, (9) what the major concerns of the culture are. Documentaries and "educational programming" illustrate art, history, and literature.

Students can focus on the physical differences between cultures if they view segments without sound. After watching a street scene, beginners might be asked to mark "same" or "different" from their own beside such items as clothing, cars, sidewalks, and storefronts. More advanced students can explain similarities and differences. They can observe a conversation and then attempt to establish the status of the speakers, the subject under discussion, and the attitudes conveyed; they can check their conclusions by watching with the sound on.

Colorado State University has produced a series of videotapes to help international students adjust to life on that campus (Telatnik and Krose, 65). The series uses situational dramatizations to serve as a means of introducing the foreign students to different—i.e., American—cultural perspectives. Followup discussions and exercises based on the tapes serve to expand their meaning. Appropriate classroom behavior can also be effectively taught through videotaped minidramas that depict misunderstandings between professors and international students (Todd-Chattin, 66). Another method of aiding overseas students in their adjustment to a new academic environment is described by Geddes (22). Videotapes of lectures— "talking heads"—were made, and students were then assigned to take notes on the lectures. The television helped to focus their attention and provide additional visual clues to meaning.

Video for Special Purposes. Because it excels at showing language in context, video has found a place in courses that teach language for specific purposes. At the University of Hawaii, video is used in the successful course on language for travel industry management. Because readily available course materials emphasize tourism in the country of the target language, video is used to bring "the reality of Waikiki's hotels, restaurants, and beaches into the classroom in situations that parallel those presented in the dialogues used in the text" (Benouis, 8, p. 16). Students are videotaped as they engage in role-playing exercises so that their performance can be analyzed. In

Japanese courses, the final project is the production of videotaped skits to illustrate the students' linguistic competence in travel-related situations (Hijirida and Iwamura, 27).

Video has even been used in teaching Spanish for agricultural purposes. As described by Mainous (46), the videotapes were based on situations an agriculturist might meet when visiting a Spanish-speaking country in South America. The purpose of these tapes was to develop both the cultural perceptivity and the linguistic ability of the agriculturists who were learning Spanish.

Evaluation. In an era when language teachers stress oral communication and cultural competence rather than written production, video provides a better medium to evaluate student performance than the traditional written exam. The advantage of video recording over audio for evaluation lies in its ability to show the visual as well as the oral aspects of communication. A model for this evaluative use of classroom video is Wylie's class in "Communication with the French" (Crook, 18). Professor Wylie stresses the acquisition of "the rhythmic patterns characteristic of the motion of the filmed French models" (p. 787). Kinesics and proxemics are studied as well as speech. After an exercise session designed to change the students' habitual American posture and carriage, class time is spent in the analysis and practice of the movements of native speakers filmed in conversation. Students use videotape to evaluate their own performance; videotapes of the original film are available for comparison. The operator of the camera can focus on the hands or the face, for example, or show the movement of the entire body. Videotape is the prime medium for students to evaluate themselves attempting to combine appropriately the linguistic and paralinguistic elements of a conversation.

Televised Teaching Redux

As the demand for languages in the schools has increased, there has been a revival of interest in televised classroom teaching as a means of offering courses that would not otherwise be available because there was no one to teach the language or because the number of students was insufficient to justify giving a class. Educators stress, however, that television teaching is not to be preferred to traditional methods (Brown, 13).

TWIT. Two-way instructional television (TWIT) is a fairly recent development. As the name implies, the system uses a video and audio hookup to link two or more remote points. Various degrees of interaction are possible. The simplest interactive system consists of a televised lecture with a telephone hookup between originator and viewers. The teacher is thus able to hear and respond to questions or comments from the audience. Typically, however, the lecturer/presenter cannot see the class. A more sophisticated system utilizes cameras at both points so that the teacher and students can see and hear each other via either projection TV systems or monitors. In addition, some systems have the capability of transmitting written documents immediately to and from the remote classroom(s).

The transmission of video, audio, and other information is accomplished through (1) broadcast TV with two-way hookup of telephone lines for audio and other materials, (2) microwave transmission of video and audio, (3) television cable hookup between sites and, (4) TV through a satellite up-link at the point of origin and down-links at remote sites with audio transmission back to the central site by phone lines or microwave. A fairly recent development, the compression of the video signal, permits two-way transmission of still pictures either by long-distance telephone lines or satellite broadcast. By allowing interaction between teacher and students, TWIT thus resolves one of the primary difficulties of televised teaching. Teachers have discovered that systems that permit both video and audio linking do not require much alteration of their teaching methods; and in this regard, the video classroom is very much like a conventional one. Special attention must be paid to placement of equipment and materials distribution—a small price to pay, users agree, for the advantages interactive television offers.

TWIT allows schools to band together and offer courses collectively to a small group at each one, using as an instructor a teacher in the consortium or from a nearby college or university. In districts that use TWIT, the goals are (1) to increase the number of courses available to students, particularly in advanced math, science, and foreign languages, and (2) to motivate and challenge students through contact with their peers in other schools. The practice is common in rural states where distances prevent small schools from consolidating their resources physically. Such schools often cannot offer advanced levels of the more commonly taught languages nor provide instruction in nontraditional ones because enrollments are not large enough to justify the hiring of a teacher (Jaschik, 30).

Evaluation shows that TWIT can be an effective way to teach. Jones (35) reports on eight TWIT systems that have been used to teach foreign languages. School districts in Iowa, Illinois, and Wisconsin, for example, have in place fully interactive systems that use cable or microwave transmission (Hagon, 25; Robinson et al., 55; Volkman, 73). Oklahoma State University uses a satellite TWIT system to offer German to rural high schools and plans to expand its offerings to include Japanese and other languages (Joggerst, 34; Lloyd, 40). (See Part II, pp. 171-203, this volume.) Designed as a complete foreign language/culture package, the course integrates live satellite programming with telephone conferencing, textbooks, workbooks, computer software, and audiotapes. Participating high schools pay a subscription fee and purchase a receiving system and support computer and audio equipment.

Videotaped Classes. Another method for offering language courses via television has been developed by North Carolina State University (Kataoka, 36). Institutions that participate in the Televised Japanese Language Program receive unedited videotapes of an NCSU Japanese language class within one day of each session. Students watch the videotapes with a native-speaker tutor who leads them in the taped drills and who may stop the tape when there are questions or problems. Tutors also lead students in one hour of drill per week without a videotape. Because the tutors are not trained in foreign language methodology, they are not expected to devise drills, provide materials, or answer questions about grammar. The instructor at NCSU creates the coursework, sends out all necessary materials, holds telephone office hours for participating students, and assigns grades. Evaluation of this project has been encouraging, and this type of televised course is perceived by the people involved as an improvement on self-instructional language programs. However, it is still inferior to programs staffed by trained on-campus instructors.

International Video Teleconferencing. Satellite technology has made international video teleconferencing a reality, and the National Committee for Internationalizing Education through Satellites (NCIES), established in 1977, has designed a model for using teleconferencing for second/foreign language and cultural training. Bimonthly live, audio-video interactive transmissions are to be supplemented by preparatory and followup sessions in the classroom and lab. The transmissions will provide a cultural context in which meaningful conversations can take place in a target language (Kavanaugh, 37). When the model is fully implemented, students will be able to interact with a native speaker in an everyday situation—talk to a chef about food, order a meal from a waiter—without leaving the classroom.

In a pilot project at Dickinson College (Eddy, 21; McMillen, 47), a modified version of the model was used with students of German who were able to see and talk with staff members at the National Maritime Museum in Bremerhaven and with a German rock star. The transmission was not two-way, so the Germans could hear but not see the students. To personalize the teleconference, the students' photos were shown to the Germans as they talked. Contrary to the NCIES model, which assumes that no modification of cultural setting will be undertaken by the native informants, the Dickinson project required that the German professors, used to teaching German to foreigners, modify their classroom behavior in order to conform to the expectations of the American students. The students prepared as well, using a preview videotape to become accustomed to the voice and mannerisms of the principle speaker. (See Part II, pp. 197-203 of this volume.)

Responses of students who participated actively in the Dickinson project indicate that the chief benefit of this kind of instruction is psychological. Although they had had ample opportunities to converse with native Germans on campus, the students did not believe they had heard "real" Germans until the teleconference itself. Thus it seems that international teleconferencing is effective in demonstrating to students that they have indeed learned to communicate with other language groups. This realization will reinforce what they have learned and motivate them to strengthen their skills in order to participate in the next transmission.

Limitations and Implications of Video in the Classroom ___

While there are convincing pedagogical reasons for using video in the foreign language classroom, it is clear that the medium has limitations, which fall into two general categories: technological and pedagogical. Extensive use of television technology also has implications for language students, teachers, and the larger community.

Technological constraints include the mechanical limitations of the equipment and the expense involved in its acquisition and use. Although searching for a particular segment on a videotape is certainly easier than on a film, it is nevertheless time-consuming to wind and rewind the tape, a fact that effectively discourages nonlinear viewing. Too long a "freezeframe" of a single image may damage either the tape or the equipment, tapes do break and, when students are using them independently, they may hesitate to report the problem (Townsend and Lewis, 67).

The price of video equipment and materials has decreased dramatically, but it is still too expensive for many school budgets. The cost of using video includes the initial investment in equipment as well as the expense of maintaining it. The purchase of security devices to guard the equipment against theft and vandalism may also be necessary. Program cost is another consideration. Movies are much cheaper on videotape than on film, but they are still far more expensive than an audiotape program that might fulfill the same instructional objectives. Video materials from publishers are generally even more expensive. Off-air taping from cable or broadcast TV is not a perfect solution: only a few languages are available, and most programs are not designed for instruction and are of limited value unless much time is spent planning their integration into classroom activities. In most cases, copyright law severely limits the time available for this.

Lack of preparation time is, in fact, one of the most severe limitations for the teacher who would use video. The integration of video into the curriculum requires careful advance planning, ranging from the viewing of a number of programs to the production of one's own videotapes. High school teachers in particular do not have adequate time at school to preview available materials nor, often, have access to the two VCRs necessary for editing their own. Moreover, when video is an integral part of classroom activities, time is needed each day for the preparation of ancillary materials and exercises. The teacher who uses videotapes tied to a textbook may solve this problem temporarily, but all may be lost when a new edition of the text appears.

Another pedagogical limitation is the inadequate training teachers receive in the classroom use of media. They are unaware of such factors as screen size, placement of monitors for good viewing, audio enhancement through the use of larger speakers or supplementary amplifiers, and different standards of recording. This lack of knowledge is not an insoluble problem, but teachers of the humanities often fear technology and resist its use. In higher education, faculty members are often reluctant to learn to use technology because there are no incentives to do so in the promotion and tenure system (Coder, 17). All teachers have had too much experience with "recalcitrant language laboratories, incompatible video recorders, incomprehensible computer programmes or intricate film-lacing systems" (Hill, 28, p. 142). Such problems can be overcome only by including training in the use of media at all levels of teacher preparation.

In the case of video, the effective use of the equipment and materials is not the only topic of media education. Teachers, who are traditionally taught to deal with printed texts, need practice in interpreting visual ones as well. If, as Postman (53) states, "no TV set or film projector ... should be brought into the classroom unless the teacher intends to call attention to how the medium controls both thought and behavior" (p. 8), then the effect of the visual emphasis of television on student thinking becomes another topic to be included in the education of teachers who use video.

More extensive training and the addition of incentives to use media are only two of the modifications needed in the professional development of teachers. Anyone who watches American TV and films realizes that, despite the realistic details and dialogue, these media distort the culture they present. The same is true of foreign media, thus, familiarity with the target culture becomes essential for those who use "authentic" materials in the classroom.

Cultural differences also affect students who view foreign television. They may be exposed to vocabulary (metaphors, epithets, swear words) not normally heard on American TV. Cultural attitudes about what is acceptable on television (nudity, for example) vary from country to country, and students will certainly be exposed to political ideas different from those that dominate American society. While the discussion of such differences contributes to the broad education of the students, it is to be expected that students, parents, and even other members of the community will question its value unless teachers are prepared to explain the cultural background of the programming and the reasons for including it in the language curriculum.

Research on Television in the Foreign Language Classroom

There is almost no research on the use of television in foreign language teaching at the present time, in contrast to the sixties (Svobodny, 63) and seventies, but the increasing use of video has not engendered any comparable studies except in the case of videodisc—a topic in Chapter 3 of this volume. (See also the various projects in Part II of this volume.) Research in related areas, however, seems to support the effectiveness of video technology. VanPatten (70), in a report on acquisition research, concludes that for successful language acquisition learners need to have meaningful and communicative inputs. One of the "inputs" he mentions is television. VanPatten also states that "Unless what is offered to listen to is interesting, it is doubtful that truly attentive listening will happen" (p. 215). Graziani

(24), summarizing research on the comprehension of Italian television programs by native speakers of Italian, notes that understanding of program content depends on the pleasure the viewer experiences from watching the program and the degree to which the viewer's own opinions match those expressed. These results mean that the television materials used for comprehension activities in the classroom should be entertaining and challenging, but that the intellectual content cannot be radically different from the students' view of life.

In a study by Mueller (49) to determine the effect of visuals on listening comprehension, contextual line drawings proved to have beneficial effects on comprehension. Perhaps this study also has relevance to the use of video, since its visuals too would provide "a framework within which the passage could be understood" (p. 335). Graziani's (24) research, however, indicates that even native speakers have difficulty in understanding content when the connection between visuals and spoken texts of the broadcasts is not immediately apparent.

In spite of studies that seem favorable to the use of television for language learning, research is needed to provide data that will support the large sums of money currently being spent in the development and dissemination of video programming. Teachers need to know which programs are most useful and how different types of programs are understood. Do the visual clues provided by TV have the negative effect on students' listening skill that von Faber (74) postulates? Are students watching, listening, and learning— or simply watching?

Funded Projects for Using Television

In recent years, various projects intended to increase the use of foreign language television have been funded by private and government sources. These projects range from the production of foreign langauge programs to the dissemination of programs produced in other countries. Recognizing the difficulty that most schools have in obtaining NTSC standard tapes of foreign language broadcasts, several institutions have developed plans to produce tapes in NTSC standard or to obtain tapes in PAL or SECAM, secure rights for their use, and convert them to NTSC for distribution. The Project for International Communication Studies (PICS) (Altman, 3) is one of the more important of these projects and is described in detail in the "Projects" section of this volume. (See Chapter 1 of Part II of this volume, pp. 171-78.)

The following projects are representative of current trends in the use of television technology in language teaching.

Yale-Wellesley/Annenberg Grant

The Yale-Wellesley proposal has resulted in the production of a series of videotapes, French in action, designed to present French culture and language in an interesting dramatic series shot on location. Awarded by the Annenberg Foundation, the $2 million grant is one of the largest ever given to the field of foreign languages. The purpose of the grant is to determine the best application of video in the classroom as well as to teach language and culture. Videotaping has been done by professional crews associated with WGBH in Boston. The project director, Pierre Capretz, was able to gain permission to shoot scenes in various locales in France not normally open to the public. Two assumptions determined the type of material to be taped: (1) student interest can best be maintained by a dramatic series in an authentic language; (2) the visual element can support comprehension of both concrete meanings and "related situational images that extend meaning to include cultural associations that native speakers make automatically" (78, p. 53).

The content is designed for students at the intermediate and advanced levels. Support materials will be available to schools using the programs, and the planners have designed the course so that it can be adapted to emerging technologies and be made interactive. Distribution began in fall 1987 both through the PBS system (which should make the materials available to a broad spectrum of viewers) and on videocassettes.

Howard University

Howard University in Washington, D.C., received a grant from the Office of Education to obtain television programs from Third World countries in Africa and Latin America. The purpose of the grant was to develop teaching modules designed to motivate minority students to study foreign languages and to provide practice material for interpreters (Dailey, 19). Modules were adapted for student viewing by using an on-camera host and voice-over narration to provide cultural information, linguistic cues, and a clarification of the story line. In some instances subtitles of difficult dialogue were provided for the modules, which are condensed versions of the programs. A study guide contains program synopses, vocabulary, cultural information, and other relevant material (Warner, 75).

University of Maryland—Baltimore County

The University of Maryland—Baltimore County began in 1985 to make French television broadcasts available to any school that had a satellite dish. Excerpts of a broad spectrum of television programs were converted to NTSC standards and were broadcast to schools throughout the country via satellite.

Schools are able to use this material free of charge because the purpose of this project is to determine if they would eventually subscribe to an ongoing series of broadcasts at a cost sufficient to cover the price of renting the satellite time and acquiring rights to the materials. The project currently provides a variety of materials from French television selected to meet the needs of both high school and college language teachers. The French Ministry of External Affairs has given support to this project and all indications are that it will continue in the future (Aulestia, 5).

SCOLA (Satellite Communications for Learning Associated)

SCOLA is a consortium of some 500 colleges and universities organized in 1983 to import news programs via satellite from countries around the world. Four down-link earth satellites (Gloucester, England; Colombo, Sri Lanka; Tokyo, Japan; Winter Beach, Florida) receive live news in several foreign languages (including Arabic, Japanese, Chinese, Russian, Spanish, Portuguese, Italian, German, and French) and "feed" the SCOLA main distribution point at Creighton University in Omaha, Nebraska (Lubbers, 43). The programs are sent daily, again by satellite (C-Band up-link), from Creighton to the SCOLA membership in North America. This global network, completely operational in December 1987, was created to help students develop a broad international awareness of peoples and cultures in the full spectrum of political, economic, and social interdependence. In addition, it provides the language departments of participating institutions with a wide range of authentic journalism for instructional purposes.

Conclusion: The Evolution of Classroom Television _____

The use of television technology in the language classroom is gaining wide support within the language profession. Schools at all levels are purchasing video equipment and materials, in part because television, although it is constantly changing, is an "old" technology that teachers and students are comfortable using. Second, despite problems of copyright and expense, there are many video programs to choose from; few complain about the lack of "good software." Third, the use of television does not require radical changes in methodology; materials can be used like any other texts. Teachers are learning how to interpret texts in print.

Speculation about the future of classroom video is fraught with possibilities for error, but current trends in technology do offer a glimpse of what may happen in the next decade. Both digital television and flat-screen monitors are available, but neither is yet widely distributed. Both have the potential for enhancing classroom video use. Aside from a much sharper picture, the digital TV sets and VCRs have two functions that could be of particularly immense value to the foreign language teacher: freeze frames for extended time periods and zoom enlargement. The teacher using digital equipment will be able to freeze the action and discuss the still picture on the screen, although the program in progress will continue. Digital TV also allows the viewer to zoom in on specific sections of the picture and view the enlarged image without picture distortion. This could be an excellent means of focusing student attention on specific vocabulary items displayed in a larger picture. Sets available now in Japan use digital technology to double the number of lines on the monitor's picture and, therefore, double the sharpness of the image (Kenny, 38).

A large viewing screen will allow the best appreciation of these capabilities of digital TV. At present, the only way to achieve this is through the use of video projection systems, but most experts believe that flat-screen monitors as large as current projection screens will become available before the end of the decade. Such screens will eliminate the use of bulky monitors or projectors and, because of their larger size, will serve as a better focus for students' attention.

In the areas of video recording, one certain development is an inexpensive videodisc recorder. Videodisc recorders are now available only at the cost of a luxury automobile, but videotape recorders were just as expensive when they were first introduced. A videodisc recorder will provide the teacher with the ability to record foreign language television on a disc and then take advantage of all of the capabilities of the videodisc medium—almost instant access to any frame on the disc, freeze frame, and the capability of student interaction via computer. The CV (compact video) player, a compact disc with limited video capability, will provide still pictures described by an audio track. Enhancement of the videocassette recorder and improvement in videocassette quality will continue. Less mechanical means of storage and retrieval than videocassettes and videodiscs may make video playback and storage so accessible that students will use "take home" video programs as they now use audiocassettes.

Sources of video materials will increase as two present impediments to the reception of programming from other countries are overcome—the incompatibility of television broadcast standards and the need for large satellite dishes. New equipment that inexpensively "translates" from one television standard to another (Gerson and Stern, 23), will allow exchanges of programming throughout the world. An increase in the number of direct broadcasting systems (DBS), which send programs directly into the home or school via a small satellite dish (3 feet in diameter), will increase the amount of specialized programming available. The transmission of programs across international boundaries, however, has serious social and political implications. France and members of the European Common Market are presently trying to establish a standard for HDTV (high density television) and this group will directly oppose efforts by the Japanese to establish a different standard. South Korea is already protesting the reception of programming originating in Japan. Technology cannot solve political problems, and potentially useful technological developments may be delayed by long debates on such topics.

Whatever the future brings, the evolution of television technology cannot affect the foreign language classroom without the involvement of the teacher. If teachers learn how to use the new media equipment effectively and if they are involved in the production and selection of materials, television teaching will make a major contribution to the learning of languages and to increased awareness of the differences and the similarities in other cultures.

References, Television Technology in the Foreign Language Classroom

1. "A Is for Apple." *Technology Review* (February/March 1982) :47.

2. Allan, Margaret. "A Guide to Hardware Options," pp. 10-34 in Marion Geddes and Gill Sturtridge, eds., *Video in the Language Classroom.* London, Eng.: Heinemann, 1982.

3. Altman, Charles F., and James P. Pusack. *Project for International Communication Studies—Consortium Proposal.* Proposal submitted to the U.S. Department of Education Undergraduate International Studies and Foreign Language Program Office of Post-Secondary Education, November 14, 1984.

4. Aulestia, Victor. "The Impact on a Foreign Language Curriculum of Foreign Language Television Signals Received from Geosynchronous Earth Satellites." *NALLD Journal* 18, 1 (1983) :21-23.

5. _____. "Satellite Communications and Foreign Language Learning," pp. 20-23 in Jerry W. Larson, ed. *Planning and Using Language Learning Centers.* The CALICO Monograph Series, vol. 1. Provo, UT: CALICO, 1986.

6. Banning, Bernardine, and William D. Yerrick. "SIN in the Language Lab." *Hispania* 70, 1(1987) :187-88.

7. Beeching, Kate. "Authentic Material." *The British Journal of Language Teaching* 20, 1 (1982) :17-20.

8. Benouis, Mustapha. "French for Specific Purposes: The Hawaiian Experience." *Foreign Language Annals* 19, 1 (1986) :13-17.

9. Berwald, Jean-Pierre. "Teaching French Language Skills with Commercial Television." *French Review* 50 (1976) :222-26.

10. _____.*Au Courant: Teaching French Vocabulary and Culture Using the Mass Media.* Language in Education: Theory and Practice, no. 65. Washington, DC: Center for Applied Linguistics, 1986.

11. Bragger, Jeannette. "Materials Development for the Proficiency-Oriented Classroom," pp. 79-115 in Charles J. James, ed., *Foreign Language*

Proficiency in the Classroom and Beyond. The ACTFL Foreign Language Education Series, vol. 16. Lincolnwood, IL: National Textbook Company, 1985.

12. Brooks, Robert J. "The Video Projector Comes of Age." *EITV: Educational Industrial Television* 16, 5 (1984) :108-11.

13. Brown, Francis C. "Televised Classes Help Rural High Schools Offer Fuller, More Demanding Curriculum." *"The Wall Street Journal,* 12 November 1985.

14. Bufe, W. "L'Enseignement des langues à l'aide de la télévision." *Le Français dans le monde* 157 (1980) :87-98.

15. Campana, Phillip J. "And Now a Word from Our Sponsor: Radio Commercials for Listening Comprehension in German." *Die Unterrichtspraxis* 17, 1 (1984) :39-43.

16. "Clarification Concerning Use of Home Use Only Prerecorded Videocassettes." *Northeast Conference Newsletter* 18 (1985) :32.

17. Coder, Ann. "Why Do Community College Faculty Resist Media as an Instructional Delivery System?" *Educational Technology* 23 (1983): 7-11.

18. Crook, Jere L. "Teaching Communication with the French." *French Review* 58 (1985) :786-92.

19. Dailey, Stephanie. *Final Performance Report: Foreign Language Training through International Media.* Washington, DC: Howard University Department of Languages, 1985.

20. Ecklund, Constance L., and Peter Wiese. "French Accent through Video Analysis." *Foreign Language Annals* 14, 1 (1981) :17-23.

21. Eddy, Beverly D. "Live from Germany: A Look at Satellite Instruction." *Die Unterrichtspraxis* 19, 2 (1986) :213-19.

22. Geddes, Marion. "Talking Heads and Study Skills," pp. 62-68 in Marion Geddes and Gill Sturtridge, eds., *Video in the Foreign Language Classroom.* London, Eng.: Heinemann, 1982.

23. Gerson, Robert, and Jennifer Stern. "Digital—At Last." *Video Review* 5, 11 (1985) :34,36,39-42.

24. Graziani, C. "Messages télévisés et publics: quelques remarques sur la nature propre de la communication télévisée." *Bulletin CILA* 42 (1985):8-20.

25. Hagon, Roger. "Two-Way Cable TV Links Rural Schools." *Tech Trends* 31, 1 (1986) :18-21.

26. "Here's How Schools Use Instructional Media." *Tech Trends* 30, 5 (1985) :19, 39.

27. Hijirida, Kyoko, and Susan Grohs Iwamura. "Languages for Travel Industry Managers: Focus on Japanese." *Foreign Language Annals* 19, 1 (1986) :19-24.

28. Hill, B. "Some Applications of Media Technology to the Teaching and Learning of Languages," pp. 142-56 in Valerie Kinsella, ed., *Cambridge Language Teaching Surveys*. Cambridge, Eng.: Cambridge University Press, 1982.

29. "In Box." *The Chronicle of Higher Education* 31, 16 (1985) :19.

30. Jaschik, Scott. "Oklahoma Tries to Turn National Reports into State Action." *The Chronicle of Higher Education* 31, 11 (1985) :19.

31. _____. "Use of Telecommunications for Instruction across State Lines Attracting Official Notice." *The Chronicle of Higher Education* 31, 10 (1985) :13,16.

32. Jensen, Eva Dam, and Thora Venther. "The Authentic versus Easy Conflict in Foreign Language Material—A Report on Experiences with Production and Exploitation of Video in FLT." *System* 11, 2 (1983) :29-41.

33. Jeppson, Cordell E. "Dealing with Television Standards Conversion and Copyright," pp. 34-49 in Jerry W. Larson, ed., *Planning and Using Language Learning Centers*. The CALICO Monograph Series, vol. 1. Provo, UT: CALICO, 1986.

34. Joggerst, Jo. "Satellite Scholastics." *Satellite Orbit* 3, 4 (1986) :31-35.

35. Jones, Maxine Holmes. *See, Hear, Interact: Beginning Developments in Two-Way Television*. Metuchen, NJ: Scarecrow, 1985.

36. Kataoka, Hiroko C. "Televised Japanese Language Program: The First Year." *Foreign Language Annals* 19, 6 (1986) :491-98.

37. Kavanaugh, Andrea. "NCIES Satellite Learning System." *ADFL Bulletin* 15, 2 (1983) :61-63.

38. Kenny, Glenn. "Video's Next Dimension." *Video Review* 7, 11 (1987): 32-34, 93-94.

39. Lee, David. "Television Commercials for German Listening Comprehension." *Die Unterrichtspraxis* 17, 1 (1984) :133-35.

40. Lloyd, Linda A. "Teaching with Technologies: Oklahoma Leads the Way." *Educational Technology Update* 3, 2 (1985) :1-3.

41. Lonergan, Jack. *Video in Language Teaching*. Cambridge, Eng.: Cambridge University Press, 1984.

42. Long, Mark, and Jeffrey Keating. *The World of Satellite Television*. Mendocino, CA: Quantum, 1986.

43. Lubbers, Lee. "What is SCOLA? (Satellite Communications for Learning Associated)." SCOLA Project Report. Unpublished. Creighton University, Creighton, NE, 1987.

44. Lynch, Anthony J. "'Authenticity' in Language Teaching: Some Implications for the Design of Listening Materials." *The British Journal of Language Teaching* 20 (1982) :9-16.

45. _____. "The 'Unreality Principle': One Use of Television Commercials." *ELT Journal* 39, 2 (1985) :115-20.

46. Mainous, Bruce H. "Spanish for Agricultural Purposes: Another Use of Video," pp. 83-95 in Junetta B. Gillespie, ed., *Video and Second Language Learning*. Studies in Language Learning, vol. 5, no. 1. Urbana, IL: University of Illinois at Urbana-Champaign, 1985.

47. McMillen, Liz. "Learning Languages by Satellite: Using Videos to Improve Lectures." *The Chronicle of Higher Education* 32, 3 (1986): 25.

48. Meigs, James B. "Shoppers Guide to Satellite Receivers." *Video Review* 6, 5 (1985) :28-34.

49. Mueller, Gunther A. "Visual Contextual Clues and Listening Comprehension: An Experiment." *Modern Language Journal* 64 (1980) :335-40.

50. Omaggio, Alice C. *Teaching Language in Context: Proficiency-Oriented Instruction*. Boston, MA: Heinle & Heinle, 1986.

51. Pennycook, Alastair. "Actions Speak Louder Than Words: Paralanguage, Communication, and Education." *TESOL Quarterly* 19 (1985) :259-82.

52. Phillips, Blayne. "Student Video Production," pp. 86-100 in Marion Geddes and Gill Sturtridge, eds., *Video in the Foreign Language Classroom*. London, Eng.: Heinemann, 1982.

53. Postman, Neil. "Critical Thinking in the Electronic Era." *National Forum* 65, 1 (1985) :4-8,17.

54. Reimers, Theresia. "The Use of Video in Elementary Language Instruction." Presentation at First International Conference on Foreign Language Education and Technology, Tokyo, 1981.

55. Robinson, Rhonda S., Keith M. Collins, and Peter C. West. "No Funds? No Teachers? Share Advanced Courses with Other Schools via Interactive Cable Television." *Tech Trends* 30, 2 (1985) :17-19.

56. Rothblatt, Martin, and Noah Samara. "The Legal Picture." *Satellite World* 2, 7 (1985) :15-17.

57. Schultz, Jill M. *A Teacher's Guide to Television Evaluation for Children*. Springfield, IL: Charles C. Thomas, 1981.

58. Sinofsky, Esther R. "A Report from the AECT Copyright Task Force on Copyright Issues." *Tech Trends* 30, 4 (1985) :12-17.

59. Skirble, Rosanne. "Television Commercials in the Foreign Language Classroom." *Hispania* 60 (1977) :516-18.

60. Smith, Stephen. *The Theater Arts and the Teaching of Second Languages.* Reading, MA: Addison-Wesley, 1984.

61. Steele, F. "Venior, Video, Vinco—or—The Rubicon before Communicative Language Teaching and How to Cross It." *Bulletin CILA* 42 (1985) :71-84.

62. Svensson, Sture E., and Malmore Borgarskola. "Video, Authenticity, and Language for Special Purposes Teaching." *Foreign Language Annals* 18 (1985) :149-52.

63. Svobodny, Dolly D. *Research and Studies about the Use of Television and Film in Foreign Language Instruction: A Bibliography with Abstracts.* New York: MLA/ERIC, 1969. [ED 026 936]

64. Tamarkin, Toby. "Hurray for Hollywood." *Northeast Conference Newsletter* 19 (1986) :26-27.

65. Telatnik, Mary Ann, and William D. Krose. "Cultural Videotapes in the ESL Classroom." pp. 171-81 in Marion Geddes and Gill Sturtridge, eds., *Video in the Foreign Language Classroom.* London, Eng.: Heinemann, 1982.

66. Todd-Chattin, Ruth. "Teaching Culturally Appropriate Classroom Behavior through the Use of Video-Taped Mini-Dramas." *TESL Reporter* 18, 3 (1985) :43-46.

67. Townsend, Barbara K., and Larry Lewis. "Beyond Production: Some Solutions to Problems." *T.H.E. Journal* 11, 3 (1983): 125-27.

68. Ur, Penny. *Teaching Listening Comprehension.* Cambridge, Eng.: Cambridge University Press, 1984.

69. Utz, Peter. *Do-It-Yourself Video.* Englewood Cliffs, NJ: Prentice-Hall, 1984.

70. VanPatten, Bill. "Second Language Acquisition Research and the Learning/Teaching of Spanish: Some Research Findings and Implications." *Hispania* 69 (1986) :202-16.

71. "Video Exchange Network Founded." *Modern Language Journal* 70 (1986) :20.

72. Vizard, Frank. "Digital TV Arrives." *Video* 10, 3 (1986) :61-62.

73. Volkman, Anne. "Two-Way Instructional Television: A Technological Alternative for the 1980's." *NALLD Journal* 18, 1 (1983) :5-19.

74. von Faber, Helmut. "Codierungsformen medialer Kommunikation im Sprachunterricht." *CILA Journal* 42 (1985) :21-33.

75. Warner, Keith. "Francophone African Television and the Teaching of Cultural Elements to American Students." Presentation at the Georgetown Roundtable of Languages and Linguistics, Washington, DC, March, 1986.

76. Weissenrieder, Maureen. "Listening to the News in Spanish." *The Modern Language Journal* 71, 1 (1987) :18-27.

77. Wilson, John. "The Global Picture." *Satellite World* 2, 5 (1985) :16-19.

78. "Yale-Wellesley-WGBH Awarded Major Grant in Foreign Language by Annenberg/CPB." *Northeast Conference Newsletter* 16 (1984) :52-53.

Appendix

Guidelines for Off-Air Videotaping

1. The guidelines were developed to apply to off-air recording by nonprofit educational institutions.

2. A broadcast program may be recorded off-air simultaneously with broadcast transmission (including simultaneous cable retransmission) and retained by a nonprofit educational institution for a period not to exceed the first forty-five (45) consecutive calendar days after the date of recording. Upon conclusion of such retention period, all off-air recordings must be erased or destroyed immediately. "Broadcast programs" are television programs transmitted by television stations for reception by the general public without charge.

3. Off-air recordings may be used once by individual teachers in the course of relevant teaching activities, and repeated once when instructional reinforcement is necessary in classrooms and similar places devoted to instruction within a single building, cluster, or campus, as well as in the homes of students receiving formalized home instruction during the first ten (10) consecutive school days in the forty-five (45) calendar day retention period. "School days" are school sessions days—not counting weekends, holidays, vacations, examination periods, or other scheduled interruptions—within the forty-five (45) calendar day retention period.

4. Off-air recordings may be made only at the request of and used by individual teachers, and may not be regularly recorded in anticipation of the requests. No broadcast program may be recorded off-air more than once at the request of the same teacher, regardless of the number of times the program may be broadcast.

5. A limited number of copies may be reproduced from each off-air recording to meet the legitimate needs of teachers under these guidelines. Each such additional copy shall be subject to all provisions governing the original recording.

6. After the first ten (10) consecutive school days, off-air recordings may be used up to the end of the forty-five (45) calendar day retention period only for teacher evaluation purposes, i.e. to determine whether or not to include the broadcast program in the teaching curriculum, and may not be used in the recording institution for student exhibition or any other nonevaluation purpose without authorization.

7. Off-air recordings need not be used in their entirety, but the recorded programs may not be altered from their original content. Off-air recordings may not be physically or electronically combined or merged to constitute teaching anthologies or compilation.

8. All copies of off-air recordings must include the copyright notice on the broadcast programs as recorded.

9. Educational institutions are expected to establish appropriate control procedures to maintain the integrity of these guidelines.

Interactive Videodisc in Language Teaching

Maj. Michael D. Bush
Maj. Jill Crotty
United States Air Force Academy

Introduction

This chapter will describe a sampling of existing training and educational applications of interactive videodisc instruction (IAV), and will explore briefly the relationship between IAV and current theories of second-language instruction. Additional topics included are strategies to develop IAV courseware to enhance the instructional process, a summary of projects at the U.S. Air Force Academy that incorporate videodisc technology in language teaching, and an overview of research that is needed for future IAV implementations.

Cognitive psychologists assert that the single most important element in instruction is the teacher's awareness of what the learner knows prior to any teaching effort (Ausubel et al., 4). Reinforcing the importance of this principle, these same psychologists propose that what is to be taught must be related to what the student knows. Learning enough about each student to achieve this goal, however, defies accomplishment in conventional educational settings. Corbett and Smith (7), for example, found difficulty in applying results of a measure of learning style to "groups in aptitude by treatment analysis," yet state that the use of the same measure "seems consistent and interpretable for the individual student" (p. 220).

Despite the value of measuring individual differences, teachers who wish to use such assessment as a tool to meet each of their student's needs in a conventional classroom setting will encounter virtually insurmountable obstacles. The difficulties arise from the enormous amount of necessary information about each student these measures produce, information that is virtually impossible to interpret without extensive data processing due to its volume and complexity.

Directly related to the problem of information overload in conventional educational settings are research findings on the effects of class size cited by Klein (19, p. 578), who notes that the greatest gains in achievement occur among students taught in classes of fifteen pupils or less. Although the observations by Klein support the idea that teachers can work more effectively with smaller groups, no reason substantiates why. It is true that more time is available for each student, but perhaps the benefit is simply that in smaller classes the teacher can better address an individual's special needs. While large classes present the teacher with the aforementioned problem of data management, budgetary restrictions disallow much improvement in the teacher/student ratio because of the need to increase the efficiency of the teaching/learning process.

Teachers in conventional settings often attempt to solve the problem by providing a wide variety of materials and methods to reach the maximum number of students. Addressing the obvious lack of efficiency of such approaches, researchers at the Waterford School (established in Provo, Utah, by WICAT Systems), are using the computer to help identify learner profiles and then to tailor instruction.

Diagnosing learner profiles is only the first step. The computer is equally essential in the second task, providing instruction to address each learner's needs as they are identified. The computer's ability to manage information, control auxiliary devices, and mediate instruction—combined with the storage and retrieval capabilities of optical media technology—helps formulate a workable solution to the extremely complex instructional problem alluded to above. The potential of the current generation of computers and optical media, and others on the horizon, will make it possible to combine the strengths of these two technologies into one integrated and interactive instructional environment. This environment, in turn, will be able to meet the special needs of each individual second-language learner.

To become an effective means of instruction, interactive foreign language learning depends upon the computer's ability to diagnose learner profiles and to mediate instructional delivery. This environment also depends upon the development of a growing family of optical media to store and retrieve instructional material. Interactive videodisc is one of the most mature members of this family and is the primary focus of this chapter. This focus is justified in light of a growing awareness of the potential of interactive video for foreign languages (Rowe, 34), and the results of some experimental research on its effectiveness (Schrupp et al., 37; Crotty, 10; Gale and Barksdale 13; and Verano, 47).

Definition of Terms

Optical Media

Optical media are means of storing information as billions of nonreflective pits on the surface of a reflective material, which modulate the reflection of a laser light source. Although optical media are often used for "memory cards," more common forms are the LaserVision videodisc and the more recent Compact Disc-Audio (CD-Audio). Where CD-Audio discs have their information stored digitally (much as computers store information), laserdiscs have their information stored in analog form (like FM radio or television signals).

Videodisc. As the first commonly available form of optical media, the videodisc is a revolutionary storage device that will have a far-reaching impact on education, government, industry, and entertainment (Lambert and Sallis, 22). Although other types of optical media exist, the videodisc used most widely in interactive applications is the laser/optical version described above. A videodisc, similar in size to a long-playing record, contains prerecorded video and audio information suitable for playback through a standard television receiver or monitor connected to a videodisc player. There are two types of laser videodiscs: constant angular velocity (CAV), and constant linear velocity (CLV).

Each frame of video on a CAV disc is embedded in a separate 360-degree track. Each frame begins at the same place on its track, allowing the random-access capability that makes interactive applications possible. Each side of a CAV disc holds up to thirty minutes of video or 54,000 individual frames of visual information. In addition, two audio tracks furnish stereo or alternate audio programs (target language/English or dialog/narration) for the corresponding video.

CLV discs are formatted more densely to allow for up to one hour of full-motion video per side, but the process sacrifices many of the special features of the videodisc player (freeze frame, frame-stepping forward and reverse, and random access of specific frames). Because most commercially released movies are found in the CLV disc format, these materials cannot be used for interactive applications.

Compact Disc. Compact disc (CD) is a special form of optical media similar to the CLV videodisc but different in size (4.7″ or 12 cm in diameter) and format. As with videodiscs, the user cannot record onto or erase a CD, but because its information is recorded digitally, each CD has the advantage of being able to store an enormous amount of computer data and programs—up to 550 megabytes of digital data (the equivalent of 220,000 typed pages or 1,500 floppy discs), a capability that is receiving a great deal of attention in the microcomputer world in the form of CD Read Only Memory (CD-ROM)) (16).

For the most part, CD-ROM has limited application in education and training not only because full-screen, full-motion video with sound is difficult to obtain from digital data, but also because authoring systems have trouble handling visual information that is stored digitally. Nevertheless, there are at least three technologies that show promise in solving the motion problem mentioned above (14, 27): (1) CD-I (Compact Disc-Interactive), (2) DVI (Digital Video Interactive), and (3) ICVD (Interactive Compact Videodisc). One CD-I disc can store as many as 7000 natural pictures in 256 colors, as well as up to 16 channels of audio. DVI uses sophisticated data decompression capabilities and will allow up to 72 minutes of full-motion, full-screen digital video from CD-ROM. Software development requires a mainframe computer to compress the digital audio. ICVD is a nonstandard yet CD-based technology that combines the capabilities of videodisc with the digital storage capabilities of CD-ROM. The problem of authoring mentioned above is being resolved by powerful software made possible by increasingly advanced hardware.

Because of the popularity of CD-Audio in the computer marketplace and the resultant price drops in the cost of that technology, CD-based interactive instruction may also prove to be equally cost-effective and, if the problem of obtaining full-motion video from digital data is resolved, may demonstrate an even wider impact on education than the videodisc.

Interaction

A basic assumption underlying the teaching/learning process is the importance of interaction and the active participation of the student in the learning process. Such interaction can take a mostly mechanical form such as the degree to which the learner can control the learning environment. There is, however, another form of interaction that involves the learner's "psychological" interaction with the material as well as with the learning environment. The first form will be discussed below under the heading "Videodisc System Interaction," and the second under the heading "Learner Interaction."

Videodisc System Interaction. With IAV systems, students can control the pace and sequencing of instructional events and their components. The degree of interactivity of videodisc systems is cataloged by numbers.

Level 1 systems, composed of the videodisc player and a videodisc, allow random access to specific materials. The videodisc may contain embedded codes that direct a program to stop at predetermined locations and wait for an input from the user. Interaction is minimal because the user must follow the sequences programmed on the disc by the authors.

Level 2 videodisc systems include videodisc players with a built-in microprocessor. Such systems can run fairly sophisticated interactive programs with a small amount of branching and answer processing. The computer program must be stored on one of the videodisc's audio tracks from which it is automatically downloaded to the player's built-in microprocessor.

Level 3 systems include a random-access videodisc player controlled by a separate microcomputer and offer the greatest interactive capability. Such systems can run highly sophisticated interactive programs involving simulation and complex answer processing. The CAV laser disc used with Level 3 systems can be very simple; all the "intelligence"—branching, graphic overlays, instructional strategies—is provided by the microcomputer. Students interact with Level 3 systems through a keypad, touch screen, light pen, joystick, mouse, or bar-code reader. All Level 3 systems can switch between computer-generated and video disc images. Some systems have the capability to overlay computer text and graphics on the videodisc image.

Learner Interaction. The noted education journalist George Leonard (23) stated that learning in general takes place when learners interact with their environment. Supporting this notion, Frank Smith (41) writes that learning itself "is an interaction between the world around us and the theory of the world in our head" (p. 119). Smith also notes that learning is a process of problem solving: we learn when we cannot relate what we know to what we observe around us, when we do not understand, when we cannot predict. Otherwise stated, everything we presently know is a consequence of previous attempts to make sense of situations we have not understood. We have learned by formulating hypotheses, testing them, evaluating them, bringing about a modification of our cognitive structure. Interaction of this type may or may not be present in a typical educational setting owing to the limitations caused by class size, but using the system described above, interactive learning can be made an integral part of an interactive video lesson to help students attain a "depth" of cognitive processing (Stevick, 44) that signifies understanding.

Introduction to Interactive Videodisc

In the mid-seventies, "intelligent videodisc" (also referred to as interactive videodisc) was billed as an educational revolution. In 1985, Shaw (39) reported that corporate and educational Americans were just beginning to recognize the capabilities of the disc. In December of the same year, the U.S. Army released specifications for a videodisc-based electronic information delivery system (EIDS). The EIDS system may well become the standard hardware delivery system for all interactive video and computer-based training in the military branches. According to Miller (26), EIDS also adds credibility to videodisc technology.

The Society for Applied Learning Technology (SALT), has promoted interactive computer-based concepts since 1972; SALT's director (Fox, 11) agrees with other industry pioneers that the EIDS initiative will act as a detonator for the predicted explosion of the videodisc industry. In addition to military applications, Fox foresees a call for generic software that will affect the educational domain, including foreign languages. The military commitment will add credibility and clout to the videodisc technology and should make prices more competitive. According to Shaw (40), the reduction of prices along with an increase of available software is just what corporate America has been waiting for.

Why has the "revolution" predicted in the 70s taken so long to materialize? What has happened to the early enthusiasts who labeled interactive videodisc the greatest instructional innovation since movable type? According to Miller (25), there are three evolutionary stages in the life of most new technologies:

1. unbridled optimism—the technology is heralded as a universal panacea
2. pessimistic depression—limitations and obstacles become apparent and realism curbs optimism
3. real benefit and real value—the true potential of the technology is explored with cautious optimism.

According to Miller, the videodisc industry is poised for major advances and thus seems to be moving beyond step 3. There have been several successful innovations in videodisc technology and its use in a variety of markets that are certain to lure the competition into the fray (40). Such success is sure to have a positive effect on the application of IAV to the educational process in general (Ofeish, 31).

IAV in Education in General

Attitudes

Education has lagged behind industry and the military. Limited funding combined with the teaching profession's inherent reluctance to embrace new technologies has hampered educators who are enthusiastic about IAV and would like to use it in their classes. Higgins and Johns (17) note that negative experiences with computer-enhanced instruction do not reflect limited capabilities of the technology but rather highlight the limited imagination of program writers.

Applications

One of the earliest projects that investigated the feasibility of IAV instruction was conducted by Bunderson et al. (6). In this study, an intelligent (Level 3) videodisc system was used to teach a semester-long introductory course in biology, including laboratory practice, to university students in Texas and Utah. Results indicated that students who received videodisc instruction scored significantly higher on posttests than students who received instruction from a traditional classroom lecture/textbook/lab approach. The videodisc group scored 8-16 percent better on objective test items; 24-75 percent better on short-answer items; and 15-27 percent better on achievement tests. And the average total study time of the videodisc group was 30 percent less than that of the regular classes.

The University of California, Los Angeles (UCLA), and the University of Nebraska at Lincoln (UNL), have addressed the problems of laboratory instruction in science education (Russell, 36). The UCLA project evaluated the effectiveness of videodiscs compared with videotapes as a delivery system for instruction of freshmen chemistry students. The UNL project compared videodisc training with traditional laboratory instruction for six experiments, two each in biology, chemistry, and physics.

The UCLA evaluations revealed that videodisc users achieved significantly better results both on a prelaboratory quiz and on the accuracy of their experimental data. The evaluation team for the Nebraska project found the time required by the two groups to complete the experiments to be the most salient and significant difference: videodisc users in the biology experiments, for example, required about 10 percent less time than students in the traditional lab group; in chemistry, experiment completion time decreased by 65 percent for videodisc users.

Project Leader (42), jointly supported by the League for Innovation in the Community College (California), National Education Corporation, and Sony Communications Products Company, was completed in 1986. Under Project Leader, the National Education Training Company made available 60 videodisc sides with programs on electrical, electronic, and mechanical technologies. The League for Innovation in the Community College in turn selected schools where the programs were to be implemented. The interactive work stations were supplied by Sony Corporation. Participants believe Project Leader will encourage an increase in the use of interactive video-based educational programs in other colleges and universities. No evaluation of any of the programs has been reported to date, but a catalog with descriptions of available courseware has been published by Sony (43). Project Leader is of interest because of the unique blend of corporate and educational purposes it embodies; such cooperative efforts may provide a model for future and more extensive educational applications of interactive videodisc instruction in a wide variety of disciplines. A unique aspect of Project Leader is the courseware, which, in addition to offering a videodisc component, is print-based; that is, students also use workbooks containing text and pictures not included in the interactive lessons.

Another collaborative effort—involving the Center for Applied Linguistics, the Media Group, and Interactive Training, Inc.—has produced an interactive videodisc program designed to teach English and cultural skills for petroleum workers in Indonesia (Crandall, 8). The courseware, Skillpac: English for Industry, provides language instruction in an industrial context and focuses on usage. As yet, there is no published evaluation of the project.

The Videodisc Design/Production Group of the University of Nebraska recently attempted to compile an update of existing educational videodisc initiatives. A summary of the results along with the names of individuals to contact can be found in Schutz (38). Those projects most relevant to this chapter are outlined below:

1. A study skills disc (Tassler, 45), The Lost Civilization Expedition, produced by the Society for Visual Education, allows students to participate in three stages of an imaginary archaeological dig, first skimming for information, next recording facts, and finally drawing inferences. The lesson integrates on-line and off-line activities; hard-copy skill sheets are used before, during, and after working with the IAV system.
2. The Interactive Video Language Laboratory at the University of Massachusetts and the Laboratory for Instructional Technology at Boston University have produced a sample educational disc that includes an advanced lesson in conversation for English as a second language and a foreign language and a library simulation for nonnative speakers of English (Meskil, 24). Prototype lessons based on disc materials are under development.
3. Under a contract from the Department of Education, the Pennsylvania State University (Prinz, 33) has produced a Level 3 videodisc application designed to assist hearing-impaired and other handicapped children in the language development process. Children select words that are illustrated with pictures or sign language. Illustrations may be in motion or still-frame. Children can then use the words to create sentences. The created sentences are illustrated by computer graphics. The vocabulary on the disc can be heard in English or Spanish according to which audio track is selected by the user.

IAV In Foreign Language Education

Specific IAV applications in foreign language instruction are not numerous. Some of the same reluctance that has slowed the implementation of interactive instruction in education in general has taken perhaps a greater toll in foreign language education. In fact, many language teachers who have adopted an attitude of wait and see remember promises of other "technological revolutions"—i.e., educational television and the language laboratory. Others warn of a parallel between the enthusiasm that accompanied the latter and the recent excitement surrounding applications of computer-assisted language learning and interactive videodisc instruction (CALL/IAV). Fortunately, it is generally accepted that the problems with the language laboratory were caused by inappropriate use rather than any inherent problems with the technology available at that time. As Underwood (46) points out, the "success or failure of any technological aid will have less to do with what it can do than with what we are actually doing with it" (p. 39). In spite of this reticence, there are several examples of CALL/IAV implementations.

Specific Projects

The first videodisc containing video conceived for language learning was created at Brigham Young University (BYU) as part of the Montevidisco Project funded by the Fund for the Improvement of Post-Secondary Education (Gale, 12). The material was filmed in Mexico and was used to create a video-based interactive adventure game to teach Spanish (see also Part II, Report 7, pp. 221-34, this volume).

VELVET (Video Enhanced Learning, Video Enhanced Teaching), a joint project of the Defense Language Institute (DLI), BYU, and the National Security Agency (NSA) has been ongoing for several years (Hendricks et al., 15). This project also has included on-location filming of materials to support DLI's German Gateway program, a seven-week immersion program designed for senior military officers. Field testing was completed in July 1986. Preliminary results indicated that students who studied via videodisc increased their average score on oral interviews from a 0+ to a 1 on the DLI scale of oral proficiency.

The United States Naval Academy is able to access foreign language materials via satellite dish. (See Part II, Report 8, pp. 243-48, this volume.) With attention to copyright restrictions, materials are reviewed and selected for transfer to the videodisc medium. To date, three videodiscs have been produced, two in Spanish featuring excerpts from the Mexican version of "Sixty Minutes" and one in French with selections from Antenne 2. Courseware designers have developed templates which allow instructors to author interactive, computer-mediated lessons using the videodisc materials.

Three IAV projects at the United States Air Force Academy have made positive statements about the potential power of IAV instruction for second-language teaching.

Schrupp et al. (37) investigated the effectiveness of IAV instruction for use with first-year students of German. The project was limited in scope and did not involve integration of IAV technology into an entire course. Students in existing beginning German courses were tested on comprehension and retention of material contained in a 12-minute film. The film was presented in three applications ranging from completely noninteractive to IAV presentation. The experiment lasted 10 class days. A short (8-item) comprehension quiz was given immediately after the initial viewing of the film and then again 6 to 8 days later. Results indicated an advantage for IAV presentation over more conventional methods.

In a second study, Crotty (10) compared the effectiveness of IAV instruction versus traditional classroom presentation of materials from *De vive voix* (Moget and Neveu, 28) for students in beginning French. The study involved two class sessions (90 minutes of instruction). Although the results were not statistically significant, the videodisc group outperformed the classroom group by a margin of 8 percent on posttest measures covering general comprehension as well as discrete vocabulary and grammar items. Analysis of the completion questions on the posttest revealed a significantly superior performance by members of the videodisc group in terms of content and spelling accuracy.

In the third study, Verano (47) investigated linear, segmented, and interactive modes of IAV presentation and their impact on achievement and retention of materials from *Zarabanda* (Ariza et al., 3) in beginning Spanish. Results of this short-term study indicated that university students who received instruction in an interactive manner (branching, hints, remediation on demand) outperformed those limited to less interactive study when tested on their understanding of content (see Part II, pp. 235-42, this volume).

One of the most extensive foreign language initiatives in the academic community is the Annenberg-CPB-sponsored Athena Language Learning Project (ALLP) at MIT. The ALLP is creating courseware for a four-course sequence in each of five languages—French, Spanish, Russian, German, and English as a second language—that will make use of artificial intelligence and include interactive video and audio. The materials are being developed on the basis of a sociolinguistic theory that "linguistic competence, i.e., the ability to use correctly the grammatical and lexical structures of a foreign language, is a subset of a more general discourse competence that includes the ability to express, interpret, and negotiate meanings within the social context of interpersonal interactions" (Murray et al., 30, p. 32). The focus of instruction is shifted from learning the mechanics of the target language to actually using the language to explore situations and solve problems. According to project developers, the computer serves as the facilitator in a multimedia learning environment and requires higher-level cognitive operations than found in most current applications. (See Chapter 4 in this volume for further information.)

A Theoretically Sound Rationale for IAV

The establishment of the theoretical foundations for IAV begins with an examination of the extent to which applications of the technology reflect tenets from a theory of second-language acquisition. Krashen (20) has summarized five hypotheses from the research into the second-language acquisition process over the last decade. Of these, the input hypothesis and the affective filter hypothesis seem most relevant to the concept of IAV instruction.

The input hypothesis suggests that language is acquired in direct relationship to the amount of comprehensible input to which the student is exposed, where comprehensible input is defined as language at the student's current level of ability (i) as well as some content somewhat beyond the learner's current level of competence ($i + 1$). The student understands ($i + 1$) content from the context and makes use of extralinguistic elements (pictures, objects, gestures) that relate to the world experience he or she brings to the situation or context under study. Comprehension is also made possible by the manner in which the input is selected and controlled by the lesson.

IAV delivery systems allow course designers to select and manipulate the input that students receive according to effective pedagogical strategies. Contextualized and extralinguistic information provided by the video material help students infer meaning from materials above their current level of competency.

The Affective Filter hypothesis is equally relevant. According to Krashen (20), success in acquiring a foreign language correlates with the following variables: (1) anxiety (the lower the better), (2) motivation (the more positive the better), and (3) self-confidence (the greater the better).

Since all input to the student must pass through an "affective filter" formed by these variables, a negative attitude will act as a dense filter, reducing the impact of input on the student's cognition and therefore blocking acquisition. The affective filter hypothesis prescribes the ambiance that will optimize the language acquisition process: it must be a low-anxiety atmosphere in which students are attentive and interested in what's taking place. In accordance with the input and affective filter hypotheses, the effective language teacher is someone who can provide input and make it comprehensible in a low-anxiety situation. Krashen (20) suggests that theory resulting from research over the past decade predicts that successful language programs will do the following:

1. Supply a great deal of relevant and interesting comprehensible input to the student in which the goal of the input is to transmit meaning.
2. Enable students to begin to speak when they are ready.
3. Tolerate errors in early efforts.
4. Shift the focus from grammar to meaning.

The IAV instructional system allows the teacher to create such an environment. Students are placed in control of the input they receive, thus eliminating the anxiety caused by not understanding the instructor or being unsure how to respond. Learners work through the materials at their own pace; they are not asked to "perform" in front of peers. Their confidence in their ability to handle the materials has time to develop before being made "public."

In summary, IAV instruction appears to embody many of the principles emerging from the growing foundation of theoretical research in the field of second-language acquisition. Justification for its use in the instructional process is thus straightforward. The problem is one of effective transfer of IAV into classroom activities. In order to mesh with proficiency-based, communicative language-teaching approaches of the 80s, IAV instruction needs to reflect these characteristics common to most of the communicative approaches:

1. Meaningful rather than mechanical practice
2. Priority of listening over speaking
3. Exclusive use of target language
4. Implicit rather than explicit grammar

5. Modeling instead of correction
6. Special efforts to create a low-anxiety atmosphere in the classroom

The incorporation of these guidelines into any model of instruction is a function of lesson design. Unimaginative or unsound IAV courseware will not be much better than an unimaginative classroom presentation. Each of the characteristics listed above will be discussed in the following section.

A Theoretical Basis for Lesson Design Strategies _____

Meaningful Rather than Mechanical Practice

The use of video-based exercises makes practice inherently more meaningful than traditional text-based exercises. Video gives students an understandable context in which to work while providing many extralinguistic clues. The control options built into the interactive lesson allow students an array of problem-solving strategies to choose from.

Priority of Listening over Speaking

An IAV system places priority on listening over speaking. Emerging technologies may eventually make a speaking component a feasible addition to an IAV system; whether or not such an addition will be an enhancement is another issue. Informal evaluations of students using IAV systems at the Air Force Academy indicate that pronunciation and intonation improve as a result of the intense auditory input that typically accompanies IAV instruction. In one instance, a less-than-gifted student of beginning French who had created his own sound-symbol correspondence for the French language made what his instructor felt to be miraculous progress in pronunciation after working through a videodisc-based lesson. The student was asked to relate what one of the video characters was talking about. He replied, "Il est [est] derrière vous [vus]." Pronunciation, accent, and intonation were decidedly Americanized. The instructor asked if that was how the video character had spoken. The student replied without hesitation "Oh no, he said, 'Il est [e] derrière vous [vu].' " Accent, intonation, and pronunciation were near native! Does this mean that IAV input results in more accurate replication of speech? More research is needed to find the answer.

Exclusive Use of the Target Language

Videodiscs designed for foreign language instruction can be made language-intensive. The use of both tracks of audio allows IAV lesson designers to maximize the use of the target language according to the needs of the learner and in accordance with course objectives. The video context and individual control over the flow of the lesson allow students to process meaning without translation. Apparently, the audiovisual delivery of lesson materials via IAV motivates the student to understand all of the second-language examples. In short, students using IAV seem more willing to take risks and guess at the meaning of what they hear than they are with traditional teaching techniques alone.

Implicit Rather Than Explicit Grammar

Videodisc materials allow students to "participate" in "real-use" language situations where the focus is on meaning rather than grammar. Student tasks are centered on deciphering what is happening rather than identifying grammar rules in action. Being able to respond to a situation is perfectly possible without understanding the specifics of the grammar in each utterance. This focus on meaning, in turn, seems crucial in helping the learner come to an intuitive grasp of the mechanics of the second language without recourse to conscious processing of input or monitoring of output.

Correction/Corroboration through Modeling

The videodisc materials provide continuous, consistent, and readily available modeling of language in action. The courseware can be designed to provide this modeling automatically in response to incorrect student responses or can allow students to ask for a modeled answer as they feel necessary. Students are forced into self-evaluation and correction of errors. Modeling can be incorporated in any of several formats, according to design strategies. For example, the student can be directed to or can select to repeat disc segments containing the desired content.

Special Efforts to Create a Low-Anxiety Atmosphere

An IAV system eliminates many potential causes of anxiety. Students control the pace and sequencing of the lesson. Help in the form of repetition, paraphrasing, access to a dictionary, and other on-line resources such as video and graphics is available on command with appropriately designed courseware. Thus, an IAV system acts as an equalizer, reducing the gap between the most talented and the less talented students. The less talented can improve their skills and increase their confidence before being asked to perform in front of more talented classmates. Talented students are encouraged to expand their skills in a similar confidence-building milieu.

Strategies for IAV Lesson Design _____

One of the challenges in introducing IAV into a language program is deciding which tasks should be relegated to the technology and which ones should be left with the classroom teacher (Ariew, 1; Ariew and Frommer, 2). A first analysis suggests that activities that are static, predictable, and convergent are prime candidates for IAV implementation. On the other hand, activities that are dynamic, unpredictable, and divergent seem to be best kept in the classroom, under teacher control. This leads to the second notion that should guide the development of IAV lessons: class time should not be used for activities that each student can do individually (watch a film or work on a written assignment). Both are exercises that can be done outside of class with CALL/IAV materials.

To cite an example, in 1982-83 the French Section of the Department of Foreign Languages at the U.S. Air Force Academy prepared several interactive lessons based on French films designed for teaching French via broadcast television. These lessons met with great success, even given the limited capabilities of 3/4" U-Matic videotape players controlled by Texas Instruments 99/4A computers. In these out-of-class lessons (the stations were set up in the computer center and later in the library's media center), intermediate students watched short segments of each film and then answered questions on the content of the segment. Wrong answers caused the program to respond with written hints and a replay of a short segment of the film that revealed the correct answer.

In spite of their simplicity, these lessons prompted very positive comments from students as well as instructors. Students liked the instant feedback to answers, and teachers were amazed at the quality of class discussion in French about the films that was possible following the assignment.

Where the above illustration included students who had a certain experience with the language (two to three semesters), the second has to do with students who had no prior experience in the target language. Students were divided into two groups: one received the presentation of the new material in the classroom using innovative instructional techniques while the second group was presented the new material in the laboratory using some very simple and straightforward exercises with IAV. The lab students did as well on an informal posttest of achievement and comprehension as did the classroom group, and gave very positive comments on the experience.

Teaching Basic Language Concepts

Following Bloom (5), strategies for teaching basic language concepts to beginning students fall in the range of knowledge of facts. Specifically, they allow the student to acquire the basic elements of the target language—sound-symbol correspondence, word order, etc.—and meaning (both global and specific) through four types of self-paced exercises.

The first, called "student control," is made available after an initial presentation of the video sequence being learned. It allows students to hear each phrase at will, as often as they desire, moving forward and backward from phrase to phrase until they feel comfortable with the new sounds. After this initial presentation phase, the computer displays in random order the words of each utterance in turn from the scenario on the screen. The student's task in this second exercise is to reassemble the sentence in its correct order. Each time a word is misselected, the computer replays the video scenario with the utterance.

The third type of exercise presents each utterance and asks the student to infer its probable meaning from several paraphrases that are displayed on the screen. In the fourth exercise, the computer randomly removes a word from each phrase and checks the student's ability to recreate the word that is missing.

Experience has shown that this simple array of exercises sufficiently introduces the students to new materials to enable them to use the newly acquired structures in more creative exercises in the classroom. Albeit mechanical, these exercises limit the treatment of language to the elements that are in fact mostly mechanical, leaving more meaningful use of language for a setting more suited to the open-ended nature of meaningful language-learning activities.

Teaching Global Comprehension

Of great importance in foreign language learning is the need to teach students how to understand spoken language from authentic sources. Much effort has been spent on using the language laboratory for this purpose, but the absence of true interaction and the lack of visual cues have limited its success. IAV enables courseware designers to take advantage of visual cues, asking comprehension questions on the dramatic content of the video sequences. Correct answers are confirmed as correct with appropriate comments to the student, while incorrect answers are remediated with hints, followed by an additional presentation of the video segment that contains the correct answer.

This teaching strategy appears to conform to Krashen's theories on comprehensible input noted above. Through the use of these simple confirmation and remediation activities, the materials are more likely to address each student's $i + 1$ level than is possible through more conventional means of instruction.

Future Strategies

Two of the more promising IAV capabilities for the future are (1) real-time access to extensive, multimedia dictionaries and other "help" features made possible through compact disc technologies, and (2) the capability of artificial-intelligence techniques to provide powerful answer-processing functions for IAV lessons. Both of these innovations are based upon technologies that exist today in prototype form and will be widely available as the price of personal computers and optical-media peripherals continues to drop.

Real-time access touches on one of the primary challenges to designers of IAV lessons: the requirement to anticipate the needs of learners encountering any new material for the first time. Even if the writer is able to anticipate the learner's need for help, designing the necessary help material is no trivial task. Placing multimedia "help" resources (dictionaries and grammar explanations) on compact disc and at the disposition of the learner from within any given lesson frees the instructional designer to concentrate on the lesson's instructional objective rather than on the elements of help screens that may or may not be needed.

Another often criticized aspect of IAV materials is the limitation of the multiple-choice and fill-in-the-blank exercises that are required by present technology. Artificial-intelligence techniques will allow future applications to give the computer a basic grammar and vocabulary, thus permitting a more informative treatment of wrong answers than simply "Wrong, try again!" "Expert systems" will make it possible to match response errors with an extensive database of cataloged errors that students have made in the past keyed to suggestions for remediation. Although these possibilities will be somewhat limited at first, systems of the more distant future will develop into intelligent tutors, having a rather complete knowledge of the target language and the ability to effectively remediate mistakes made by the student.

Needed Research

Research needed to increase the effectiveness of IAV can be classified into three basic categories, (1) learner profile research, (2) materials development research, and (3) learner/materials interaction research. The variables that make students different need to be studied closely. Advanced IAV systems will be able to collect significant data on the effectiveness of learner strategies and provide feedback on the numerous possible instructional approaches. Equally important is the study of how students with different cognitive and affective profiles are able to learn using various types of materials (Krashen, 21). Each of these areas of research is elaborated below.

Learner Profile

For IAV to achieve its maximum potential, much research must be accomplished to identify how and why individual students learn differently. The affective and cognitive domains have been identified as sources of individual differences (Rubin and Thompson, 35; Oxford, 32) but the knowledge base in both areas must be extended if foreign language instruction is to address individual differences by means of educational technology. The basic questions that must be answered are (1) What makes some students more successful than others at language learning, and (2) How can mediated instruction best help all types of learners?

Materials Preparation

Related questions to be addressed for IAV courseware include: What types of materials are best suited for beginning, for intermediate, and for advanced students? What constitutes an essential vocabulary and how fast should new words be presented? For what concepts is an inductive approach more suitable than a deductive approach?

Two main areas for needed research thus are (1) the development of resource materials such as on-line multimedia dictionaries and easily accessible grammar summaries and (2) the development of various databases and programming capabilities to mediate instructional efforts that invovle artificial intelligence.

Aptitude x Treatment Interaction

Determining how students of differential learning styles and abilities react to each type of presentation is the logical next step. The important question thus is, What types of materials and methods of presentation are interesting and effective for what types of learners?

Carefully designed experimental strategies are required to study these "student to materials to machine" interactions. Something along the lines of interaction analysis techniques found commonly in classroom research (Cronbach and Snow, 9) may hold some promise in this regard. One obvious necessity is to classify the various types of interactions possible between the student and the material.

The fully developed computer-based configuration of the future will respond to students beginning each session in a manner totally unlike today's bland welcome. Instead, the computer will search its database for information on the student's performance during previous sessions in consonance with "knowledge" about his or her learning profile. In short, the computer will "know" the student and adjust the instruction he or she receives accordingly.

Conclusion

Some of the notions described above are feasible today; others are not. Falling hardware costs, however, combined with the increased power and options available from a variety of new technologies are sufficient reason to be optimistic about the continued potential of applying technological resources to second-language teaching. In any case, true success is dependent upon learning about the language-learning process itself. Not enough is known about how people learn languages and why they learn at different rates (Jarvis, 18). Nor is it known how best to develop good IAV materials to reach each individual learner. If technology is to be exploited to its fullest, it is essential that answers be found to questions in these areas. But the development/application process must begin somewhere. It is not necessary to develop "perfect" IAV activities in order to get the ball rolling. Implementing *a priori* hypotheses about how best to use technology and then studying the results will lay the foundation for improvements in the future. To paraphrase Andrew Molnar (29) of the National Science Foundation, "the only way to learn how to do interactive videodisc, is to do it."

References, Interactive Videodisc in Language Teaching

1. Ariew, Robert. "Integrating Video and CALL in the Curriculum: The Role of the ACTFL Guidelines," pp. 41-66 in Wm. Flint Smith, ed., *Modern Media in Foreign Language Education: Theory and Implementation.* Lincolnwood, IL: National Textbook Company, 1987.

2. _____, and Judith G. Frommer. "Interaction in the Computer Age," pp. 177-93 in Wilga M. Rivers, ed., *Interactive Language Teaching.* Cambridge, Eng.: Cambridge University Press, 1987.

3. Ariza, F., M. Sperber, and M. Fernandez-Gasalla. *Zarabanda.* St. Paul, MN: EMC, 1972.

4. Ausubel, David P., Joseph D. Novak, and Helen Hanesian. *Educational Psychology: A Cognitive View.* New York: Holt, Rinehart & Winston, 1978.

5. Bloom, Benjamin S., ed., *Taxonomy of Educational Objectives.* Handbook I, Cognitive Domain. White Plains, NY: Longman, 1969.

6. Bunderson, C. Victor, James B. Olsen, and Bruce Baillo. *An Intelligent Videodisc System: Evaluation in Developmental Biology.* Orem, UT: WICAT, Inc., 1981.

7. Corbett, Stephen S., and Wm. Flint Smith. "Identifying Student Learning Styles: Proceed with Caution!" *The Modern Language Journal* 68 (1984) :212-21.

8. Crandall, J.R. Personal communication.

9. Cronbach, L. J. and R. E. Snow. *Aptitudes and Instructional Methods.* New York: Irvington, 1977.

10. Crotty, Jill. "Instruction via an Intelligent Videodisc System versus Classroom Instruction for Beginning College French Students: A Comparative Experiment." Unpublished Ph.D. dissertation, University of Kansas, 1984.

11. Fox, Ray. "Observations of an Industry Leader." *Training Solutions* 2, 4 (1985) :2.

12. Gale, Larrie E. "Montevidisco: An Anecdotal History of an Interactive Videodisc." *CALICO Journal* 1, 1 (1983) :41-46.

13. _____, and Karl Barksdale. "The Development and Formative Evaluation of 'Interactive Dígame' Courseware." Department of Instructional Science, Brigham Young University, Provo, UT, 1986. Mimeo.

14. "Games Companies Go Interactive." *The Videodisc Monitor* 5, 7 (1987):4.

15. Hendricks, Harold, Junius Bennion, and Jerry Larson. "Technology and Language Learning at BYU [Brigham Young University]." *CALICO Journal* 1, 3 (1983) :23-30.

16. "Here Comes the Compact Disc." *Instructional Delivery Systems* 1, 4 (1987) :8-10.

17. Higgins, John, and Tim Johns. *Computers in Language Learning.* Reading, MA; Addison-Wesley, 1984.

18. Jarvis, Gilbert A. "The Psychology of Second Language Learning: A Declaration of Independence." *The Modern Language Journal* 67 (1983) :394-402.

19. Klein, Karen. "The Research on Class Size." *Phi Delta Kappan* 66, 8 (1985): 578-80.

20. Krashen, Stephen D. *Principles and Practice in Second Language Acquisition.* Oxford, Eng.: Pergamon, 1982.

21. _____."Applications of Psycholinguistic Research to the Classroom," pp. 51-59 in Charles J. James, ed., *Practical Applications of Research in Foreign Language Teaching.* Lincolnwood, IL: National Textbook Company, 1983.

22. Lambert, Steve, and Jane Sallis, eds., *CD-I and Interactive Videodisc Technology.* Indianapolis: Howard W. Sams and Comp., 1987.

23. Leonard, George. *Education and Ecstasy.* New York: Dell, 1968.

24. Meskil, Carla. "An Advanced ESL Conversation Lesson and Library Simulation." *NEWS (Newsletter of the Videodisc Design/Production Group, University of Nebraska, Lincoln)* 8, 1 (1986) :3.

25. Miller, Rockley L. "The Ripple Effect of EIDS." *The Videodisc Monitor,* 4, 1 (1986) :2.

26. _____ "CD ROM and Videodisc: Lessons to be Learned," pp. 37-42 in Steve Lambert and Suzanne Ropiequet, eds., *The New Papyrus: CD ROM*. Redmond, WA: Microsoft Press, 1986.

27. _____ "Fear [of Losing in the Marketplace]." *The Videodisc Monitor* 5, 7 (1987) :2.

28. Moget, Therese, and Pierre Neveu. *De Vive Voix*. Paris: Didier, 1972.

29. Molnar, Andrew R. "Intelligent Videodisc and the Learning Society." *Journal of Educational Technology Systems* 8, 1 (1980) :31-40, (1983) :11-16.

30. Murray, Janet H., Claire Kramsch, and Douglas Morgenstern. "Designing Materials for the Language Lab of the Future: An Overview of the MIT Athena Language Learning Project." *CALICO Journal* 2, 4 (1985): 31-34.

31. Ofeish, Gabriel D. "Interactive Information Technologies and Their Potential in Education," pp. 161-67 in Steve Lambert and Jane Sallis, eds., *CD-I and Interactive Videodisc Technology*. Indianapolis: Sams, 1987.

32. Oxford, Rebecca. "Second Language Learning Strategies: What the Research Has to Say." *ERIC/CALL News Bulletin* 9, 1 (1985) :3-4.

33. Prinz, Philip. "ALPHA Interactive Language Project." *NEWS (Newsletter of the Videodisc Design/Production Group, University of Nebraska, Lincoln)* 8, 1 (1986) :3.

34. Rowe, A. Allen. "Interactive Language Simulation Systems: Technology for a National Language Base." *CALICO Journal* 2, 3 (1985) :44-47.

35. Rubin, Joan, and Irene Thompson. *How to Be a More Successful Language Learner*. Boston, MA: Heinle & Heinle, 1982.

36. Russell, Arlene. "Videodisc Based Training Explored for Classroom Laboratory Instruction." *Video Computing* (April 1985) :8.

37. Schrupp, David M., Michael D. Bush, and Gunther A. Mueller. " 'Klavier im Haus'—An Interactive Experiment in Foreign Language Instruction." *CALICO Journal* 1, 2 (1983) :17-21.

38. Schutz, Mary N. "Education Videodiscs." *NEWS (Newsletter of the Videodisc Design/Production Group, University of Nebraska, Lincoln)* 8, 1 (1986) :2-7.

39. Shaw, Michael. "Observations on an Industry Leader." *Training Solutions* 2, 4 (1985) :2.

40. _____ "Training and POS [Point of Sale] Drive Disc into Limelight." *Video Computing* (April 1985) :1.

41. Smith, Frank. *Comprehension and Learning*. New York: Holt, Rinehart & Winston, 1975.

42. Sony Corporation of America. Press release. 18 October 1985.

43. _____. Software catalog., NJ: Sony Communications Products Company, Park Ridge, NJ, 1986.

44. Stevick, Earl W. *Teaching Languages: A Way and Ways.* Rowley, MA: Newbury House, 1980.

45. Tassler, Nancy. "Study Skills: The Lost Civilization Expedition." *NEWS (Newsletter of the Videodisc Design/Production Group, University of Nebraska, Lincoln)* 8, 1 (1986) :2-3.

46. Underwood, John H. *Linguistics, Computers and the Language Teacher: A Communicative Approach.* Rowley, MA: Newbury House, 1984.

47. Verano, Miguel. "Achievement and Retention in Spanish Presented via Videodisc in Linear, Segmented, and Interactive Modes." Unpublished Ph.D. dissertation, University of Texas (Austin), 1987.

4

The Athena Language-Learning Project: Design Issues for the Next Generation of Computer-Based Language-Learning Tools

Janet H. Murray
Douglas Morgenstern
Gilberte Furstenberg
Massachusetts Institute of Technology

Introduction

The Athena Language-Learning Project (ALLP), the largest of MIT's Athena Projects and funded by the Annenberg/CPB Foundation, represents an attempt to shape the emerging workstation-based computer medium for the purposes of communication-based language learning. The educational goals of the project have been clear from the start and represent the impetus for exploring the computer medium. ALLP is currently exploring ways to turn the promise of the new workstations for these communicative learning tasks into realities. This challenge has resulted in an ongoing design effort focused simultaneously on the creation of prototypical materials under the LINCS rubric (Language Instruction through Communication-based Software) and on the shaping of the workstation medium to support these materials. This chapter traces the design decisions facing the project in its first three years.

Educational Principles

Communicative Approach

At the base of ALLP are the major principles of a communicative approach to language learning (see Kramsch, 8; Widdowson, 21). Language is seen as a negotiable system of meanings, expressed and interpreted via the social interaction of reader and text, or between speakers in a culturally coded situation rather than as a closed system of formal lexical and grammatical rules. Accordingly, the aim of the materials being developed is not so much the mastery of the grammatical and syntactic code as the ability to use this code to perform or have others perform certain actions, e.g., access useful information or give orders to protagonists in a story. Language is thus learned through its use in communication.

The conversation-based programs are meant to use both the artificial intelligence (AI) and the "artificial unintelligence" of computers to motivate students to learn and use the foreign language. This use of language on the computer, at this stage of technology, however, cannot include speech recognition. Messages are typed in by the student and the answers are displayed on the screen. One might argue that the process of silent and visual communication using spoken langauge is an unnatural one. Whether students can learn to treat the machine as a human being and use more natural forms of discourse to "converse" with it rather than the primitive computerese they are used to remains to be seen. In the learning process, however, slowing down the speech by having students type in their utterances—allowing them time for both self-monitoring and self-reflection—could be a distinct advantage.

ALLP is exploiting MIT-based techniques of natural-language processing and knowledge representation to develop a system with maximal tolerance of errors and minimal tolerance of ambiguity. The goal of the AI portion of the Project is to develop a natural-language processing system that can intelligently "guess" the meanings intended from minimal clues, and check its understanding with the user. Frequent requests for clarification, suggested meanings ("Do you mean X?"), and restatements and paraphrases by the computer should serve both as a "natural" correction behavior and as a model for the negotiation of meanings in natural face-to-face interaction. Another key goal is to understand the surface structure of utterances and their intentionality within given frames of reference. It is hoped that, by operating within the restricted lexical and grammatical resources of second-year students, the range of unpredictable behavior to which the system has to respond can be narrowed. (The question of predictability is dealt with in more detail below.)

It is likely, however, that the students' imaginations will exceed the limits of the natural language the computer can understand, in which case the "unintelligence" of the system becomes an asset. Whether the "failures" of the computer are integrated into the fiction narrative (the persona in the machine claims amnesia) or whether they imitate natural breakdowns in communication ("I don't quite get what you meant."), the goal is always to encourage the student to repeat, restate, paraphrase, or circumlocute as in natural conversation.

In addition, the material is designed in such a way that it trains students to recognize topics and follow them up. For example, rather than initiating exchanges and offering tasks to be solved, No Recuerdo (a program in Spanish described below) involves students in conversation with an amnesiac scientist (see Morgenstern 12 and 13) and invites them to identify which topics to pursue in order to reach a certain piece of information and decide which questions to ask and with what degree of politeness or indirectness. This concept was created by Claire Kramsch as "Reverse Eliza" because unlike Weizenbaum's Eliza therapist program (20), the user rather than the computer examines and manipulates the interlocutor's speech in order to elicit further revelations.

Finally, the materials are based on the interaction of the student and the computer as well as on that of students and teacher in the classroom. These are not "stand-alone" lessons for self-instruction. They find their ultimate meaning in the way they are integrated into a communicative approach to language learning and teaching. The materials are to be followed up and supplemented by reports, role-plays, simulation activities, and written texts in the classroom, based either on a gradient of differing information gathered by individual students at workstations or on the result of discussions among groups working in cooperation at one common station. Toward this end the Project is designing a new Language Learning and Resource Center that will feature multiperson computer-based carrels and adjacent classrooms with large-screen computer projectors.

The interactive nature of cooperative learning, one of the major principles of communicative language instruction, calls into question traditional means of evaluating the effectiveness of the material because the intended effect— the encouragement of a different pedagogy by the teacher and of a different mode of learning by the student—cannot be measured by the usual psychometric devices of the input-output variety. In contrast, the impact of the material on the students' motivation, interest, and general cognitive and linguistic abilities will have to be assessed in ways approximating more the method of the social sciences (students' reports, teacher diaries, thinking aloud protocols, etc.) than those of the natural sciences.

Simulations

Simulation, long used in fields as diverse as urban studies and military planning, offers a means of implementing two important language-learning goals. First, simulation provides a highly contextualized environment (created by the simulation's designer) that transcends the computer and classroom space. Learners use the target language to talk about something and to accomplish a series of tasks leading to the fulfillment of specific objectives. Although role-playing occurs during this process, simulations are not dramatic skits; participants think and act strategically, motivated by the need to cooperate and compete with one another. A full range of discourse functions arise naturally in this situation, e.g., in a business simulation a salesperson may have to convince a client, while in a political simulation an official may need to threaten, promise, or make excuses.

A second feature is the transfer of discourse power from the instructor to the language learners. In classroom simulations, once the ground rules have been set, the students do most of the talking and must open and close conversations and control topics if they are to accomplish their tasks. The instructor's role is limited largely to facilitating the activity, offering help (as unobtrusively as possible) with vocabulary, syntax, etc., and filling in holes in the context by means of guiding questions or probes. This instructor posture continues into the final debriefing, which includes feedback on content (whose goals were met and why) as well as the linguistic and cultural appropriateness of participants' behavior.

In addition to offering rich context and high learner control, computer-aided simulation can be less subject to the constraints of real-time interaction. A move-based simulation gives participants time to reflect on their actions and obtain available linguistic or cultural help. If the activity also includes access to videodisc or a similar information-storage device, the added advantage of authentic settings and native-speaker models can at least partially simulate interaction in the target-language environment. The most rewarding system will encompass and integrate both classroom and computer-simulation phases.

The Technological Base

The Athena Language Learning Project is using computer technology that models what will be available to colleges and universities in the 1990s. As part of the $70 million campuswide Project Athena, ALLP has access to a network of workstations (UNIX-based DEC microvaxes and IBM RTs), some of which have interactive video and the capability of advanced graphics. The Language Learning and Resource Center being planned will have thirty of these workstations, including some in adjoining classrooms. Prices are expected to come down in the 1990s to the point at which other universities can adopt the same workstation technology at costs close to those for the current generation of microcomputers.

The advantages of the networked workstation over the microcomputer are increased speed and memory (at least 1 million instructions per second and 3-4 megabytes of running memory, as well as 40-megabyte hard disks and increased remote storage on the network). Speed and memory translate into the ability to use artificial intelligence programming for real-time natural-language processing. The addition of laserdisc players, of CD ROM players (eventually), and of audio-to-digital boards to the basic work station allows for storage and retrieval of video and audio data along with large textual and visual databases (dictionaries, slide libraries), and processing of spoken input.

ALLP's use of digitial audio and speech processing steers away from speech synthesis and speech recognition, both of which are underdeveloped for language teaching purposes. Instead, the computer is used to give repetitive practice first in speech perception and then in speech production, both with immediate feedback. The challenge of this side of the project will be the building of spectrographic displays that convey appropriate information.

The potential capabilities of this new computer medium are quite promising. Noteworthy are (1) the encyclopedic information usually associated with print that can be recalled with the speed of a computer, (2) the extensive models of the language provided by multiple speakers (including native speech in its appropriate cultural context) usually associated with television or film materials, and (3) the engagement of interactivity usually associated with more primitive drill-and-practice routines. The new Language Learning and Resource Center is expected to model the ways in which these multiple computer-based technologies can be combined with innovative classroom techniques to reinforce communicative language learning. The first step in modeling this combination is to create exercises that exploit the promising aspects of the new technology but that are open-ended enough to lend themselves to a variety of learning activities. These exercises should develop each of the individual technologies as fully as possible while also modeling the strategies by which they may be combined.

Building Block Design

It seems clear that the best way to develop individual technologies while modeling the strategies to combine them is to build prototypes that are in themselves building blocks. Although these building blocks would derive from designs for specific exercises, they would not be single-purpose systems, but rather components capable of supporting numerous exercises. Most importantly, the building blocks would address the important capabilities of the new workstation medium, particularly natural-language processing and interactive video.

In designing these building blocks, ALLP has been operating in large part independently of previous CAI applications despite some carryovers from existing uses of the computer for instruction—the grammar drills and adventure games from early interactive videodiscs—to the purposes of communicative and humanistic learning. But for the most part the Project has had to design its own medium with conventions and constructs that are invented as the need arises.

Prototypes of Natural-Language Processing: Structured Conversations

ALLP began consideration of natural-language processing on the workstation with the clear goals of communicative teaching and a knowledge of the technological resources at MIT in mind.* Existing uses of natural language processing include:

1. *Parsing systems*, which presumably could be used for more effective grammar drills, but which have been chiefly explored for support of machine translation
2. *Query systems*, which answer questions capable of predicate calculus representation, such as "Which battleship is nearest Cuba?" or "What trains leave for Toronto tonight?"
3. *Blocksworld Systems*, after the pioneering SHRDLU of Terry Winograd (22), which allows users to manipulate objects by very limited natural-language commands
4. *Adventure games* (pioneered at MIT by hackers who went onto form the Infocom company), whose games send players through a series of "rooms" through "board move"-like commands ("go east" "kill troll with sword")
5. *Script-based systems*, pioneered by Weizenbaum (19 and 20), and Schank and Abelson (17), which do little syntactic analysis but create believable dialogs based on preconceived models of exchanges.

ALLP has incorporated some elements of all of these applications, but has had to go beyond them to invent a sixth form called *structured conversations*.

Structured conversations privilege conversational quality over grammar correction, query accuracy, command serving, game moves, or ritual predictability. They aim to carry on a believable conversation using a knowledge base in order to answer queries or to construct answers containing knowledge of the world; they also contain a knowledge base of discourse structure to determine what are appropriate responses. The discourse structure covers a full range of functions, the most important of which is the tracking of topics.

The overall plan for the Athena Structured Conversation System (SCS) encompasses three goals:

1. to use the highest possible quality of natural-language processing to capture syntax and meaning
2. to structure discourse for the computer according to pedagogically defined discourse goals
3. to make the conversations literally engaging and to enhance believability by covering computer failure with literary inventiveness.

Although it emphasizes discourse tasks, the SCS includes extensive and precise processing of syntactic elements. There are two reasons for this

---

*Technical adviser for this project is Professor Robert C. Berwick of MIT's Department of Electrical Engineering and Computer Science and the Artificial Intelligence Laboratory. We have also had the advice and support of Professors S. J. Keyser of the Department of Linguistics and Patrick Winston, Head of the Artificial Intelligence Laboratory.

processing. First, the system must be able to recover from misunderstanding or poorly formed input. Careful parsing helps to guess at the intended meaning. Second, language teachers are concerned with tracking and correcting students' errors; however, the major concern of structured conversations is keeping the communicative exchange going so that the student has the opportunity to initiate language and to learn discourse skills.

The design for the SCS is given in Figure 1. The cross-hatched boxes represent processes that are independent of language knowledge. The shaded boxes represent tables that are created individually for each of the languages the system can deal with. The white boxes represent language-processing routines that are designed generically to be independent of any knowledge of particular languages.

There are three important points to make about the SCS system. First, its modular construction is particularly well suited to experimentation. It ensures that there will be useful components made in support of any exercise, although the exercise itself may later be modified extensively or even discarded.

Second, the SCS design provides linkage between syntactic and semantic information, particularly in the Object Lexicon and the Case Frame Interpreter (CFI). The Lexicon provides information on meaning as well as part of speech. It is here that the system encodes information such as that the verb "eat" takes an object that is a "food" and that "apple" is a kind of "food." The Case Frame Interpreter includes stencils of verb-arguments with information on the semantic role of syntactic elements. For instance, it is in the CFI that the system learns that in the sentence "Janet threw the computer out the window" the subject of the verb "threw" is the agent or person throwing, the object of the verb is the thing thrown, and the prepositional phrase beginning with "out" will give the location of the action. The linking of syntax with semantics increases the reliability of the system in figuring out the students' meaning, as well as in formulating questions to clarify meaning. For instance, the system can respond to the statement "Put the book" with a request for a location: "Where should I put the book?"

Third, the SCS maintains a representation of knowledge of the world separate from its knowledge of particular languages. The system uses this knowledge to interpret students' input as well as to construct responses. This knowledge representation gives the system much greater flexibility of response than a reliance on "canned" answers. Furthermore, the knowledge representation is constructed in an object-oriented way that allows for generically defined operations. For instance, the system knows about "containers" as a category, not merely about the particular vase, beer stein, and bottle in its first scenario. Therefore it can apply the properties of containers (e.g., capacity) to later additions (e.g., samovars or tea cups).

In general, then, the modular design of SCS allows it to be easily altered for changes in task and in language. The extensive parsing mechanism allows it to be adapted for variable levels of error correction and analysis processing (see below for pedagogic concerns in this regard). Most importantly, the

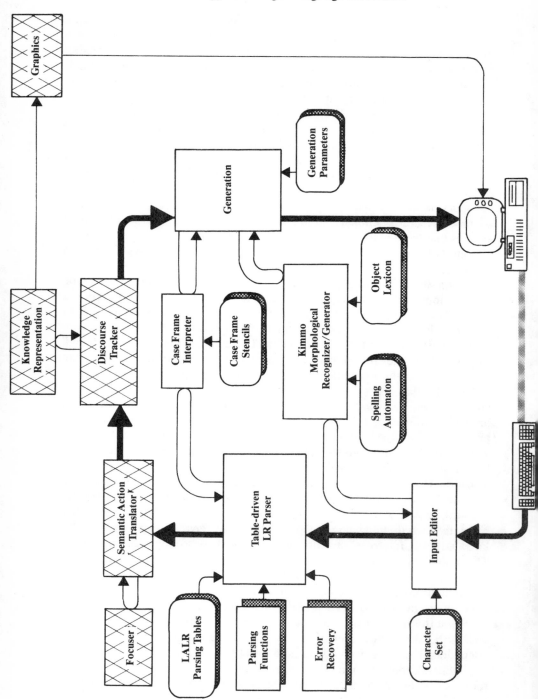

Figure 1. Athena Structured Conversation System.

modular design allows for changes in discourse structure to accommodate a range of exercises. To take advantage of this feature, the two prototypes that are in active development are quite different in topic and form, but both are predictable, structured conversations.

The first and simpler of the two is Lingo, a conversation with a poltergeist about manipulating objects in a room. The objects are displayed on the screen in graphics with a conversation line underneath them into which the student can type responses to the invisible interlocutor. The student is given the task of messing up the room (or of cleaning up a messed-room screen that was created by a previous student). The poltergeist comments on the appropriateness of tasks and encourages the student toward the goal. For the messing-up version, the game is terminated when the student scores enough (internal) messiness points. Meanwhile, the poltergeist keeps track of the topics under discussion (so that students can use pronoun reference) and simple discourse tasks such as saying "please." The poltergeist is constructed in such a way that she does not merely respond to imperatives, but requires the student to carry on a conversation, to comment on the mess, and to receive her comments and suggestions for further action and respond to them.

Here is a sample dialog (in English for demonstration purposes) illustrating the capabilities of the system as of spring 1987:

POLTERGEIST: Hello. My name is Drulla. I am a poltergeist. I can help you to mess up the room. You can ask me to do things and you can ask questions. Let's start to play now, OK?

STUDENT: No.

DRULLA: Play, please!

STUDENT: Okay.

DRULLA: Thank you! What should I do?

STUDENT: You should tell me where the glass is.

DRULLA: The glass is on the table.

STUDENT: Try laying it inside the fridge, please.

DRULLA: Very good. I have laid the glass in the refrigerator. Now what should we do?

STUDENT: Tell me where the book is.

DRULLA: I don't know which book you're talking about.

STUDENT: The red book.

DRULLA: The book is lying on the bed.

STUDENT: OK, put it upside-down under the bed.

DRULLA: OK. I have put the book under the bed upside down. What do you think I should do now?

STUDENT: Look inside the closet.

DRULLA: The closet isn't open. I can't see the contents.

STUDENT: Open it, then.

DRULLA: OK. I have opened the closet. Do something to the shirt!

STUDENT: Put it in the fridge.

DRULLA: Very good. I have put the shirt in the refrigerator. What should
we do now?

STUDENT: Try putting the closet on the rubbertree.

DRULLA: Are you kidding? The closet is too heavy!

STUDENT: Try the chair, then.

DRULLA: I like that! I have put the chair on the poor rubbertree. The
poor rubbertree has been killed. What should we do now?

STUDENT: Pour the milk in the vase.

DRULLA: There isn't enough space in the vase.

STUDENT: Try the beer, then.

DRULLA: A wonderful idea! I have poured the beer in the vase. The poor
flowers have been killed. I think you have done enough damage now.
Goodbye!

Since this exercise uses an object-oriented knowledge representation that
keeps track of physical objects, it is not referring to a set of "canned" potential
answers. Instead, the program refers to representations of the room itself,
with all the objects in it, and with some generic information about objects
in general (the category of chairs as well as two specific chairs). It keeps
track of size, location, and qualities such as whether an object can be opened
and closed. The poltergeist converses about this room by constructing
sentences "on the fly" to match semantic content arising from this
representation. Separating knowledge of the "world" about which the
poltergeist is talking from "answer construction" produces greater flexibility
of response, which is displayed as less repetition and greater naturalness
in the conversational exchanges.

As of spring 1987 Lingo is still a development system, not yet ready
to deliver to students. This is largely due to delays in establishing the hardware/
software environment on which to implement the system. The natural-
language processing system that underlies Lingo, however, has substantial
components in place for processing French, Spanish, English, Russian, and
German. This modular system forms the basis of the structured conversations
mentioned above.

While Lingo continues in development, work is also going on with the
other more powerful use of the SCS. No Recuerdo grew out of a more
general design for an ideal series of conversations with strong narrative
interest and a topic-based discourse structure. This framework was first made
the basis of a design for Encuentros, a simulated environment made up
of a number of dramatic situations, personae, and localities. The protagonists
were selected for representativeness of cultural and economic diversity within
a Latin American situation. Encuentros is in a draft structure at this writing
and has not been implemented.

No Recuerdo thus grew out of the Encuentros concept with the addition
of these learning goals—that the student "draw out" the computer, and that
the computer respond with increasing helpfulness based upon the student's
mastery of discourse tasks such as echoing, keeping on topic, and asking
for clarification. These tasks, articulated as a "Reverse Eliza" (see

"Educational Principles," p. 85, above) were given life by Douglas Morgenstern in the form of an amnesiac interlocutor. In keeping with these discourse tasks, Gonzalo, a Colombian scientist who has lost his memory and with it the clue to the location of some dangerous material that could cause a biological catastrophe for all of Latin America, refuses to answer questions that are put too bluntly, and demands that the student lead him on gradually, paying close attention to the development of topics and to clues that he drops from time to time. The amnesiac situation provides the dramatic basis for computer default situations: when the system cannot process a student's input, Gonzalo can claim he "can't remember" or is developing a headache. When the computer understands partially, the student is given pedagogically valuable tasks of paraphrase or clarification.

No Recuerdo, then, represents the most ambitious ALLP project and the most challenging application of the Structured Conversation System to date; consequently, it is being developed in several parts. The video components of the conversation are already taped (see below). Two computer interfaces, however, are in development. One is the full implementation described above. The SCS as it exists for Lingo is the first draft of this system, along with a separate knowledge representation that depicts the subjects in Gonzalo's memory. At the same time, the Project is producing a preliminary pattern-matching protocol to gather data on students' range of input. These data will be used in the development of the more complete system.

No Recuerdo is also important as a prototype of an integrated exercise that combines natural-language processing with interactive video.

Prototypes for Interactive Video

Communicative Goals

The main goal of ALLP with regard to interactive video has been to fully utilize its specific advantages for communicative language learning. Interactive video can provide students with a sense of immersion that no other technology can duplicate, as the students are "surrounded" by a multiplicity of language sources—video, stills, audio, graphics, texts—which allows them to see, hear, and read the language simultaneously. This variety of language sources has the advantage of recreating the multidimensional nature of language as it exists within the visual, social, and cultural world, allowing for immersion in the truest sense of the word. Furthermore, the very nature of interactive video technology provides students with a degree of involvement heretofore unparalleled, allowing them to manipulate the video at will, and even to interact directly with characters in a story.

ALLP sets out to exploit the immersion advantage to the fullest by "parachuting" the students into the middle of Paris or Bogota where they are involved in a fictional story, with characters and a plot, and are also able to "wander" around. As a result, the learners find themselves in a completely authentic cultural and linguistic environment and come face to face with a very complex reality. Although this degree of authenticity and cultural density would present a clear problem with linear video, it is particularly well-suited to interactive video, since the computer can provide learners with all the tools they need to decipher and understand the whole cultural context in addition to the language.

Objectives for a New Approach

Both existing materials and existing authoring systems were unsuitable for the creation of the materials for interactive video. Existing materials, no matter how compelling they might be as video, are typically shaped for relatively passive viewing. Generally speaking, they do not encourage active involvement except in the form of seeking further information in aids to comprehension. Nevertheless, ALLP is exploring the use of existing materials in two projects—one a Japanese videodisc under the supervision of Michio Tsutsui made from a broadcast television drama, and the other a German videodisc made under the supervision of Robert DiDonato from authentic text materials, slides, and realia. Activities using these discs and others like them will focus on context-based listening and reading comprehension.

On the other hand, videodisc materials specifically designed for interactivity give students a direct control over what happens on the screen—the story might develop a different way or the path through a real geographical space might change. This capability creates a much richer learning environment, because students can be thrust into a foreign world and made to function totally within that context.

Similarly, existing authoring systems set a rigid path of lesson-followed-by-quiz, which gives the learner too little control over the experience. Therefore, the Project determined to create its own programming environment and to make its own materials. The goal is to create the most malleable medium that would support the two major uses of interactive video: manipulative and participatory interaction.

In manipulative applications, the user can locate and repeat video segments at will and obtain access to help or to further information from text files, stored slides, graphic overlays, or their combination. Manipulative capabilities permit users to confront an authentic visual and auditory environment that, in a real target-country interaction, might be confusing or frustrating. Deciphering and glossing can make what has been experienced more comprehensible, as well as provide a means to investigate a particular phenomenon in more detail; thus, materials designed specifically for videodisc should elicit a high degree of manipulation.

In participatory applications, the user's input influences the program's output, perhaps leading to a particular video segment whose content is different from an alternate version also stored on the videodisc. The nature of this particular segment naturally influences the user's next response, leading to a series of interactions that forms a particular path through the program. Multiple routes that differ substantially allow for different experiences by each program user, as well as diversity of repeated uses by the same user.

Although the first language-learning interactive videodisc program, "Montevidisco" (Gale, 5), was a narrative designed to permit participatory interaction (using a multiple-choice format for input processing), subsequent efforts have tended to adapt existing materials for manipulative purposes. While effective manipulative capabilities are absolutely vital for successful interactivity, the addition of participatory capabilities alter the user's experience dramatically. The learner now has much greater control (or the illusion of control) over the content of the video program. The probable result is increased engagement with the simulated environment. Ideally, participatory use should incorporate student input in natural language.

Documentary as well as narrative material can be participatory. Students can choose their own geographical route and the extent they wish to experience different characters and places. They can be given the power to edit and reshape material in order to create their own version of reality, their own "mini-documentaries." To accomplish this end, the students must be freed from simple menus and arbitrary presegmented bites of information. They must be able to get from one segment to another as simply as possible and to view, repeat, or even edit video footage in the lengths and combinations that they find appropriate.

The system being built by the Visual Courseware Laboratory of ALLP is designed to support the flexibility necessary for successful language applications. The system provides a quarter-screen digitized video window with excellent resolution. On the same screen, there are video-manipulation buttons, subtitling below the video frame, glossary and cultural notes windows, a word-processor window to be used as a student notebook, and video "still" windows in which students can capture single frames to display on the screen in a variety of sizes and store for future reference. The ability to manipulate the video and to store single frames will be used as the basis for a visual notecard system (which will combine text and pictures) and for a system of editing the disc material (to be used by students as well as faculty with mini-films for class presentation).

Characteristics of Narrative versus Documentary Material

There are basically two kinds of material that can be put on a videodisc, as there are two filmic genres: the narrative and the documentary. ALLP is developing both side by side (in the case of Direction Paris, for French) and in an integrated fashion (in the case of No Recuerdo, for Spanish). The narrative and documentary modes serve different but highly complementary purposes and provide complementary learning paths for the foreign language learner.

In the case of a narrative, students enter a fictional world that contains its own characters and plot, which provides a very engaging and involving environment. Students are thrust into a highly active role as they enter the story and become its central character, since the development of the story hinges entirely upon their actions. The story can go forward only based upon the student's understanding of its parameters, thus learning becomes highly functional.

A documentary allows students to be immersed in a completely culturally authentic environment and to receive a first-hand look at a specific cultural reality. Experiencing that cultural reality through discovery becomes the entire focus of the interaction, since there is no plot to uncover nor characters that address the students directly. In this way students are free to explore the material, on their own, in a much more deliberate and reflective fashion, thus allowing for a more observational approach to language learning.

As the ALLP workstation medium evolves to accommodate more extensive storage of visual and text materials via CD-ROM (See Part I, Chapter 3 pp. 65-66 in this volume), the documentary opens up to the capabilities of a hypermedia environment, in which students can gain further information on cultural points through an extensive databank of related cultural and linguistic material. Students exploring St. Gervais with the ALLP French disc, for example, could be provided with slides and text files describing this Paris neighborhood at different times in history and expanding upon the lives of historical and literary figures associated with the quartier. Visual, textual, and video explanations combined would create an interrelated super-glossary that would represent a rich source of discovery in itself.

A documentary necessarily invites students to work with images as well as words. For instance, the students' ultimate task is to make their own documentary of Le Quartier St. Gervais. Visual elements become central to this task and, in the process of visually constructing their own vision of the neighborhood, students will learn to understand and interpret correctly the cultural reality around them.

In comparison to documentary-based interaction, interactive fiction entails more meditation of reality and less authenticity of situation. Scripted fiction offers the greatest artistic and linguistic control; it also tends to offer less redundancy than authentic speech, and therefore can be especially challenging for learners. The two French videodisc projects of ALLP offer both ends of this spectrum—documentary material and scripted narrative.

Direction Paris is a sequence of activities based on three half-hour videodiscs, one of which is a narrative. The narrative, "À la rencontre de Philippe," revolves around a young Frenchman, who invites the student to help him find an apartment in Paris. The student can travel around the city via the videodisc and see a variety of apartments. In Philippe's current apartment the student can use the telephone and answering machine and find written clues to other apartments for rent. By careful listening, the student is able to see a variety of possible activities and help Philippe make choices. The narrative is influenced by the students' choices at various branch points where the film stops and the student is consulted directly; the narrative is also influenced by the students' spontaneous decisions on which apartment to visit and whether or not to relay information from one character to another.

There is a link between the narrative and the two half-hour documentary French discs. The link occurs in the first scene, in which Philippe gives the student the choice of helping him make a guidebook to Paris instead of helping search for an apartment. If the student chooses the guidebook option, a partial guide is presented and the student is sent to the documentary material to find the information to complete it.

The documentary, called "À la découverte d'un quartier," also stands on its own as a sequence of video, stills, and audio that are accessed by students as they move around a map of the St. Gervais neighborhood. Beginning students can be given this material with the task of finding functional vocabulary within the scenes. Advanced students can be asked to construct their own documentaries based on thematic rather than geographical arrangements. The vocabulary and cultural information available on the computer make it possible to use the material at a variety of levels for a variety of tasks.

The Spanish project No Recuerdo uses a hybrid approach. Documentary segments and settings are integrated with the fictional base. The student "converses" with both imaginary and real people. The imaginary people hold lengthy conversations based on the story, but real people can also be queried briefly about more mundane subjects, such as their names, ages, and professions or the prices of food. There are several sequences of about two minutes each that show representative parts of the city of Bogota. The student is able to explore Bogota in this way at crucial times in the story in order to get ideas for conversational topics to pursue with Gonzalo. The narrative part of No Recuerdo also has a documentary character that uses Latin Americans who are not actors but portray the characters by improvising to fit preconceived situations.

Experience with students will demonstrate the best mixture of documentary and narrative elements, but it seems clear that both have a role to play in the design and content of interactive video materials.

Design Choices for Constructing a Narrative

ALLP has implemented two models of narrative design. The model for "À la rencontre de Philippe" is based on a realistic scenario and a situation that is eminently practical. A common thread to the various paths is that all action occurs during a single day. Learners interact with the protagonist, Philippe, and influence events at various junctures by using—or failing to use—their own initiative in noticing details and transmitting messages effectively. Secondary characters and episodes provide romantic interest and humor.

In designing the choice points, emphasis was put on encouraging the students' observational powers. For example, if students realize that the phone message from Philippe's boss is important, they will relay that fact in time for Philippe to learn that he has a job and thereby make it more likely that he is offered a desirable apartment. If the student relays the message to Philippe's girlfriend, then the romance will resume and he will no longer need a new apartment.

The characters in the narrative were chosen to represent different social classes and registers of discourse: there is a plumber and a very genteel aunt, as well as scenes with realtors and with friends. The student is free to follow the romantic or the practical side of the story—furthering either the romance or the search for a new place to live. Many of the choices are value-free: they are only alternatives rather than right/wrong tests. The story will move, therefore, as much according to the student's temperament and whim as according to his or her linguistic ability, a fact that ensures a variety and engagement.

The model for No Recuerdo blends realism with fantasy. Through the use of numerous flashbacks, the program treats time elastically and exploits opportunities for visual reinforcement of linguistic content. Learners interact with several characters, but are permitted gradual access to dramatic material according to successful interaction with two protagonists, Gonzalo and Elena. Much of this interchange is centered on general topics such as weather, food, and sports. The documentary interludes reinforce these themes.

The French project offers higher visual contextualization, with numerous slides of Paris neighborhoods and apartments. Focus is less on the characters than on the target culture itself. In No Recuerdo the focus is reversed. The characters are highly detailed, and it is through interchanges with them that the user learns about the culture. The learner in "À la rencontre de Philippe" is given power to influence outcomes by making a series of choices throughout the narrative; the quality of learner decisions improves with more exploration of the simulated environment. Although the Spanish project offers several explorations that can help the user advance through the storyline, power is based largely on the wise use of conversational strategies during extended text interaction with the characters.

No Recuerdo has a conversational structure that emphasizes the language the student originates. Direction Paris requires much less production of language but a more intense effort at listening comprehension and alertness to cultural context. Yet, in spite of their differences, both narrative models offer the two principal features of simulations: high contextualization and the transference of power to the user.

These prototypical exercises are not intended as either/or choices. Direction Paris is meant to be a demonstration of the uses of interactive videodisc and was made with a higher level of production values for the video itself. No Recuerdo is meant to demonstrate the integration of natural-language processing with interactive video. Both models will no doubt continue to be useful exemplars for a long time to come.

Interactive Narrative as a Language-Learning Tool

The production of the two videodiscs has made clear some useful elements for interactive narrative as a language-learning tool:

1. *Multiplicity of Protagonists.* This allows for the story to be told from different points of view. For example, in No Recuerdo, students receive different versions of events from Gonzalo and Elena. In this way gaps are created for students to share information in class.

2. *Multiplicity of Plot Events.* This is the simplest way of creating variety, based on simple branching at choice points, or more subtly based on "invisible" choices—actions the student performs (like listening to or relaying a message) that do not have immediate effects but influence the story at a later point.

3. *Knowledge-Based Choice Points.* Listening tasks embedded in the story can form the basis for choices. In "À la recontre de Philippe," for instance, Philippe asks where the check for the plumber is, and students will know the answer only if they have listened carefully and understood a previous message.

4. *Choice-Points Based on Temperament of the Learner.* Multiple protagonists and plot events should allow for different ways of going through the same material, stressing different topics of conversation with Gonzalo, for example, or choosing to follow a romantic or a practical approach with Philippe's situation. In this way the learner adapts the material to suit a comfortable modality.

5. *Whimsy.* The sense of playfulness created by the computer environment should be encouraged through inclusion of material that is there merely for enjoyment. This material should be intrinsic to the story and culture, however, not just gratuitous joking. It should also call attention to the multiplicity of the form. (For example, Philippe at one point receives flowers intended for his girlfriend and he crushes them in a variety of amusing ways in different versions of the story.)

6. *Multiple Media for Presentation.* Students should be given the opportunity to choose the mode of presentation of material. For instance, news about Gonzalo can be read in a newspaper or heard on the radio. Although listening comprehension should always be foremost, activities should be designed to mix aural and visual language skills (e.g., writing a guidebook about the Marais).

7. *Intrinsic Rather Than Extrinsic Tasks and Rewards.* Progress through the story should be based on language acquisition, and the story should motivate the acquisition, rather than merely serve as an occasion for quizzes. Involvement in the story and involvement in the learning task should be one and the same thing. This is in distinction to exercises that use the continuation of the story as the "reward" for completing irrelevant drills.

Design Issues for Interactive Documentaries

Although the notion of an interactive documentary has not been tested yet, it seems clear that a certain number of traits need to be present for it to be engaging to the student. In the case "À la découverte d'un quartier," over 30 hours were shot in Paris with much careful preparation beforehand to produce 60 minutes of successful sequences. In producing these 60 minutes, some clear values have come to the fore.

To begin with, a documentary should show people in their own usual environment and at an unstaged moment in their lives. In this way the viewer can obtain an insight into the larger cultural whole. For example, one should not film people exclusively at times and places when there are no interruptions. On the contrary, interruptions allow the students to grasp the daily dimensions of the subjects' lives.

By the same token, a successful documentary should present issues that are real to the people filmed and that other people can relate to. Individual sequences should contain several layers that students can explore at different depths according to their interests. For example, interviews should range over personal and professional subjects, and they should touch on historical and sociological issues reflected in everyday experience. There should be an overlap among a series of interviews with pieces that students can connect so that inferences can be drawn and differing points of view compared. Finally there should be variety, including some interviews that are more prosaic (a youth hostel manager describes his accommodations) and some that are more intense (a Holocaust survivor describes Paris during the Occupation). Because the effect is cumulative, the student begins to achieve a sense of what it is like to live in that time and place as, for example, when each interviewee comments on changes in the neighborhood (gentrification) in his or her own way. The goal is for all of these details to add up to a whole that has richness and depth.

Some Generic Tools for Interactive Video

In order to function within the foreign universe described above, language learners obviously need tools to comprehend what is going on and what they see. Two kinds of tools are needed: those that aid linguistic comprehension and those that aid cultural comprehension.

Subtitling is the most obvious tool that students need for foreign language study. The opportunity to access a text-window that helps the learner decipher difficult listening passages is an important feature of the interactive videodisc environment. ALLP plans to experiment with several strategies. The one constant is that only the target language will be used.

One strategy is to present the passage in a cloze format, but with only the difficult words or phrases offered. Another option is to give a simple list of key words without the extra spatial hint offered by the cloze procedure.

Finally, passages that are extremely difficult, whether because of enunciation, speed, dialogue overlap, or ambient noise, can be transcribed in their entirety. In any case, the user will be encouraged to repeat the passage before calling up a subtitle.

Treatment of differences between oral and written speech is one of the interesting questions that subtitling of authentic speech raises. In French, for instance, the dropping of the "ne" from the negative form "ne (verb) pas" is extremely commonplace. Substitles that point out this difference must be prepared without confusing the students about the demands of written speech. One way of accomplishing this is to include the omitted particle but put in in brackets (e.g., "si je [ne] trouve pas un boulot"). However it is carried out, the inclusion of written versions of speech should be the occasion for explicit learning about these differences, rather than confusion.

A glossary is another obvious tool to help the learner. Thus, students would also be given access to a glossary, which would be rendered as visually as possible (graphics to illustrate the meaning of "socks" for instance). They could also access a simplified audio track that would present either slowed speech or paraphrase depending on the difficulties of the passage. Access to a full transcript would also be possible, but would be discouraged until students have tried to understand the passage without attempting to decode every word.

In the area of cultural information, students need help with a variety of problems, including historical references, tone (is a person being straighforward? sarcastic? ironic?), and nonverbal cues (what attitudes are reflected by posture or gesture or facial expression, and how need they be interpreted?). Since the learner may not even be aware of some of these cultural difficulties, they will be "flagged" by the appearance of an icon. The learner will thus be alerted that there is something there that needs clarification and can choose to see an explanation. At other points, the program will check with brief comprehension questions to make sure that students understand the material beyond the literal level.

Conclusion and Remaining Issues

The work accomplished on the Athena Language Learning Project so far has amounted to a "first draft" of the workstation medium. The computer environment on which these applications are being built is still too unstable to be able to judge the efficiency of the approaches either technically or pedagogically. The largest uncertainty is the degree to which natural-language processing is able to mimic conversations. Some time will be needed before work in this area is consolidated to a sufficient degree to put it to a realistic test.

Interactive video has proven so far to be even more promising than anticipated, especially within the context of the workstation environment where students can have flexible tools at their disposal. The creation of new materials at MIT for this purpose has been extremely expensive but is not likely to remain so. Therefore, it is important to assess the effectiveness of these products for learning to understand if they are worth the considerable expense of creating them.

Perhaps the biggest question facing ALLP in terms of design is the question of error correction and error analysis. Since the tools described above were originally designed for communicative purposes, their use for coaching and research in students' errors has been of secondary importance. At the same time, however, the Project is aware of a large demand by the profession for computer-based tools that use pseudo intelligence to track student errors in a scientific manner. Since the materials developed for ALLP incorporate extraordinarily sophisticated language-processing tools, the MIT researchers feel a responsibility to make the system open to these purposes.

Second-language acquisition research has concentrated on two separate areas of student errors and reaction strategies: (a.) performance errors during oral communication in the classroom (often as indicative of the nature of the learner's interlanguage and level of self-monitoring) and (b.) errors encountered in compositions written outside of class, with opportunities for revision generally present.

Recent studies that place the treatment of errors in theoretical perspective include Horwitz (7), Krashen and Terrell (10), VanPatten (18) and Kramsch (9). These researchers advocate either the total lack of correction, specific types of correction, or correction only in particular circumstances. Recent studies about the effects of different kinds of errors in communicative situations include Chastain (2) and Eisenstein (4). (The most complete catalog of possible teacher strategies in dealing with oral errors is still to be found in Chaudron, 3.) In the case of CALL—error identification, analysis, and remedial guidance are generally claimed as significant advantages of the computer medium (Ariew and Frommer, 1). Those who advocate systematic treatment of written errors include Lalande (11) and Rogers (16). Higgs (6) includes a model for different types of feedback. Others rejecting the usefulness of such attention to written errors include Robb et al. (15)

The type of interaction in the LINCS programs, and especially in No Recuerdo, is a hybrid of the situations described above. Learner production is written, not oral, with opportunity for revision. However, the move-based environment of a simulated text conversation will create more time constraints than those present in a typical assigned composition. It is therefore probable that in this particular environment the intersection of fluency and accuracy will be found somewhere between the errors committed while speaking and the errors made while writing, with time to monitor one's composition (as described under a. and b. above). Expectations as to performance therefore should be adjusted accordingly.

From the wide variety of error-reaction strategies espoused by various theorists, ranging from total avoidance of intrusion to immediate interruption with detailed feedback, ALLP favors modeling of the correct response. The computer interlocutor would react with "Did you mean to say X?" or a more subtle variant. However, because individual teaching and learning styles affect error treatment, the goal is to offer a system that will be adaptable, i.e., the nature and frequency of responses will be at least minimally modifiable.

Although the initial Annenberg/CPB Project funding will expire in 1990, it is hoped that the work begun by ALLP will continue, at MIT and elsewhere. The design decisions made so far will have to be tested through active use by students and through incorporation of the materials into a communication-based classroom methodology. It is exciting to look at the Project at this point, however, and see the shape of a new learning medium emerging from what seems to be a fortuitous combination of ambitious teaching aims and an increasingly malleable modern technology.

References, The Athena Language Learning Project

1. Ariew, Robert, and Judith G. Frommer. "Interaction in the Computer Age," pp. 177-93 in Wilga M. Rivers, ed., *Interactive Language Learning.* Cambridge, Eng.,: Cambridge University Press, 1987.
2. Chastain, Kenneth. "Native-Speaker Reactions to Instructor-Identified Student Second Language Errors." *The Modern Language Journal* 64 (1980) :210-15.
3. Chaudron, Craig. "A Descriptive Model of Discourse in the Corrective Treatment of Learners' Errors." *Language Learning* 27 (1977): 29-46.
4. Eisenstein, Miriam. "Native Reaction to Non-Native Speech: A Review of Empirical Research." *Studies in Second Language Acquisition* 5 (1983) :160-76.
5. Gale, Larrie E. "Montevidisco: An Anecdotal History of an Interactive Videodisc." *CALICO Journal* 1, 1 (1983) :41-46.
6. Higgs, Theodore V. "Coping with Composition." *Hispania* 62 (1979) :673-78.
7. Horwitz, Elaine. "Some Language Acquisition Principles and Their Implications for Second Language Teaching." *Hispania* 69 (1986) :684-89.
8. Kramsch, Claire. *Discourse Analysis and Second Language Teaching.* Washington, DC: Center for Applied Linguistics, 1981.
9. _____ "Interactive Discourse in Small and Large Groups," pp. 17-30 in Wilga M. Rivers, ed., *Interactive Language Teaching.* Cambridge, Eng.: Cambridge University Press, 1987.
10. Krashen, Stephen D., and Tracy D. Terrell. *The Natural Approach: Language Acquisition in the Classroom.* Oxford, Eng.: Pergamon; Hayward, CA: Alemany, 1981.
11. Lalande, J. F. II. "Reducing Composition Errors: An Experiment." *The Modern Language Journal* 66 (1982):140-49.
12. Morgenstern, Douglas. "The Athena Language Learning Project." *Hispania* 69 (1986):740-45.

13. _____ "Simulation, Interactive Fiction and Language Learning: Aspects of the MIT Project." *Bulletin de l'ACLA/Bulletin of the CAAL (Canadian Association of Applied Linguistics)* 8, 2 (1986):22-33.
14. Rivers, Wilga M., ed. *Interactive Language Teaching.* New York: Cambridge University Press, 1987
15. Robb, Thomas, Steven Ross, and Ian Shortreed. "Salience of Feedback on Error and Its Effect on EFL Writing Quality." *TESOL Quarterly* 20 (1986):83-95.
16. Rogers, Margaret. "On Major Types of Written Error in Advanced Students of German." *International Review of Applied Linguistics* 22 (1984):1-39.
17. Schank, R. C., and R. P. Abelson. *Scripts, Plans, Goals and Understandings.* Hillsdale, NJ: Erlbaum, 1977.
18. VanPatten, Bill. "On Babies and Bathwater: Input in Foreign Language Learning." *The Modern Language Journal* 71 (1987):156-64.
19. Weizenbaum, Joseph. *Computer Power and Human Reason: From Judgment to Calculation.* San Francisco: W. H. Freeman, 1976.
20. _____ "ELIZA—A Computer Program for the Study of Natural Language Communication between Man and Machine." *Communications of the ACM* 9, 1 (1966):36-45.
21. Widdowson, Henry. *Teaching Language as Communication.* London: Oxford University Press, 1978.
22. Winograd, Terry. *Understanding Natural Language.* New York: Academic Press, 1972.

The CLCCS CALL Study: Methods, Error Feedback, Attitudes, and Achievement

Gail L. Robinson

Center for Language and Crosscultural Skills

Overview

This report presents a summary of the CLCCS CALL study (Robinson et al, 19) in which the computer was used as a research tool to compare the effectiveness of (1) different pedagogical principles applied to instructional presentation and (2) different answer-judging strategies for error feedback.

Theoretical Framework

One of the major trends in pedagogy reflected in second-language literature during the last decade has been a shift in emphasis from the structure and form of language to communicative or discursive meaning (e.g., Rivers, 14, 15; Robinson, 16, 17, 18; Savignon, 21; Stevick, 26). This distinction between form-centered practice and meaning-centered practice through authentic communication has been interpreted through a variety of somewhat overlapping theoretical frameworks, referred to variously as the distinction between linguistic and communicative competence (Politzer, 13), learning versus acquisition (Krashen, 7), and grammatical versus notional/functional syllabuses (Wilkins, 29). While approaches that focus on acquisition and functional/notional syllabuses differ on many levels, they share a common emphasis on meaning as opposed to form. Within this framework, the key questions become "What does *meaningful* mean?" and "Do meaning-centered activities lead to greater language acquisition than form-centered ones?"

The CLCCS CALL study reported herein investigated a variety of factors related to "meaningfulness" in order to compare their effects on language achievement in contrast with other factors related to "form." For example, computer exercises in Spanish were designed to measure the following pedagogical principles (Figure 1): effect on achievement of integrated context versus discrete items, personally meaningful versus impersonal material, student choice of background content versus program choice, and the effect of problem-solving activities on the acquisition of language skills. (Proficiency measures were not applicable due to the relatively short time-span of instruction in the field study.) Through varied error-feedback strategies (Figure 2), the study considered the relative effectiveness of student-controlled help versus program-controlled error correction, types of error repetition, and the role of student discovery in the error-correction process (e.g., location of error versus commentary as in hints, and implicit versus explicit feedback).

Figure 1. Pedagogical, content variables

Experimental Group		**Control Group**
1. Known others	vs	Anonymous characters
2. Integrated material	vs	Nonintegrated items
3. Meaningful practice	vs	Manipulative practice
4. Emotional/humorous content	vs	Dry facts
5. Background Content:		
Student choice through menu	vs	Program designation
6. Problem-solving activities	vs	Descriptive activities

Figure 2. Error feedback variables

Experimental Group		Control Group
1. Student discovery of error correction	vs	Program disclosure of error correction
• Error location		• Correct answer
• Error location with hints		• Correct answer with explanation
2. Implicit feedback	vs	Overt correction
3. Student-controlled or combined help	vs	Program-controlled or no help
4. Recycling of missed items:		
• Repetition of missed item at random intervals	vs	• Immediate repetition of missed item
• Immediate introduction of parallel item	vs	• Repetition of all missed items together at end

The hypotheses central to this study have their foundations in theories related to language acquisition, psycholinguistics, and human memory, in particular the various factors that influence the learner's retention of linguistic material on *delayed* recall tasks (Clark and Clark, 4; Lindsay and Norman, 9). Therefore *cumulative* differences between experimental and control groups based on posttests were of greater interest than daily results based on immediate testing. To that end, each pedagogical principle and error-feedback variable was examined independently in order to identify clearly what made up the respective experimental and control treatments, should any cumulative differences be found.

Design

The field study population consisted of all students in the second semester of second-year Spanish at Montera Junior High School, Oakland, California. Eighty-three students in three Spanish classes, normally taught by two different teachers, took part. The students were ethnically quite mixed (50 percent minority) and many (43 percent) were from professional families.

For a 45-minute period each day and in the absence of the classroom teacher over a period of nine days, all students received instruction in Spanish exclusively by means of computer materials designed for this project.

Assignment to Experiment and Control Groups

Students were randomly assigned to experimental and control treatments that were maintained throughout the study so that comparisons could be made of the cumulative effects of the variables of interest on achievement. Each day, the experimental treatment consistently isolated variables related to meaningfulness; the control treatment consistently isolated contrasting variables related to form. The CALL activity for each day was based on a single and different hypothesis so that variables accounting for any observed differences in daily and/or cumulative achievement could be identified for future application to courseware, and for replication of the research.

Pre- and Posttesting

Students completed three types of pretests in order to identify prior attitudes, abilities, and achievement in Spanish, and their potential relationship and mediating effects on daily and cumulative treatment: (1) the Pimsleur Language Aptitude Battery (PLAB), (2) a background questionnaire identifying students' experience with computers, interest in the study of Spanish, and attitudes toward Spanish-speaking people, (3) a specially constructed Spanish achievement test of prior knowledge, based on the material to be covered in the different CALL activities of the project. The pretests were conducted on the day prior to the onset of the CALL treatments. The same pretest of Spanish achievement was used as the post-achievement measure to ensure high content validity. In addition to the latter, project staff collected scores for each student from the school files on the California Test of Basic Skills (CTBS) Composite tests of Language and Reading.

At the conclusion of the study, students repeated the achievement test and the PLAB and completed a shorter version of the initial attitude survey. Overall achievement in the study could not be accurately assessed solely on the basis of gains between pre- and posttests but needed to be considered in light of the several mediating variables—different backgrounds, aptitudes, abilities, and prior achievement in Spanish. The results, mediated by these prior factors, are reported below.

Achievement Testing in Spanish

Achievement testing was carried out in two ways: (1) daily achievement tests, and (2) a cumulative posttest (following the nine-day instructional period and after a weekend's delay). While it would have been desirable to retest the students after an even longer period of time, the results of a delayed posttest would have been confounded by the intervention of the classroom teachers once students returned to their normal modes of study.

The posttest was a composite of representative contents from the daily tests. Each section of the posttest thus corresponded to the daily tests, which, in turn, reflected the instructional goals for a particular hypothesis of interest. The daily tests and posttests were common to both experimental and control groups and both included a variety of forms associated with integrative and discrete testing, and included production and recall tasks. However, within the short run of the study, only finite curricular goals could be measured. Each test, thus, focused on common instructional material including new structural and/or vocabulary items introduced on a given day; however, the material was practiced according to a particular hypothesis and its corresponding experimental and control treatments.

Statistical Procedures and Data Collection

Tasks

Four data-analysis tasks were undertaken. The first examined student scores on the pre- and postachievement measures to determine if a cumulative difference existed in student achievement between the experimental and control groups in light of prior aptitude, attitudes, abilities, and achievement in Spanish (Table 1). The second tast examined student test scores on the daily activities, which isolated each particular pedagogical principle and error-feedback variable (Table 2). The third task explored possible changes in student attitudes as well as in aptitude, the latter again measured by the PLAB (see Table 1). Finally, responses to the daily tests were examined in order to determine if the measures clustered along a priori dimensions of "integrative" and "discrete" types of tests (Robinson et al., 19, pp. 40, 68).

Procedures

The data analyses proceeded in the following manner:
1. A table of intercorrelations identified possible covariates for subsequent analyses of covariance. Significant covariates identified included preachievement scores, several of the PLAB subscales, CTBS scores,

Table 1. Cumulative achievement test gain scores:
Mediated by Pretests
Analysis of Covariance

Covariate	Ns	CONTROL	EXPER	p*
Achievement pretest	42/37	30.81	34.43	< 0.01 (e)
CTBS Composite Language	35/33	32.91	35.27	< 0.05 (e)
CTBS Reading	35/33	33.11	35.27	< 0.03 (e)
Interest in Learning Spanish	36/35	32.44	34.54	0.51
Enjoyment of Spanish Class	36/35	32.44	34.54	0.76
Pimsleur Pretests Composite Score	41/36	31.12	33.69	< 0.02 (e)
PLAB Pre-Post Gain Scores				
Language Analysis	39/34	1.00	1.00	1.00
Sound/Symbol Assoc.	39/34	0.82	0.85	0.96
Sound Discrim.	39/34	0.18	1.06	0.40
Vocabulary	39/34	0.44	2.15	< 0.02 (e)
Composite	39/34	2.44	5.06	0.12

* P values preceded by "<" are judged significant. The letter in parentheses indicates the direction of difference: c = Control; e = Experimental.

Table 2. Daily test means by group:
Mediated by achievement pretest (Covariate)
Error-Feedback Variables

Variable	Day	Test Type	No. of Items	N1/N2/N3/N4	1	2	3	4	p*
student	3	Test 1: DR (6)		22/16/13/20	5.59	5.87	5.77	5.65	0.86
discovery	3	Test 2: IR (7)		22/16/13/20	5.27	5.62	5.23	5.70	<0.01(e)
recycl. errors	6	Test 1: IP (6)		20/16/10/18	3.45	3.81	3.50	3.06	<0.01
program/ stu-	8	Test 1: IP (8)		21/16/16/17	4.57	5.44	5.62	4.94	<0.05(e)
dent control	8	Test 2: DP (5)		19/16/15/17	3.68	4.12	3.07	3.94	0.42
explicit/ implicit	10	Test 1: IR (6)		34/32	4.06	4.09	—	—	<0.02(e)
	10	Test 2: DP (18)		33/32	11.39	11.75	—	—	<0.01(e)

Pedagogical Variables					EXP	CNTRL			
known/anony-	2	Test 1: IR (10)		35/35	8.11	7.94			<0.01(c)
mous characters	2	Test 2: IP (5)		34/34	3.06	2.68			<0.01(c)
	2	Test 3: IR (5)		34/29	4.41	4.41			0.34
integrated/	4	Test 1: IR (10)		35/32	9.23	9.19			<0.02(c)
nonintegrated	4	Test 2: IR (5)		34/32	3.82	3.97			<0.01(e)
material	4	Test 3: IP (7)		34/32	6.50	6.28			0.63
emotion/	5	Test 1: DR (5)		38/34	4.47	4.47			0.25
dry fact	5	Test 2: IR (5)		38/34	3.74	3.97			<0.01(e)
	5	Test 3: (9)		38/34	4.79	4.12			<0.01(c)
problem-solv/	6	Test 2: IR (7)		36/28	3.64	3.61			<0.02(c)
non-prob.solv	6	Test 3: DP (5)		36/28	3.44	3.12			<0.01(c)
meaningful/	7	Test 1: DP (10)		36/35	6.19	5.11			<0.01(c)
manipulative	7	Test 2: IP (5)		36/35	3.78	2.57			<0.01(c)
menu choice/	9	Test 1: None (12)		37/34	8.22	8.47			<0.01(e)
no topic choice	9	Test 2: DR (5)		37/34	3.97	3.82			<0.01(c)

Tests were categorized according to the following types:
DR = discrete recall; IR = integrative recall; DP = discrete productive; DR = discrete recall
* values preceded by "<" are judged significant. The letter in parentheses indicates the direction of difference: c = Control; e = Experimental.

and preattitude scores. Analyses of covariance were performed for daily tests and for gain scores on the cumulative posttest.

2. A one-way analysis of variance tested the difference between group means for daily test scores involving the error-feedback hypotheses, followed by multiple pairwise comparisons for any of these tests that proved significant.

3. T-tests were applied to the difference between (1) the two answer-judging group means involving implicit versus explicit feedback, (2) control and experimental group means for daily tests involving the pedagogical hypotheses, (3) control and experimental group means on the achievement tests, (4) the PLAB, (5) the attitude measures, and (6) the difference between control and experimental group means for each gain score on the achievement, PLAB, and attitude measures.

4. The attitude scales were also analyzed pre- and poststudy to determine if students changed their feelings toward the computer as a medium of instruction, the Spanish language and/or Spanish-speaking people, and their reasons for taking Spanish classes. Simple t-tests (for testing the null hypothesis that total group mean gains were zero) were used for these analyses.

Quantitative Results

1. The greatest predictors of achievement for students in both the experimental and the control groups were initial interest and enjoyment of Spanish in comparison to other school subjects, information that students had indicated on a questionnaire before the study. This finding coincides with previous research regarding the relationship between motivation and language achievement (Lambert and Tucker, 8).

2. The major quantitative result of the study is that pre-post achievement gains clearly favored the experimental group ($p < .05$) when the influence of prior knowledge, aptitude, and abilities were taken into account (Table 1). (It is interesting to note as well that the pre-post language aptitude (PLAB) vocabulary subtest gain score also favored the experimental group ($p < .02$.) In contrast, the control group did not outperform the experimental group on any post measure.

3. On a daily basis, when experience prior to the study was taken into account, three of the four experimental hypotheses for error feedback were confirmed (Table 2): location of error with hint, (Day 3, Group 4) combined program and student-controlled help (Day 8, Group 3), and implicit feedback (Day 10, Group 2).

4. On a daily basis, results for the different pedagogical hypotheses, when mediated by the pretest, were inconclusive: the control group was favored on three days and the experimental group was favored on one. Most often, however, the results balanced out (Table 2).

There are several interpretations for these apparently inconclusive findings regarding the pegagogical variables of the study and the resulting discrepancy between daily and cumulative results: First the distinction between immediate recall activities and longer-term, delayed recall may apply; that is, rote learning activities and structural drills, while they may be effective on a short-term basis, may not contribute as much to long-term retention (Brown, 3). Methods that might appear to be equally or even more effective in the short term, thus, may actually prove to be less effective in the long run. This circumstance would account for the difference between the daily results and the cumulative posttreatment gains by the two groups, since the former were based on immediate recall tests and the latter were based on cumulative, delayed recall tasks.

Second, the daily tests as well as the postexperiment achievement tests may have favored the control group. While the research intended to test both communicative competence (via integrative tests—cloze, etc.) and linguistic competence (via discrete tests—grammatical fill-in-the-blanks, etc.) the actual achievement testing tended to measure linguistic more than communicative competence. Post-experiment cluster analyses of achievement scores disclosed that both types of tests frequently appeared to have tapped similar factors (Robinson et al., 19, p. 68).

A third factor that may have confounded the results of the daily tests is the distraction that may have resulted from certain experimental treatments in the shorter term, which actually increased retention in the longer term. Since portions of the posttest corresponded to the daily achievement tests, further analysis of the data could disclose whether particular variables introduced daily were consistently more influential in affecting students' overall scores. For the present, it is important to iterate that the most significant gains appeared as a *cumulative* effect of all the experimental variables taken together, when mediated by prior experience, rather than the effects of one particular treatment on one particular day. This circumstance points to the importance of applying the above-mentioned experimental features to instructional programs in combination rather than in isolation. An elaboration of the pedagogical principles and error-feedback variables follow below for both the experimental and control groups.

Pedagogical/Methodological Treatments

Figure 1 outlines the variables that distinguished the experimental from control treatments each day. All other variables were constant, e.g., content, vocabulary, structure. Daily results are reported in Table 2.

Known versus Anonymous Others

Research in cognitive psychology suggests that learners remember things that refer to themselves (or to known others) two or three times as often as those that refer to anonymous others, objective facts, or word rhymes (Smith, 23).

In this CLCCS study, students in the experimental group were first asked to type in the names of their favorite male TV or movie star and their favorite male singer. These names were then used by the program as key characters in the activities that followed. New material was introduced in a narrative concerning the daily life of these known, famous people, with visuals to aid comprehension. The control exercise was identical except that the narrative was about the anonymous "Roberto" and "María."

Integrated versus Non-integrated Material

Drill-and-practice exercises in CALL as well as in language texts are often marked by a variety of discrete items that lack an episodic relationship despite their similar grammatical structure. Psycholinguistic research has shown that memory for otherwise discrete lexical items is improved by providing the learner with an integrated context (Bower and Clark, 2).

In this CLCCS study, students in the experimental group read a sequenced chronological narrative about two characters. The control group read unconnected sentences about different and unrelated individuals. Sentences for both groups were identical in vocabulary and syntax; they differed only in names of characters and sequence of presentation.

Meaningful versus Manipulative Drills

Research also suggests that contextual and meaningful practice that requires the student to comprehend the meaning of an utterance may be more effective than manipulative practice that does not (Clark and Clark, 4).

In this CLCCS study, students in the experimental group were presented new forms and vocabulary by means of a dialog between schoolmates regarding a problem one of them was having—falling asleep in algebra class. Practice consisted of a set of true-false comprehension questions based on the meaning of the conversation. This type of experimental practice was termed "meaningful" rather than "communicative" because the information requested was already known from the dialog (Paulston, 12). Students in the control group were presented the same new forms and vocabulary but in uncontextualized sentences; practice then consisted of typical pattern drill on forms.

Emotional Content (Humor) versus Dry Fact

Research suggests that affective associations may be more critical to language acquisition than those that are purely cognitive (Stevick, 26; Robinson, 17,

18). Emotional associations tend to be more deeply encoded in memory (Lindsay and Norman, 9).

In this CLCCS study, students in the experimental group were presented new forms and vocabulary in the context of a humorous dialog. Follow-up practice consisted of having students answer similar silly questions about themselves ("¿Te lavas el pelo con champú o champán?" [Do you wash your hair with shampoo or champagne?]). For the control group, the dialog was intentionally lacking in humorous content ("¿Te lavas el pelo con champú?" [Do you wash your hair with shampoo?]).

Choosing from a Menu for Background Topic versus No Choice

Psycholinguistic research suggests that comprehension involves integrating new information from assertions about things the listener (or reader) already knows (Clark and Clark, 4).

The CLCCS research reported herein hypothesized that students able to choose from a "menu" of topics to provide the background for the topic of instruction would achieve the lesson goals more effectively in comparison to those who were assigned a topic automatically by the program (assuming the menu reflected students' interests). The research assumed that people are generally interested in things that they already know and would like to learn more about.

To ensure that the menu choices reflected student interests, all students completed an interest survey prior to the courseware development for the study from which four menu choices were made available. During the field study, students in the experimental group thus were able to choose the context for the lesson under study. Students in the control group had no choice of topic and read whatever passage the program assigned them. All versions of the stories and subsequent activities for the experimental and control groups were parallel, except for background content.

Problem Solving versus Description

Research suggests that good learners actively draw inferences about what they read or hear, using both inductive and deductive reasoning (Naiman et al., 11; Rubin, 20). Activities that require students to draw inferences as in problem solving are thus more meaningful than those that engage them solely in description.

In this CLCCS study, the computer "drew" the same picture of a house for both the experimental and control groups, identifying the location of each new object with a sentence (e.g., "La bicicleta está delante del árbol" [the bicycle is in front of the tree]). In subsequent practice, the control group was shown the same picture and asked to describe the location of objects; the experimental group was shown a scrambled picture (e.g., the bicycle on top of the tree, the dog on the car) and the student was given the problem of unscrambling these pictorial scenes by answering questions about where the object should logically appear (providing the correct answers caused the object in question to return to its proper place).

Error Feedback Treatments

Figure 2 outlines the variables that distinguished the experimental and control treatments with respect to differential error feedback. While a particular error-feedback variable was being tested, the lesson presentation was identical for both the experimental and control groups. Feedback differed only in the event the student made an error. Daily results are reported in Table 2.

Student Discovery Strategies

Since research suggests that good learners actively make use of inference when they read or listen (Naiman et al., 11; Rubin, 20), it follows then that CALL feedback strategies that guide students to discover errors should improve achievement more than strategies of error feedback that merely give the correct answer and/or explain it automatically following the learner's incorrect trial or request for help.

In this CLCCS study, forms of error feedback were developed and compared in order to isolate different degrees of student discovery. The experimental and control groups were each subdivided accordingly. Both groups completed the same exercise, but each group received a different type of feedback on errors (see Table 2): correct answer only (Group 3); correct answer with explanation (Group 2); error correction only by blanking out incorrect letters (Group 1); error location with hints related to meaning (as opposed to form) (Group 4). The content of this hint varied according to which incorrect response the student had chosen. As hypothesized, the latter type of feedback led to greater achievement on the daily tests.

Implicit Feedback versus Overt Correction

The theoretical benefits of implicit feedback versus explicit, overt correction are also related to the issue of student discovery learning. For example, suppose a native speaker of Spanish responds to the English question, "What did you eat for breakfast?" with "I eated bananas." Overt correction would involve modeling the correct answer (No, I *ate* bananas" or "No, you *ate* bananas"). Implicit modeling would embed the correct structure within a conversational response: "Oh, you *ate* bananas. I *ate* some too. What else did you eat?" Implicit feedback thus allows for the conversation to continue through reflective listening with student discovery of errors rather than be interrupted by an overt indication of speaker/learner error (Terrell, 27).

This CLCCS study compared achievement on identical exercises that differed only in implicit versus explicit feedback. Daily test results favored the use of implicit feedback, as hypothesized (Table 2, Group 2).

Student Controlled versus Program-Controlled Help

Many investigators argue in favor of the actual benefits (Merrill, 10; Smith and Sherwood, 24) and potential benefits of CALL (Higgins and Johns, 5; Underwood, 28) because students may "control" their learning experience. In contrast, other researchers point to the detrimental effects of student control (Howe and DuBoulay, 6; Stevens, 25).

In this CLCCS study, it was hypothesized that a midway position would be favored that allowed "student control" to decide whether help is desirable and "program control" to act as the teacher or "expert" to designate which particular kind of help is appropriate. Four variations of program-controlled feedback and student-controlled help were compared. The experiment and control groups were again subdivided as in Figure 2. Results are reported in Table 2.

1. No help, programmed correct answer (Group 1): After each mistrial, the program gave the correct answer and instructed the student to type it again.

2. Total program-controlled help (Group 2): After each mistrial, the program displayed a help screen automatically with hints related to the type of error the student had made; after looking at the screen, the student could try again.

3. Combined program and student-controlled help (Group 3): After each mistrial, the student could try again without help or seek help by pressing the "escape" key. After the student requested help, the program automatically called up the help screen pertinent to the particular error, and allowed the student to retype the response.

4. Total student-controlled help (Group 4): After each mistrial, the student could try again or seek help by pressing the "escape" key, which called up a "help" menu. Students then chose the type of help screen, (e.g., Do you want to review the vocabulary? the grammar? the story? etc.) and retyped the response.

The daily test results supported the combined position as hypothesized (Group 3). Students may have been unable to diagnose their errors when given full control over their progress through a lesson, for they appeared to lose time while reading and responding to the "help" menu choices. On the other hand, perhaps total program control decreased their motivation to respond to the lesson overall.

Recycling of Missed Items

Social learning theory (Bandura, 1) and conditioning theory (Skinner, 22) suggest that repeated exposure to similar or parallel material, with spaced practice over time, produces greater behavioral changes than one-time learning trials.

The CLCCS study compared four ways of recycling missed items (see Table 2):

1. Immediate repetition of same item (Group 1)
2. Immediate repetition of a parallel item (Group 2)
3. Repetition of missed item at spaced intervals (Group 3)
4. Repetition of all mistakes together, at the end of the exercise (Group 4)

Both experimental and control groups read the same narrative on clothing and practiced completing the same sentences about things they wear. The mistakes were handled in the four different ways described above. While it was hypothesized that repetition of the same item at random intervals would lead to the greatest achievement, daily test results favored the immediate repetition of a parallel item (Group 2)—which had been hypothesized as the second-best feedback strategy.

Attitudes toward CALL

While quantitative measures of pre-post student attitudes did not reveal any statistically significant differences between experimental and control groups, both positive and negative attitudes toward CALL emerged through qualitative, ethnographic evaluations (Robinson et al., 19). These included (1) a review of videotaped interviews with students held in the computer lab and in the postexperiment discussion session, (2) the examination of staff logs including staff observations and daily student comments, and (3) videotaped interviews with the principal of Montera Junior High School and the senior project adviser.

On the positive side, the CALL activities challenged students and encouraged them to develop their own learning strategies, while proceeding at their own pace. Students commented that the computer was a forgiving and patient tutor. On the negative side, students complained that the computer was mechanical, impersonal, and inflexible. Even the students most enthusiastic to be away from their classroom teachers at the beginning of the study looked forward to returning to the classroom by the study's end.

Summary, Limitations and Implications for Future Research

In summary, the CLCCS CALL study resulted in these findings:

1. On a cumulative basis, the pre-post achievement gains favored the

experimental group significantly when the gain scores were mediated by prior knowledge, aptitude, and abilities.

2. On a daily basis, three of the four experimental error-feedback hypotheses were confirmed when prior experience was taken into account.
3. On a daily basis, results for the different pedagogical hypotheses, when mediated by the pretests, were inconclusive: the control group was favored on three days, and the experimental group was favored on one day. On four days, however, the results balanced out.
4. The greatest predictors of achievement for students in both experimental and control groups were initial interest and enjoyment of Spanish in comparison to other school subjects.

These findings are limited in the following ways:

1. The short duration of the study limited evaluation to measures of achievement rather than proficiency, and to measures that reflected discrete more than integrative language goals.
2. Achievement posttesting was limited to one cumulative evaluation; delayed retesting was not possible owing to teacher intervention following the study and the probable confounding of the treatment conditions.
3. Due to funding limitations, the overall posttest gain scores were not analyzed to identify which particular variable(s) studied day by day, if any, would account for overall cumulative achievement more than others.

Nevertheless, the experimental variables as a whole did lead to greater cumulative achievement. The common denominators for these variables were "meaningfulness" and "student discovery." The particular contribution of this CLCCS study for CALL, thus, has been to examine and define in lesson presentation and mode of error feedback to students the ingredients that make up "meaningfulness" and "discovery strategies." In summary,

1. In organizing material for CALL (or textbook) lesson presentation, language-learning materials may be more effective, over time, when presented and practiced within an *integrated context* in which students' attention is focused on the *meaning* of the material and language is used to *draw inferences* as in *solving a problem*. Material may be more meaningful when students *relate personally* to it, either because the materials contain *reference to themselves* or to *people they know*, because it is amusing or otherwise *emotionally appealing*, and because they *select it (from a menu)* out of *personal interest*. While these features did not appear to have any *immediate* effect on second-language learning in this study, their *cumulative* effect is noteworthy and merits further investigation.
2. Feedback to students appears to be more effective in the short and the long term if it guides students to discover the answers, as opposed to merely displaying the correct response with or without an explanation after "Wrong, try again." More effective feedback via CALL includes *locating errors* by highlighting or by blanking out wrong characters, accompanied by *hints*, and *rephrasing* the question to offer *implicit*

correction through modeling within a meaningful, communicative context. *Combined student-controlled and program-controlled help* may also encourage students to discover answers by joining active student involvement with teacher or program expertise. Lastly, following missed items by a *parallel item* may foster repeated practice while encouraging students to apply reasoning to a new instance of the problem.

While several of the above features are usually found in existing CALL programs in some form, the challenge is to apply them together in the same units of work that integrate CALL with classroom instruction. In short, the impersonal quality of computer-assisted instruction can only be remedied by balancing CALL with the human element. Ensuring that CALL is an integral rather than separate component of the total program of instruction and that the teachers are likewise an integral part of the CALL laboratory is the necessary first step.

The next stage of this research at CLCCS will be to create such an integrated instructional program incorporating the elements mentioned above in order to combine and coordinate instructional content and teacher training between the classroom and CALL lab. To evaluate program effects on language proficiency, such a program will need to be taught during the normal yearly course of instruction.

References, The CLCCS CALL Study

1. Bandura, Albert. *Social Learning Theory*. Englewood Cliffs, NJ: Prentice-Hall, 1977.

2. Bower, G. H., and H. Clark. "Experiments in Story Understanding and Recall." *Quarterly Journal of Experimental Psychology* 28 (1976) :511-34.

3. Brown, H. Douglas. *Principles of Language Learning and Teaching*. Second edition. Englewood Cliffs, NJ: Prentice-Hall, 1986.

4. Clark, Herbert H., and Eve V. Clark. *Psychology and Language*. New York: Harcourt, Brace Jovanovich, 1977.

5. Higgins, John, and Tim Johns. *Computers in Language Learning*. Reading, MA: Addison-Wesley, 1984.

6. Howe, J. A. M., and B. DuBoulay. "Microprocessor Assisted Learning: Turning the Clock Back?" *Programmed Learning and Educational Technology* 16, 3 (1979) :240-46.

7. Krashen, Stephen. *Second Language Acquisition and Second Language Learning*. Oxford, Eng.: Pergamon, 1981.

8. Lambert, Wallace E., and Richard Tucker. *Bilingual Education of Children: The St. Lambert Experiment*. Rowley, MA: Newbury House, 1972.

9. Lindsay, P., and D. Norman. *Human Information Processing*. New York: Academic Press, 1977.

10. Merrill, M. D. "Toward a Theory of Intrinsically Motivating Instruction." *Cognitive Science* 5, 4 (1980) :149-85.

11. Naiman, Neil, Maria Frohlich, H. H. Stern, and Angela Todesco. *The Good Language Learner*. Toronto: Ontario Institute for Studies in Education, 1978.

12. Paulston, Christina B. "Structural Pattern Drills: A Classification." *Foreign Language Annals* 4, 2 (1980) :187-93.

13. Politzer, Robert. *Linguistic and Communicative Competence*. Final Report NIE G-79-D130. Palo Alto, CA: Stanford University School of Education, 1980.

14. Rivers, Wilga M. *Teaching Foreign Language Skills*. Rev. Chicago: University of Chicago Press, 1986.

15. ———, ed. *Interactive Language Teaching*. New York: Cambridge University Press, 1987.

16. Robinson, Gail L. "Magic-Carpet-Ride-to-Another-Culture Syndrome." *Foreign Language Annals* 2, 2 (1981) :135-46.

17. ——— *Issues in Second Language and Crosscultural Education*. Hayward, CA: Alemany, 1981.

18. ——— *Crosscultural Understanding: Processes and Approaches for ESL, FL, and Bilingual Educators*. New York: Prentice-Hall, 1986.

19. ———, John Underwood, Wilga Rivers, José Hernández, Carollyn Rudesill, and Clare Malnik Enseñat. *Computer-Assisted Instruction in Foreign Language Education*. San Francisco: Center for Language & Crosscultural Skills, 1985. [EDRS ED 262 626.]

20. Rubin, Joan. "Study of Cognitive Processes in Second Language Learning." *Applied Linguistics* 2, 2 (1981) :117-131.

21. Savignon, Sandra. *Communicative Competence*. Philadelphia: Center for Curriculum Development, 1972.

22. Skinner, B. F. *Science and Human Behavior*. New York: Macmillan, 1953.

23. Smith, Edward. "Human Memory." Lecture in cognitive psychology, Department of Psychology, Stanford University, March 1979.

24. Smith, S., and B. A. Sherwood. "Educational Uses of the PLATO Computer System." *Science* 192 (1976) :344-52.

25. Stevens, Vance. *Annotated Bibliography of Articles Concerning Computers in Education*. Honolulu: University of Hawaii, Department of English as a Second Language (ESL), 1982.

26. Stevick, Earl. *Memory, Meaning and Method.* Rowley, MA: Newbury House, 1976.

27. Terrell, Tracy. "The Natural Approach: An Update." *Modern Language Journal* 61 (1982) :325-36.

28. Underwood, John H. *Linguistics, Computers and the Language Teacher: A Communicative Approach.* Rowley, MA: Newbury House, 1984.

29. Wilkins, David A. *Notional Syllabuses.* New York: Oxford University Press, 1976.

The Computer and Foreign Languages in the High School

James E. Becker
University of Northern Iowa
Malcolm Price Laboratory School

Introduction

Technology all by itself is rigid. It offers no solutions and often causes confusion through the questions it engenders and the problems it leaves unresolved, yet everyone has been touched or transformed by the current technological revolution and the capacity of the computer to store and manipulate vast quantities of information. The impact of this transformation on education, however, and its nature and speed of assimilation does not depend on technology alone but on how successfully the educational community comes to accept it and find ways to use it. Haavind (14), among others, has noted that the ultimate greatness of the machine will depend more on the wisdom of the users than on the brilliance of its creators.

Thousands of high school language teachers have been challenged (and in some states mandated) to develop an understanding of computer-assisted instruction (CAI) and to demonstrate how the medium can influence student achievement (Dunnaway, 9; 10). Educating the public along these lines is not an easy task; there is hardware to examine and even more courseware to review and integrate into the curriculum. Moreover, despite the growing interest and excitement generated by the computer in almost every school in America, only a small proportion of language teachers seem to be working toward exploiting the tremendous power of the medium. Perhaps this is understandable, since computer-assisted language learning (CALL) is still in its infancy. Nevertheless, given the importance of computers in business and industry, and in almost all other aspects of American life, it seems clear that computer literacy is bound to take its place with the "three Rs" and, sooner or later, noticeably affect second-language learning and teaching.

This chapter is intended to provide an overview of CAI for the high school language teacher and to encourage the computer novice to investigate the immense potential of CALL. To these ends, the following pages are organized under these larger topics: achieving literacy in CAI, hardware considerations, standards and evaluative criteria, and common types of CALL software. The end portion of the chapter holds an overview of a wide range of general-purpose software and contemporary materials for computer-assisted language learning, including many in the public domain.

Achieving Literacy

It is apparent that a large part of the computer's attractiveness in education lies in its novelty and intrinsic allure. Some educators are positive CAI is the most valuable teaching tool since the blackboard; others are convinced it is no more significant than the typewriter (Ruthven, 22). For many parents, however, instilling computer literacy in their children has become as important as teaching table manners. Acquiring literacy in computer routines can be compared to developing skill in reading. There are no clear-cut stages of discernible progress (aside, perhaps, from learning the basic terminology); rather, a more complete understanding of the process reveals itself gradually with practice over time (11).

Training

The move toward computer literacy is no less important for language teachers, according to Hoch (15), who stresses the value of extensive hands-on experience over "quick fix" inservice programs as the only means of coming to grips with the value of the medium in different disciplines and at different grade levels. Inservice instruction that focuses on answering pertinent questions and providing experience on the computer in a sine qua non if CAI is to become effective and economical, especially in the foreign language curriculum. Inservice training can take various forms, including released time and workshops. Released time for teachers to explore the use of CAI plus full use of computer systems and access to a wide range of software has paid off in the city of Ladue, Missouri (Schwartz, 23) thanks to a system of novel grants for faculty development and familiarization with the medium.

Saturday workshops and after-school seminars that focus on CAI/CALL have proliferated elsewhere, but they vary greatly in format, content, and quality. Some reflect the view that learning to program should be part of an initial encounter with CAI; others demonstrate that programming is not an important first step and should be delayed until teachers have learned some of the basic interactive skills with the medium. Few teachers want or need to become sophisticated programmers; nevertheless, some learn to author simple drills with the help of a programmer friend or to use the various template programs available commercially. Some even learn to write simple routines with the help of students. More important than programming as an initial encounter with the machine, however, is for the novice to become comfortable with the ways the computer can enhance teaching and learning generally. The greatest challenge is for the teacher to explore what the computer can do best for languages, then to become an expert in types of hardware and software and to learn how to integrate their use effectively in the classroom.

Across the Nation

Some states have taken the lead in training teachers to use hardware and software. Dearborn (8) discovered many state education departments, as in California (6), have designated experts to advise teachers on CAI and to help them sort through and evaluate software. Nine states require teachers to take a course in computer literacy; two others and the District of Columbia mandate CAI throughout the curriculum. Five others require schools to offer students at least one computer course toward literacy and have mandated demonstrable competency. Texas, Utah, and the District of Columbia require teachers to take a computer course prior to state certification; nine others require math, science, and business education teachers to take a computer course for continuing licensure. (For a summary, see Figure 1).

Educational leaps forward are usually followed by reflection as the profession considers how best to benefit from innovation and where to go next. The last half decade, perhaps, has exemplified this pause in CAI. Still, there are indications that, while computer hardware has become more sophisticated (and a bit less expensive) and technologically advanced systems and high-grade software have fallen into place, a new step forward is underway. Laggards will ignore this initiative at their peril. How well schools

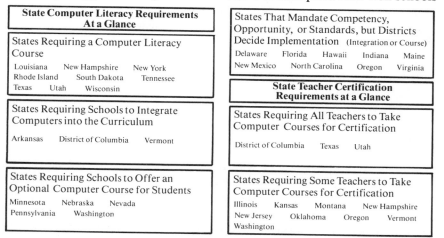

State Computer Literacy Requirements At a Glance

States Requiring a Computer Literacy Course

Louisiana   New Hampshire   New York
Rhode Island   South Dakota   Tennessee
Texas   Utah   Wisconsin

States Requiring Schools to Integrate Computers into the Curriculum

Arkansas   District of Columbia   Vermont

States Requiring Schools to Offer an Optional Computer Course for Students
Minnesota   Nebraska   Nevada
Pennsylvania   Washington

States That Mandate Competency, Opportunity, or Standards, but Districts Decide Implementation (Integration or Course)
Delaware   Florida   Hawaii   Indiana   Maine
New Mexico   North Carolina   Oregon   Virginia

State Teacher Certification Requirements at a Glance

States Requiring All Teachers to Take Computer Courses for Certification

District of Columbia   Texas   Utah

States Requiring Some Teachers to Take Computer Courses for Certification

Illinois   Kansas   Montana   New Hampshire
New Jersey   Oklahoma   Oregon   Vermont
Washington

Figure 1. States with certification requirements   ELECTRONIC LEARNING OCTOBER 1985

and teachers exploit the medium will separate the winners from the losers. In short, there is increasing and substantial agreement that the computer can be an effective and economical tool for instruction. The question is *how*.

Levinson (16) believes the major challenge for CAI, regardless of the discipline, is to match software to teaching style. In language teaching, for example, if teachers believe students must memorize rules and conjugations, they should use courseware that focuses on drill and practice. On the other hand, if they hold language is acquired through social interaction and role play, they should seek software that applies language in conversational settings. Levinson writes that CALL should encourage teamwork among pairs of small groups of students and contain an "intermittent-reinforcement pattern" in which easy and difficult tasks are intermingled. The same courseware should also repeat questions that students are likely to have answered *correctly* so that learning is reinforced and available for further practice. Whatever the case, there is evidence the computer does give students a sense of control over learning and can be especially helpful for slow achievers who have difficulty wih school subjects that require memorization and repetition. And CAI is reputed to increase the opportunity to experience a variety of contexts for the gifted learner, and can teach decision making and logical thinking. Moreover, the fact that the computer lacks the human quality of empathy and reinforcement seems to be a virtue rather than a deficiency (Robinson et al., 20). Taken together, CAI and CALL seem to work best when integrated into classwork, whether "hands-on time" takes place at home or at school.

Some Survey Data

More and more Americans are becoming computer users and, while the varied applications of the medium continue to gain favor with the average citizen, a clearly defined minority refuses to become literate with the machine. In 1986, for example, a poll by the National Science Foundation reported 37 percent of roughly 2000 adults surveyed had used a computer or word processor with some frequency; 24 percent had a very good idea of how computer software operates, but 29 percent wanted nothing to do with the medium (1).

In 1985, H. J. Becker, an eminent sociologist from Johns Hopkins University, reported the results of a comprehensive survey incorporating 2300 schools in the public and private sector (2). Becker found there were over one million computers in American elementary and secondary education but although one fourth of the nation's teachers—some five hundred thousand—had access to computer equipment, only one or two in a given subject in a typical school made use of the medium. The same survey (3) revealed half of all U.S. secondary schools have at least fifteen machines. In fact, one quarter have enough computers to serve between one-half and one full classroom of students at the same time. Becker further discovered subject-area teachers who use computers were business, science, industrial arts/agriculture, English, and social studies. Foreign langauges were conspicuously missing. Principal problems the Becker survey identified included (1) schools lack equipment, software, and funds to purchase them, (2) teachers do not have enough time to develop computer-based activities on their own, and (3) teachers generally lack interest in learning to use the machine. The least-reported problem Becker noted was substandard courseware. The best use of the medium was reported to be in classrooms designated as a computer laboratory rather than when the equipment was moved from room to room, a common practice in many schools.

Central Missouri State University and FLAM (Foreign Language Association of Missouri) sponsored a series of seven workshops throughout the state in the fall of 1985 and spring of 1986. In these workshops high school teachers asked questions about CALL, observed demonstrations, and evaluated a wide range of software for French, German, Spanish, Latin, and ESL. Responses to a questionnaire (summarized below) by more than 150 participants offer some clues about how language teachers view computer-assisted instruction. Teachers new to the medium were queried with respect to questions they thought should be asked prior to adopting CALL. Those already using CAI were asked what they liked and disliked most. Finally, separate comments were solicited from other high school teachers who use CALL in their classes every day. Taken together, these responses may be considered representative of what classroom teachers in general think about computers in language teaching:

Teachers new to CAI want to know:

- How do I incorporate programs into my classes?
- How do I share one computer with a class of thirty-five students?
- Are computers cost-effective?
- What software is available?
- Is it worth the time I will spend using it?
- How much time should I devote to CAI?
- Will the students learn more with the computer than with classwork?
- How does one convince the administration that CAI is important?
- Can I use the same software with different computers at the same time?

Teachers already using CALL in some degree responded:

- It often meets the learning style of a student who might not otherwise be reached.
- I like the variety of subject areas available.
- The idea of making mistakes in private while teaching yourself is excellent.

- I have never had anything work as well in teaching vocabulary.
- It helps me with individualized instruction, even with large or multilevel groups.
- It really holds the students' attention.
- It provides needed grammar drills for advanced students.
- It enables me to have more than one level of instruction in one classroom with each group having sufficient time for drill.
- It makes FL learning more up-to-date in our computer-oriented society.

When asked what they like and dislike about CAI/CALL, these same teachers reported:

- Not enough students can use the computer at the same time.
- There are too many mechanical malfunctions and program quirks.
- There is no audio.
- It is hard to manage all the different levels and activities.
- It is difficult to find time for students to use the computers.
- It is expensive.
- Some students do not work well in a depersonalized framework such as presented by CAI.
- Only one student in my entire class can use it during a given time.
- It makes for lots of extra work for me.
- It is difficult to use some programs.
- The computer is too impersonal.
- CAI takes students away from the oral practice they need.

Teachers who use CALL on a regular basis with high school students demonstrate the obvious:

Fort Dodge High School (Fort Dodge, Iowa). Galbraith (12), a teacher of German, uses CALL daily "because it has proven successful." The school has installed a Corvus Hard Disk laboratory equipped with twenty-eight Apple IIe computers. Half of Galbraith's students use the lab in groups of two or three per computer while the other half of the class listens to audiotapes. Galbraith notes that a major problem is finding time for language classes to use the computer lab as CAI gains popularity with other faculty and other disciplines.

Lyons Township High School (La Grange, Illinois). Schwartz (23), a teacher of Spanish, uses CALL as supplementary review. Her school has eight computer labs equipped with TRS-80 Model III machines. All labs are networked. Schwartz and her colleagues have written CALL tutorials on grammar topics that incorporate drills and games specific to the adopted textbook, noting that "in house" materials are preferable over commercially available programs since the latter either demonstrate too many errors or contain vocabulary not central to the basic course materials.

University High School (University of Illinois, Urbana). Curtin (7) reports that when preparing for specific tests the entire foreign language department makes use of CALL for review work in class-size contact periods of 25 minutes. The hardware consists of two labs equipped with both Apple family computers and IBM PCs. Students are assigned two or three to a terminal and both enjoy and profit from the cooperative work. Single microcomputers, to be used for reward or for special individual student projects, are kept in individual classrooms.

Glenbard West High School (Glen Ellyn, Illinois). Level I and II students of Gillespie (13), a teacher of French, are required to spend 20 minutes in the computer lab for each unit of study in their respective texts. Working with programs developed in house, Gillespie reports that low and below-average students who use CALL regularly are generally able to raise and maintain their foreign langauge grade at average or above.

Cupertino High School (Cupertino, California). Morrey (18) a teacher of German, oversees a variety of Radio Shack TRS computers in his school, some networked, some on hard-disk systems; Morrey counsels teachers must have a lighter load if they are expected to devote time to integrating CALL into their instructional programs. Furthermore, Morrey advises, teachers should read widely about CAI/CALL, visit classes where CALL is in use, read CALL software reviews regularly, and preview as many CALL programs as possible.

There are many significant challenges associated with adapting to a new technology; as teachers (and students) learn more about the computer and CALL, they will help to decide whether this new tool will survive the test of time.

Hardware Considerations

What hardware and peripherals to buy is not an easy decision. The ideal system must be flexible, reliable, relatively inexpensive and certainly "user friendly." The system should be easily upgraded or enhanced, and service should not be far away. Buying any equipment usually requires some compromise; visiting with experienced persons who have gone through the process will help in making the correct decision.

CAI/CALL does not have to be complex. At minimum, one needs a computer with at least one disk drive, a monitor, and of course quality software. Dozens of peripherals can be added as needed—additional memory, a modem, a second disk drive, a CD (compact disk drive), a drawing pad, mouse, accelerator, and speech synthesizer cards, etc. Computer magazines that cater to microcomputer use in the schools such as *Computers in Education, The Computing Teacher,* and *Classroom Computer Language* feature new and interesting enhancements in each issue. More speed, better color graphics, improved sound, and easier-to-use programs are all promising additions for CALL.

Despite a wide range of quality hardware to choose from, a problem for CAI/CALL users is the lack of compatibility among computer brands. In 1983, Market Data Retrieval reported Apple as the leading hardware (29 percent) in the school marketplace, followed by Radio Shack TRS (21 percent) and Commodore (15 percent). In 1987, IBM and the IBM-compatible Zenith held the edge in higher education, while Apple products had gained in popularity (85 percent) in high schools (24). Apple software will not run on IBM or the Commodore and the TRS programs will not run on either. The IBM-compatible machines accept IBM software but the majority of programs for secondary schools are written for the Apple, a problem ameliorated for Radio Shack users by the TRACKSTAR 128 board for the Tandy 1000 SX that emulates the Apple family (and accepts Apple Pascal) and supports IBM DOS 3.3 and Pro-DOS. This technology opens direct user access to an extensive library of educational software as well as business applications without significant cost for extra equipment; other innovation is sure to follow.

Hard Disk and Networking

The national trend in schools is to install computers in a laboratory setting and to "network," or link, several computers to each other and/or a central source, usually a hard disk. The Corvus Omninet (Corvus Systems, Inc.) for example, permits the simultaneous use of several programs via a network of twenty-five or more microcomputers; the same program can be used by more than one student at the same time, obviating the need to purchase a "lab pack" (up to ten diskettes of a single lesson) when multiple copies of the same lesson might otherwise be needed. Moreover, since several programs can be loaded into memory at once on a hard-disk system, students may have access to more than one hundred programs without having to change disks. Unprotected disks (those that can be copied legally) must be purchased to set up such a disk storage system and/or licensing agreements must be negotiated from vendors for this purpose. The primary challenge for the user, however, may be finding software that will work on the hard-disk system in the first place.

The LINK Video Networking System (Applied Computer Systems) connects several computers in the same manner that console and student stations are conjoined in an audio-active language laboratory. The teacher is able to receive a display on a console screen from any student monitor in the class and has the option of transmitting the display from the master console to any or all student stations (or class monitor). The LINK system also allows all terminals to operate independently for library work and is available for computers with either composite or color monitors.

Schools that cannot install individual computers in a permanent laboratory or in a classroom that becomes a designated computer lab often place the equipment on mobile carts that are rolled from room to room. Others may assign a single machine to each classroom. What to do with a single computer and twenty-five students is a compelling challenge. Some suggestions are (1) rotating hands-on experience among two or three students for short periods of time; (2) connecting the computer to a large screen monitor to enable everyone to see what is happening on the screen as one or more students work through a game, a drill-and-practice routine, a tutorial, or any other variety of CALL programs; (3) limiting computer time to individuals who either merit the experience or need remedial instruction.

Projection Systems

Projection systems that permit the image on the computer monitor to be projected to a large daylight screen have been available for a number of years. Recently developed "computer projection panels" offer an attractive alternative. These liquid crystal displays, when placed on a standard transmission overhead projector, are able to project a bright, wide-angle, high-contrast image in monochrome onto a standard movie screen. Text, graphics, charts, computer animation and other data are all displayed with excellent clarity, even in normal room light. These projection panels (available from Kodak, Magnabyte, Sharp, and Vivid, among several companies) interface with a wide range of computers. Although their cost is still significant (as much as the source unit itself), the computer projection panel is a viable way to offer large-screen viewing convenience for large group presentations.

Standards/Evaluative Criteria for Courseware

There are generally three comprehensive and highly simplified areas on which the value of most software can be judged—content, instructional purpose, and technical soundness.
1. *Content.* Is the program accurate, of educational value, and free of stereotypes? Does it develop communication skills? How much material is on the disk? What are the prerequisite skills needed to use it?
2. *Instructional Purpose.* Is the purpose well defined? Is the presentation clear and logical and the level of difficulty appropriate for the target audience? Are the graphics, color, and sound used appropriately? Does the program motivate and stimulate student creativity? Is feedback effective? Does the learner control pace and review? Are the instructions integrated? Is the learning generalized?
3. *Technological Aspects.* Are the support materials comprehensive and effective? Is the display of information effective? How easy is the operation for the intended audience and for the teacher? Are the uses relevant to the computer capabilities? Is the program reliable?

Charp (5) writes that the improved quality of educational software can be attributed to a variety of reasons, but primarily to the fact that the educational user is becoming more knowledgeable (p. 10). Although much of what has occurred in the development of software for secondary schools heretofore has been merely a translation of print media onto computer disks, there is a wide array of computer materials available beyond simple drill and practice, including tutorials, games, simulations, problem solving, authoring, word processing, testing, classroom management, and demonstration. Having a variety of software available is one requirement for maintaining student interest, motivation, and achievement. The sections that follow give a capsule description of common CALL software types.

Common CALL Software Types

Drill and Practice

By far the most common type of CAI software, drill and practice requires short answers that are typed by the user. The drills can be repeated many times, in succession, in order to assure mastery. Fill-in-the-blank, true-false, multiple choice, and one-to-one translation of words or phrases are the most common formats and are designed to reinforce or remediate knowledge that has been presented previously. Some drill-and-practice programs keep track of student performance, store the results for the printer, and provide a list of missed items at the end of the lesson.

CALL drill-and-practice software has been labeled as "electronic worksheets" by critics owing to the short-answer format it typically contains and an emphasis on rote memory. Higher-level thinking skills such as analyzing and evaluating are not part of drill-based software, but that is not the purpose of this form and exercise. Drill-and-practice software is designed to review skills that have been taught previously. Although some drill-and-practice software is poorly written and deserves the negative publicity that it has received, many programs are well done and, frankly, some students enjoy using them.

Games

Games entertain and many instruct as well. Subject-matter mastery is often necessary to score well. Games used in foreign language software usually provide some type of incentive for correct responses in the form of scoring points or moving a graphic on the screen (aiding a mountain climber scale a peak, etc.). Some software packages include separate game disks, others simply incorporate the game into a drill or insert the game at the end of the program as a reward for mastering lesson material.

Tutorials

Tutorial programs are designed to take the student from ground zero at an individual rate. Concepts are presented in small, manageable segments to help students move step by step toward mastery. Usually, students need little additional help to proceed. Tutorials are part of many popular software programs such as Apple Works and Apple Presents Apple that introduce the novice to CAI. (The latter is highly recommended for a first look at the Apple IIe.)

Simulations

Simulation programs mimic real-life situations. The computer demonstrates what happens when certain decisions are made by providing the student an opportunity to play "what if." The student has control over certain variables and the means for testing hypotheses about them. Judgment and skill are required to make choices and perform appropriate tasks. For example, No Man's Land (NNELEC) is a popular simulation game in French that challenges the user to navigate across the Atlantic Ocean in thirty days from La Rochelle to Halifax (U.K.) by choosing the proper type and number of sails, resources, and winds. The student quickly discovers the fastest route is not the most direct.

Problem Solving

Problem solving programs require higher-order thinking usually associated with complicated plots. Students work step by step toward a solution. Good programs offer feedback and provide branching to keep the student on task. Mystery House (Sierra-on-Line, Inc.), in French, is one example of a mystery game that requires logic and problem solving as well as a good knowledge of imperative verb forms. As the commands are typed, the scene changes on the screen during the student's attempts to solve a series of murders in an old Victorian mansion.

Overview of CAI/CALL Software

Today's teachers are seeking and using materials that reinforce the content of the textbooks they teach. Yet a full array of textbook-specific CALL materials is still far off. Extant text-specific CALL is due to teacher demand (and written almost exclusively for the Apple family of computers). The scope and content focus primarily on vocabulary building and grammar. Software for French for Mastery and Spanish for Mastery (D. C. Heath) is typical. Self-contained and easy-to-use "canned" packages are what teachers seem to be asking for; ready-to-go software that drills vocabulary, verb conjugations, and cultural points are the most popular. Since teachers do not have time to create lessons with authoring systems nor to program lessons themsleves.

Most software also now has many built-in aids; the sound can be turned off and on at will; the menu is accessed easily, as are accents and other diacritics; branching provides additional help, hints, or practice exercises. And returning to the main menu can be as simple as pressing an asterisk (*), the escape (ESC) key, or the letter 'S' to exit a lesson.

Audiocassette tapes accompany the programs *Spanish for the Traveler* (Roger Wagner Publishing), ¡Vamos! (Heinle and Heinle), Le grand concours sonore (International Software), and Allons-y! (Heinle and Heinle). Sliwa Enterprises, Inc., offers a Spanish program for the Street Electronics ECHO II speech synthesizer that digitizes speech; with it, students can hear "Spanish" via a small speaker built into the computer. Several other programs "talk," but most have a "computer voice." The new generation of Apple GS computers may change that perception thanks to improved speech chips.

Most teachers search American catalogs and resources for quality foreign software. A few Apple users also have discovered a London firm, Wida Software, that supplies a wide array of both authoring programs and CALL software for the Apple family hardware. Two of Wida's very popular programs available in French, German, and Spanish are Storyboard and Clozemaster (see also pp. 155-56). The former is a challenging authoring program in which a full screen text typed in (and saved) by the teacher is replaced by a series of asterisks and punctuation marks. The student's task is to restore the entire text word by word through inference and problem solving. For example, *** *** ** **** could be The boy is tall. After typing in "The" and RETURN, the text would read THE *** ** ****. Storyboard is an ideal program for full-class or group participation around a computer owing to the problem solving and inferencing it invites.

Clozemaster allows the teacher to input text and then the student decides how often he or she wants a word deleted (from every fifth word to every fifteenth word). Language teachers who find value in the cloze procedure will discover that Clozemaster's powerful editing and drill features will greatly enhance the student's ability to guess words. When the correct word is guessed, the program places it in the text appropriately with all attendant accents and diacritics.

There is a wide variety of additional courseware that foreign language teachers find useful. Programs in Latin, Italian, Russian, Hebrew, and other exotic languages are being developed as demand increases for each. The following are examples of standalone software that teachers report students enjoy using on a regular basis.

Spanish

The Spanish Contest (International Software), similar in format and content to the AATSP National Spanish Contest, tests grammar and culture. Correct Behavior the Mexican Way (Roger Wagner Publishing) presents a series of 28 cultural assimilators available in English and Spanish, each reflecting a situation in Mexico in which a visitor might commit a social blunder. ¿Cómo se dice? (International Software) holds 200 beginning-level sentences to translate into either Spanish or English. An authoring program on the disk allows the teacher to create additional vocabulary or sentence translation drills. Batalla de palabras (Gessler International Software) is a two-disk game program that focuses on vocabulary found in school settings, sports, daily life, travel, and occupations. An editor mode permits the teacher to create additional word files for the colorful arcadelike game. Sound, graphics, and the ability to print out vocabulary all add to the popularity of this program.

Drill and Filler (Twenty-First Century Software, Inc.) is an easy authoring program for Spanish that offers teachers templates to create drill-and-practice lessons using student textbooks and supplementary materials. French and German versions are also available, each with complete sets of accents. Each reflects a wide variety of formats including matching, fill-in-the-blanks, true-false, translation, and reading comprehension. The same program for ESL students is called CreataDrill (Twenty-First Century Software) and can be adapted to any discipline. Let's Practice Spanish (20) is a three-disk package for beginning students that features a variety of simulations, tutorials, and drill-and-practice exercises. Basic vocabulary and colloquial phrases within a lively cultural context are used to stimulate student interest. Banco de palabras (Mindscape, Inc.) consists of four games that provide practice in recognizing and classifying basic Spanish vocabulary. The program encourages students to review words in logically related groups. Each game contains four graded levels of words from the beginning course to the third or fourth year. The user is able to call up a list of words for review, add more words, and change or delete words.

Spanish Achievement I (Microcomputer Workshops) presents vocabulary questions in a multiple-choice format and is designed to prepare students for the College Entrance Examination Board. Levels II and III of the series both offer practice in a wide variety of grammar problems. Taken together, this series provides an excellent review of Spanish for the advanced levels. Una visita a México (Heath) is a three-disk package that introduces the historical origins of Mexico while giving information on the Aztec and Mayan cultures. Episodios elementales (Newbury House) has twenty-five short reading lessons presented with special vocabulary and practice activities. An authoring mode in the program allows the teacher to create additional reading lessons following the templates therein.

Poker Listo (Gessler International Software) is a culture game. Students are dealt seven topics chosen at random from fourteen subjects covering hundreds of questions on history, literature, and vocabulary. The program can be used as a quiz, tutorial, or game. Spanish Grammar Computerized I and II (Microcomputer Workshops) are designed to accompany and reinforce the beginning textbook by presenting review and practice of basic grammar structures. Each disk contains over 1000 practice questions and test items. CompuCat QuizWare (Webster/McGraw-Hill) for Spanish Level One and Level Two tests a variety of subject areas in a colorful game format. A cat leaps across the screen to simulate a timer as students select both the topic and level of difficulty in an effort to score points. Features such as bonus points and "beat your own score" keep students' interest alive.

A popular disk among students is Spanish Hangman (George Earl, Inc.). While the program is simple, students enjoy guessing elements to complete common sentences or words. Un día típico (Heath) teaches the fundamental vocabulary and structures associated with daily routine, leisure time, and classroom activities. The program introduces the concept of reflexive verbs graphically while providing drill and review of vocabulary.

French

Le Grand Concours (International Software) contains many items of the type found in AATF-sponsored National French Contests. The program provides a good review of grammar and culture on all levels. An audiotape version of this program called Le grand concours sonore is available from the same publisher, but requires a special interface to enable the computer to stop or play the portable audio recorder in consonance with the program. The Utilisons l'ordinateur series (Heath)—Le Métro, Un repas français, Le déménagement, Les sports, En vacances, and En ville—are popular owing to their high-quality color, good graphics, sound, clear scoring formats, menu-driven selections, and many games. All are intended to complement a beginning course. Jeu de vocabulaire (Mindscape) offers four games that reinforce association, understanding analogy, and definitions for more than 1000 French words. Each game offers vocabulary items at six levels of difficulty appropriate for students at the first through fourth years of study. Additional words may be entered as needed. Each drill is presented in a game format with optional sound accompaniment.

Bataille de mots (Gessler International Software) reviews hundreds of French words via an arcadelike game that includes color, sound, and perhaps most importantly, an editorial mode that allows the user to create additional games. To play the game, the student attempts to match and "shoot down" a word in English before a time limit expires with one of four French words that appear overhead. With the two-disk edition now available for the Apple, IBM PC, and Commodore 64, the teacher can create and print out vocabulary, exercises, and tests.

Langenscheidt Publishing carries both an English and French version of Correct Behavior. Each program contains several songs at the end of the disk complete with the words and music to encourage sing-along or cloze activities. CompuCat QuizWare (Webster/McGraw-Hill) contains 760 multiple-choice questions in French in a fun and fast-paced game format available in two levels of difficulty. Students are tested on factual information in a variety of subjects by grade level. In each game, the computer selects up to thirty questions that are graded according to difficulty. A colorful jumping cat keeps track of the time as students attempt to respond as quickly as possible.

Comment dit-on? (International Software) contains dozens of sentences to be translated either from French to English or vice versa, as well as an editor mode and template for teachers to create drills. The challenge to the student is to do a good job as a translator/interpreter and to be paid for the level of performance/achievement. Mésaventures culturelles (Gessler International Software) is a reading program that reveals differences between the American and the French cultures. Students learn how to avoid typical cultural faux pas made by visitors to France. French Grammar I and II, and First and Second Byte in French (International Software) are popular for reviewing, drilling, and testing grammar. Purchased together, they are very helpful for introducing and reviewing verbs, numbers, pronouns, comparatives, and tense.

The French Review Packet (COMPress) is one of the most comprehensive grammar series of French CALL on the market. The total materials comprise thirteen disks that drill, test, and provide games for a wide array of grammar points. COMPress offers similar grammar packages in Spanish, German, and Russian.

Perspectives françaises (EMC Publishing) is a popular software package that accompanies a French text by the same name. Students enjoy Poker Pari (Gessler International Software) a culture program presenting multiple-choice questions on French culture and civilization, grammar, and vocabulary, which, like the Spanish version, can be used as a tutorial, game, or quiz. La Carte de France (from the same publisher) employs graphics to teach aspects of geography, history, industry, and culture for each of the major regions of France. Review quizzes are presented in a variety of formats; a final exam reviews the entire program.

French Achievement I, II, and III (Microcomputer Workshops) are based on the College Entrance Board Examination and in 1983 were judged software of the year by the Learning Periodicals group. The three disks in French and Spanish and a recent addition in German are excellent preparations for the College Level Entrance Proficiency (CLEP) exams offered at many colleges and universities, and for the Advanced Placement (AP) exams. Somewhat controversial, yet extremely popular among younger students, is La guillotine (George Earl, Inc.). To save an aristocrat from losing his head, the student must guess the letters of a word presented by topic on two levels of difficulty. A vocabulary review and matching exercise are included for each category. If the student wins, the prisoner turns and smiles to the tune of the Marseillaise; if not, down comes the blade and off goes his head.

German

High school students and teachers alike enjoy Correct Behavior the German Way (Langenscheidt) available in either German or English. It presents a series of twenty-eight slices of life in Germany each followed by multiple-choice questions on typical social blunders faced by a visitor. German Hangman (George Earl, Inc.) like the French and Spanish versions, also contains words and sentences to be either translated from German to English or vice versa. German Language Review Packet (COMPress) contains ten disks plus a game disk and is among the most complete packages for German grammar currently on the market.

The German Contest (International Software) tests grammar and culture as well as providing an excellent review of elementary and intermediate German vocabulary. Drill and Filler (Twenty-First Century Software) permits teachers of German to create many types of drill-and-practice exercises and to store them on the same disk. Wie Sagt Man? (International Software) challenges students to translate dozens of phrases from German into English or vice-versa and to be rewarded in dollars according to speed and accuracy. An editor feature invites the teacher to create drills of additional vocabulary or sentence translation.

Poker Parat (Gessler International Software) is a computer game based on the card game that quizzes grammar, literature, and culture. Gessler also publishes German Word Order, which requires the student to make logical sentences from scrambled lexicon, and Deutsche Grammatik "Der-Die-Das," a three-part program that reviews the nominative, accusative, and dative cases, the declension of the definite article, strong and weak verbs, and prepositions. Each section explains pertinent grammar and is followed by a drill containing fill-in-the-blank sentences.

Let's Practice German (EMC Publishing), based on approximately one thousand of the most frequent words, is comprised of three disks that supplement the study of vocabulary for students in any introductory course. The lessons, which describe famous people, places, and things in reading passages, teach and drill cultural information as well. Wortgefecht (Gessler International Software) is available in a new edition that drills common vocabulary in an arcadelike game that requires the student to select the correct match from four choices to "shoot down" the English prompt. Students enjoy the graphics, sound, and speed requirements. Additional words may be added by using the editor mode, which is part of the program. The program is available in three versions: Apple, IBM PC, and Commodore 64.

Latin

As the popularity of Latin returns in American schools, CALL materials to help teach the language are increasing in number as well. Latin Flash Drill (Centaur Systems) is drill-and-practice software for the many paradigm charts of Latin forms and endings. The program is for the Apple IIe and requires an 80-column card. All drills offer command options for help and hints, and a special reference section on grammar explanations on ten topics helps the student review or study new forms. Latin Exercises for First Year Latin (International Film Bureau, Inc.) is a series of four disks with sixty lessons divided into fifteen units of study. Quo modo dicis? (International Software) is a sentence-translation game using a "hangman" approach on three levels of difficulty. Some two hundred preprogrammed sentences are arranged by grammar structure on the disk. An editor module permits the teacher to add sentences that the students are studying in class. International Software also features approximately one thousand practice items in Latin Grammar Computerized I, which contains twenty lessons of materials normally covered in one year of study. Latin Hangman (George Earl, Inc.) drills students on famous Latin quotes and sayings in the familiar "hangman" format.

Russian

CALL materials for Russian are scarce. A multiple-disk set of materials called Russian Language Review Packet (COMPress) is one of the most complete sets of program materials available for the Apple (9 disks) and IBM PC (4 disks). Students may drill for hours the varied aspects of Russian grammar using the Cyrillic alphabet. Each lesson also contains an introduction, vocabulary practice, and a final exam. The Russian Disk (International Software) contains one set of programs to teach the Russian alphabet while another teaches Russian vocabulary and word recognition. The Linguist (Broderbund Software) is a general-purpose language-translation and tutorial program for the Atari, Commodore 64, IBM PC and Apple, with typefaces for twenty different languages, including Russian. The teacher is able to create lists preparing two languages. These lists may be word/word, word/definition, or phrase/phrase.

Other CALL programs appear almost weekly. The teacher can keep abreast of the best of them by reading the software review section of *The Northeast Conference Newsletter, Hispania, Die Unterrichtspraxis, The French Review,* and *The Modern Language Journal.*

Courseware Creator Software

Passport: The Courseware Creator (Gessler International Software) is an integrated two-disk authoring program that enables the teacher to create lessons and tests without knowing how to program. The program uses color and high-resolution graphics, and contains accents for French, Spanish, German, along with fonts for Russian, Hebrew, Japanese, and thirteen other languages. A user's manual provides the necessary information for constructing questions with up to five different answer possibilities, which can be paired with a feedback response so that a correct response can be reinforced and incorrect responses can receive corrections and additional instruction. The teacher may also write questions and provide automatic remediation and multiple levels of explanation.

Dasher (CONDUIT) is another versatile program for teachers who would like to create computer drills and who have little or no experience with programming. The package includes a user's guide and four diskettes for the Apple IIe and II+ and contains the programs and test materials needed for creating exercises in English, French, German, or Spanish. Dasher's most distinguished feature is the manner in which it handles errors. Visual clues are provided to errors in word order, extra characters, missing accents, and extra words. The teacher can create the full-sentence questions and answers along with all instructions, answers, and messages. No programming knowledge is necessary to create a wide range of exercises for elementary and intermediate students including transformations, scrambled sentences, sentence construction, fill-in items, and vocabulary review.

The GreatCreator (The Professor, Inc.) is an impressive program that enables teachers to prepare exams, drills, and homework quizzes on the computer quickly, easily, and creatively. The program contains all the accents for seventeen different languages. Through a text-entry system, the teacher selects between two different types of multiple-choice questions or a fill-in-the-blank format. The program then aids the teacher to create, edit, and save these questions. Multiple-choice questions may have up to five possible responses and an automatic explanation when the student chooses the wrong answer. The package includes a demo disk, utility disk, three data disks, and a user's guide.

Textbook Correlated Software

Mellgren (17) feels strongly, as do many educators, that for CAI to become a reality in more public school classrooms, teachers are going to have to see a wider variety of text-related software. Three recent examples of such CALL courseware are published respectively by D.C. Heath, EMC, and Heinle and Heinle.

D.C. Heath's popular *French for Mastery* and *Spanish for Mastery* both have software components. EMC Publishing has courseware available for *Deutsch Aktuell* as well as *Perspectives françaises.* Supplementing Heath's *Face à Face* textbook for grades 8-12, a software package by the same name offers original drills not found in the French text or workbook. Exercises drill vocabulary from the text and stress the mastery of grammar. Two exercises for each lesson follow the scope and sequence of the text's grammar and vocabulary presentations. Each disk contains a graphics-based review of the materials in a creative context. Back-up disks are provided with the five two-sided disks along with a key reference card and a teacher's manual.

A new EMC Spanish text, *¡Mucho gusto!*, with courseware, is in preparation. Heinle and Heinle have developed courseware and cassettes for two college texts: *Allons-y! Le français par étapes* and *¡Vamos! Bienvenidos al mundo hispánico*. Ten two-sided diskettes, a complete set of back-up diskettes, and an audiocassette tape enable students to hear authentic language in context for *Allons-y! Le français par étapes*. Nine two-sided diskettes, back-up diskettes, and an audiocassette tape accompany the Spanish text *¡Vamos! Bienvenidos al mundo hispánico*. Graphic representations of various scenes appear along with the dialogues that students may hear on the tape. Many language teachers think that the addition of sound to computer programs via cassette recordings is a step in the right direction and is another good means for enhancing CALL.

The D.C. Heath *Foundation Course in Spanish* software is for grades 8-12 and complements the text by the same name. The four two-sided disks, complete with back-up diskettes, a reference card for the keyboard, and a teacher's manual, offer a variety of computer drills featuring original material not in the text.

Word Processing for Language Teachers

Word processing on the computer is a timesaving and helpful aid. Examples of time saving include the creating and storing of examinations that can be used over and over, updated, changed in any portion and later printed as needed. The same work-saving use applies to student worksheets, vocabulary lists, and other handouts in addition to personal correspondence. Since the dot-matrix and letter-quality printer will cut a ditto master easily and quickly, word processing has rapidly become one of the primary uses of the computer as teachers learn of its usefulness and have access to both the computer and a printer. Newer word-processing programs put accents on the screen and print them as well.

MultiScribe (Styleware, Inc.) is an excellent example of a powerful word processor that furnishes the Apple IIe or IIc the type of flexibility previously available only on the Apple Macintosh. With MultiScribe the language teacher can choose from a wide range of fonts, character styles, and text formatting options. Unlike many other word processors, what you see on the screen is what you get; with MultiScribe, this is the highest resolution available on Apple. The easy-to-use program also permits the user to customize fonts, that is, make any letter shape and size desired. With the "pull-down" menus, the user never has to leave the document. Seven categories of word processor functions (File, Edit, Search, Format, Fonts, Size, Style) appear across the top of the screen to be pulled down as if they were a window shade. Either a keyboard or a mouse can be used to choose options. The exclusive FontEditor permits the user to either create fonts with accents or edit an existing one. The newer 2.0 version of MultiScribe features a near-letter-quality print option for a wide range of dot-matrix printers and cards. Several language versions complete with various font styles are under development. Five additional FontPak disks contain a total of ten additional fonts to complement the standard font assortment. Each FontPak disk includes a special utility program (Font Manager), which makes moving the fonts from disk to disk an easy task. A Spell Checker uses a 40,000-word dictionary to search for spelling errors in each document.

Two other powerful related word-processing programs for language teachers are Gutenberg Jr. and Gutenberg Sr. (Gutenberg Software, Ltd.). The programs are for multipurpose, multilanguage word processing and text formatting for the Apple family of computers. Gutenberg Jr. is among the most comprehensive word-processing and text-formatting capabilities ever designed for a microcomputer. Gutenberg Sr. comes with ready-made format files easily supplemented as needed. The availability of special characters for both the screen and printer, the mixing of text with graphics, and the page layout options make the program a very useful one for foreign language teachers. The twenty-one different printer font styles and the fourteen print pitches also add to the power of the special printer capabilities. With both programs, the accents for Spanish, French, German, Italian, and Portuguese are in place and ready to go. Both allow the teacher to create characters for other alphabets, such as Greek and Russian. The print commands permit subscripting and superscripting, underlining and double underlining, bold, italics, and more. The Sr. edition is much more powerful and does not impose as many restrictions on the user. Text created on the Gutenberg Jr. may be printed with the Gutenberg Sr. The Jr. edition provides only italic and bold type styles while the Sr. version includes five styles and many special symbols. The programs are not as easy to learn as MultiScribe; however, the many features place them among the most powerful word-processing packages for language teachers on the market and make them the preference of many experienced users.

Word Prof (Interkom) permits the teacher to create documents on the screen and to print with all requisite accents. Novice teachers appreciate the simplicity of Word Prof despite its limited editing features and printing options. The program is available for both the Apple IIe and IIc, and in Spanish, French, German, or Italian keyboard versions. The four editing commands remain on the screen as the teacher types the text and permit quickly and efficiently changing a line of text previously written, centering the text, changing the side margins, and ending work on the text.

Teachers using the IBM have access to a powerful word processor called Multilingual Scribe (Gamma Productions). The program performs a wide array of word-editing features for creating and storing documents in several languages. Users may type, edit, and print any combination of alphabets— English (including most European characters), Hebrew, Greek, Arabic, and Russian all within one file, even within one line. Foreign languages are displayed on the computer screen complete with all accents and vowel points, and are easily printed on most popular brands of dot-matrix printers. No hardware modification is required to the computer or the printer. Multilingual

Scribe is a full-featured word processor with powerful text-editing and print-formatting features. Custom character and custom keyboard layouts, even with complete new alphabets, can be created with a powerful Font Generator.

Popular Generic Software

Five generic programs that are not language-specific but that teachers find to be easy to use, fun, and worthwhile are The Print Shop (Broderbund), Crossword Magic (Mindscape), The Newsroom (Springboard Software), PrintMaster (Unison World), and Certificate Maker (Springboard Software).

The Print Shop, one of the most popular programs in the nation among all computer users, is designed to write and print greeting cards, signs, banners, and letterhead using eight type styles and a wide variety of graphic designs. Language teachers can use the program to create interesting verb charts and bulletin boards. Transparencies can be made from the final product. Additional disks accompany The Print Shop and contain dozens of varied graphics and designs including a special holiday edition.

PrintMaster, while similar to The Print Shop, differs in that it offers an on-screen version of the final printout as part of the program before it is printed. The various print styles may be changed on any line within the document, a special feature not available with The Print Shop. Both programs are fun and easy to learn. An additional data disk is available containing eight other type styles and 140 graphic designs. No programming or drawing skills are necessary to use and print with either program.

The Newsroom is a dynamic program designed to stimulate the creativity in journalists of all ages. Informal publications may be created that are formatted electronically and "typeset" without any knowledge of programming. The program provides a simple two-column page layout into which the writer enters text and graphics. While The Newsroom is more difficult to use than The Print Shop or PrintMaster, with a little practice the result can be a quality desktop newsletter that foreign language clubs and classes can share and enjoy.

A highly popular program for language teachers that creates crossword puzzles with ease is called Crossword Magic. The puzzles can be sized automatically as the words are typed, thus fitting the words into adjacent connecting spaces. The clues may be in the foreign language or in English and all this with just a few simple keystrokes. No provisions are made for accents, so all the letters in the puzzle are in capitals. Multiple class copies can be made by printing a ditto master. A wide variety of printing options are included with Crossword Magic, including the capability of storing puzzles on a separate disk for future use, editing, and printing.

Certificate Maker provides an easy and effective way to recognize, reward, and encourage all kinds of foreign language achievements. The teacher may select from over two hundred ready-to-go formats and, after filling in the details, may print a professional-looking certificate. Creating a certificate is a matter of selecting a border, entering the message, providing the signature and date line, and placing a colorful sticker on the certificate for the finishing touch. The Most Improved Student, Student of the Month, Best Idea Award, and many more make this program a popular addition to any software collection.

Electronic Grading Software

A wide variety of software is available for storing student grades on the Apple or IBM computer. One of the most popular programs is Report Card (Sensible Software). With this easy-to-use grading system, the process of compiling students' marks become more accurate and efficient. Grading is made more flexible by allowing the teacher to weight activities according to importance. Students can be shown their grade instantly as progress is made through the school year all from data that can be stored on a single diskette. Report Card allows a special "no grade" mark whenever a student is absent. Typical capabilities of each diskette are forty students per class (fifty on IBM), fifty graded activities per class, twelve classes per diskette (ten to fifteen on IBM), and three hundred students per diskette. Students may be ranked by last name, first name, selected activities, or grade. Printouts can list class averages, letter grades, a student's grades, activities of a class, results of an activity, and a class roster. A printer is optional (but recommended) with both the Apple and IBM versions. Teachers will find that an electronic gradebook helps to keep more accurate records, saves time, and adds credibility to any grading system.

Public-Domain Software

The public-domain arena offers a wide array of software that can be reprogrammed easily for classroom use (Bell, 4). For example, computer clubs almost always have extensive lists of free software shared among members (19). Since 1983, over 10,000 Apple computer clubs have been formed worldwide to help students learn more about what they can do with Apple personal computers. By conservative estimates, there are more than 10,000 programs available that range from complex programming languages to challenging games; they provide a good means of building a library of software at almost no cost. Many public-domain programs that focus upon concentration game exercises, word matching, or the unscrambling of words and expressions that flash on the screen are for CALL or are CALL-related. They do not, however, contain accents and in most cases must be accessed using all capital letters.

Software Fairs and Clearinghouses

Software fairs and clearinghouses are two good means of learning more about the kinds of programs available for foreign language instruction. There are two kinds of software fairs. The first is vendor-sponsored and vendor-oriented to introduce new products to the general public. (Apple World, held in January 1986 in San Francisco and again in March 1987 in Los Angeles sponsored by Apple Computer, Inc., is a good example.) The second type of software fair is non-profit-oriented and does not seek to promote one particular publisher.

A major drawback of software fairs, no matter their size, is the limited geographical area served, most often only the large metropolitan communities. Nevertheless, software fairs provide an excellent means of viewing a wide variety of courseware. In Iowa, for example, sixteen area educational agencies have set up libraries of software with review centers to provide teachers with the opportunity to have a hands-on experience with the hardware and to view a wide range of programs; experts are also available to answer questions. Given limited budgets, language teachers are hesitant to invest in software unless they can first judge for themselves that it fits their needs, and the preview centers are effective for this purpose. To that end, every two years a large educational fair is held in Fort Dodge. A wide variety of classroom materials is previewed. Hundreds of teachers are invited to view displays and to visit with vendors. Computer displays and demonstrations are only one part of the day's activities. Many software distributors provide demonstration lessons as well for teachers using computer programs.

Iowa is also representative of several states (along with Minnesota, Texas, Illinois, Wisconsin, South Carolina, California, and Florida) that have allocated funds to establish clearinghouses to evaluate and distribute educational software and make available a variety of services for interested teachers. The regional Area Educational Agencies purchase rights for unlimited duplication of diskettes by paying several times the normal price of the program. The programs are then duplicated and sold at low cost exclusively to schools in that area. Vendors are usually willing to work with this arrangement and schools gain access to programs at minimal expense. By purchasing software and duplication rights, programs can be put into the hands of teachers in all areas of the curriculum at a nominal cost for the disk and its documentation.

Conclusion

The jury is still out on just how successful the power of the computer is as a surrogate teacher or as a means of increasing student achievement. Will the millions of dollars being spent on computers strengthen what goes on in the secondary schools, or will the computer of the 1980s gather dust alongside the language laboratory of the 1960s? It is difficult to imagine what the future of CAI/CALL will offer, but even the critics admit that computer technology has become a fixed part of modern media. Still, despite a growing interest in the medium, few schools appear to be exploiting the tremendous power of the machine.

Computer proponents will continue to stress the potential of CALL to relieve teachers of tedium, thus freeing them from all but the most creative interactions with students. The use of CAI will suffer most in secondary schools where students have grown dependent upon the teacher to disseminate information. A radical and new outlook toward teaching methods and teacher-student roles is required. As teachers develop skills and understanding of the machine, they will discover uses of the medium that they could not have imagined in their initial encounter.

Research will have to become more sophisticated on all levels of instruction as teachers and administrators together explore how the microcomputer can help students to better master all subjects in the curriculum. Computer use in secondary foreign language classrooms will rise significantly in the next decade as mammoth memory and storage capacities make switching disks unnecessary and the centralized laboratory setting grows in popularity. Hard-disk drives that can hold homework accumulated over an entire semester from thirty students will become commonplace.

Predicting certainties is almost always risky, but one can predict with some assuredness that computer use will continue to challenge teachers in all areas of the curriculum as much as any technological innovation in the history of education.

References, The Computer in the High School Classroom

1. "America at Ease with Computers." *U.S. News and World Report* 100, 6 (1986) :72.

2. Becker, Henry Jay. "The Second National U.S. School Uses of Microcomputer Survey." Paper presented at the World Conference on Computers in Education, Norfolk, VA, 29 July 2-August 1987.

3. _____. "Our National Report Card: Preliminary Results from the New Johns Hopkins Survey." *Classroom Computer Learning* 6, 4 (1986):30-33.

4. Bell, Jack. "Fun and Games in the Public Domain." *Personal Computing* 10, 2 (1986):81-85.

5. Charp, Sylvia. "Editorial." *T.H.E. Journal* 13, 3 (1985):10.

6. *Computers in Education: Goals and Content.* Sacramento, CA: Bureau of Publications, California State Department of Education.

7. Curtin, Constance O. Personal correspondence, 1986.

8. Dearborn, Donald E. "How States Evaluate Software." *Electronic Learning* 5, 2 (1985):27-31.

9. Dunnaway, James. "Computer-Based Instruction: A Status Report." *Streamlined Seminar* 4, 2 (1985):4.

10. *Electronic Education* 5, 7 (1986):19

11. *Electronic Learning* 6, 6(1987):18-23

12. Galbraith, Stanley. Personal communication, 1986.

13. Gillespie, Barbara L. Personal communication, 1986.

14. Haavind, Robert. "The Pyramid of Our Age: A New Set of Tools." *High Technology* 6, 2 (1986):4.

15. Hoch, Frances S. "Computer Literacy and the Foreign Language Teacher." *CALICO Journal* 3, 1 (1985):17-18,32.

16. Levinson, Cynthia Y. "Quick Reference: Computer Technology and Foreign Language Teaching." *SEDL/RX Newsletter* 1, 6 (1985):10-12.

17. Mellgren, Millie Park. Personal communication, 1986.

18. Morrey, Robert A. Personal communication, 1986.

19. *Personal Computing* 19, 2 (1986) :86-87.

20. Robinson, Gail, John Underwood, Wilga Rivers, José Hernández, Carollyn Rudesill, and Clare Malnik Enseñat. *Computer-Assisted Language Instruction in Foreign Language Education.* San Francisco: Center for Language & Crosscultural Skills, 1985. [EDRS: ED 262 626]

21. Roger Wagner Publishing, Inc., P.O. Box 582 Santee, CA 92071

22. Ruthven, Carol W. *Electronic Education* 5, 1 (1985):15.

23. Schwartz, Martha. Personal communication, 1986.

24. "Technology in the Classroom," pp. 26-27 in *Educational Mailing List and Marketing Guide, 1987.* Shelton, CT: Market Data Retrieval.

CALL and NCCALL in the United Kingdom: Past, Present, and Future

Graham D. Davies
National Center for Computer Assisted Language Learning
Ealing College of Higher Education

Introduction

This chapter holds two principal parts. The first traces the recent history of computer-assisted language learning (CALL) in the United Kingdom, highlights current trends in software development, and speculates about its possible future direction; specific references are made to examples of software produced by British educational institutions and by private software houses. The second part describes NCCALL (the National Center for Computer Assisted Language Learning) and its projects and activities.

Recent History of CALL in the UK

Early Efforts

In the 1970s CALL was regarded by most teachers in the UK as the pursuit of the lunatic fringe of language teaching methodologists. At the time of this writing (May 1987), it is probably true to say that CALL has finally attained a position of respectability if not complete acceptability. It is difficult to gauge precisely how many language teachers now make use of CALL materials, but figures obtained from selected publishers, combined with intelligent guesswork, indicate that about 20 percent of secondary schools and further and higher education colleges (which serve the 16-plus age group), along with significantly higher proportions of universities and polytechnics, are now using CALL software packages. NCCALL (the National Center for Computer Assisted Language Learning—described in detail in the second half of this chapter) at Ealing College of Higher Education, London, set up with the aid of central government funding to service the nonadvanced further education sector, has been gathering information on the use of CALL since 1985. The picture beginning to emerge is very patchy. Most local education authorities now have a nucleus of CALL enthusiasts, but there are a few spots where there is virtually no interest in computers among language teachers and language advisers, and apparently little support for anyone wishing to take part in appropriate training courses.

Before the 1970s there was little activity in CALL outside the universities. This author's involvement with CALL began in 1977. Rex Last, then at the University of Hull, was the first kindred spirit identified. Both of us had been working independently toward similar goals, and it was only after 1979 that we discovered coincidentally that we had both been working on multipurpose programs that could be adapted to produce an infinite variety of question-answer sequences (Last, 14; Davies, 8). A typical computer-student dialogue looked like this:

COMPUTER: What is the German for "the car"?

STUDENT: Der Wagen

COMPUTER: Correct! You could have also said 'das Auto'.

In retrospect, this low-level, first-blush approach reflected the author's rudimentary knowledge of BASIC and the hardware available at that time— a Prime 300 minicomputer running under a slow and unreliable time-sharing system that students accessed via noisy teletype terminals. The hardware situation improved with the advent of the microcomputer. The Microelectronics in Education Programme (MEP), which was initiated with the aid of central government funding in late 1980 and continued until early 1986, gave schools the necessary financial resources to enable them to purchase microcomputers, and selected institutions were given funding for software development. As the new hardware was introduced into schools in the early 1980s, new interest in CALL grew and amateur programmers were quick to jump on the bandwagon, producing an abundance of programs generating random items of vocabulary to be translated and out-of-context verbs to be conjugated.

The early micros were not particularly suited to CALL. The Apple II, for example, on which the first version of the Apfeldeutsch package was written in 1981, came without a standard lowercase character set and required elaborate programming to enable the learner to type commas in his or her answers. Apfeldeutsch was originally written in uppercase only and lacked Umlaute and the Eszett character. Apfeldeutsch did, however, include a pattern markup facility that highlighted minor spelling errors, and alternative answers were accepted. But it took months to find someone with the expertise to create software that could generate a full upper- and lowercase German character set—a feature now taken for granted on all microcomputers.

Apfeldeutsch, and indeed most of the software developed in the UK in the early 1980s, fell into the right-wrong-try-another-one quiz category. Clearly CALL could and should offer more (Holmes and Kidd, 13). There were hints of more interesting uses of CALL at a conference held at the Polytechnic of Central London in 1980 (Leather, 15). Farrington (10) of Aberdeen University described materials now known as LITTRE for guiding students through the process of translating French prose, and Roach (19) of Leeds University showed a video recording of oriental students practicing listening skills and pronunciation with a Commodore Pet linked to an audiocassette recorder. In 1981 at a CALL conference organized jointly by the Council for Educational Technology (CET) and the Center for Information on Language Teaching (CILT), the Atari conversational packages for French, German, and Spanish were demonstrated (2). These packages can be considered a breakthrough in that they included recordings of human voices, but the interactive sequences were primitive. The multiple-choice test was the only form of assessment, and all the programs were completely linear. Feedback was limited to "right" or "wrong" responses and branching; remedial reviews and discrete error analysis had been totally ignored. By this time CALL had ceased to be the pursuit of a handful of academics. In 1982, CILT held its first annual CALL workshop and the newsletter *Callboard* was set up. Most CALL software was unimaginative, however, and it seemed difficult for old hands and newcomers alike to break from repetitive drills. As a result, CALL became associated with the behavioristic rather than the communicative/functional approach to language teaching (which was by now the methodology favored both by practicing teachers and by local authority advisers for modern languages) and CALL was therefore given a cool reception.

New Hardware, New Software

One of the major factors contributing to the development of more imaginative CALL software in the UK was the establishment of the BBC Microcomputer as the dominant machine in education, which in turn gave encouragement to software writers, who could now rely on a more stable market. The "Beeb" was a computer designed specifically with the educational market in mind. It was a dream to program. Its extended version of BASIC offered Pascallike procedures, user-defined strong functions, and excellent facilities for producing graphics. Generating foreign character sets presented few problems. Furthermore, the "Beeb" knocked the spots off its closest competitors—Commodore PET and the Apple II—in speed. But the attractiveness of the machine—particularly its facilities for producing color and graphics—did have some disadvantages. Multicolored graphics became the yardstick by which new programs were judged, and any programs containing just text were considered dull and boring.

Two programs produced at Chelsea College, London (now King's College) and available from the Longman Group, for the BBC micro—known as METRO and COPROB—were typical products of this new enthusiasm. METRO simulates a trip on the Paris Métro, testing the learner's ability to understand the meanings of essential signs and public notices. The aim is to reach a specified destination by answering a series of multiple-choice questions. The learner moves from station to station in accordance with correct responses. A map of a section of the Métro is drawn, irritatingly slowly, after each correct response, showing the station at which the student has arrived. If the learner fails to recognize that a change of train is necessary— a test of skill in map reading rather than in recognizing French—off he or she goes in the wrong direction and has to backtrack.

The idea in METRO is essentially a good one; the attention devoted to the graphics, however, seems to have resulted in the sacrifice of important pedagogical features. The program offers little feedback apart from indicating that the learner's response is right or wrong; the French text is all in capital letters and, apart from the questions themselves, there is little French on the screen. Moreover, the program lacks variety. The quesitons are always presented in the same order with the same arrangement of correct answers and distractors. The section of the Métro is always the same, as is the specified destination. METRO therefore turns out to be little more than a linear recognition exercise in which the learner's role is essentially passive.

COPROB offers even less language. It is basically a guessing game in which the learner plays the role of a policeman whose task is to preempt a series of four crimes about to be committed in a French town. There are twelve locations where the crimes might take place. The learner is given a list of them at the beginning of the program, and it is suggested (in English) that four thieves are about to steal various items (for example, money or gasoline). The learner's task is to identify the likely locations of these items in order to catch the criminals in the act. The locations are given in French, in capital letters (so no accents appear). A graphic representation of the town is then displayed, and the learner indicates the four possible locations of the crimes. At level 1 this is done in multiple-choice format, but at level 3 the learner has to type whole words from memory. Guesses including the article, for example LA BOULANGERIE, are rejected. The program is similarly weak in the way it handles input from the keyboard—for example, an extra space is considered a misspelling (Davies and Higgins, 9, pp. 24-26). Feedback is minimal if the guess is incorrect, but a correct guess causes a little square representing the police car to race to the scene of the crime to catch the criminal. The locations themselves are depicted symbolically, but the graphic symbols are unclear and sometimes misleading. (It takes some considerable mental gymnastics to work out that the drawing of an elephant represents the hypermarket: elephant = mammouth = Mammouth = famous French hypermarket chain.) But apart from these criticisms, learners who use COPROB will learn very little French. At best they will end up with the ability to recognize a dozen nouns.

One is inclined to ask whether it is worth the effort (and expense) to develop such programs considering how little language they contain in relation to graphics. In fairness, however, their effectiveness could be enhanced by imaginative work on the part of the classroom teacher through eliciting oral responses from the class in reaction to what appears on screen. But METRO and COPROB did help to establish the use of the microcomputer as a presenter of authentic French, which was a move in the right direction, and both programs marked a break with the drill-and-practice tradition in CALL.

Recent Trends

Graphics

Software that makes intelligent use of graphics, without sacrificing language, has been produced by Netherhall Software (a software house that emerged from within Netherhall school, Cambridgeshire). Netherhall's French Connections software package (marketed by Cambridge Micro Software) for the BBC micro consists of two programs that aim to familiarize the learner with the langauge of giving directions and with the geographical locations and features of important French towns.

The first of the programs in the package, Directions, depicts a street map and an animated figure, Pierre, whom the learner instructs to move in different directions: "Tournez à gauche," "Allez tout droit," etc. The learner is congratulated when Pierre reaches his goal or, if a mistake is made, errors are highlighted and the correct French phrase is displayed accompanied by an animated graphic sequence. The animated sequences are well-executed and help clarify the meaning. Apart from the language associated with giving directions, there is plenty of French on the screen and instant translations into English are available if required.

The second program in the package, Villes de France, is for more advanced learners. In an accompanying booklet, a number of important towns in France are described (in French): where they are located, what kinds of industries they have, and other notable features. The program consists of two guessing games that tie in closely with the printed material. The object of the first game is to pinpoint the locations of ten different towns by moving the cursor across a map of France. The second game requires the learner to identify towns marked with crosses on the map from clues given in French, which in turn requires the learner to use the knowledge gleaned from the booklet. This approach to CALL, in which printed information has to be consulted in order to make use of the program, is a positive development and is featured in a number of new packages. Quelle Tête (also from Cambridge Micro Software), which is based on the police "Photofit" principle, uses graphics to familiarize the learner of French with the vocabulary of physiognomical description and to demonstrate the agreement and position of adjectives. Its companion program, Jeu des ménages, focuses on the vocabulary used to describe the rooms in a house and the items with which they can be furnished. There are German versions of the last two programs, respectively called Kopfjäger and Umziehen. The programs can be used by individual learners but, as the accompanying booklet suggests, they are especially effective as visual aids for stimulating conversation and group activities.

The idea of the teacher using the computer as a stimulus in group activities is a relatively new development and contrasts with the more traditional view of CALL, which stresses the importance of individualized instruction and the ability of the computer to adapt itself to the learner's own pace. The disadvantage of the traditional approach to CALL is that it assumes that there is one computer available for each student—which is still the exception rather than the rule in most classes in the UK. One reason for the popularity of CALL in group activities in the UK is the difficulty language teachers experience in gaining access to the microcomputer laboratory, but there is also a strong feeling that this approach is more in line with communicative language teaching methodology (Beaton et al., 3).

Jeu des ménages also offers possibilities as a means of stimulating oral work. The program draws a cross-section of a house as a means of displaying the various rooms: la cuisine, la salle à manger, etc. The learner is asked in which rooms a succession of items of furniture are to be located and the computer dutifully positions them as requested. Jeu des ménages is fun for the individual learner, but it is also effective in group activities.

It can be argued that Quelle tête and Jeu des ménages are no more useful than a poster or overhead projector. The advantage, however, is that the images can be easily varied and, if the printout facilities of the programs are used, a valuable source of handouts is immediately available to the teacher. The computer thus becomes a useful tool without attempting to take over the teacher's role.

So far the main distinguishable trends in CALL in the UK are a movement away from drill-and-practice toward the development of programs incorporating graphics and the use of the computer in group activities. Drill programs continue to be popular among students (the *most* popular according to the borrowing pattern from NCCALL's software library). It is clear that the well-designed drill with appropriate feedback and remediation will always play an important role for the self-access learner, but school teachers in the UK seem to be more in favor of exploratory or task-oriented programs, including simulations. Unlike the programs described above, simulations do not necessarily rely on graphics, but they are ideal for group activities, with or without the presence of the teacher.

Simulations

The Granville package (Cambridge Micro Software) is probably the best examle of a language simulatioh. This excellent and ambitious software package consists of a disk and an illustrated booklet and aims to give the learner an idea of what it is like to spend a short holiday in France. The booklet gives detailed instructions to the teacher on using the program and includes numerous authentic texts and photographs that convey an accurate image of the town.

Granville consists mainly of descriptive text in French and may be compared to the popular adventure games. The difference, however, is that the program is set in a more down-to-earth environment. The learner begins by filling in the "fiche" to register in a hotel. From this point on the learner can explore the town, going shopping, taking a bus or boat ride, or visiting the beach or casino! The computer program constantly monitors the learner's thirst and hunger and may whisk him or her off to a bistro for lunch. It is essential to pay the bill, however, for otherwise a warning appears. Moreover, it is vital to stay within one's budget and not indulge in luxuries. If necessary, it is possible to phone home, which causes the instructions found in a French kiosk to appear on screen. So authentic is the simulation, even the sound of the phone being taken off the hook and the dial tone can be heard. Granville is a good example of an exploratory program that offers hours of amusement to the individual learner and a whole range of activities for group use under the supervision of the teacher.

Most language teachers seem to like the idea of simulations and would like more of them, but they take a long time to write. There are a few good simulations written especially for language learners. Apart from Granville, there is Incendie à l'hôtel (Wida Software) for the BBC mirco, which faces the student with the problem of escaping from a burning structure, Faisons des achats (also Wida), which simulates a shopping expedition, Manoir des oiseaux (Camsoft), which calls upon the student to detect the perpetrator of a crime in a French country house, and Schloss Schattenburg (Camsoft), a German-language adventure in the more traditional vein.

NCCALL also has two simulations under development for use with the BBC—Airline Booking Simulation (to be marketed by McGraw-Hill UK) and Por Favor (owned by the Ealing College School of Language Studies), both scheduled for completion in early 1988. The former simulates the purchase of airline tickets on a French teletext system and is based on an English version. The program will be accompanied by a detailed workbook (in French) and is aimed at students who need to acquire experience using French for practical purposes. The second program simulates a visit to Caceres, Spain. The learner is required to produce appropriate responses in Spanish in a variety of situations. Both programs, which make use of authentic materials, should prove interesting to teachers who favor the communicative approach.

Text Reconstruction Programs

Another useful development in CALL in the UK is the emergence of a variety of text-reconstruction programs (also called information-gap programs). Like simulations, these programs are task- rather than form-oriented and mark a break with traditional drill-and-practice CALL. One of the most inventive programs of this type is Higgins's Storyboard (Wida), from which this author's Copywrite (Camsoft), Moy's Developing Tray (Inner London Educational Computing Centre) and numerous similar programs were derived. In these programs a short text is presented and then reduced to punctuation and dashes representing the original letters. The student's task is to restore the text by entering any words he or she can remember or guess. Correctly guessed words are then located on the screen in the right places.

Text-reconstruction programs call upon a wide range of skills. The student has to apply knowledge of grammar and vocabulary as well as common sense and general knowledge. The idea is an extension of Taylor's cloze procedure (20), the removal of words from a text at regular intervals, which the learner has to replace. Jones's Clozemaster and the author's Clozewrite (both available from Wida) are examples of more traditional cloze programs.

An unusual application of the principle of masking a text is Higgins's Pinpoint (Wida), in which the computer begins by displaying a word from one of a selection of six texts. At the top of the screen is a set of six possible titles for the text. The user's task is to guess the title of the masked text from the minimal amount of information. One word rarely gives enough information; however, more context can be "bought" until the learner can guess more confidently. As a group exercise, this is an exciting and competitive activity.

Such text-reconstruction programs represented another breakthrough in CALL. They offered new exercises that could not be easily done by any other means. They often puzzle traditionally minded computer-assisted learning experts, particularly nonlinguists, because they do not focus on clearly defined areas of vocabulary or grammar. They are not structured teaching programs but computer-controlled activities that encourage the user to work out his or her own learning strategies. This may sound contradictory in view of what was said about programs that fail to offer feedback. In language teaching, however, one needs a mixture of activities, some of which focus on specific structures and lexicon (in which feedback and appropriate branching may be called for) and some of which set the student tasks that call upon an undefined range of skills. Text-reconstruction programs fail into the latter category; they force students to search and use their store of linguistic knowledge and to rely upon their own initiative. They are an excellent way of concentrating the attention and exercising the learner's memory and of reinforcing grammar and vocabulary in context.

Authoring Packages

Most of the text-reconstruction programs mentioned above were designed as authoring packages, enabling the teacher to produce an infinite variety of new materials to be manipulated in different ways. Such packages have been well-received compared, for example, with traditional general-purpose authoring packages. Most general-purpose packages have found little favor among language teachers, probably because they usually offer little more than a quizlike structure into which a series of questions are slotted, with appropriate branching and remediation, and assume a programmed-learning approach. What language teachers seemed to want is the possibility of longer contexts and more imaginative activities.

Gapkit (Camsoft) by the author is an example of an authoring package that copes adequately with longer contexts—up to three pages of eighteen lines apiece. It allows the teacher to set up a series of screen pages from which any individual words, groups of words, or parts of words can be deleted—in effect, a selective cloze exercise. Discrete clues can be built in to assist the student and a "help" panel can be provided. Gapkit is not particularly exciting as a program, but it does enable simple structural drills and controlled vocabulary exercises to be written with a minimum of effort. Gapkit can also be used in conjunction with printed material, town maps, and descriptive texts, for example, in order to produce exercises on the giving of directions and to test reading comprehension of French.

Other authoring packages for language teachers, from Wida, include Vocab, which consists of a set of games centered on items of vocabulary and appropriate contexts; Speedread, which enables rapid-reading exercises to be created; and Wordstore, which the teacher or student can use to create a context dictionary.

There is also the Fun with Texts package (Camsoft) by the author, which offers for French, German, EFL, and Russian a range of decoding, reconstruction, unscrambling, and predicting activities, two of which, Copywrite and Clozewrite, have been mentioned above.

Word Processor and Writing Skills

The move away from series of short drills and the improvements in authoring packages have helped the progress of CALL, but much work remains to be done to foster writing skills. This is where the word processor comes into its own. A questionnaire produced, distributed, and analyzed by NCCALL in 1985 to all further and higher education colleges and polytechnics in the UK (see pp. 161-62 below) revealed that the single most popular piece of software used by language teachers was the word-processing package. There is no doubt that the humble word processor provides an invaluable focus of attention for students of languages. Piper (18) of NCCALL, who teaches students of English as a foreign language, has produced a set of text files and printed materials that exploit the BBC Microcomputer's VIEW word-processing package as an aid to teaching word-processing skills and the English language simultaneously. These materials offer the student a variety of proofreading, transformation, blank-filing, and reordering tasks in the form of text files that are called up in sequence. The student begins with the simple, which may require the correction of a spelling error in a text or the conversion of all the verbs from the present to the past tense. The students have the impression that the main aim of these tasks is to offer a series of grammatical exercises, but the covert purpose is to familiarize them with the functions of the word-processing package. A French version of Piper's software is being developed at NCCALL, and Congdon (6) of South Manchester Community College is producing similar materials in Spanish provisionally known as VISTA. Both will be available through NCCALL. The biggest single advantage of such packages is that files created on one word processor on one type of machine can easily be recreated on a completely different word processor with minor modifications on another type of computer.

Once students are completely conversant with the basic word-processing functions, they may be given free-writing tasks. The teacher circulates around the class, checking the work on screen for obvious errors and offering guidance where necessary. Using the word processor for composition is a much more effective way of handling free-writing tasks than setting topics to be written at home and corrected at a later date. The students derive much more satisfaction from the "clean" copy they take away at the end of the session and are more likely to look back on their work when it is not covered in red ink. One advantage of this approach that has become obvious to the authors when working with students of German is that minor irritating errors, such as incorrect adjective endings, wrong plural formations, and misplaced verbs in subordinate clauses can be picked up on the spot, before the student reinforces them by repetition, and then checked and changed globally if necessary.

Speech

Most CALL programs in the UK still ignore the most important aspect of language: the human voice. Voice synthesizers are available for most computers, but synthetic speech is so poor an imitation of the human voice that it is doubtful synthetic speech will provide an answer in the foreseeable future. Research in this area is being carried out predominantly by computing enthusiasts who are more interested in the challenge it presents that in producing a usable system for language teachers. Speech synthesizers can produce a range of completely natural-sounding male and female voices with different regional accents, but only on the most expensive computers. Digitized speech is another question, but it will be some time before the necessary equipment is available at a price most educational institutions can afford.

In any case, it is debatable whether the computer is an appropriate device for reproducing speech. The audiocassette recorder appears to be much better suited to this task. Tandberg's specially adapted random-access audiocassette recorder (the TCCR 530) can be linked to a computer, and it is then possible to set up a useful range of activities. Page (17) of Luton College of Higher Education has created dictation exercises (Dictation, available from Forlan Software) that have been designed for students in secretarial-linguist courses. The student hears a letter being dictated in French, phrase by phrase, and can attempt to type in any phrase, listen to it again, or give up and see what the correct form is. The computer automatically checks the student's answers and provides the necessary feedback. Page has also created a number of gap-filling and text-reconstruction exercises (Gapfill, also available from Forlan) that make use of the same technique. For students who may have to cope with a telephone in a foreign country, Page has produced a simulation (Phone, again through Forlan) in which the student has to dial a certain number and indicate an understanding of the information conveyed by the authentic telephone voice at the other end of the line. The added dimension of authentic (not synthetic) sound is undoubtedly a major step forward in CALL.

Interactive Videodiscs

Research in the area of interactive videodiscs and modern languages is still in its infancy in the UK, but interesting work is being carried out under the direction of Hill (12) at Brighton Polytechnic's Language Center on a videodisc derived from the BBC TV series *Dès le début* and the *Bid for Power* videodisc for learners of English as a second language. Other interactive videodisc projects for modern languages include a videodisc under development in schools within the Shropshire local education authority that simulates a walk through a French town; a package recently completed at Preston Polytechnic that exploits the BBC TV's *Ensemble* videodisc (for beginners of French); Expodisc (from the Ealing College School of Business Administration), a collaborative videodisc project in progress at this writing aims to teach the language of export marketing recently proposed by NCCALL and Buckinghamshire College of Higher Education. At present, few schools are equipped with the necessary hardware but, largely as a result of the BBC's initiative in the production of the *Domesday Project* (which was released in early 1987), a number of schools are now purchasing interactive videodisc equipment. The *Domesday Project,* which has led the way in the use of this exciting new medium, is essentially a document of life in the UK in the 1980s, an elaborate database of still and moving images, simulated walks, maps, statistics, and descriptive texts. Although it was not designed with language teaching in mind, a number of teachers of English as a foreign language, both in the UK and abroad, have begun to explore its possibilities as a language-learning resource.

The Future

As for the future of CALL in the UK, progress is foreseeable on a number of fronts. While the microcomputer laboratory for private study will continue to play a role, there will be increased emphasis on teacher-directed and student-directed communicative and role-playing CALL activities. To a large extent this reflects the recent shakeup in the secondary schools' public examination system—the biggest in over thirty years. The replacement of the General Certificates of Education (GCE) "O" level and Certificate of Secondary Education (CSE) examinations, which were taken by secondary school children at about age sixteen, by the combined General Certificate of Secondary Education (GCSE) has brought about a significant change in the way modern languages are examined and taught. The emphasis is now firmly on communication and authentic language rather than on grammar and contrived texts to be translated (which characterized the GCE "O" level examination in particular). Listening, speaking, reading, and writing skills now carry equal weight. It is likely, therefore, that the computer will be appreciated more as a tool or as a classroom aid—as a stimulus for activities that reflect the new syllabuses—rather than as a device that attempts to take over the teacher's role. There will probably be more use made of interactive videodiscs in order to enable authentic language and authentic images of foreign countries to be presented.

There will undoubtedly be increasing interest in electronic mail as a means of communication between schools in the UK and continental Europe, and in using the computer to access foreign databases. Hewer (11) of the Brealey Center, St. George's School, Sleaford, Lincolnshire, has already established an electronic link with a school in Luxemburg, and other educational institutions are beginning to explore the possibilities of international electronic communications. The role of NCCALL as a catalyst in all of these endeavors is described below.

NCCALL

Since the early 1980s, the British government has invested considerable sums of money in education in order to promote awareness about computers and their applications. The Microelectronics Education Programme (MEP), which ran from 1981 to 1986, established a national center and a network of regional centers through which schools were able to purchase hardware and teachers were awakened to the possibilities of the new technologies. Selected educational institutions were also able to develop courseware—although relatively little was produced for CALL. The MEP funding has now come to an end, but some of the centers are still operating and the government continues to support its successor, the new Microelectronics Education Support Unit (MESU) based at the University of Warwick.

Under the new program of funding, which began in 1985, the Department of Education and Science has provided Educational Support Grants (ESGs) to enable a number of regional and national centers to be set up and maintained in further and higher education colleges to promote awareness about information technology in the so-called nonadvanced further education (NAFE) sector. Broadly speaking, NAFE covers the education of students of sixteen and over who have completed secondary or vocational nature. Some centers in receipt of ESG funding are more concerned with the development of courseware in specific subject areas, while others are more concerned with the running of training courses for teachers or the gathering and dissemination of information.

It was under this new program of funding that NCCALL, the National Center for Computer Assisted Language Learning, was set up in the School of Language Studies in Grove House at Ealing College of Higher Education, London, in April of 1985.

Activities and Projects

NCCALL is concerned mainly with the following languages: EFL/ESL, French, German, Spanish, and Russian. Although NCCALL aims to promote CALL in the sphere of nonadvanced further education, it also maintains close contacts with schools, universities, and other educational institutions in the UK and abroad. A large number of demonstrations and lectures on CALL have been given by NCCALL staff throughout the United Kingdom and in Norway, France, Denmark, Belgium, Holland, Switzerland, Sweden, Finaland, East Germany, West Germany, Poland, Hungary, Canada, South Africa, India, and the USA.

The activities of NCCALL can be summarized under the following seven headings:

1. Gathering information about CALL
2. Dissemination of information about CALL
3. Acting as a CALL resource center
4. Evaluation of CALL courseware
5. Development of CALL courseware applications
6. Staff training and development
7. Collaboration with other institutions

Gathering Information about CALL

NCCALL's first major attempt to gather information took place in April 1985 when a questionnaire was sent to approximately 500 colleges and polytechnics in England and Wales. The main aims of the questionnaire were to identify which colleges were active in CALL, what hardware and software they were using, and what languages were being taught with the support of CALL.

176 responses were received. The most important conclusions of the questionnaire can be summarized as follows:

1. 62 institutions indicated they used CALL, but most teachers complained of the lack of software, the lack of inservice training, and the lack of time to learn about the new technology.
2. The stand-alone BBC Micro was used by over 80 percent of institutions that responded to the questionnaire, followed by the RML 380Z/480Z, used by under 20 percent of institutions. Use of other computers was insignificant.
3. Most institutions were using commercially produced software, but a significant number were producing their own. BASIC was the commonest programming language, but many institutions were using authoring packages. Somewhat fewer were using authoring languages. Word-processing packages were by far the commonest form of software used by language teachers. Gapkit, and Copywrite, Clozemaster, Storyboard, and Choicemaster were the most popular named CALL packages.
4. French figured as the main language being taught with the support of CALL, followed by German, English, Spanish, ESL/EFL, Italian, and Russian. Public examinations and general interest or adult education were indicated as the main goals for language students.
5. Increased motivation among students, the experience of using a computer, and the opportunities for self-access learning were cited as the major benefits of CALL.

Since the issue of the 1985 questionnaire, NCCALL has received a steady flow of information on the CALL activities of a wide range of educational institutions, mainly through direct contact by individuals. The most recent indications (in 1986-87) were that, although language teachers are becoming more aware of CALL, a great many—possibly as high as 80 percent—have still had little or nothing to do with computers. A disturbing fact that has emerged since NCCALL was established is that many language teachers do not appear to have easy access to computing facilities, and some local education authorities are unwilling to offer financial support to teachers wishing to attend training courses. This appears to indicate that a significant number of headteachers and educational administrators still associate computers only with the scientific disciplines.

Dissemination of Information about CALL

The volume of inquiries received by NCCALL, from all sectors of education in the UK and abroad, now runs about 20 to 25 per week. General inquiries are always answered with the current issue of NCCALL's Information Sheet, which contains the range of NCCALL's activities and includes a short, select bibliography on CALL. Where possible, NCCALL endeavors to provide more detailed information if requested, but the large volume of inquiries means that it is not always possible to answer everyone personally.

NCCALL now produces the newsletter *Callboard*, which was established in 1982 with the aim of keeping language teachers informed about new developments in CALL. *Callboard* appears at regular intervals and there are now over 500 subscribers mainly in the UK, but also as far away as Papua, New Guinea! Subscription inquiries are welcomed.

NCCALL subscribes to the Times Network for Schools (TTNS) and can be contacted on HFE027, the NCCALL ID on TTINS. Of particular interest to NCCALL are the international links being investigated at TTNS by Julia Cooper (7). NCCALL regularly uses TTNS mailing and bulletin-board facilities for disseminating information. NCCALL's current Information Sheet, announcements of forthcoming courses, and extracts from *Callboard* are already accessible via TTNS under the FHE (Further and Higher Education) database. It is also planned to build up a keyboard-searchable database of available CALL software on TTNS.

Acting as a CALL Resource Center

A large number of teachers from the UK and abroad visit NCCALL—an average of four visitors per week. Some simply wish to consult the software library, but most are more demanding and can easily occupy the attention of a member of the staff for a whole morning or afternoon.

NCCALL is equipped with the following hardware:

24 BBC micros
1 BBC Master 128
1 Apple IIe
1 Commodore 64
1 RML 480Z
1 RM Nimbus
1 IBM PC XT (10 megabyte hard disk)
1 Apple Macintosh
1 Tandberg TCCR 530 (Computer-controlled cassette recorder)
1 Interactive videodisc workstation (BBC Micro, Philips VP831 videodisc player, and Nordmende TV set)
1 Sony universal projector
2 Salora VHS cassette recorders
1 Tandata Modem (plus TTNS communications software)

This hardware is located in three rooms: the NCCALL office, the programmer's office, and one large open-access room in which teaching also takes place. Most of the BBC micros are used regularly by language students on courses in the School of Language Studies, by visitors, and by teachers on training courses. The Sony projector is invaluable for teaching and for software presentations. The other computers are used mainly for administration, for running software not available on the BBC micro, and for viewing software for reversioning.

While the BBC micro will probably continue to be the main machine used by students and staff for some time to come, it is becoming clear that NCCALL should think about seeking funding to bring itself into line with the rest of the world, which currently appears to favor IBM PCs and compatibles.

The BBC micros are stand-alone units. Each machine is equipped with the VIEW word-processing ROM. Two machines also contain Wordwise Plus. Three others contain AMX mouse software, a speech synthesizer, and LOGO. The IBM PC XT and Apple Macintosh, which are used almost exclusively for administration, are equipped with word-processing and database software.

The college computing center houses a Prime minicomputer system, which is used by NCCALL mainly for text-analysis tasks. The computing center can be accessed from terminals in Grove House, including a BBC micro equipped with Kermit.

NCCALL's software library now has a stock of about 300 disks, mainly for the BBC micro. These materials are used extensively by language students, by visitors, and by teachers on training courses. A list of titles is available for each of the languages taught in the School of Language Studies: EFL, French, German, Russian, and Spanish. NCCALL's library of books on CAI/CALL now includes some 100 titles. This library is available for consultation by students, staff, and visitors.

Evaluation of CALL Courseware

All newly acquired software/courseware packages undergo a quick initial evaluation. Ideally, each package should be evaluated more thoroughly with the aid of NCCALL's own CALL evaluation form, but his is an extremely time-consuming process—at least three hours per package is required—and many packages still await thorough evaluation. One way of evaluating software is to observe it in use. Having watched a countless number of students and staff working with various packages, NCCALL staff now have a good idea of the robustness and popularity of most of the packages and are able to pass this information to inquirers. An analysis of the pattern of borrowings from the software library is currently being carried out, which at first sight indicates that the most popular packages among students are grammatical drills and text-reconstruction exercises.

Development of CALL Courseware Applications

Dedicated CALL software of high quality is still in poor supply in the UK, and NCCALL has therefore concentrated its efforts on producing new software and developing strategies for using it and existing context-free software (e.g., word-processing packages) in the language classroom. The goal is to produce (and market where appropriate) courseware that can be used in general language courses from beginning to intermediate level, leading up to a wide range of public examinations. Most of the courseware is suitable for secondary education (11-16-year-olds) as well as further education students (over 16).

In view of the responses to the 1985 questionnaire and the continued high demand for BBC micro software, the BBC micro has been targeted as the main machine for developing new software, but NCCALL is keeping a close eye on the RM Nimbus and the IBM PC/compatibles, as both types of machines seem likely to come to the fore in education in the future.

Several courseware projects are under development; some are in the planning stage, others have reached field testing in-house or at sister institutions. Taken together, these projects represent a broad spectrum of media applications and purposes for language teaching. For example, NCCALL has an agreement with the University of Western Ontario, Canada, to revise CLEF—a self-access package of some 60 diskettes from Gessler Publishing for the beginning and intermediate student of French—for the BBC micro. Almost half of the materials are completed at this writing. Other projects include the authoring and development of simulations like Airline Booking Simulation (NCCALL will publish the French version), Mazes (for EFL)—based on the book of the same name by Berer and Rinvolucri (4), and Por Favor, for Spanish. Still others reflect the collection of data files in several languages through the use of various authoring packages like Gapkit and Fun with Texts, and the development of a handbook on the use of computers to teach bilingual students by Lewis (16). Also worthy of mention is the collection of data toward establishing a multilingual database for commercial correspondence in several languages. The idea is to help a student "compile" a business letter in the target language using English source expressions. The database will make use of an elementary word processor and a multilingual business handbook.

Three videodisc projects are also underway at NCCALL. A pilot program written in Microtext exploits the telephone sequences in the short French videodisc film "Le Dossier Pons" (Distrimage, Paris). Expodisc, by the Ealing College School of Business Administration, is planned as instruction in export marketing in French and Spanish to teach business people and students basic negotiating and social skills. Discussions are underway with the BBC toward selecting extracts from the "Deutsch Direct" TV series for transfer to videodisc format and computer mediation for instructional purposes.

Finally, in addition to projects involving word processing in EFL, French, and Spanish, NCCALL is using the Oxford Concordance Program to analyze the General Certificate of Education (O-level) examination papers in German produced by the University of London Examination Board. The goal is to produce a list of frequencies of occurrence (with contexts) of all German words used in the Board's O-level papers during the last fifteen years (and to update this database as the new General Certificate of Secondary Education examinations come on line—see pp. 159-60 above). This analysis is designed to give teachers an indication of what examination candidates were really expected to know and what shifts in emphasis have taken or are taking place.

Staff Training and Development

Regular one-day training courses for teachers are held at NCCALL—two to three per term. Longer courses, of four to five days, have been offered during Easter vacation. All so far have been aimed at beginners or near-beginners in CALL, the area of continued highest demand. The courses usually consist of a mixture of presentations of a variety of CALL packages to the whole group, with suggestions on how to make use of them in the classroom, backed up by plenty of hands-on sessions in which teachers can familiarize themselves with selected programs. In the longer courses, teachers are also offered training in the use of computer operating systems and an introduction to programming.

NCCALL also welcomes requests from organizations that wish to make use of NCCALL's facilities for training and can arrange for staff to travel to other institutions to give guest lectures or to help run courses.

Collaboration with Other Institutions

NCCALL maintains close links with a number of educational institutions worldwide. Institutions in the UK wishing to initiate CALL projects are encouraged to approach NCCALL for financial support to enable them to release staff from teaching on a part-time or temporary basis so that they can devote their attention to approved projects. Staff involved in such projects can also call upon NCCALL's expertise and resources.

NCCALL belongs to the EUROCALL group, founded in January 1986, which includes members from the UK, West Germany, Belgium, France, Denmark, The Netherlands, Italy, and Portugal. The main purpose of EUROCALL is to promote the exchange of information about new developments in CALL in individual European countries. A number of EUROCALL meetings and conferences have taken place in Belgium, West Germany, England, and The Netherlands with the support of national or institutional funding. The conferences have attracted a wide range of speakers and participants from various European countries. The EUROCALL group has also applied to the European Community for funding for a joint research project on CALL and has considered the possibility of collaborative software development.

The Future of NCCALL

When the present program of funding for information technology in nonadvanced further education comes to a close, it is hoped that NCCALL will continue as a viable unit, but additional funding will have to be sought, probably from industrial sources. NCCALL is currently trying to identify sympathetic business organizations. It is hoped NCCALL's reputation will appeal particularly to computer companies or businesses that have a strong interest in the promotion of foreign languages, especially multinationals with a large export market.

NCCALL's constantly expanding volume of work, the steady flow of inquiries, and visitors from all over the world seem to indicate that what NCCALL does is of value and appreciated. It is clear, however, that we have only begun to scratch the surface of the possibilities of computer applications to language and language learning, and we are now considering installing a machine translation system and familiarizing the staff with desktop publishing and expert systems. Since 1985, a lot has been achieved, but much more remains to be done.

Readers interested in further information about NCCALL are invited to write to any of the staff who devote their time exclusively to the National Center for Computer Assisted Language Learning: Graham Davies (Project Leader), Sarah Aspinall (Project Liaison Officer), Garry Marshall (Programmer). Inquiries should be addressed to NCCALL, School of Language Studies, Ealing College of Higher Education, Grove House, 1 The Grove, London W5 5DX, England.

References, CALL and NCCALL in the United Kingdom

1. *Airline Booking Simulation.* English version. Maidenhead, Eng.: McGraw-Hill (UK), Under development.

2. *Atari Conversational French.* Harlow, Eng.: Longman, [German and Spanish also available.], 1983.

3. Beaton, Richard, Eric Brown, Les Churchman, Lynette Heath, Sue Hewer, Barry Jones, David Little, Roger Sparkman, and Berthold Weidman. *CALL for the Computer.* London: Council for Educational Technology, 1986

4. Berer, Marge, and Mario Rinvolucri. *Mazes: A Problem-Solving Reader.* London: Heinemann, 1981.

5. Brown, Eric, ed., *Composite Report of the CILT/CET Conference "New Technological Developments for Language Teaching and Learning" and of the CILT/CET Workshop "Learning and Teaching Foreign Languages: What Has CALL to Offer?"* London: Center for Information on Language Teaching (CILT), 1982.

6. Congdon, Richard. Personal correspondence.

7. Cooper, Julia. The Times Network Systems, Ltd. P.O. Box 7, 200 Gray's Inn Road, London WC1X 8EZ. Personal Correspondence.

8. Davies, Graham. "New Technologies for Linguists." *Computer Age* 9 (1980) :23-26.

9. _____, and John J. Higgins. *Using Computers in Language Learning: A Teacher's Guide.* London: Center for Information on Language Teaching (CILT), 1985.

10. Farrington, Brian. *Scottish Computer-Based Learning Project.* Aberdeen, Scot.: University of Aberdeen, 1984.

11. Hewer, Sue. "E-Mail: A Cautionary Tale," pp. 5-7 in Eric Brown, ed., *CALL Report 5.* London: Center for Information on Language Teaching (CILT), 1987.

12. Hill, Brian. Personal correspondence.

13. Holmes, Glyn, and Marilyn Kidd. "The Evolving Case for Computers in the Study of Modern Languages." *ALLC Journal* 8, 1 (1980) :7-10.

14. Last, Rex W. "The Role of Computer Assisted Language Learning in Modern Language Teaching." *ALLC Journal* 7, 2 (1979) :165-71.

15. Leather, Jonathan. "The Computer in Language Teaching." *CALNEWS* 16 (1980) :4-6.

16. Lewis, Charlie. *Language, Computers and Bilingual Students.* London: National Center for Computer Assisted Language Learning, Ealing College of Higher Education, 1987.

17. Page, Alan. Personal communication.

18. Piper, Alison, "Helping Learners to Write: A Role for the Word-Processor." *ETL Journal* 41, 2 (1987) :119-25.

19. Roach, Peter. "The Microcomputer as an Aid to the Teaching of Pronunciation," pp. 9-10 in Eric Brown, ed., *Composite Report of the CILT/CET Conference "New Technological Developments for Foreign Language Teaching and Learning" and of the CILT/CET Workshop "Learning and Teaching Foreign Languages: What Has CAL to Offer?"* London: Center for Information on Language Teaching (CILT), 1982.

20. Taylor, Wilson L. "Cloze Procedure: A New Tool for Measuring Readability." *Journalism Quarterly* 33, 4 (1953):415-33.

PART II
Projects

PICS:
The Project for International Communication Studies

Rick Altman
University of Iowa

The Project for International Communication Studies (PICS) was created in January 1983 at the University of Iowa under the direction of James Pusack and Rick Altman.* The original purpose of PICS was to foster the use of international video materials in courses at the University of Iowa. However, PICS has grown into a major distributor of authentic foreign language videos and is now supported by a consortium of universities and a national network of collaborators on projects involving pedagogical applications of international video. During the course of this expansion, many individuals from around the world have contributed efforts to make international video materials into a major teaching resource. The following discussion of PICS's history and mission will be divided into the major concerns that have occupied PICS during the last few years.

Technological Resources

Though faculty members at the University of Iowa had long been interested in possible pedagogical uses of European video programs, it was not until 1982 and the general availability of multistandard videocassette recorders that appropriate programs could be easily played in this country. However,

---

*The original proposal was conceived and drafted by Janet G. Altman (Department of French and Italian), C. F. (Rick) Altman (Departments of Communication Studies and French and Italian), Sue E. K. Otto (Language Media Center), and James P. Pusack (Department of German).

PICS has never had to rely entirely on multistandard VCRs, thanks to the University of Iowa's purchase of two standards converters, permitting conversion of PAL and SECAM video materials into NTSC, the American standard. In addition, the University of Iowa Video Center now has facilities (including time-base correction) for 1″ PAL, 3/4″ BVU PAL, 3/4″ U-Matic SECAM, and 1/2″ VHS and Beta in both PAL and SECAM. Coupled with the Video Center's existing professional NTSC studio, this international video technology gives PICS access to extraordinary technical resources for standards conversion, subtitling, foreign language production, and all forms of electronic manipulation of video formats. These resources have facilitated PICS's increasing inquiry into the possible pedagogical benefits of modifying original authentic video materials (through simplified second sound tracks, original-language keyword subtitles, edited versions for elementary courses, and so forth).

Grant Support

Since its inception in 1983, PICS has been the recipient of three major national grants. The first, from the United States Department of Education Undergraduate International Studies and Foreign Language Program, provided funds for the development of new international video-supported courses at the University of Iowa. Between 1983 and 1985, participating faculty members from the School of Journalism and Mass Communication, the Department of Communication Studies, and three language departments (French and Italian, German, Spanish and Portuguese), developed six new courses and introduced international video materials into fourteen existing courses. Though this initial grant had significant local impact, its most important long-term result was to convince participants of both the pedagogical value of international video materials and the time commitment necessary to maximize their usefulness. For these reasons, as early as 1984 PICS adopted a new strategy. No longer concentrating on video programming acquired informally for use exclusively at the University of Iowa, PICS instead recognized the need (1) to negotiate agreements permitting distribution of international video programming throughout the United States, and (2) to establish a national consortium of institutions and a network of individuals eager to participate in the elaboration of pedagogical materials facilitating appropriate use of international video in American education.

In recognition of the national nature of PICS's mission, the U.S. Department of Education Undergraduate International Studies and Foreign Language Program in 1985 awarded a second grant to PICS, now constituted as a consortium including Brigham Young University, Clark University, Middlebury College, and Ohio University, with administrative staff and technical services (as well as legal responsibility) located at the University of Iowa. Under the aegis of this second grant (1985-1988), twenty-five new or revised courses in ten different fields have been or will be developed at the five participating institutions. Perhaps more important, individuals throughout the PICS Consortium have contributed to the acquisition of video materials from numerous countries, while at the same time helping to develop more effective and more sharable strategies for using international video programs in the teaching process.

The major resources required for PICS to attain national distribution of these materials rapidly became clear. Funds for the purchase of distribution rights would be needed, along with support for necessary international travel and correspondence. A broad marketing effort would require trained personnel and extensive publicity. Development of supporting pedagogical materials would need coordination, as well as honoraria for authors and funds to cover duplicating costs. To these ends, successful application was made in 1986 to the Annenberg/Corporation for Public Broadcasting Project for major funding covering the entire range of PICS's operations. A substantial award has assured basic support for PICS's activities through 1990. Under the provisions of this grant, PICS will acquire and distribute international video materials and will also constitute a national clearinghouse for the development and exchange of pedagogical strategies and materials related to international video.

Further attempts to secure grant support include application for funding to underwrite acquisition of Japanese video programming. Future grant applications are expected to include a major subtitling effort aimed at making international video materials more accessible to monolingual students.

Acquisition

PICS's European programming has been anchored since 1985 by the PICS/ BBC coproduction of *Telejournal*, a weekly thirty-minute news program recorded in one of four languages from any of fifteen channels in nine Western European countries. Currently, major PICS acquisition efforts are concentrated in three languages and their related geographical zones: German, French, and Spanish.

German-Language Programming

Thanks to the efforts of Kimberly Sparks (Department of German, Middlebury College), in 1985 PICS signed a far-reaching agreement with the Austrian national broadcasting system (Österreichischer Rundfunk), providing distribution rights for a broad spectrum of Austrian programming. Working with the Oregon-based Eurotel (American agent for Transtel/Cologne), PICS has acquired rights to important literary and cultural programs from West German regional broadcasting systems. Further acquisition efforts center on West German commercial programs (ZDF-Mainz) and pedagogical productions (Institut für Film and Bild in Munich), as well as representative

East German programs. James Pusack directs the PICS German-language series.

Francophone Programming

Since 1985, PICS has had a wide-ranging agreement with France's Antenne 2, covering the monthly news summary entitled *Panorama* and numerous other programs. A broad range of Francophone public-service consumer-relations programs (PIT, EEC) has also been available since 1985. As of 1986, PICS began distribution of a series of programs prepared especially for American teachers of French by the Mission Inter-universitaire pour la Coopération Éducative Franco-Américaine (MICEFA). In 1987, PICS signed a broad agreement with the Centre National de Documentation Pédagogique (CNDP), calling for American distribution of numerous CNDP productions originally produced for broadcast over Télévision Française 1 (TF1) or for face-to-face pedagogical situations. Over twenty hours of CNDP programming were added to the PICS catalog in 1987; more can be expected each year. Further negotiations are currently underway with the French national video archive (Institut National Audiovisuel), a government-sponsored distributor (France-Média International), and France's largest advertisement agency (Publicis).

In order to balance this attention to programs originating in France, PICS signed an agreement in 1987 with the Institute pour la Coopération Audiovisuelle Francophone (ICAF). Beginning in 1987 with twenty-five programs from the Espace Francophone series originally seen on France 3 (FR3), PICS plans to distribute the continuing ICAF production, concentrating on Francophone countries throughout the world. In addition, PICS has recently established contact with Louisiana producers in the hope of adding to the PICS catalog programs from American French-speaking regions. Québecois programs are expected to follow. Eventually, PICS also expects to acquire distribution rights to Francophone programming from other regions. Rick Altman directs the PICS Francophone series.

Hispanic Programming

With the support of PICS consortium members in Madrid, in early 1987 PICS began negotiations with Radio-Televisión Española (RTVE), the Spanish national network. It is expected that PICS will shortly be able to offer for distribution in the United States a variety of Spanish television programs. At the same time, PICS is following up contacts in a number of Latin American countries. During the course of the Annenberg/CPB grant, PICS hopes to offer a broad selection of Hispanic materials from Europe, South America, and Central America. Sue Otto directs the PICS Hispanic series.

Programming in Other Languages

Since 1985, PICS has received Soviet programming by satellite. Until recently, legal uncertainties have slowed distribution of this material. In the near future, however, PICS expects to begin distribution of Soviet video programs.

Current initiatives by PICS collaborators target the acquisition of Portuguese, Brazilian, Chinese, Korean, and Japanese materials. If requested grant funding becomes available, Japanese video will be the target of PICS's first major acquisition effort in the Orient. Thomas H. Rohlich (Department of Asian Languages and Literature) will direct the Japanese series.

Distribution

PICS remains dedicated to a broad distribution through teaching-oriented policies and sensible pricing. From the beginning, PICS has made a conscious effort to negotiate agreements that include the right for the acquiring institution to make multiple copies for use exclusively on the same campus or within the same district. In 1986, PICS staff made a decision to fix the prices for all PICS videotapes at a single, affordable price. All 30-minute tapes are thus priced at $50, all 60-minute tapes at $75, and so forth in increments of $25 per half-hour. A further decision assures inclusion of short pedagogical supplements (when available) at no additional cost.

In late 1986, the hiring of a marketing and business director made it possible for PICS to undertake its first serious effort at national marketing, including direct mailings, journal publicity, and systematic representation at important conferences. At the present time, PICS distributes programs primarily on videocassette, with an increasing number of key programs available on videodisc. In addition, PICS has acquired the broadcast or cablecast rights to numerous international programs; at a later date a more active effort will be made to explore this distribution channel.

Cataloging the PICS Archive

With the creation of PICS began an effort to establish a major teaching and research archive of international video materials at the University of Iowa. The PICS Archive now holds over fifteen hundred hours of video programming representing dozens of countries from around the world— from Iceland to Australia and from South Korea to the Basque-speaking provinces of Spain. Programs of all types are included, as well as continuity recordings of full-evening broadcasts. The archive is especially rich in French material and, as it grows, will take on increasing importance for scholars of communication studies and individual cultures.

In anticipation of the archive's eventual role, PICS has devoted significant effort to devising appropriate strategies for cataloging the collection.

Principles for cataloging domestic audiovisual materials are still in the developmental phase, and few standards exist for cataloging non-U.S. video materials; nevertheless, PICS has developed a series of forms and principles—and an on-line catalog—that should help to facilitate access to the archive and make it easier for libraries and other depositories around the country to codify international video materials for cataloging purposes. In support of this activity, the University of Iowa Library has recently created the position of international nonprint archivist.

Pedagogical Research

While PICS has recognized from the start the importance of making international video materials available to the American teaching profession, PICS has become increasingly aware of the necessity of providing instructors with guidance in the use of international video in and around the classroom. To this end, PICS has embarked on two separate projects designed both to expand the range of video's usefulness and to help instructors use video materials to maximum advantage.

Manipulation of Programs

Authentic international video has enormous benefits for the teaching of language and culture at all levels. Still, it is clear that broadcast video programs from another country are easier to use with experienced language students than with beginners. In order to bridge the gap between the aspirations of beginners and the complexity of many authentic video programs, PICS is spending an increasing amount of energy to adapt original programs for use in the American classroom. The first strategy applied was careful selection and recombination of short programs, leading to the creation of the second-year French compilation Télé-douzaine, a special selection of news features. In late 1986, PICS began to experiment with a simplified second sound track for Nachrichten I (now available on videodisc), making it easier for beginners to work their way up to the original announcer's voice preserved on a separate sound track. In early 1987, PICS signed coproduction agreements authorizing development of simplified versions of certain productions by CNDP, Antenne 2, and Espace Francophone. These will involve re-editing of existing footage in order to produce programs appropriate for first-year students of French.

The re-edited programs will make heavy use of original-language subtitling. Indeed, subtitling has played an important part in PIC's development, both in the target language (for language learners) and in English (for students of history, political science, communication studies, and the like). Thanks to the efforts of James Pusack and Cordell Jeppsen (University of Iowa Video Center), the University of Iowa has developed a highly sophisticated automated subtitling system, permitting PICS to effect subtitling for organizations like MICEFA, France's Agence du Court Métrage, and New York's distinguished public broadcasting system WNET. Through judicious use of original-language subtitles and careful subtitling of programs that interest monolingual faculty and students, PICS hopes to make a growing spectrum of international programs available to the American public.

In addition, PICS has undertaken a limited program of indigenous productions, using native voices and original international materials. The first group of productions will shortly be available for distribution. These include four versions of *Little Red Riding Hood* (Perrault and Grimm in French, Perrault and Grimm in German), with the Perrault versions using computer-enhanced nineteenth century French folk drawings from Epinal, and the Grimm versions built around modern German illustrations. Future developments in this area will depend on the availability of production funds.

Strategies for Development

With the help of collaborators around the country, PICS is developing a series of pedagogical supplements designed to provide guidance in the use of selected video programs. The first series of pedagogical materials, developed with the assistance of Edward Knox (Director of Language Schools, Middlebury College) is designed for use with selected CNDP, Antenne 2, Espace Francophone, and French public-relations video programs. These materials, which will soon be followed by pedagogical supplements for programs in other languages, will help instructors achieve effective use of international video in classes at all levels.

An alternative to the printed word approach is being developed by Sue Otto and James Pusack, who together direct PICS's interactive video project. Working with video programs that have been carefully chosen and edited for videodisc mastering, Otto and Pusack are elaborating strategies for the interactive use of international video with the help of such experienced researchers as Randall Jones (Department of German, Brigham Young University) and others. By the end of the decade, PICS expects to have pressed some thirty videodisc sides, many of which will be accompanied by level-two programming, which permits convenient disc control with low-cost hand controllers.

Future Projects

In the years to come, PICS expects to become increasingly aware of worldwide video production at all levels. Thus far attention has been directed at major commercial and government producers. In an effort to represent minority groups, unofficial languages, unsanctioned political movements, and other important activities often avoided by national broadcasting, PICS will continue to negotiate agreements with organizations that work to provide balanced representation of local and international news, as well as special programs devoted to the world as Americans are not always privileged to see it.

Through expanded distribution and increased pedagogical support, PICS expects to make effective use of international video materials far easier and rewarding. A long-term program of subtitling (assuming appropriate funding) will help PICS to make international video accessible to a broader audience. Eventually, subtitled programs, along with appropriate original programs, will make it possible for PICS to offer to broadcasters and cable channels a fund of international programs. During this time, the PICS Archive will grow to the point where it will become a major resource for scholars whose work depends on international video programming.

During July of 1988, PICS will sponsor at Middlebury College the first International Symposium on the role of video in teaching world languages and cultures. This symposium will provide an opportunity to broaden the PICS Network to an ever-widening circle of collaborators.

For information about the materials PICS distributes, contact Deborah Bjornstad, Assistant Director, or Susan Skoglund, Marketing and Business Director (1-800-335-2335). Individuals interested in participating in the activities of PICS should contact the appropriate series editor at the following address: Project for International Communication Studies, International Center, University of Iowa, Iowa City, Iowa 52242.

French Media Courses for Journalism and Communications

Lois Vines
Ohio University

Introduction

In the fall of 1984 under a grant from the U.S. Department of Education's Undergraduate International Studies and Foreign Language Programs, the Department of Modern Languages at Ohio University launched two sequences of courses designed to teach French and Spanish to students in journalism and communications through the extensive use of foreign language television and video materials. This report details the program for French.

The purpose of the project (which continues at this writing) is to encourage the study of foreign languages among American students planning careers in journalism and in other communication fields by providing new courses based on print and broadcast media in French and Spanish. The goal is to motivate students to study the target language for a minimum of six quarters beyond the beginning level and to acquire second-language skills that will be useful professionally. This curricular focus reflects Krashen's concept of "sheltered subject-matter teaching" through which a specific subject is made comprehensible in the target language (4, p. 63). Students learn the target language through studying how media are represented in cultures where the foreign languages are spoken. Television via satellite dish, video and audio tapes, and the Ohio University Laboratory for Computer Assisted Language Learning play a major role in the curriculum.

Scope and Content

Students are admitted to the special six-course sequence at the intermediate level after having completed two years of foreign language study in high school or one year in college. The special sections reserved for journalism and communications majors are indicated in the schedule of classes each quarter. These courses run parallel to the regular sequences of intermediate and advanced foreign language courses as can be seen in Figure 1:

Prerequisite: 2 yrs. h.s. or 1 yr. college French

French for Journalism and Communications Majors (one section—25 students)

Regular sequence for all other majors (four sections—100 students total)

211 Intermediate French (fall)	211
212 Intermediate French (winter)	212
213 Intermediate French (spring)	213

Prerequisite: 4 yrs. h.s. or 2 yrs. college French

French for Journalism and Communications Majors (one section—15 students)

Regular sequence for all other majors (two sections—30 students total)

341 Advanced Conversation and Composition (fall)	341
342 Advanced Conversation and Composition (winter)	342
343 Advanced Conversation and Composition (spring)	343

Figure 1. French classes for communications majors

The first three quarters (intermediate French) hold a structured review of grammar to sharpen oral and written skills. To this end, students interact with a wide range of software in the CALL lab (drill and practice, vocabulary review, etc.), freeing classtime for activities related directly to journalistic applications of radio and television.

Since many students entering from high school have had no experience in the language laboratory or have never heard the foreign language spoken except in pattern drills, the French sequence begins with Aérodrame, a twenty-five-episode audio program that dramatizes the adventures of a young French journalist pursuing a scoop that involves espionage and the sale of arms. Students are not given the tape script. For most, thus, this exercise is the first time they have been required to depend entirely on listening for comprehension. Questions on each episode are prepared in advance to guide the listening experience and to serve as a basis for discussing the program in French. Students continue listening to Aérodrame at the intermediate level while short video segments on other topics are introduced gradually.

Video Materials

Three types of video programs are used throughout the six-course sequence: (1) materials produced specifically for teaching the foreign language, (2) broadcasts intended for native speakers, and (3) video recordings produced by the teacher and students themselves.

At the intermediate level, the video programs are short, have a clear sound track, and focus on a single topic. In French, videos produced by John Rassias (Dartmouth College) and Bernard Petit (SUNY-Brockport) offer short, unscripted segments with native speakers talking about their work or accomplishing everyday tasks. Tape 11 ("Accents") of Rassias's Contact French (2) offers a variety of interviews with Parisians who talk about their work in 3 to 5 minute segments. Three video programs produced by Petit provide excellent sources of short segments presenting authentic French situations: France from Within (Tapes 1 and 2) and The French Way (3). In addition to the videotapes, all programs include supplemental materials designed to guide their use in class. The segments vary in level and difficulty, and can be used throughout the intermediate and advanced levels. The selection of a specific segment is also based on its relationship to topics discussed in class. For example, after reading a press article on the TGV *(Train à grande vitesse,* the high-speed French train), students view two segments, one on the same topic from France from Within (Tape 1) and another from The French Way (Program 5, "Travel by Rail"). The video materials have been found most effective when used in conjunction with subjects whose vocabulary and background have been introduced first through the written press so that students are more attentive to the visual and spoken presentation.

Television broadcasts intended for native speakers are a second major source of materials. These programs come from several sources, including live broadcasts from Montreal transmitted to the Ohio University Language Lab through a satellite reception system. A television monitor with four individual headsets provides the opportunity for students to view live broadcasts at will eleven hours a day. Each week students select three programs that interest them and keep a log of their individual viewing, including key vocabulary and synopses of program content. The purpose of the assignment is to encourage students to become familiar with the variety of programming available and to improve comprehension skills. Program segments to be used as class assignments are recorded from the live broadcast and held on videocassette in accordance with copyright restrictions so that students can review them as needed.

In addition to broadcasts from Montreal, television programs from France via satellite are transmitted to WOUB, the local PBS station, once a month under the auspices of the University of Maryland-Baltimore. (See Part I, Chapter 2, in this volume on television technology.) These programs are recorded on videocassette in the Ohio University Language Lab and also made available on a demand basis to increase news coverage from France.

The third source of television programs from abroad is PICS (Project for International Communication Studies, see Part II, Report 1, pp. 171-78, in this volume). Taken together, these three sources offer a wide variety of programs that provide exposure to many subjects and language experiences. Students have the opportunity to hear different registers and accents within a given language—which are normally not used in materials produced specifically for classroom use.

Television programs intended for native speakers can be obtained through two additional sources that record the broadcasts from French television and include additional pedagogical materials. Middlebury College (5) offers a selection of videocassettes entitled *La télé des Français* that includes a variety of programs and suggestions for class use. The packet also comes with a glossary directly related to television, thus providing the basic vocabulary needed to discuss various aspects of the subject. The McLean Company has marketed a selection of three French news broadcasts from 1984 along with complete tape scripts of the programs. Students gain comprehension skills by listening to televised news, which is reported quickly and with very little redundancy.

Using Video Segments

Two VCR stations in the language laboratory allow students access to materials on videocassette. Each station is equipped with headsets so that the audio does not disturb other students in the lab. Students sign up to use the station ahead of time to avoid last-minute requests for the assigned materials and to ensure enough time to replay the tapes as much as necessary for comprehension.

Each video assignment is first introduced in the classroom by showing a short segment on a portable VCR and monitor. The segment is most often related to prior reading of a related subject in the press and lasts no longer than ten minutes. Students are given prepared assignment sheets that include various types of activities to focus their attention on detail, including questions in the target language, true-false questions, use of specific vocabulary, and subjects for general discussion. After viewing the video individually in the language lab, students are usually well prepared to discuss the program in class using the target language. This very structured assignment is alternated with one that is based on a longer video segment and requires less attention to detail. For example, students watch a half-hour news broadcast and make a list of the major events with a few notes about each one.

Video Practicum

Videos produced in class play an important role in the special foreign language courses for journalism and communications majors. The original federal grant and the College of Arts and Sciences have provided funds to invite to campus professional French- and Spanish-speaking journalists so that students can learn more about the foreign media from experts in the field. An important activity associated with these visits is the preparation the students undertake to interview the guests in the target language. The practicum follows five steps: (1) preparation of questions, (2) practice of delivery, (3) the interview (which is videotaped), (4) review of the interview in the language lab, and (5) writing a report on the interview. In addition to interviews with foreign correspondents, French- and Spanish-speaking students at the university are also invited to participate in interviews, thus giving the American students the opportunity to learn more about different cultures and to practice both the language and the interview process.

La Voix de la presse

At the advanced level (third-year conversation and composition courses) students in French produce "La voix de la presse" (The Voice of the Press), a news program recorded on video. The program presents four "journalists" and a moderator discussing the top news stories in France during a given week. Each student gives a three-minute presentation of a topic and responds to questions by other panel members before the moderator introduces the next "journalist." Information and vocabulary for each presentation is gathered from French newspapers by small groups assigned to the project. The presentation is written and corrected before the student begins practicing orally. Although the students may refer to the written reports for their presentation, they prepare orally so that they can look at the camera rather than simply read from the written page. Adequate preparation requires a great deal of individual and group practice, which are accomplished out of class. The final videotaping is done in class, however, so that each group can see what the others have produced. A videocassette of each program is placed in the language lab so that students may view their performance. "La voix de la presse" has proven an important means of students' development of speaking skills along with reading and listening comprehension.

Evaluative Efforts and Results

Evaluation of the six-quarter media courses in French and Spanish for journalism and communications majors is based on (1) retention rate of journalism and communications students enrolled in the sequences (shown below) as compared to the 10 percent retention rate of these students before the special program was initiated, (2) students' written evaluations of the courses, and (3) the report of an outside evaluator.

The purpose of creating special courses based on the media is to encourage students to continue study of French or Spanish with the aim of professionalizing their skills in a second language. Students in the College of Communications at Ohio University are required to take only one quarter of a foreign language at the intermediate level. During the first year of the program (1984-85), the retention rate in the second quarter of intermediate (an elective) was 85 percent for French and 87 percent for Spanish. The impact of the media courses vis-à-vis holding power is noteworthy. The enrollment figures at the intermediate level reflect that a significant proportion of students elect to continue.

		Fall	Winter	Spring
1984-85	Intermediate French	28	24	19
	Intermediate Spanish	24	21	17

The figures below reveal that for French the attrition between the inter-mediate- and advanced-level courses is negligible (Spring 1985, 19 → Fall 1985, 17) while attrition in Spanish is higher.

		Fall	Winter	Spring
1985-86	Intermediate French	23	18	17
	Advanced French	17	13	12
1985-86	Intermediate Spanish	16	12	12
	Advanced Spanish	6	4	3

Data for the 1986-87 academic year show enrollment figures that are very similar to the previous year in both languages. Enrollments can be affected by a wide variety of factors, and it would be speculative to draw hard conclusions on limited experience. One development does seem clear, however: in French an average of 45 percent of the journalism and communications students who begin the intermediate sequence continue for five quarters *beyond* the college requirement as compared to a 10 percent average before the special sequence was offered. Students' written evaluations reveal a very positive attitude toward the special sequences of media-based foreign language courses and toward the relationship between these studies and their majors. The opportunity to do live interviews and use television and video are aspects of the course often receiving favorable comments. One student wrote: "The course is excellent for journalism majors—it is relevant to what we are studying in other (journalism) courses."

The federal grant provided funds to bring in an outside expert to evaluate the first two years of the program. Dr. Marie Galanti, noted educator and publisher of the *Journal Français d'Amérique*, spent three days on campus in 1986 visiting classes and talking individually with students in the special media courses. In her written report, Dr. Galanti made the following observation: "In the language lab I was given the opportunity to meet students on an impromptu basis. These students were watching and taking notes based on the video of the previous guest lecturer, a reporter from *Le Monde*. The students said that they were watching the interview for the third time, to make sure that they had perfectly understood the replies given to their questions. It had been my experience that students will only do this if they are greatly interested and motivated." The motivation and interest are inspired, at least in part, by the use of the modern media to teach students who are preparing careers in various fields of communications.

An additional source for evaluating the special courses is somewhat limited but nonetheless important. Two journalism majors who completed the six-course sequence of media courses in French were selected for internships abroad. One served as an intern at *Le Soleil* in Quebec and, while there, wrote an article in French that was selected for publication in the *Journal Français d'Amérique*. The other worked as an intern for UPI in Paris. Both returned to campus to praise the training they had received in the special sequence of French courses.

Conclusion

Introducing modern media into courses designed for journalism and communications students has been beneficial. Because of the training they received in their majors, students are particularly receptive to using television and video to increase their foreign language skills and knowledge of the world. Their positive attitude encourages faculty members to continue developing courses that make intensive use of the media. The success of these innovative courses confirms Krashen's point that sheltered classes, especially those related to specific professions, "help students cross the bridge from the language class to the real world" (4, p. 66). Through modern technology, the "real world" can be transmitted to the classroom. Foreign language teaching techniques designed to make use of media are in the early stages of development. Continuing experimentation will lead to more refined pedagogical utilization of the enormous resources available through modern communications systems.

Readers interested in further information about the French Media Courses may write to the author, Department of Modern Languages, Ellis Hall, The Ohio University, Athens, Ohio 45701-2927.

References, French Media Courses for Journalism and Communications

1. *Aérodrame* (1974). EMC Publishing, St. Paul, MN.

2. *Contact French* (1984). CBS Fox Video, Farmington Hills, MI 48024.

3. *France from Within* (1986). *The French Way* (1986). *The Spanish Way* (1987). Boston: Heinle & Heinle, Boston, MA.

4. Krashen, Stephen D. *Inquiries and Insights.* Haywood, CA: Alemany, 1985.

5. *La télé des Français* (1986). Middlebury College Language Schools, Middlebury, VT.

German by Satellite: Technology-Enhanced Distance Learning

Harry S. Wohlert
Oklahoma State University

Introduction

The *German by Satellite* educational television program is a two-year accredited high school course that combines two 45-minute live television broadcasts with three hours of computer-assisted language learning (CALL) each week. The program, which represents the exact equivalent of an elementary one-year college German course, is designed for schools without a German teacher on their staff. This unconventional method of language instruction was originally developed to improve the level of achievement of high school students and to increase the number of academic courses available to smaller, mainly rural schools. The initial stimulus occurred when Beaver High School, a progressive rural school in the remote Panhandle region of Oklahoma, was unable to hire a foreign language teacher and, encouraged by the dean of Arts and Sciences at Oklahoma State University, approached the author to develop a distance learning course for the school. Based on an already established computer-assisted language learning program in the German section of the Department of Foreign Languages and Literatures, a pilot project was started in the spring of 1985.

In this initial program, fourteen students with various academic backgrounds enrolled to learn German over the telephone from a professor who was 250 miles away. Two certified teachers without any knowledge of German agreed to coordinate and supervise the German class at Beaver High School. The learning materials, tests, quizzes, and grading procedures were the same as used at the university. The only adjustment made was the speed of progression, i.e., the course for five hours of college credit (one semester) was extended to two school terms for one year of high school credit. This pilot high school German course was conducted with the following support system:

1. The German teacher at the university and a coordinating teacher at the school who was not required to know German
2. Learning materials—college textbook, lab manual, workbook, language cassettes for homework
3. Technology to enhance distance learning: CALL programs with voice input/output and a communication system

Initially the students worked with the professor three times a week for 50 minutes over the telephone and were required to practice with an Apple IIe computer during the remaining two days of the school week. However, it soon became apparent that the students did not have sufficient time allotted for practicing German on the computer. The schedule was therefore changed to two lectures and three computer sessions a week, which proved to be a more effective arrangement.

The Oklahoma State Department of Education, which had given its approval for the project, evaluated the German course through interviews with students, coordinating teachers, and administrators and through class observations. The report results were positive and led to guaranteed continuous support. The performance of the high school students was evaluated through validated tests used for the Oklahoma State University German students. A statistical evaluation was not possible, but a comparison of test results indicated that the performance of students in the pilot project was similar to that of average college freshmen.

Because of the success of the pilot project, it was decided to continue the distance learning course on a larger scale as the *German by Satellite* program.

The remainder of this report will be devoted to teaching by television, technology in the telecommunication program, evaluation measures used in the program, the impact of *German by Satellite* on education, and conclusions drawn from the program.

Teaching by Television

One of the reasons *German by Satellite* is currently considered a model for educational television is its combination of fast-paced TV programming, computer learning technology, and conventional teaching methodology.

The CALL package used for the pilot project was kept unchanged for the *German by Satellite* program; however, the delivery system was significantly transformed from a telephone hookup to a televised program requiring a television studio with a satellite up-link (transmitter) connected via a satellite to a receiving system at the participating school, which consists of a satellite dish antenna with its complementary electronic equipment.

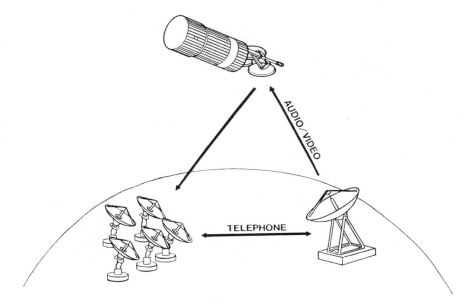

Figure 1. Satellite telecommunication link between university and high schools.

Cost of the Learning System

To an average-size school, the one-time cost is several thousand dollars for the required equipment—dish antenna with receiver and monitor, video and audio recorders, computers, modem, software, video and audio tapes, and installation. The only recurring expenses are the university's enrollment fee (in-state or out-of-state) and an annual per-student fee for every student beyond the tenth enrolled. Schools with much larger enrollments are encouraged to try finding a qualified language teacher.

Structure of Programming

During the fall term 1986-87, the twice-weekly German I lecture was transmitted at 9:10 CST to the Westar IV satellite and was then available to the schools or anyone with a dish antenna in the continental United States and Hawaii. After a ten-minute break, the broadcast continued at 10:05 for German II. Every broadcast opened with a brief report about the prevailing weather in Germany superimposed on a computer-generated map, currency exchange rate, homework, and detailed classroom assignments for the nonbroadcast days. Each broadcast day, one school was selected to be the host and participated for the whole show either over a voice bridge from the home location or live in the telecommunications center studio.

After the introduction of the host school, the lesson proceeded with activities such as pronunciation exercises, explanations of grammar, and dialogue practice that are typical for foreign language teaching. The lessons presented, within the limits of a beginning course, all four aspects of a spoken language (listening, speaking, reading, and writing) in the cultural setting of a German-speaking country. The presentation of each lesson segment stayed within the average attention span of young students and was separated from others by taped breaks such as German TV commercials or cultural vignettes about Germany, Austria, or Switzerland.

Questions coming from the host school were answered immediately as in any classroom setting. Questions from other schools could be taken simultaneously, but they were screened for topics of common interest before the call was connected to the studio.

At home, in preparation for the broadcast, students were required to listen to language tapes, practice reading, and do written exercises. To involve every student in the active learning process, each one had to practice in the classroom with the aid of computer technology and had to react to every item presented in the exercises.

Technology

Oklahoma State University entered the era of satellite telecommunication in 1983 with the dedication of its telecommunications center. The nationally recognized center represents the latest in the state-of-the-art equipment, and its studios are comparable to those at any of the three major television networks. The center is staffed with 18 full-time professional and 40 part-time staff members.

The *German by Satellite* schools receive the talk-back satellite-television broadcasts via a 10 meter C-Band up-link (transmitting antenna) and the Spacenet satellite. (The university is the first in the nation to have a center that can also transmit on the Ku-Band, but since a number of schools can receive only on C-Band, the program uses only the latter at this time.)

The Receiving System

The required size of the dish antenna depends on the strength of the signal at the receiving site. Most schools buy a 10-ft. antenna with receiver and monitor from a local dealer who is also responsible for measuring the signal, installation, and maintenance. A video recorder is required to tape shows for absent students or reviews.

Computer-Assisted Language Learning

The vital hub of the German program is the software and hardware used in the CALL system, which is enhanced with the satellite broadcasts and an extensive communication setup for vital interaction between student and teacher.

Wortschatz: Vocabulary Practice. Normally, no German-speaking person who could assist the students with German pronunciation is present in the participating schools. Since poor pronunciation quickly fossilizes, it is most important not to let beginning students guess and practice speaking unfamiliar words on their own. The students are therefore required to work first with the Wortschatz program when new vocabulary is assigned. In Wortschatz, automatically controlled cassette recorders integrate sound with the German text on the screen. When learning vocabulary, a student who sees a German word or phrase for the first time can then immediately hear the correct native pronunciation.

The Wortschatz program contains an algorithm that does not just simply turn a cassette recorder on via a cassette control device but also turns it off at the appropriate time (Wohlert and McCormick, 4). When the students achieve mastery of the vocabulary, they usually continue overlearning for long-term memorization without the recorder.

This technology for sound output was developed because of its cost-effectiveness; quality speech digitizer or random-access cassette recorders are far more expensive than the $80 system described above. As mentioned previously, for most schools it is the low cost of the *German by Satellite* program that allows them to offer a class with about ten students.

Speech Recognition: Pronunciation Practice. To further enhance and establish good pronunciation, the Scott Instrument Voice-Based Learning System, a speech-recognition unit with software, was adapted for beginning German students (3). This system stores the pronunciation of a native speaker in the computer for comparison with a spoken input.

Each week, students are encouraged to practice fifteen to twenty minutes with the speech-recognition unit, which prompts them to speak precisely determined words, phrases, or short sentences into a microphone for evaluation. If the student's vocal response falls within set parameters of the pronunciation stored in the computer, the program will continue to the next item. Another variation of the program displays a thermometer whose column falls or rises with the accuracy of the student's pronunciation.

Dasher: Grammar Practice. All suitable exercises in the Houghton-Mifflin college textbook *Deutsch Heute* are contained in Dasher (1), a commercial software shell program. Exercises assigned during the television broadcasts are done on the Apple IIe allowing students to receive an instant evaluation and to correct grammar or spelling errors. Dasher, like all other CALL programs, can record performance if the student wishes.

Diktat: Listening-Comprehension-Spelling. Possibly the most difficult assignment for the students is practicing dictation with the Diktat program. Using the same controlled audio technology described for the Wortschatz above, students listen to longer phrases from a continuous text and then type them into the computer for evaluation. With step-by-step assistance from the computer, corrections are again made before a student can proceed.

Communication Technology: Interaction between Student and Professor

Live interaction takes place during the satellite transmission via an audio bridge that makes it possible to connect one or more schools at the same time with the professor in the studio. In practice, a flood of calls to the broadcast studio never occurs because every lesson seems to elicit only a certain number and type of questions, i.e., one answer will generally satisfy most questions. In addition, the participating schools requested that calls be screened to bring only questions of common interest into the studio. Questions that are not put on the air are answered by telephone after the broadcast.

An electronic mailbox allows students, language coordinators, or school administrators 24-hour-a-day access to the professor. The caller can simply type the message into the computer, which will send the text over an attached modem to a centrally located electronic mailbox, in this case an IBM mainframe computer. The receiving party can retrieve the message by calling the mailbox at any convenient time. The professor checks and answers the mail mainly at night when the telephone is not busy. Any participant can send a message to all *German by Satellite* schools at one time.

An in-state and out-of-state toll-free number is a third way to contact the professor or an assistant directly. Since each line can be switched to an answering machine, access is made available 24 hours a day. Over 1100 calls were received from the 108 participating schools during the school year, which was twice as many as were handled by E-mail. The toll-free phone is occasionally also used to set up sessions as decribed in the pilot project with Beaver High School when longer discussions with an individual school are necessary.

Evaluation of Student Performance _____

Comprehensive tests covering the chapters in the college textbook *Deutsch heute* and vocabulary quizzes are sent in by the schools for correction and grading. The grades, based on university standards, and the tests are typically returned within 48 hours. It is then the prerogative of the school to either accept the grades or adjust them according to their own criteria.

The unadjusted grade distribution of 34 schools offering the *German by Satellite* course for high school credits are shown in Figure 2.

An anlaysis of schools with low averages indicated that they were mainly caused by long delays in obtaining hardware, software, or even textbooks. In cooperation with the Oklahoma State Department of Education, school administrators, and teachers, arrangements such as changing the course from a credit-bearing to an enrichment course were made in such instances to avoid assigning invalid grades to the students.

A more formal evaluation with the standardized AATG college test for elementary German was undertaken, but since the test forms arrived late in the school year, only four schools could administer the test. The average scores were equal to a grade of C. Boise City, a small town in the Panhandle of Oklahoma, scored three A's, two B's, and two C's. Preliminary figures show a similar performance for the 1986-87 school year for the 14 students enrolled at Boise City. The same data indicate that 18 percent of all the students in the *German by Satellite* program were earning an unadjusted grade of A!

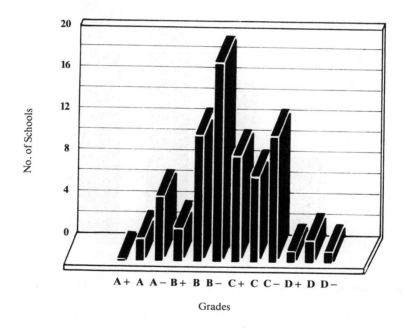

Figure 2. Average grades of schools completing first year *German by Satellite* 1986.

Among other indicators measuring academic performance are seven inter-scholastic contests for high school students at various Oklahoma colleges, where *German by Satellite* students either swept the first three places in their category or placed among the top three in the contest.

Impact on Education

The *German by Satellite* program has shown a controlled growth in three years going from one pilot school in Oklahoma to 108 German classes in five states. The projected enrollment for the coming fall indicates a total of over 220 classes for German I and II in ten states, including school districts that have not offered a foreign language in decades.

The impact on foreign language enrollments in Oklahoma can be shown in the following comparison. The *German by Satellite* program increased the number of public schools in Oklahoma with German in their curriculum by 321 percent since 1986.

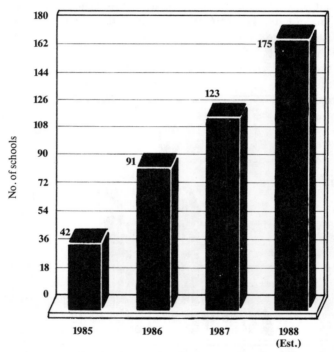

Figure 3. Oklahoma schools offering German courses (1987-88 enrollment is estimated)

The effect of the *German by Satellite* on a high school depends on the support and involvement of the school administrators and, most of all, the coordinating teacher. With their involvement and enthusiasm, substantial increases in ACT scores and attitudes toward learning can be documented. Several schools reported increases in numbers of students planning to attend colleges and universities. Members of the communities often get involved either by studying with the students or assisting in the program. In addition, a number of coordinating teachers have been studying German along with the program with the intention of completing a teaching minor later at a college or university.

Over 1,500 inquiries and visits about the *German by Satellite* program indicate that its impact was felt not only in the participating states but across the country where it has been discussed and described in over 200 newspapers and journal articles.

Conclusions

The *German by Satellite* program was developed to provide equal access to an educational opportunity for schools that have to operate with a limited curriculum.

The effort to teach students to read, write, and speak German guided by a professor in a television studio without a German teacher present at the school may have met initially with some skepticism. However, because of the combination of traditional instructional methods and a technology-enhanced learning system consisting of satellite television, CALL programs, and communication systems, *German by Satellite* differs fundamentally from earlier unsuccessful television-based instruction courses and has won strong support and approval among administrators, educators, and students. Testing of student achievement, evaluative interviews by the Oklahoma State Department of Education in the participating schools, and top placements in state interscholastic high school competitions attest to the academic success of this program.

German by Satellite, which has been supported by Oklahoma State University, several state departments of education, and the Oklahoma Chapter of the American Federation of Teachers has shown a steady growth since its inception in 1985. The number of participating schools has doubled every year. During this time period, the satellite program clearly has not replaced any teachers but increased the number of schools offering German, thus adding to the total foreign language enrollment in several states.

Programs such as *German by Satellite* are certain to play a major role in the educational system during the next few years and will affect every state across the country. Recognizing the potential of satellite telecommunication, the United States Senate Labor and Human Resources Committee already approved legislation to strengthen the curriculum in the area of foreign languages, mathematics, and natural sciences (2). Bill S 778 intends to provide $100 million through 1992 for such satellite telecommunication programs in isolated schools.

It can safely be assumed that the less commonly taught languages will especially benefit from long-distance teaching. As long as courses of this nature maintain high academic standards, strive for overall excellence and attention to details, and make use of the rapidly developing technology, they will make a significant contribution to better educational opportunities for a large number of students.

References, German by Satellite

1. Pusack, James P. *DASHER: An Answer Processor for Language Study.* Oakdale, IA: CONDUIT, 1983 [Foreign Language Authoring System].

2. "School Technology Bill Okayed by Senate." *Technological Horizons in Education Journal* 14, 10 (1987):26.

3. Wohlert, Harry S. "Voice Input/Output: Speech Technologies for German Language Learning." *Die Unterrichtspraxis* 17, 1 (1984): 76-84.

4. _____, and Martin McCormick. "An Algorithm for Controlled Integration of Sound and Text." *CALICO Journal* 3, 2 (1985): 19-21, 37.

4

Interactive Tele-Classes from Germany

Beverly D. Eddy
Dickinson College

Introduction

Providing language students with the opportunity to interact with native speakers within a truly European setting is a challenge that faces all second-language teachers. The experience is especially critical for students at the intermediate and advanced levels of study. The former profit from having their fledgling attempts at communication substantiated when a meaningful conversation or information exchange takes place; the latter gain as well, but across a broader spectrum of language and in more elaborate subject matter.

This report describes one school's effort to bring language students and the parent culture into interesting and meaningful contact through three types of interactive tele-classes: live by television and telephone from professional television studios in the parent country, live by video teleconferencing from designated sites, and live by enhanced audio teleconferencing *in situ.*

The Satellite Classroom

Since the spring of 1984 Dickinson College has worked with Intel-Ed (International Tele-Education, Inc., an organization formally known as the National Committee for Internationalizing Education through Satellites) to conduct experimental language classes by satellite between the Federal Republic of Germany and the United States. Through this program, Dickinson students in the third and final semester of the required language sequence are able to converse once each term by telephone line with German informants

211

whose images and voices are carried live by satellite into the Pennsylvania classrooms.

The first of three experimental classes to this end originated in the National Maritime Museum in Bremerhaven (see Reference). The television studios of Radio Bremen handled picture production and transmission for this class, whose predetermined content focused on German emigration to the United States. The 60-minute class was structured in a question-and-answer format; four German scholars asked the American students general questions about emigration and famous German-Americans while offering new information about the conditions facing the nineteenth century emigrants who departed for the United States from the port city of Bremerhaven.

Despite difficulties with echo feedback, the student response to this satellite class was startling. Subsequent surveys and interviews revealed that the participants thought they had listened more intently to the German informants than to their German instructors or to native German guests and students in their classrooms; moreover, they concentrated more on the simple act of communication than on the particulars of lesson content. Perhaps because of this concentration, for the first time, students believed they had participated in a real German conversation. All previous conversational experience with German visitors on campus or in the classroom were seen as having been conducted in watered-down German tainted by the American experience.

Subsequent classes by satellite have had similar results. Whether talking with the German rock star Klaus Lage from a Bremen studio or with German university students speaking from the old Aula of the University of Heidelberg, students have maintained that the German they have heard seems more genuine than what they hear in this country. When asked, for example, on a postclass questionnaire whether conversation with German exchange students at Dickinson wasn't really as valuable as conversation with German students by satellite, students uniformly responded in the negative. One put it this way: "Although they are true Germans, they are too aware of our language level and aren't as challenging"; another noted, "They really don't give you the same effect. They are very much Americanized in the few months they are here."

These responses suggest the importance of conducting international tele-classes with third-semester students. Apparently, no amount of classroom conversation, laboratory quizzes and drills, or oral proficiency testing convinces them they are, at the close of the required language sequence, able to converse with Germans in the German spoken in Germany. Students need to face the reality of a true German setting. Ideally, all language students would be flown to a parent country to make this discovery themselves. Since that is impossible, the interactive tele-class clearly offers a dynamic and viable alternative.

Still, for all practical purposes, the satellite model of live, interactive exchange developed with Intel-Ed is too cumbersome and costly to be integrated widely into regular language classes. For example, each of the three satellite classes offered through Intel-Ed (with Rutgers University students joining Dickinson in two) was made possible only through funding from outside sources. In addition, negotiations were necessary with German television studios well in advance, informants had to be found and trained in television studio work, and participating language teachers had to compete with journalists and potential funders who disrupted the classes in progress in their eagerness to observe the process of satellite instruction in action.

Nor had an ideal model for satellite classes evolved. It seemed, in fact, that in their zeal to perfect the technical and visual aspects of the classes, television studio personnel and native language informants forgot the students for whom the classes were originally intended. Pedagogical concerns were played down when the visual production took on more importance than the learning process. Nervous teachers cued students to ask rather than answer questions, so that they would not have to concentrate so intently on what the informants were saying. It was at this point that Dickinson began to look for means to link its language students with German informants that were less costly, less flashy, and less dependent on nonpedagogical interests.

Video Teleconferencing

The first alternative, and in many ways the most attractive one, was video teleconferencing. This technology does not require working with German television studios, because video teleconferencing originates from conference rooms and thus avoids the flashiness of studio production. Participants simply sit at a table and, via a television screen, speak directly with informants abroad seated at another table. The technology provides a two-way video link, so that the informants in Germany can see the language students as they talk with them. Although an hour-long class is costly, a video teleconference is still significantly less expensive than a private studio production.

There are, of course, disadvantages. The major one is that students are required to travel to Washington, D.C. (the only center for international video teleconferencing presently available), while the German informants must travel to Frankfurt-am-Main. Thus it is nearly as hard to justify the expenses and inconveniences of the video teleconferencing class as it is to justify the satellite studio production.

Nevertheless, there are Dickinson students for whom the video teleconference may prove worth the effort of traveling to the teleconferencing "studio" in the nation's capital. Dickinson is planning annual video teleconferences for senior German and international studies majors whose German is fluent. These students will interview German professionals on mutual career interests in a variety of fields (law, business, media, etc.) to discuss international career options. Following the video teleconference with Germany, the students will be encouraged to visit businesses and agencies in Washington for information interviews with American professionals in similar fields, in the hope that the combined experience will make them more attractive employees in the international arena. Dickinson hopes from these video teleconferences to further refine the guidelines (explained below) it is establishing for a successful international classroom experience.

The major concern from a language standpoint, however, remains the intermediate students taking language as a graduation requirement with no real expectation of putting that language to any real or practical use. It is precisely these students who need to be convinced of their language abilities. Such students often find written and oral testing more punitive than helpful; both too often succeed in persuading the tester of the student's language abilities rather than in confirming for the student that substantial learning has taken place. This is where Dickinson finds the live conversation from Germany so helpful. And if a school cannot afford to transport Germans into the classroom by satellite or by video camera, it can afford to transport them by telephone.

Enhanced Audio Teleconferencing

Dickinson's first effort in audio teleconferencing was taken with great trepidation. Language teachers know it is extremely difficult for intermediate-level students to carry on a telephone conversation in the foreign language. Without visual cues it seemed likely the students' stammering conversation would falter completely, and the audio class would be a dismal disaster. Dickinson took great efforts to minimize these problems by incorporating some of the video aspects of satellite and video teleconferencing into the audio teleconference. Prior to the broadcast, for example, the German informants made and sent a videotape of themselves to the Dickinson campus. This tape let the students see the speakers prior to the teleconference, and get an idea of their natural flow of conversation. The format of this video was left up to the German informants, and resulted in a lively discussion about the United States' bombardment of Libya.

The Dickinson students, too, were videotaped. Each student introduced him- or herself, and spoke a little about life on the Dickinson campus. From this introductory video, the Germans learned something of each student's language level, assertiveness, and areas of academic and extracurricular interest.

As a result of this video exchange, neither the students nor the informants were complete strangers when they took to the telephone lines. To further ease the students into the teleconference class, telephone conversations were made part of the last two weeks of the class syllabus, and exercises in the language lab allowed each student to practice the experience of conversing with foreign "bodyless" voices.

This first audio teleconference was conducted with students at the University of Bremen, which is Dickinson's partner school and had served as a vital link in all the satellite and video teleconference classes. Half of the Dickinson language class had already participated in the satellite exchange with the German rock star, and there was some concern that the remaining students would feel cheated by having neither a television picture nor a celebrity during their audio class. Once again, the students proved the language experts wrong. When asked to compare their experience with that of the students in the satellite class, one student commented, "Our way was more difficult, and as a result we paid less to learn more"; another noted, "I think the teleconferences are even more helpful, because they force you to use better listening skills. When you can't see (the Germans), it's more of a challenge."

Audio teleconferences are much less expensive and much easier to mount than the video tele-classes. The only costs are the purchase and postage on a videocassette and the price of a trans-Atlantic telephone call. The German informants need not travel to a studio or conference center; all they really need is a room large enough to accommodate their numbers and a telephone with a speaker. There is no need to schedule these classes weeks in advance, and they can generally be arranged at the informant's convenience.

Characteristics of a Successful International Tele-Class _____

The enhanced audio teleconference would not have been successful had it not followed guidelines established during the earlier video experiments with Intel-Ed. The following seven principles are equally viable for video and audio tele-classes.

1. The language informants must have pictures and background information on the American students with whom they will be speaking prior to the class. Audio or video cassettes aid even further in giving the informants an idea of the students' personalities and linguistic abilities. The exchange should be as personalized as possible so that the informants can call on the students by name, and refer to their special interests or abilities.
2. The classroom teacher should either leave the room during the tele-class or, at the very least, remain out of sight. At no point during the tele-class should the teacher speak up, signal, or try in any way to direct or aid the conversation. As soon as the teacher mediates in the discussion, the students relinquish their responsibility to carry the burden of conversation.
3. Students should be seated in an open semicircle so they can maintain eye contact and solicit help from one another when they cannot think of a word or have difficulty with the answer to a question. Each student should be within reach of a microphone. Dickinson has purchased a conferencing device so that multiple microphones can be used in the interface to the telephone line, which makes it possible for every two students to share a microphone, with no more than ten students participating actively in the conversation at a given time. This arrangement means that half the class may be seated behind the semicircle

of active students and change positions with their classmates halfway through the class hour.

4. The informants should be instructed to ask concrete questions that can be answered from personal knowledge or experience. The informants should not test the students' knowledge; rather, they should solicit information, so that the students can be "experts" in that aspect of the conversation. Teachers acquainted with oral proficiency elicitation techniques can aid the informants in suggesting appropriate areas for questioning prior to the tele-class experience.

5. Students should introduce themselves by name each time they volunteer information and, in audio teleconferencing, the language informants should do the same. The informants should also call on the American students by name for most questions, rather than asking general questions directed to no specific person.

   The language informants should have a check list of all student participants to guarantee that each speaks at least once during the class hour.

6. A stationary videocamera should be aimed at the semicircle of participating American students, and the entire class videotaped for class analysis the following day. By reliving the class experience and studying errors or difficulties in comprehension, the students can better understand why they found a particular exchange gratifying or frustrating.

   The teacher can also study the classroom videotape for areas that need to be modified or changed before the next tele-class.

7. Finally, the teleconference or satellite class must be incorporated topically into the rest of the course material and, wherever possible, segments of the informants' conversation should be worked into a scheduled class quiz. The success of the tele-class rests on the students' perception that the experience contributes to and is an integral part of the course syllabus.

Conclusion

Technologies are changing so rapidly that it is difficult to say if or when the costs of video teleconferencing will be reduced and conferencing sites made readily accessible. The video teleconference is the most desirable circumstance for international tele-classes, with enhanced audio teleconferencing the only cost-effective one presently available.

Dickinson intends to continue exploring both areas, while concentrating on the latter technology for its third-semester language students. During the next two years, audio tele-classes are projected in a variety of languages, linking Dickinson's intermediate language students with students and faculty at partner institutions throughout Europe and Asia. Participating faculty will endeavor to refine evaluative procedures for measuring motivation and classroom behavior before and after each experiment. Dickinson has no intention of increasing the number of international tele-classes per classroom;

these will instead remain a single, culminating experience for the intermediate langauge student, with video teleconferencing an occasional offering to senior language and international study majors.

To date, Dickinson can point to two apparent benefits from the tele-class experience. One is a greater spontaneity among tele-class participants and willingness to speak up in class. Another is an increased percentage of nonmajors applying for study programs in Germany. Of the twenty-seven participants in the first satellite class, for example, fourteen elected courses beyond the required language sequence, with nine of these enrolling in Dickinson's summer or year-long programs in Bremen. Of the participants in last year's teleconferences, a similar percentage has enrolled in programs in Bremen, with a higher number opting for a full year of study.

Students are not provably better speakers for the tele-class experience, nor do they come from it with a markedly increased knowledge of German history or culture. On the other hand, they are demonstrably more confident in German conversation, and they seem to have a more realistic grasp of their own abilities and limitations, all of which has helped to strengthen Dickinson's German program. Similar benefits are expected to accrue when interactive tele-classes are expanded to other languages and other students and, to that end, the Dickinson model is a replicable prototype for other American schools and colleges.

For further information on the pedagogical aspects of this project, contact the author, Department of German, Dickinson College, Carlisle, PA 17013. Professor Robert W. Cavenaugh, Director of Instructional Media at Dickinson, can answer questions on the technology used in the three tele-class models. Dr. Thomas Naff, Director of Intel-Ed, and Project Director Mr. William Johnston can be reached at Intel-Ed, 2400 Chestnut Street, Philadelphia, PA 19103-4316.

Reference, Interactive Tele-Classes from Germany

Eddy, Beverly D. "Live from Germany: A Look at Satellite Instruction." *Die Unterrichtspraxis* 19, 2 (1986):213-19.

Using Interactive Audio with Computer-Assisted Language Learning

Randall L. Jones

Brigham Young University

Introduction

One of the standard criticisms of most computer-assisted language learning (CALL) programs is their failure to simulate real language activities (e.g., Ariew, 1; Underwood, 8). By far the majority of CALL lessons stress grammar in some fashion, often in a way that they are little more than electronic versions of grammar workbooks (Ng and Olivier, 7). Recent hardware and software developments, however, provide the option of including sound with CALL lessons, thus making it possible for students to listen to authentic samples of the language as part of their computer language experience. This report will describe four methods of implementing external audio into CALL lessons and will discuss the relative advantages and disadvantages of each.

Terminology

Because of the rapid development of audio technology during the past few years, it is important first of all to clarify some of its principles. This discussion will be confined to three sets of "either-or" concepts: magnetic vs. optical storage, analog vs. digital recording, and sequential vs. direct access.

Magnetic vs. Optical Storage. The information on an audiotape or cassette is recorded and read using a magnetic process. The recording head arranges the magnetic particles on the tape in such a way that they correspond to the patterns of the original sounds. The read head then detects these patterns and converts them into electronic signals that are amplified and transmitted to a speaker or headphones. Optical storage differs primarily in the way the sound patterns are recorded and read. The sound waves are "printed" on a disk using optical laser technology, and the information is read and interpreted using a similar laser device. Most optical storage media today become permanent records, i.e., they cannot be erased or recorded over.

Analog vs. Digital Recording. A record or audiocassette is said to be an analog recording, as the recorded sound patterns are analogous to the actual sound waves. A digital recording, on the other hand, represents a total restructuring of the information. A periodic sampling of a sound waveform is taken and recorded as binary digital data—in a format that is understandable by the computer. This process is known as analog-to-digital (A/D) conversion. The reverse process, D/A conversion, is used to convert the data back into a sound signal. The quality of the signal is dependent on the sampling rate (expressed in kilohertz or thousandths of a second) and the number of bits used to store each sample. Typical compact disk (CD) sound recordings use 16-bit A/D conversion at a 44-kHz sampling rate. For speech, such fidelity is not necessary, and in fact would be a waste of precious disk space.

Sequential vs. Direct Access. In order to find a specific piece of music on an audiocassette it is necessary to fast-forward and check a number of times. This is sequential access. A phonograph record, on the other hand, allows placing the needle at random directly at the beginning point of the desired piece. This is direct access. Direct access is much faster and offers significant advantages for CALL, but it does not come without a price to pay.

Evaluation Criteria

Because the features of each audio device are so different, it is important to establish a set of criteria against which one can make a comparison. Listed here are seven criteria that can be used to evaluate available devices. In many cases the criteria are closely related to each other, e.g., one is achieved at the expense of others.

1. *Quality of speech.* The quality of speech delivered by peripheral computer hardware ranges all the way from barely comprehensible to very high fidelity. For language-learning purposes the voice quality should be at least as good as telephone speech. It should sound authentic with natural intonation and stress.

2. *Speed of access.* Ideally an utterance that is part of a language lesson should be accessed and played immediately. Long delays can cause frustration and eventually defeat the purpose of the lesson.

3. *Ease of use.* Excessive demands on the instructor or student in using a device can be a serious problem. It should be possible to prepare materials without extensive training, and the whole operation should be as transparent as possible to the user.

4. *Reliability.* A piece of broken equipment is worse than having no equipment at all.
5. *Flexibility.* Can the same device be used for any language? How easy is it to modify the utterances for a revised version of the lesson?
6. *Resource requirements.* Some devices are wholly self-contained, others require additional hardware or disk space.
7. *Cost.* In addition to the initial outlay, the cost of maintenance and supplies may be significant.

Specific Devices for Interactive Audio

The four devices discussed below are said to be "interactive," i.e., the computer can interact with each in order to locate and deliver specific utterances. (Names and addresses of representative models within each category of interactive device mentioned in the paragraphs below are found in the Appendix to this report.) It would, of course, be possible to write a CALL lesson that instructs the student to turn a cassette player on or off manually, and there are even cables that connect a cassette player to a computer for the purpose of controlling the "pause" and "play" functions. Such methods, however, cannot be said to be interactive.

Random-Access Cassette Player

Tandberg and Sony manufacture special cassette players that allow all functions to be controlled by a computer. In addition, it is possible to access and play any section of the tape randomly. This means that, as the lesson branches, one of a variety of samples can be selected, or that the same sample can be repeated indefinitely. It is important to stress that the information on these machines is accessed sequentially, not directly. Thus there can be a delay of up to several minutes before the segment is located and played. With thoughtful programming, however, most delays can be kept to just a few seconds.

Collett (2) reports on several CALL projects that use the Tandberg TCCR 530, most notably a French dictation program developed at the University of Waikato in New Zealand. He points out that it is advisable to leave three-second gaps between recorded speech segments in order to allow for a margin of safety (p. 38). Other users have learned that the accuracy of accessing segments on a cassette diminishes as the cassette is used. The Sony Series 5000 players with CAX-50 Computer Adapter is said to be more resistant to accessing problems because it uses a different technology for locating segments.

Random-access cassette players deliver very good speech quality, are easy to use, and are reliable and flexible. They require a serial interface card, a connecting cable, and cassettes. The cost depends on the adaptatation required and options, and can be substantial. The biggest disadvantage is the slowness in accessing speech segments.

Direct-Access Audio Disk

The Instavox is an interesting blend of technology: a magnetic direct-access analog audio device. The basic recording medium is a 15-inch flexible disk made of the same material as audio tape. It is contained in a paper envelope and fits into a drive very much like a floppy disk. Each disk has a capacity of 27 minutes of high-fidelity audio, or 44 minutes of lower fidelity. (The lower fidelity is perfectly adequate for most language-learning situations.) Any speech segment on the disk can be accessed in 0.4 seconds or less. The disk may be recorded over as often as one wishes, although it is advisable to re-record the entire disk instead of "patching in" new segments.

Henry et al. (5) at Northern Illinois University have used the Instavox to develop what they call "hyper-speech" lessons (See Part II, Report 6, pp. 221-34 in this volume). An authentic sample of language is recorded and transferred to the Instavox. The computer is used to control the presentation of the spoken language as well as to provide assistance to the learner in comprehending the utterances. Harold Madsen of the ESL Program at Brigham Young University (6) uses the Instavox for the listening-comprehension section of a computerized adaptive test for ESL placement. The entire test is computer-controlled and offers great flexibility for this type of testing.

Weinstein (9) uses the Instavox as part of his VOCAL System, especially for listening comprehension, pronunciation, and dictation. The pronunciation exercises use the record feature of the Instavox, which allows students to record their voices and compare them with the model. The Instavox delivers very good speech quality virtually instantaneously. It is definitely more difficult to work with than the Tandberg and Sony devices, but with practice one can learn to use it with little problem. It also requires a serial interface card and cable, as well as a supply of diskettes. The device is larger and heavier than a cassette recorder, thus creating problems if space is an issue. It is also more expensive than a random-access cassette recorder.

Digitized Speech. As sophisticated as the technology of digitizing speech is, the process is actually quite simple. Speech samples are digitized and entered into the computer's mass-storage device through a special interface card under software control, either directly from a microphone or from a recorder. Commands are then embedded in the lesson to access any segment of speech to be used with a lesson.

Demers (3) and his colleagues (Jonathan Kent, Karl Tomizuka, and Yarko Tymciaurak) at the University of Arizona have developed a program for Chinese listening comprehension using the Dialog 1 speech board. A text is displayed on the screen using Chinese characters. The student can point to one or more characters, then listen to them as they are spoken. Demers reports (3) that the speech quality is very good and the response is immediate.

Fischer (4) has found the Audio Tool Kit for the Victor 9000 to be an excellent device for writing interactive listening-comprehension lessons. He has developed a German program called Rechnung that concatenates individual segments of speech (e.g., numbers) to create the "illusion of complex continuous speech" (p. 27). Such methods can save significantly on storage.

Digitized speech offers many attractive features and appears to be the most promising option for interactive audio. The quality of speech can be very good, depending on the sampling rate of the AD/DA board. Access is immediate and it is very simple to use. The main drawback of digitized speech in the past has been the large storage requirement. For example, CD audio requires approximately 100 kilobytes (kB) of disk space for every second. Digitized speech for language purposes is adequate with a much lower sampling rate (10-15 kHz) and using an 8-bit instead of a 6-bit sample. Compression techniques reduce the requirements even more. With hard-disk storage becoming so inexpensive, the demand on disk space is now less problematic. Good boards at a reasonable price are becoming available regularly.

Synthesized Speech. Synthesized speech is familiar to everyone through the telephone. Many of the recorded messages heard after dialing a number that has been changed or disconnected are in fact not recorded at all, but rather generated through a text-to-speech process. A written message is transformed into spoken form by an algorithm that attempts to simulate the human speech mechanism.

The greatest advantage of synthesized speech is its simplicity. After installing the necessary hardware and software it is only necessary to write out the text in English and have the program synthesize it. Unfortunately, the disadvantages of synthesized speech are so great that it virtually precludes its use in second-language programs. First, the quality is not high enough to use as a model for language students. It sounds mechanical and makes numerous pronunciation errors. In addition, there are few synthesizers available that handle languages other than English. The prospects for improvement are not good. The computer industry does not see a need to invest money in the improvement of a product that is already performing adequately for most applications. Prices for speech synthesizers typically parallel the range of costs for devices that permit digitized speech.

Conclusion

External audio offers some exciting possibilities for CALL. Immediate access of good-quality speech at a reasonable cost is now a reality. The burden is now on authors' shoulders to be creative in developing imaginative courseware to match the sophisticated hardware.

References, Using Interactive Audio with Computer-Assisted Language Learning

1. Ariew, Robert. "Computer-Assisted Foreign Language Materials: Advantages and Limitations." *CALICO Journal* 2, 1 (1984) :43-47.

2. Collett, John. "CALL with Audio Output." *CALICO Journal* 3, 3 (1986) :37-41.

3. Demers, Richard. Personal communication.

4. Fischer, William. "Master(')s Voice: The Victor 9000 and High-Fidelity Voice Reproduction for CALI." *CALICO Journal* 3, 4 (1986) 21-31.

5. Henry, George M., John F. Hartman, and Patricia B. Henry. "Computer-Controlled Random Access Audio in the Comprehension Approach to Second-Language Learning." *Foreign Language Annals* 20, 3 (1987) :255-64.

6. Madsen, Harold. Personal communication.

7. Ng, K. L. Evelyn, and William P. Olivier. "Computer-Assisted Language Learning: An Investigation on Some Design and Implementation Issues." *System* 15, 1 (1987) :1-17.

8. Underwood, John H. *Linguistics, Computers and the Language Teacher: A Communicative Approach.* Rowley, MA: Newbury House, 1984.

9. Weinstein, Allen. "Adapting Programmed Materials to Learning Strategies: Overcoming the Spatial-Sequential Effect with the VOCAL System." *CALICO Journal* 4, 3 (1987) 13-24.

APPENDIX: Vendors' Addresses ————————————

1. *Random Access Cassette Players*
   Tandberg TCCR 530, TAL 812, TAL 822
   Tandberg of America
   Labriol Court
   Armonk, NY 10507

   SONY 5000 with CAX Adapter
   SONY AV Products
   Educational Electronic Corporation
   213 North Cedar
   Inglewood, CA 90301

2. *Direct-Access Audio Disk*
   Instavox RA-12
   Educational & Information Systems, Inc.
   804 North Neil St.
   P. O. Box 1774
   Champaign, IL 61820

3. *Speech Digitizing Boards*
   Audio Tool (for Victor 9000)
   Victor Technologies, Inc.
   380 El Pueblo Drive
   Scotts Valley, CA 95066

   Dialog 1
   Dialogic Corporation
   129 Little Road
   Parsippany, NJ 07054

   DSA-120
   Digital Voice Card
   Online Product Corporation
   20251 Century Boulevard
   Germantown, MD 20874

   IBM Voice Option Card
   Contact local IBM representative.

   ProTalker
   Speech, Ltd.
   3790 El Camino Real, Suite 213
   Palo Alto, CA 94366

   Supertalker II
   Mountain Computers, Inc.
   3000 El Pueblo Road
   Scotts Valley, CA 95066

4. *Speech Synthesizers*
   DECtalk
   Digitial Equipment Corporation
   146 Main Street
   Maynard, MA 01754

   ECHO IIb
   Street Electronics
   P. O. Box 50220
   Santa Barbara, CA 93150

Personal Speech Synthesizer
Votrax, Inc.
1394 Rankin
Troy, MI 48089

Speech Master
Techmar, Inc.
6625 Cochran Road
Solon, OH 44139

FLIS:
Random-Access Audio
and Innovative Lesson Types

George M. Henry
John F. Hartmann
Patricia B. Henry
Northern Illinois University

Introduction

Most computer-aided instruction (CAI) for foreign language is altogether silent, depending entirely on mute text and occasional graphics to instruct and aid the learner. A few systems incorporate a tape recorder, which either forces a rigid, invariant lesson design or requires the learner to endure delays of up to half a minute before hearing a desired speech segment. CAI systems that incorporate interactive video are a promising alternative, but they will be expensive, probably will not be customizable, and commercial versions will not be available for the less commonly taught languages due to high production costs.

The Northern Illinois University Foreign Language Instruction Station (FLIS) is based on a computer-controlled random-access audio device called the Instavox and consists of a complete lesson authoring and presentation system that can record and play back high-quality audio segments (speeches) in conjunction with computer-displayed text and graphics. Any audio segment specified by the lesson author or chosen by the learner can be accessed and played with no delay at any time during the lesson. Speech samples of any desired content can be provided by the lesson author and can be called up by the student at will as the lesson progresses. These audio segments might include hints, translations, cultural notes, interactive feedback messages or slower and more distinct re-recording of the original natural language segment.

With a moderate investment in equipment, training, and time, any individual or institution can create, modify, and use FLIS-mediated interactive audio lessons for any language (or any subject where audio via Instavox is a useful added dimension in the presentation of instruction). A preliminary version of the FLIS system was completed in mid-1985; presently some ten authors have been trained to write materials on the FLIS system, only two of whom have had any significant previous computer experience. While the rate varies with which individuals master the FLIS authoring protocols, in most cases a week or two of training and practice are sufficient; moreover, the authoring process is entirely menu-driven. Thus, no knowledge of computer programming is necessary.

This report offers first a brief description of the equipment and software that composes FLIS, including specific features seen by both lesson authors and students, and then characterizes two innovative lesson types ("interactive story" and "Hyper-speech") designed to improve listening-comprehension skills. The report concludes with some comments on evaluation efforts to date.

The FLIS System

Equipment

The current FLIS system consists of four workstations, each equipped with an Apple IIe computer and an Instavox (a direct-access audio device). The four workstations are connected by a Corvus network to a Corvus Hard Disk Drive, which holds the FLIS computer programs and student records. The data needed for an individual lesson are stored on two standard floppy diskettes, one containing pictures for the lesson, and the other holding information about sequencing of lesson material, speeches to play back, specific feedback for given responses, etc.

The audio component of the lessons is provided by the Instavox, which accomplishes what would be impossible with a tape recorder—instant access and replay of any speech at any time during the lesson with a delay of less than half a second. The Instavox is similar to the conventional floppy-disk drive of a computer but employs a Mylar disk 15 inches in diameter that holds up to thirty minutes of recorded (as opposed to machine-generated) human speech in which all the nuances, tones, and rhythms of language are reproduced faithfully.

At each workstation used in the teaching of Indonesian and Thai at the NIU Southeast Asia Center, the Instavox is controlled by the computer using lesson data that indicates corresponding software programmed to store the exact location of the beginning and ending of each speech segment. Access to audio segments is random in the sense that requests to play back speech samples may be made in random order and may differ from one use to another in the lesson. In this fashion, the lesson author may choose to have speech samples played or replayed in an order that depends on the particular responses of the learner, or the learner may be given some degree of control in the progress of the lesson, perhaps electing to hear optional hints or translations that are made available, or choosing to repeat or skip certain optional sections of the lesson at will. In either case, the Instavox audio device is able to access these random locations with virtually no delay. Immediate access and playback result in a significant saving of learner time and a greater efficiency in the learning task when compared to other systems, such as the random-access tape recorder, which demonstrate delays of up to ten seconds to access a given speech.

The Authoring System

Creating a lesson for the FLIS system is a two-part task. The lesson must be planned carefully, bearing in mind the capabilities of the system as well as its limitations. The general lesson type is determined first (four have been developed so far: drill, tutorial, interactive story, and "hyper-speech"; the latter two are described below), then individual "frames" are designed as needed. Each frame constitutes a single computer-student interaction; for example, a single frame may consist of presentation of material, followed by a question, the student's answer, and the computer's response to that answer. Frames may include multiple-choice or short-answer questions or may offer a choice of what happens next (for example, a branch at a new section, the playing of a hint), or may require no action at all from the learner. Along with this detailed planning of the scope and content of the lesson, the author may choose to provide more or less detailed remediation or feedback to incorrect answers. In addition, a script of speeches and pictures to be used at each point of the lesson must be prepared.

Once an author has produced one lesson of a given type, subsequent lessons are more easily created, since the underlying framework will be familiar, although the content and details may be quite different.

After the lesson is planned and scripted, the actual production is made easy by the FLIS Authoring System. The system is entirely menu-driven and requires only that the author know what should happen in the lesson at each point. All lesson data can be imprinted for later reference, and all data can be changed at a later time, if desired. This circumstance means that the lesson itself can be modified in light of difficulties or shortcomings discovered in the course of formative evaluation. Typical information for a frame might include the following: the speech, text, and picture to use in the "presentation" part of the frame, the specification of possible correct and wrong answers, and the response the computer should give for each answer. The computer's response can be (1) none (in which case the lesson proceeds to the next frame), (2) a message displayed on the screen, (3) an audio message, or (4) a branch to a set of remedial or speech feedback frame(s) for that particular answer.

Especially noteworthy is the Instavox component of the authoring system, which controls the recording of speeches. This, too, is menu-driven, and allows either live recording of individuals or the copying of segments of audio tape or cassette to the Instavox disk. The author simply taps the computer's space bar to initiate the recording (or copying) process and then taps it once again to stop. Audio segments may be recorded automatically one after another, or the recorded segment can be replayed instantly by tapping a key; if the recording proves unsatisfactory (too loud or soft, not lively enough, background noise, the last syllable cut off prematurely, etc.), the speech samples can be re-recorded and validated instantly. In addition, a given speech segment can be re-recorded at a later time or additional speeches added to the lesson. The extreme ease of creating and editing the audio materials for a lesson contrasts sharply with other video or CD-ROM devices.

Lessons

Each FLIS lesson may be included in a number of "courses" of lessons and made available to students. Each student is registered in a specific section of a given course. A choice of up to thirty lessons is displayed for each course with an indication of which lessons have been tried previously by the particular student. Once a choice of lesson is made, the student is responsible for obtaining and inserting the two floppy disks and the Instavox disk into their respective machines, and the lesson begins. At the end of the lesson a summary of the student's performance is displayed on the screen and written to a permanent file on disk, and the student is returned to the course menu to retake the lesson, choose another, or quit.

A primary challenge for authors who design lessons for the FLIS system is to go beyond traditional drill or tutorial lessons to other types that make use of the unique capabilities of random-access audio. While traditional lesson types are useful to a degree, the Instavox capacity for random-access audio invites teachers to create lessons that can take fuller advantage of the computer's capacity for interactive instruction.

Two innovative lesson types for FLIS developed at Northern Illinois University that appear to have great promise are "interactive story" and "hyper-speech." Both are explained more fully in Henry, Hartmann, and Henry (See Reference).

The Interactive Story

Interactive story lessons were inspired by the structure of the series of "Choose Your Own Adventure" stories written for children. In these books, at the end of each page the reader is invited to choose what will happen next and, depending on the choice, is instructed to turn to a particular page.

In short, the reader "branches" through a series of alternatives, whose election at each point determines the subsequent story line and its consequences. The story, then, has many variations, and can be read many times, each with a different outcome.

The extension of this concept to FLIS-mediated lessons is straightforward; the computer poses choices to the student at various points in the interactive story lesson and, based on the student's response, continues with the chosen part of the plot. For example, in one such FLIS lesson, the student takes the part of an Indonesian child sent to the market to buy fruit for a guest. At various points in the lesson, the student must make choices for the child in accordance with what is heard: which kind of fruit to buy, whether to buy at the offered price or to bargain; whether to accept a lower offer or to walk away (in hopes of a still lower offer); whether to buy some fruit that is not quite sweet enough, etc. At each point the student sees a picture of the situation and overhears the voices of the child and the sellers. Not all frames are "choice" frames; in some the narrative is interrupted and the student is asked a question (Does the child have enough money to accept the seller's offer?); in others the student may simply be asked to listen and understand perhaps with the aid of optional hints or translations.

Students are encouraged to undertake lessons of this kind several times, each time making different choices. In this way, a considerable amount of repetition of lexical items and syntactic patterns is experienced, but the repetition is cloaked in sufficient variety to prevent boredom. The interest inherent in discovering the unknown consequences of the choices appears to be a powerful motivating factor if the "plot" is cleverly constructed. An additional attraction of interactive story lessons of this type is the ease with which the consequences of actions in different cultural settings can be illustrated unobtrusively. For example, in Western culture, bargaining is rare, and the strategy of walking away from the seller to elicit a lower offer is not widely practiced. In the FLIS-mediated interactive story lesson, this situation (and others of cultural contrast) may be presented and the results of various actions demonstrated in a vicarious but dynamic fashion.

The Hyper-Speech

In its pure form, the hyper-speech lesson gives the student a set of speech segments to understand and, for each such segment, a set of instantly available aids to comprehension. Aids may include the following:

1. Instant repetition of the speech segment
2. A set of audio hints (lexical, grammatical, or cultural notes)
3. A picture illustrating the situation
4. A slower, clearer re-recording of the original speech segment
5. The text of the speech segment displayed on the screen
6. Written notes about the speech displayed on the screen

7. A translation of the speech segment, spoken or displayed
8. A glossary of unusual words in the lesson

Typically, a learner is required to access some of the less complete aids before full text display and translation will appear, but other than that restriction (which need not be followed by the lesson author), students are free to attack the audio passage as they please. Evaluators engaged in on-site observation of students working with hyper-speech lessons have noted that some learners prefer to repeat the passage many times before calling up any of the aids; others turn almost at once to the re-recording and then back to the original. Still others exhaust all available hints before continuing. Students exhibit considerable perseverance in trying to comprehend as long as the listening passages are not too far beyond their ability; perhaps more important, students report that the lessons are enjoyable and seem very worthwhile. This positive evaluation can be ascribed, perhaps, to these reasons: mature students apparently like the fact that they are in control of their own learning, and can set the pace of the lesson and the details of their interaction with it. In addition, the nature of the materials and the way they are presented offer the user a clear sense of accomplishment in understanding samples of authentic foreign language instead of the controlled and contrived speech typical of classroom language. Finally, the materials reflect the full range of environments where speech is natural, purposeful, and functional (taped conversations, commercial recordings of comedians, news broadcasts from the radio, songs, plays, etc.) and where the content is clear, relevant, and interesting. Hyper-speech lessons are probably not suitable for beginning students, but seem clearly suitable for students at the intermediate level or above. The concept may be applicable for beginning learners, however, with carefully selected (or crafted) materials and their equally careful workup for use on FLIS with special attention to the hints and other aids appropriate for beginning students.

Evaluation

Lessons that incorporate direct-access audio presented by an interactive computer system appear to be effective and highly motivating to students learning foreign languages. The equipment and time necessary to produce these lessons, while far from negligible, are moderate compared to any other presently available medium that can claim usable random-access audio capability; moreover, they are not beyond the means of many secondary schools or institutions of higher education. The Northern Illinois University Foreign Language Instruction Stations, together with the lesson types that have already been developed, constitute a viable means to explore further the possibilities of random-access audio in all levels of second-language learning.

For further information, readers are invited to contact the authors at The Center for Southeast Asian Studies, Northern Illinois University, DeKalb, IL 60115.

Reference, FLIS

Henry, George M., John F. Hartmann, and Patricia B. Henry, "Computer-Controlled Random-Access Audio in the Comprehension Approach to Second-Language Learning." *Foreign Language Annals* 20, 3 (1987):255-64.

7

Macario, Montevidisco, and Interactive Dígame: Developing Interactive Video for Language Instruction

Larrie E. Gale
Brigham Young University

Introduction

The young "gringo" visiting Mexico from the United States is incensed that the druggist of the small Mexican village is charging so much. The druggist picks up the phone and calls his cousin, the accountant, to see if the prices can't be changed. The druggist hangs up and, as the discussion ensues, the cousin appears but turns out to be a local police officer who invites the gringo to go with him to the police station.

The gringo is actually a language student at Brigham Young University, an intermediate speaker of Spanish, who didn't have to cross the border to visit Mexico but simply used a conversational simulator, predicated on interactive video technology, to practice Spanish and encounter a variety of different circumstances (and native speakers) while engaged in the vicarious experience of interacting and problem solving in a foreign culture.

Researchers at the David O. McKay Institute and College of Education at BYU have pursued the development of interactive videodisc technology as a natural extension of a long-term institutional commitment to computer-assisted instruction (CAI) and were among the first educators in the United States to purchase prototype interactive videodisc hardware and develop courseware for instructional purposes. Several interactive videodisc (IAV) products have been subsequently authored for investigative purposes, including materials intended to teach history, physics, social studies, and math, as well as German, French, and Spanish.

The three programs for Spanish described in this report—Macario, Montevidisco, and Interactive Dígame—are representative of the historical and progressive development of the medium at BYU; each further exemplifies some of the problems and unique approaches developed in their production.

Macario: An Annotated Film

Goals and Audiences

Early in the history of interactive video it was felt a great deal could be learned about the use of the medium without having to pay for the expense of video production. Thus, in 1975, several colleagues conceptualized how an existing film might be converted to interactive video for language instruction and, the following year, supervised the transfer of Macario, a feature-length Spanish-language film, to videodisc format. The resulting IAV courseware was then used in conjunction with intermediate Spanish classes. A Spanish instructor at BYU, Gloria Melendez, had been using Macario in her intermediate Spanish classes to help students develop listening-comprehension skills, notice culturally appropriate cues, and recognize the symbolism, metaphor, and analogy used in the film.

The research team decided to adapt Macario for interactive video and under Dr. Melendez's supervision carefully footnoted and annotated each scene. This adaptation was accomplished by creating a series of questions or comments related to key segments of scenes throughout. The objectives that guided the annotation were predicated on helping students notice the figurative language and graphic icons apparent in the film, calling to their attention the use of regionalisms and, further, providing a contextual basis to investigate other unique lexical and grammatical elements found in the dialog. The intended user would have the ability to stop the videodisc and work with the materials at will.

The Materials and Equipment

When the Macario videodisc was developed in 1980, there were no off-the-shelf interfaces between computers and videodisc players, and the few personal computers that existed were all C/PM based. These circumstances made it necessary to create a "two-screen" version in which the video images appeared on a television monitor while the computer images appeared on the computer screen. To reduce costs, all ninety minutes of the film were placed onto one thirty-minute videodisc. This reduction required the presentation of major sections of the film as still frames accompanied by audio—a sort of slide-tape presentation—while other major sections were maintained in full motion and sound. In short, after receiving permission from the appropriate license holders, Macario was edited and transferred to videotape, and then pressed to videodisc (one of the first ever pressed by 3M).

What "Macario IAV" Looked Like to the User

Students sat at a keyboard terminal with a CRT (computer monitor) and a television monitor mounted just above the computer screen. The film appeared normal in every way when played for the student, except for the message across the computer screen that said in Spanish, "To stop the presentation, press the space bar."

The student could stop the videodisc player at any time immediately after which a menu tied directly to the segment of the scene the student was viewing (see Figure 1) appeared on the screen.

Figure 1. "A screen from Macario"

A. Continue the presentation	F. Repeat the scene in English
B. Repeat this scene	G. Provide the text in English
C. Back up X seconds	H. Provide the text in Spanish
D. Repeat the previous scene	I. Get the dictionary/glossary
E. Stop at the end of this scene	J. End the presentation

1. Is there some symbolism in the falling of the tree?
2. Do the clothes of Macario give you a clue as to when the story occurred?
3. Is there a special motive behind assigning Macario the occupation of a wood cutter?
4. Why has the family lit a candle for Godmother Rosa?
5. Is there dramatic purpose behind the daughter's comment about lighting a candle for her father?
6. What does Macario use to help him carry the wood?
(Press the space bar to see more options for this scene.)

At the beginning of the film, Macario, the protagonist, is seen in the woods chopping down a tree and carrying firewood home where he is met by his wife and children. Were the student to press the space bar anytime during the first sequence, questions such as the following would appear on the screen, in Spanish (see Figure 1):

1. Is the falling of the tree symbolic?

and if the student were to press the corresponding number, the question would be repeated on screen along with the instructor's response, which (in Spanish) would read:

For some, the falling of the tree is symbolic; when a tree falls, a person falls in death. Sometimes authors skillfully convert symbols of this type into a motif, repeating it artistically with variations throughout the story. Why don't you watch throughout the rest of the film to see if there isn't something to this?

In the first scene there are twenty such questions tied to answers or further questions, or prompts tied to further commentary. Several of the questions are posed but not answered in order not to "spoonfeed" the students; rather, instructors wanted students to notice those attributes in Macario that were critical to the development of the film and to watch for recurring patterns.

As can be seen in Figure 1, there is a menu at the top of the computer screen that gives students control of the presentation. Students can interrupt the presentation, back up and repeat a scene, or have the presentation stop at a scene boundary; they can also call up the text that appears on their screen in English, as well as call for the second soundtrack recorded in English. Later versions of Macario also provided a dictionary so that students could look up unfamiliar terms or phrases; these versions also incorporated facilities that allowed the student to back up in the IAV presentation any specified number of seconds.

Students used Macario IAV individually in what is called "personalized interactive video" (PIV). Earlier viewing in groups of two to four students was found detrimental to understanding; students who wanted to stop the program to investigate scenes would defer to others who did not and less information was gleaned from the viewing than might otherwise have been the case.

Research Results

Four different comprehensive studies conducted with Macario IAV revealed essentially the same results (Gale et al., 9). In each, control groups used Macario in a traditional mode; that is, teachers lectured students for one or two class periods on what concepts should be noticed and on how the materials were to be used as the basis for a term paper and an achievement test. Following these lectures, students were sent to the BYU Learning Resource Center, where they were permitted to view the film (on videotape) in a continuous unsegmented format. Students using Macario on interactive videodisc were simply told that the materials would be the basis for a term paper and an exam that had to be completed successfully following its viewing, and were then directed to report to the videodisc lab and to sign up for viewing time. Both treatment groups were exposed to identical video footage, however students from the traditional approach had to correlate what they were seeing with class notes and handouts whereas the students in the videodisc group could stop the presentation at any time and were presented with the menus described above (Figure 1). Since the computer was programmed to capture every keystroke, tracking usage patterns and comparing them with student performance was relatively easy.

The results of all four studies showed significant improvement on the part of the videodisc groups at or beyond the .05 level of confidence. In each, the interactive videodisc groups outperformed the traditionally taught students by at least one, and in some cases, two standard deviations. Comparatively speaking, this means that students in the videodisc groups who received lower scores on an achievement test still performed as well as the better-performing lecture-and-videotape students.

These differences in performance offer several explanations. At first it was thought that being able to see the text and to hear the the second soundtrack of Macario in English might have been the major advantage. As a result, the program was altered so that students could not call up the English soundtrack until they previously had seen and listened to its corresponding sequence at least three times in Spanish. When performance on the achievement test was checked against the frequency of reversion to English prompts, fewer than 10 percent of the students (typically two in a class of thirty) were found to have elected to see the English text or to hear the English soundtrack. Moreover, among those who did call up these options, a strong negative correlation occurred between the number of times the English prompts were accessed and the student's test score. This result indicates that those few students who relied heavily on English really did not profit from the English clues; consequently, their performance on the achievement test was below that of their counterparts who interacted directly with the materials in Spanish.

The difference in scores that favored the interactive video students thus seemed attributable to two circumstances: (1) their increased degree of control over the information flow on the Macario videodisc, and (2) the inseparable nature of the symbolism, metaphor, and analogy that the teachers had wanted students to notice from the scope and content of the filmic materials themselves.

Montevidisco: A Conversational Simulator

Conceived as a conversational simulator that would make more complete use of the capabilities of IAV technology (Gale and Brown, 7) Montevidisco is predicated on a visit to a Mexican village by intermediate speakers of Spanish who will actually visit that village the following semester as part of a BYU study-abroad program. The responses that students make to queries and comments by native speakers as they appear on the screen determine what the student sees next; that is, the way in which the student interacts with the program determines where he or she is branched. In this way, each new "visit" to Montevidisco can be a different experience. (There are more than 1100 different situations and branch opportunities depending on how the user decides to respond to his or her interlocutors.)

Intended Goals and Audiences

The goals of Montevidisco were to provide students as much experience as possible in dealing with the situational and linguistic challenges they might encounter in Mexico. To this end, Montevidisco was designed to give the student the vicarious experience of listening to Spanish spoken at native speed and to produce Spanish in response to what they heard. The hope was that providing natural language in context in a visually rich environment would help students polish their listening and speaking skills. The materials were filmed *in situ* by the research team and assembled into videodisc format at BYU (Gale, 2, 3).

What Montevidisco Looked Like to the User

The Montevidisco courseware consists of an event on the screen that requires the student to respond by making a decision and speaking Spanish. For example, as the program begins, the user wanders into a plaza in a Mexican village. A young man aproaches and tries to sell himself as a tour guide. He opens (in Spanish) with:

Hello; you're an American tourist, aren't you?

At that point in the video frame freezes, and four options appear in text on the computer screen:

(1) Yes I am. Why do you ask?
(2) Yes and no. I'm an American but I'm a student from the Center for International Studies.
(3) An American tourist? Guess again. I'm a Russian sailor. Can you help me get back to my secret submarine base?
(4) What did you say?

The viewer's responsibility is to select one of the options and speak it in Spanish (into a microphone); then the conversation will proceed. After speaking, a surrogate or model can be called up on-screen to speak the phrase correctly and at native speed. The user can then choose to listen to the native speaker again and either reinitiate the spoken response or simply continue with the conversation.

Were the student to select option 3 above, the response of the tour guide would be (again in Spanish):

Oh, you really caught me by surprise that time. I'll tell you how to get back to your submarine base. All you have to do is catch bus number 13 and when it arrives at the beach ... but why are you in such a hurry? Why don't we go to the bar 'Toda Grande' first. There are a lot of good-looking girls there ..."

at which point the video again holds in freeze-frame while the user is presented with yet another set of options. And so it goes through more than a thousand different situations including scenes at the beach, police station, hospital, marketplace, restaurant, hotel, and many others.

The branching logic of Montevidisco is complex. Since each interaction typically provides four branch alternatives, the program quickly defines over 4000 branch points. In order to control production costs, many of these branch points were folded back on previously written scenes—which is why there are six different ways to take the same taxi ride, three ways to end up in the hospital, and four to end up in the police station. Because of the gender-intensive nature of Spanish, there are two treatments in Montevidisco, one for males and another for females, each held on a separate "gender-specific" disc.

There is an element of suspense in Montevidisco common to the adventure game (as can be seen in the option to be a Russian sailor). Many of the branches are surprises. This surprise element (and humor) is something like "the spoonful of sugar that helps the medicine to go down" and is instrumental in encouraging students to explore what would have happened had they selected different options and traced different paths through the program.

The types of feedback available to the student include (1) the natural consequences of each decision (for example, a wrong choice of beverage branches the user to the hospital), (2) the surrogate or model's response, (3) and the instructor's or proctor's evaluation of the student's spoken (recorded) efforts.

The Equipment System

Figure 2 shows the equipment system as it needed to exist in those early years. Two different videodisc players were used with interfaces designed and built by BYU electrical engineering students; a cassette player was also used with a BYU interface. The two videodisc players provided, respectively, the situations and the model (surrogate) responses. The computer-controlled cassette player was used to record student responses so that proctors or the instructor could later listen to and critique student speech efforts. With present equipment systems the situations and surrogate responses could be delivered through IBM InfoWindow, Sony View, or a combination of other personal computers, videodisc players, and interface cards now available on the market.

The Creative Elements of Montevidisco

Montevidisco appeared to be the first language simulator to incorporate interactive video. In its day, the materials were unique; the program used subjective camera techniques that required viewers to participate in the story and control the outcomes of their experience through the choices made to alternatives set forth in the development of a story line. The materials were equally unique in their use of the equipment systems available at the time, both in the types of feedback available and in the fact that the program

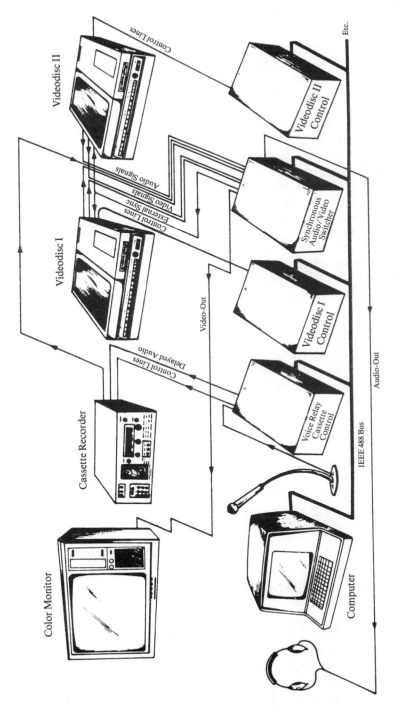

Figure 2. Equipment system for conversational simulator style

was not linear. Montevidisco enjoyed a variety of situations that provided very complex branching possibilities such that students using the program could actually create a new degree of fiction each time they used the materials. Finally, Montevidisco was unique in the authoring approaches used and in its instructional design, script format, and production techniques. (See Gale, 2 and 1.)

Research Results

Important lessons were learned about how the program ought to be modified as Montevidisco began to be used and data were collected for formative evaluation. However, plans for more formal research were thwarted when funding was reduced and the David O. McKay Research Institute at BYU was dissolved. Resumption of evaluative efforts awaits response from other funding sources (or institutions) interested in examining further the particulars of Montevidisco as a prototype for interactive videodisc-based language learning.

Despite this problem, informal evaluation results to date (Gale, 4) show that a conversational simulator is generally a good idea and that students very much like working with Montevidisco. The two-hour blocks of time initially scheduled for students to work with the materials proved insufficient. The vicarious interaction was clearly a motivating experience, and students were willing to sit in front of the television monitor for two hours without tiring appreciably. Furthermore, the data collected on patterns of student use revealed that the learner who most needed to listen to the surrogate/model and to use additional helps available in the program were the very individuals that failed to access them. Other learners, however, were able to take advantage of the help options in a fashion that exploited the model. Comparative results indicated that student scores on standardized tests were not affected appreciably by their exposure to Montevidisco, nor were such results expected. Two to four hours of experience with an interactive program is not apt to make a large difference in scores on tests that evaluate listening comprehension in content areas far afield from Montevidisco, let alone impact on writing, grammatical accuracy, etc.

Interactive Dígame: A Classroom Application _____

Interactive Dígame (Gale and Barksdale, 6) is an adaptation (with permission) of the BBC television production "Dígame" which was reedited and transferred to videodisc format. The research team then developed prototype lessons intended for personalized interactive video and tested them in a local high school. In order to compare different approaches, the same content was treated as personalized interactive video (PIV) lessons, and other lessons were created for classroom interactive video (CIV) for use with teacher intervention.

Early research results strongly supported the use of (PIV) versions but the classroom versions (CIV) also demonstrated promising results and the investigators then developed IAV courseware intended for use in the classroom alone.

Goals and Intended Audience

The goals of the classroom interactive video version of Interactive Dígame are aimed at the general improvement of Spanish listening-comprehension and speaking skills. It was also hoped that improvement in writing and reading abilities would follow as side products. The intended population for this courseware are beginning Spanish students in high school.

The Equipment System

In the classroom interactive video approach, a two-screen presentation is used. The video images and audio supplied by the videodisc player are sent directly to screen 1, a TV monitor in plain view of the class. Screen 2 is the computer monitor visible to the teacher alone. The CIV equipment system consists of an IBM PC with keyboard and monitor, a Pioneer LD-V6000 videodisc player, and a large-screen television monitor. The videodisc player is completely under computer control with the worst-case access-time somewhere under two seconds. The still frames, motion sequences, vocabulary items, etc., are available at the touch of a key.

The equipment for classroom interactive video is relatively inexpensive, and since only one system is required per classroom, virtually all high schools can afford to invest in the technology at a fraction of the cost of a typical electronic classroom or fixed-position language laboratory.

What Interactive Dígame Looks Like to the Users

The use of the courseware is difficult to appreciate through simple description. The teacher uses Interactive Dígame as an integral part of classroom instruction. In fact, the video that the students experience is very much like studying with a team teacher.

Once IAV lessons are developed and displayed on the computer monitor, the teacher can select any section of the lesson for presentation or review, or in other ways move around in the courseware easily and quickly.

In class, the teacher positions the computer monitor and keyboard for easy access and places the video screen (supplying the image from the videodisc player) such that students can readily see it. Menus of materials appear on the receiver for the class to see. A variety of different options are then available—playing an entire sequence of related scenes or segments thereof using still frames from the screen to introduce vocabulary or other materials, etc. The teacher usually requires students to view a short video clip from the longer sequence and then backs up to analyze it by introducing vocabulary while reviewing visual images on the screen, requiring students to produce those same words and phrases, thereby demonstrating comprehension. Once students appear comfortable with the new terms, the teacher then may continue to require different forms of listening and speaking practice or ask comprehension questions.

Next, the teacher changes the context and expects the students to produce a dialog on their own based on the vocabulary and experiences they have just practiced through interactive video. For instance, one of the sequences discusses ¿Qué hay en Cuenca? (What is there (to do) in Cuenca?); students learn about the different sights, activities, industry, etc. in and around this city in east central Spain. Once they have interacted with that sequence, the teacher may ask them to respond with similar information about their home town. The results have been surprising; students have been able to speak creatively in Spanish for 2 to 6 minutes without prompts or interruption.

In subsequent units students are exposed to a variety of concepts, terms, and culture associated with checking into a hotel, soliciting information from the tourist office, changing money, etc. Information from earlier units is reintroduced systematically as a reading exercise and then a few weeks later as a writing exercise.

Supplemental lessons have also been developed around cognates and the use of *tener* or *tener que*, and *hay*, etc. in Spanish. When these and other grammatical concepts are presented, situations and vocabulary are used from previous units. In this way the teacher need not be concerned that new vocabulary confound the learning of new grammar. Once these skills and concepts become second nature, students move to new information, such as describing grammatical usage while using familiar contexts.

Classroom Environment

Student attention span increases dramatically with classroom interactive video. Watching students pay attention to the instructor and television images is something akin to witnessing a tennis match with student attention being fixed first on the television and then on the instructor for a few seconds and then back to the television again. In short, students in the IAV classroom seldom exhibit anything but complete attention.

Research Results

Most of the research on Interactive Dígame conducted to date has been used to learn how best to use interactive video rather than to compare it rigorously with other approaches or media. However, in the process of trying to learn how best to use interactive video, competing approaches were inevitably contrasted. The results have revealed that IAV holds substantial promise for both personalized and classroom applications.

In the first year's study (Gale and Barksdale, 6), three different treatments of identical content were developed: (1) personalized interactive video instruction (PIV), (2) classroom interactive video instruction (CIV), and (3) traditional instruction. All three treatments were identical in content, context, vocabulary, and usage. They differed only in how the materials were treated and delivered. Students were pretested and then tested after exposure to one of the treatments. Later, each treatment group was exposed to one of the other treatments so that patterns of performance might be revealed. There were two cycles of instruction with testing occurring after each period.

Achievement after the first instructional cycle was highest in the person-alized interactive video group, second-highest in the classroom interactive video group, and lowest in the traditional class. In fact, a large gap existed between CIV and the group receiving traditional lessons. Differences occurring between traditional and CIV or PIV treatments did not occur by chance (significant beyond the .01 level of confidence) and were large. The best-performing students in the traditional setting had scores similar to the poorest-performing interactive video students.

Student performance after the second cycle of instruction again strongly supported the use of interactive video regardless of the treatment preceding it. Such large performance differences are seldom seen in educational or language-learning research, suggesting that the promise of IAV is substantial.

Results for 1987 (Gale and Barksdale, 5) were very similar to those obtained in 1986. When all groups from both years were compared, interactive video once again had a strong showing. Repeated measures analyses revealed that all interactive video treatments were significantly better than the traditional approach, but that none of the IAV treatments was significantly better than another (Table 1).

Table 1. Final Test Results by Treatment Groups for 1986 and 1987:
Tukey B Multiple Comparisons

Mean	Group		Group			
			3	2	4	1
30.65	3	1986 Traditional				
39.60	2	1986 Classroom IAV	*			
43.92	4	1987 Classroom IAV	*			
45.80	1	1986 Personalized IAV	*			

Multiple Range Test: * denotes pairs of groups significantly different at or beyond the .05 level.

Students liked both interactive video approaches—even those who complained about lesson details. In fact one IAV student discovered skills she thought herself incapable of as she moved from a D- to an A.

Summary

Early experimental use of interactive video was predicated on the supposition that the technology's advantage would exist in personalized forms of instruction and in complex simulations. Films were transferred to videodisc to avoid the high cost of video production and the results were researched with respect to any pedagogical advantage the new formatting might offer. The experiences with Macario suggest that there is value in "retrofitting" existing filmic footage, although the process is laborious without appropriate authoring software.

Montevidisco, an original complex-branching conversational simulator, was designed and produced to explore an alternative to using preexisting filmed footage for videodisc content. This experience revealed the need to create authoring tools and techniques that simplify scripting and production needs. The Montevidisco materials also revealed that more complex simulations may be very beneficial and entertaining for intermediate speakers, but other uses of interactive video may be essential for the beginner.

While evaluating the BBC Dígame in an interactive format, classroom versions of IAV were found to deliver results similar to personalized forms. Since that time, the research team has been involved in creating and testing different versions of classroom interactive video with very positive results.

The Theory and Design

While the capabilities of personalized and classroom interactive video are exciting, the need for carefully considered instructional design based on sound theory lies at the heart of any instructional paradigm. Technology is a powerful delivery medium; but by itself, it is only a vehicle (Gale and Schneider, 8).

What Was Learned

Experience to date with Interactive Dígame indicates that (1) the instructional design process and its relationship to learning theory needs to be rethought and revised, (2) the entire notion of "authoring" needs to be considered carefully along with changes in video production, and (3) programming tools need to be developed that will reduce costs and make interactive video a technology accessible to a wider range of language teachers.

Readers interested in further information about any of the IAV projects reported above may contact the author at E-509 Harris Fine Arts Center, Brigham Young University, Provo, Utah 84602.

References, Macario, Montevidisco, and Interactive Dígame

1. Gale, Larrie E. "A Theoretical Perspective for Using Interactive Videodiscs in Instruction," pp. 378-89 in Laurin F. Lewis and Benjamin Feinstein, eds., *Proceedings of the International Conference on Courseware Design and Evaluation.* Ramat Gan, Israel: Israel Association for Computers in Education, 1986.
2. _____. "Computer-Assisted Production Procedures for Interactive Videodiscs." Paper presented at the Annual Conference of AECT (Association for Educational Communications and Technology), New Orleans, January 1983.
3. _____. "Montevidisco: The Anecdotal History of an Interactive Videodisc." *CALICO* 1, 1 (1983) 42-46.
4. _____. "Results of Using Montevidisco." Occasional Technical Report. Provo, UT: Brigham Young University, David O. McKay Institute, June 1984.
5. _____, and Karl Barksdale. "1987 Results from Using Interactive Dígame in the Classroom." Unpublished Report, Department of Communication, Brigham Young University, 1987.
6. _____, and Karl Barksdale. "The Development and Formative Evaluation of Interactive Dígame Courseware." Paper presented at the Southwest Conference on Language Teaching, Phoenix, AZ, February 1986.
7. _____, and Bruce L. Brown. "A Theory of Learning and Skill Acquisition Applied to Interactive Video: Activities at the David O. McKay Institute, Brigham Young University." *Studies in Language Learning,* 5, 1 (1985) :105-14.
8. _____, and Edward W. Schneider. "Interactive Video: Medium or Pedagogy?" Working Paper for The Technology Study Group of the Fund for the Improvement of Post-Secondary Education. Department of Education, Washington, DC, 1986.
9. _____, David D. William, and D. William Quinn. "Evaluation of the Effectiveness and Use of Student-Controlled Interactive Videodiscs." Paper presented at the annual meeting of the Evaluation Research Society, Chicago, October 1983.

Vendors' Addresses

IBM, 1801 South Federal Highway, Del Rey Beach, FL 33444.
3M, Optical Recording Project. Building 225-45, 3M Center, St. Paul, MN 55144-1000.
Sony, 9 West 57th Street, New York, NY 10019.

8

USAFA Interactive Study in Spanish

Maj. Miguel Verano
United States Air Force Academy

Introduction

Technological applications to foreign language instruction continue to proliferate. New technologies appear and progress so quickly that they present a constant challenge to educators to stay abreast. Interactive videodisc (IAV) applied to second-language teaching and learning is one of the relatively new technologies that promise to provide the qualitative difference that many educators claim to be essential but find lacking in foreign language classrooms—interaction.

Depending on lesson design, interactive videodisc can display instructional video and present students with questions, vocabulary lists, video replays, hints, and explanatory statements, among other instructional strategies. An interactive videodisc system is a synthesis of the visual dimension of the videodisc and the vast storage and retrieval capabilities of the computer. DeBloois (6) clarifies further that an interactive videodisc system is not just a merging of video and computer media, but that an entirely new medium arises with characteristics that are different from each of the composites. Howe (8) calls IAV "the most powerful instructional tool [available]" (p. 8).

The Importance of Interaction

Rosenbaum (15) reports no more than four or five linguistic interactions between the teacher and each learner in a typical fifty-minute language class of about fifteen students; in an entire two-semester first-year course a student normally participates in no more than four or five hundred foreign language interchanges, considerably less than the average made in a single day between two people using their native language.

Educators recognize a difference in learning between students who are passive during instruction and those who are active (Anandam and Kelly, 2; Mahlios and Bromley, 11; Schrupp et al., 16). Rivers (13) asserts that "to promote interaction in another language, we must maintain a lively attention and active participation among our students" (p. xiv). According to Rivers, "interaction implies both reception and expression of messages" (p. xiv).

Interaction, as it relates to computer-based instruction, entails a response by the learner to stimuli in an instructional program. That same program should be capable of adapting to the needs of the learner and the content of the lesson. Nelson et al. (12) writes that "interaction is perhaps the most effective teaching technique possessed by the human teacher" (p. 30). "Interaction," as an instructional strategy, can be extended to the nonhuman teacher as well, according to Bosco (3), who explains that a videodisc can imitate three types of hypothetical teachers:

> The first teacher lectures to the students and permits no interruptions for questions or comments from students. The second lectures but at particular points in the lecture stops and ... asks a student to gauge the extent of understanding of the presentation .... The third teacher is involved in continuous dialogue with students, stopping in mid-sentence to respond to cues that some students are not getting the desired understanding (p. 17).

Bosco's rationale provides a basis for the questions the study reported herein was designed to answer: What would be the differences in effect on achievement and retention when Spanish language instructional material is presented via videodisc in a linear, a segmented, and an interactive fashion (Bosco's first, second, and third hypothetical teachers)? That is, what effect would increasing the level of interaction have on learning outcome and retention? More specifically:

1. What would be the difference in effect on achievement, as measured by a criterion-based posttest, between (a) questions introduced between segments of a Spanish language instructional videodisc and (b) the material presented in an interactive manner, with questions, feedback on incorrect answers, video replay and hint options, explanatory statements, and vocabulary lists?

2. What would be the difference in effect on retention levels, as measured by a delayed administration of the same criterion-based posttest under the conditions in the preceding question?

3. What would be the effect on achievement and retention if students viewed the same materials without interruption in a linear fashion (typical of the presentation of film and videotaped materials in language classes) as opposed to students who proceed via segmented or interactive study, as defined above?

Experimental comparisons based upon hypotheses of zero differences between groups were undertaken for data collected from the segmented study, interactive study, and control groups. Differential time on task constrained comparisons between the linear group and all others to a simple description of results (Verano, 17).

The Study

Following a variation of the randomized control group posttest-only design (Isaac and Michael, 9, p. 69), students (N = 92) were randomly selected from the seven sections of the fall 1986 basic Spanish 131 course at the U.S. Air Force Academy (Table 1), and then randomly assigned in equal numbers (n = 23) to a group included for descriptive purposes (linear), or to one of two experimental groups (segmented, interactive), or to a control group (Figure 1). The results reported herein reflect data collected before, during, and after the two-week run of the experiment.

Table 1. Biographical characteristics of sample.

	GpI	GpII	GpIII	GpIV
Sex				
Male	23	20	22	22
Female	0	3	1	1
Total	23	23	23	23
Age				
18 yrs.	7	6	6	13
19 yrs.	12	13	12	9
20 yrs.	1	2	4	0
21 yrs.	1	1	0	0
22 yrs.	2	1	1	1
Total	23	23	23	23
Mean	19	19	19	18.5
Previous Spanish				
None	11	10	12	9
2 semesters	6	7	7	4
3 semesters	1	0	0	1
4 semesters	4	6	3	9
5 semesters	1	0	0	0
8 semesters	0	0	1	0
Total	23	23	23	23
Mean	1.56	1.65	1.47	2.04
Other languages				
None	18	16	17	19
1-2 yrs.	5	7	6	4
Total	23	23	23	23
Mean Academic Composite*	3034	3027	3053	3098

*A numerical representation of a cadet's potential for success at the U.S. Air Force Academy derived from Scholastic Aptitude Test (SAT) scores, high school grades, athletic participation, and leadership positions. Approximate possible high score is 4000.

Figure 1. Variation of the randomized control-group posttest-only design

Treatment	Immediate Posttest	Delayed Posttest
Descriptive (R) Group 1 (*n*= 23)	linear	T[1]	T[2]
Experimental (R) Group 2 (*n*= 23)	segmented	T[1]	T[2]
Experimental (R) Group 3 (*n*= 23)	interactive	T[1]	T[2]
Control (R) Group (*n*= 23)	English	T[1]	T[2]

(R) = random assignment

Implementation and Procedures

The videodisc used for the experiment was mastered, with permission, from the first two edited lessons of the British Broadcasting Corporation's *Zarabanda* film series. *Zarabanda* contains a series of short dialogs intertwined by a dramatic story line resembling a soap opera. The *Zarabanda* material was selected for the study because it teaches the kind of Spanish beginning students will most likely encounter in real life.

Group I, the linear videodisc instruction group (descriptive), was presented Spanish instructional material via videodisc in a passive manner. Group II, the segmented videodisc instruction group (experimental), was presented the same material as Group I with the addition of inserted true-false and multiple-choice questions on content at selected breakpoints in the story line. Students in this group received limited feedback in the form of remarks such as "Correct" or "Wrong." Students in Group II could not return to any portion of the lesson with which they had difficulty nor attempt a missed question again. The lesson for Group III, the interactive videodisc instruction group (experimental), was interrupted by the same questions at the same breakpoints as Group II with the additional benefit of feedback on incorrect choices, vocabulary lists, video replay, and hint options for remediation. The program also provided explanatory statements on correct choices. Group IV (control), was presented with material in English totally unrelated to the material presented to the previous three groups. By administering the posttest to Group IV, information that would normally be derived from the administration of a pretest was obtained without prejudicing the results.

All students took a 40-item true-false (10 questions) and multiple-choice (30 questions) criterion-based posttest. A delayed posttest, using the same instrument, was administered to all groups one month later. A coefficient Alpha procedure was used to determine the reliability of the test (.78). In addition, all students completed pre/post experiment questionnaires.

The brevity of the lessons and the relatively short time allocated for the experiment precluded testing for proficiency. Furthermore, students were honor-bound not to discuss the material during the course of the experiment, which denied them practice opportunities apart from contact with the material during the computer-driven lessons.

Summary of Findings

The analyses of the data (ANOVA, Tukey HSD) indicated that the results of the immediate and delayed posttests for Group III, the interactive videodisc instruction group, were significantly higher ($p < .0001$) than all other groups, as shown in Tables 2 and 3. (Tables 4 and 5 provide a summary of ANOVA results for the immediate and delayed posttests; other analyses are reported in Verano, 17.)

The results are consistent with the findings of Schrupp et al. (16), in which students of German presented material in an interactive fashion outscored students who watched the same film in a linear and passive fashion. Results of another study (Abrams and Streit, 1) using interactive video compared to linear video in the teaching of basic photography skills also agree with the results of the present study.

Table 2. Means and standard deviations for achievement scores on the immediate posttest

Treatment Group	n	Mean	Percent	SD
Gp I (linear)	23	16.65	41.62	3.86
Gp II (segmented)	23	19.73	49.32*	4.63
Gp III (interactive)	23	26.26	65.65**	4.97
Gp IV (control)	23	14.00	35.00	3.19

*$P < .05$, significantly different from Gp IV only
**$P < .0001$, significantly different from all groups

Table 3. Means and standard deviations for achievement scores on the delayed posttest

Treatment Group	n	Mean	Percent	SD
Gp I (linear)	23	14.74	36.85	3.71
Gp II (segmented)	23	17.78	44.45	6.67
Gp III (interactive)	23	23.04	57.60*	7.43
Gp IV (control)	23	15.21	38.02	3.80

*$P < .0001$

Table 4. Summary of analysis of variance for the immediate posttest

Source	df	SS	MS	F	p
Between groups	3	1924.46	641.48	35.95	$< .0001$
Within groups	88	1570.08	17.84		

df = degrees of freedom, SS = sum of squares, MS = mean squares, F = F ratio, P probability

Table 5. Summary of analysis of variance for the delayed posttest

Source	df	SS	MS	F	p
Between groups	3	771.39	257.13	7.87	$< .0001$
Within groups	88	2874.08	32.66		

Group II, the segmented videodisc instruction group, scored significantly higher ($p < .05$) than the control group on the immediate posttest, but not on the delayed posttest, suggesting that the insertion of questions at selected breakpoints in the story line improved learning as was found in the study conducted by Kurtz et al. (10). However, when the same questions were asked of Group III with the addition of feedback on incorrect choices, vocabulary lists, and video replays and hint options for remediation, the results were dramatically better. The capability of the videodisc to access video materials randomly and instantly probably facilitated learning as was the case in previous studies (Bunderson et al., 4; Crotty, 5; Ebner et al., 7).

Results of the postexperiment questionnaire indicated that there were no significant differences between groups in attitudes toward Spanish, Spanish-speaking people, Spanish culture, or the technology itself. The postexperiment questionnaire also showed that students in Group III, the interactive videodisc instruction group, made frequent use of student options during instruction, including video replays and hints for remediation. The capability of the interactive videodisc lesson to focus the student's attention on a particular facet of linguistic data presented in the *Zarabanda* film by asking a question, and then offering video replays or hint options a second or third time, if needed, appears to be the factor that best explains the superior results obtained by Group III.

Given that all groups spent the same amount of time at the computer carrels during instruction, the actual time that Group II spent working with material was only three to five minutes less per lesson than Group III. One may conclude thus that interaction, a concept that includes the element of practice, is most likely the factor that best accounts for the superior results of the interactive videodisc instruction group.

Group I (linear study) was included in the investigation for descriptive purposes only. Group I was exposed to *Zarabanda* for less time per lesson than Groups II and III owing to the nature of the presentation of the materials. Determining whether the difference in achievement is attributable to difference in treatment or time on task becomes difficult. Nevertheless, Group I's mean score (14.74) was lower than that of the control group (15.21) on the delayed posttest (Table 3). These results suggest that for Group I: (1) little learning occurred during the linear showing of *Zarabanda*, an instructional approach to film presentation that very closely resembles that used in many traditional foreign language classrooms, (2) a large amount of guessing apparently transpired on both the immediate and the delayed posttests, and (3) the material was not retained because little learning initially took place, possibly due to the short exposure time. Second, the standard deviations for Groups II and III on the delayed posttest (Table 3) were much larger (SD 6.67 and SD 7.43, respectively) than on the immediate posttest (SD 4.63 and SD 4.97—Table 2) suggesting that a more heterogeneous distribution of test scores from the mean occurred as a function of time away from the material.

Conclusion

This study and previous studies involving interactive video and CAI are beginning to confirm intuitions and support the theoretical framework concerning the effectiveness of these emerging instructional technologies. The present study offers evidence in favor of the active involvement of the student in the learning process and highlights the concept of mediated interaction as a crucial element to improve the foreign language teaching/learning paradigm. Perhaps equally important has been the integration of a number of Robinson et al.'s (14) pedagogical and answer-judging hypotheses (see chapter 5, pp. 113-18), in the lesson design found in the interactive treatment for this study, making it the first comprehensive application of these hypotheses within an interactive videodisc setting.

Based on the results of this study and previous studies involving interactive video, one may postulate that interactive technology holds the potential to provide qualitative improvements in foreign language teaching and learning. Improvements in many areas of second-language instruction are possible with careful design and the judicious use of the capabilities of interactive technology. The key lies not necessarily with the media, even though the media act as a facilitating tool, but rather with the quality of the interactions within each lesson and the lesson design itself.

Readers interested in further details of this study may write to the author at HQ USAFA/DFF, United States Air Force Academy, Colorado, 80840.

References, USAFA Interactive Study in Spanish

1. Abrams, Arnie, and Les Streit. "Effectiveness of Interactive Video in Teaching Basic Photography." *T.H.E. Journal* 14, 2 (1986) : 92-96.
2. Anandam, K., and D. Kelly. "Guided Exposure to Microcomputers: Interactive Video Programs." Miami, FL: Miami-Dade Community College (1981) [EDRS: ED 205 238.]
3. Bosco, James J. "Interactive Video: Educational Tool or Toy?" *Educational Technology* 24, 4 (1984) :13-19.
4. Bunderson, C. V., J. B. Olsen, and B. Baillo. "Proof of Concept Demonstration and Comparative Evaluation of a Prototype Intelligent Videodisc System." Orem, UT: WICAT, Inc., 1981. [NSF SED 7900 794.]
5. Crotty, Jill. "Instruction via an Intelligent Videodisc System versus Classroom Instruction for Beginning College French Students: A Comparative Experiment." Unpublished Ph.D. dissertation, University of Kansas (Lawrence), 1984.
6. DeBlois, Michael, ed. *Videodisc/Microcomputer Courseware Design.* Englewood Cliffs, NJ: Educational Technology Publications, 1982.
7. Ebner, Donald G., Diane T. Manning, Franklin R. Brooks, James V. Mahoney, Henry T. Lippert, and Paul M. Balson. "Videodiscs Can Improve Instructional Efficiency." *Instructional Innovator* 29, 6 (1984) :26-28.
8. Howe, Samuel F. "Interactive Video: Salt and Pepper Technology." *Media and Methods* 21, 5 (1985) :8-20.
9. Isaac, S., and W. B. Michael. *Handbook in Research and Evaluation.* 2nd ed. San Diego, CA: Edits, 1985.
10. Kurtz, Albert K., Jeanette S. Walter, and Henry Brenner, Comp. *The Effects of Inserted Questions and Statements on Film Learning.* University Park: Pennsylvania State University, 1950.

11. Mahlios, M. C., and K. D. Bromley, "Students and Teacher Bidirectional Classroom Behavior: Effects on Classroom Interaction, Achievement and Attitude." Paper presented at the annual meeting of the Association of Teacher Educators, New Orleans, January 1984.
12. Nelson, G. E., Jean R. Ward, Samuel H. Desch, and Roy Kaplow. "Two New Strategies for Computer-Assisted Language Instruction (CALI)." *Foreign Language Annals* 9, 1 (1976) :28-37.
13. Rivers, Wilga, ed. *Interactive Language Teaching.* New York: Cambridge, 1987.
14. Robinson, Gail, John Underwood, Wilga Rivers, José Hernández, Carollyn Rudesill, and Clare Malnik Enseñat. *Computer-Assisted Instruction in Foreign Language Education.* San Francisco: Center for Language & Crosscultural Skills, 1985. [EDRS: ED 262 626]
15. Rosenbaum, Peter S. "The Computer as a Learning Environment for Foreign Language Instruction." *Foreign Language Annals* 2, 4 (1969): 457-65.
16. Schrupp, David M., Michael D. Bush, and Gunther A. Mueller. "Klavier im Haus—an Interactive Experiment in Foreign Language Instruction." *CALICO Journal* 1, 2 (1983) :17-21.
17. Verano, Miguel. "Achievement and Retention of Spanish Presented via Videodisc in Linear, Segmented and Interactive Modes." Unpublished Ph.D. dissertation, University of Texas (Austin), 1987.

9

The Annapolis Interactive Video Project

Gladys M. Rivera-La Scala

United States Naval Academy

The Annapolis Interactive Video Project, begun in 1985, has three immediate objectives: (1) to develop interactive video (IAV) programs through the use of videodiscs and the computer to enhance the learning of foreign languages at beginning, intermediate, and advanced levels; (2) to incorporate these programs as lesson materials in existing curricula; and (3) to develop a system for continuous evaluation of the effectiveness of this new approach to language learning at these levels.

Members of the U.S. Naval Academy faculty working on this project are Michael C. Halbig, chairman of the Language Studies Department; the author, 1986-87 project director and author of Spanish programs; Helen E. Purkitt, chief evaluator; John D. Yarbro, author of French programs; Sharon G. Dahlgren, 1985-86 project director and author of Spanish programs; William H. Fletcher, author of Spanish programs; Enrique Márquez, author of Spanish programs; John A. Hutchins, operations manager of USNA earth satellite receiving station; Christopher D. Buck, programmer.

The first IAV lessons, completed in 1986 and successfully integrated into the third-year French course, used TV material from France received via Canada by the Naval Academy earth satellite station. Although work continues on IAV lessons in French and Russian—and German eventually will be included—the project is now concentrating on beginning and intermediate Spanish.

Students in the first-year Spanish courses at the Academy began using IAV-based lessons in the fall of 1987 to practice listening comprehension and to a lesser extent reading skills outside the classroom through controlled exposure to the native speech provided by foreign language television programs. This report describes the rationale, scope and content of this undertaking, and outlines a plan for its evaluation.

Foreign Language Telecasts via Satellite _____

Foreign language telecasts provide listeners with samples of authentic speech—that is, speech aimed at native speakers and not at language students—in situations that native speakers encounter on a daily basis. From this standpoint, such video materials can be called "found" texts, as opposed to those termed "didactic," which simulate authentic listening situations for the express purpose of teaching students certain aspects of the foreign language and culture. Since found texts are not in and of themselves tailored to the learning needs of beginning and intermediate students, they must be treated as raw materials from which video sequences appropriate for lessons at these levels are selected and edited carefully before transfer to videodisc. The Annapolis IAV Project applies the following criteria in the selection process:

1. The content of the programs must be of significant cultural as well as linguistic value.
2. The visual elements must support directly and, whenever possible, add to the oral communication.
3. The quality of the audio and video must be in the "excellent" range, with exceptions made for programs in which the image contains some static but the audio is very clear and the content represents salient characteristics of the culture and language.

Programs judged marginal in some of the above aspects are edited as needed to form a new, shortened version. Although editing video materials requires much time and skill, the process converts a basically unusable program into a potential didactic tool.

To date, the Academy has made five videodiscs from TV segments recorded via the Annapolis earth satellite receiving station—three in Spanish, one in French, and one in Russian, and plans are underway to produce others.[1] These five videodiscs contain a wide variety of oral texts that illustrate historical and contemporary aspects of the society and culture to which they relate.

In the case of Spanish, for example, interviews recorded from Mexico touch on such subjects as problems of urbanization, Mexican elections and politics, and child development. The speakers in these interviews represent different socioeconomic groups, professions, and regions, from the poor illiterate land squatter in Guadalajara to the upper-class, middle-aged politician or child psychologist in Mexico City. From a linguistic standpoint, such texts give listeners exposure to free-flowing, unplanned discourse characterized by repetitions, false starts, rephrasings, elaborations, meaningless additions, interruptions, more errors and repairs, contractions, and less complex syntactical patterns. In addition, these segments reveal

---

1. Distribution of these discs is limited to the Department of Defense in accordance with copyright restrictions that govern the use and distribution of such materials for experimental and educational applications by the U.S. government.

mouth movements, facial expressions, and other aspects of body language. Their level of difficulty varies from novice-low to superior on the ACTFL proficiency scale.

In contrast, advertisements, songs, and TV lessons consist mostly of planned discourse or written texts delivered in oral form. Commercials and public-service announcements of ten to sixty seconds in length, for example, use fragments of language that are repeated often to communicate a specific message. Moreover, the content of this consumer-oriented language reflects popular culture and gives insights into the daily concerns of a people. Announcements that encourage public participation in preserving natural resources, developing literacy, and spreading understanding of the country's culture and history reveal, in part, the value system of a society.

A few songs, judged to be musically, linguistically, and culturally appropriate, also constitute excellent texts for comprehension. The popular "Eres Tú," for example, offers listeners practice with the familiar form of *ser* in the present indicative tense, exposure to some common vocabulary, and a chance to hear a chorus from the Yucatán peninsula.

Lessons taken from the Mexico City's Educational TV station, Channel 13, deal with the origin of Spanish words, the creation of neologisms, and with problems of orthography. Targeted for Mexican junior high and high school students, the program features an experienced instructor, a pupil, graphic and video displays, and a computer, and it employs language used regularly in a Mexican classroom. Linguistically and culturally these programs are particularly good for the mid-novice through the intermediate-high or advanced levels on the ACTFL scale where more control over linguistic structure is needed. They also offer students from another culture a direct insight into the kind of instruction young people may receive in a Spanish-speaking country.

Newscasts on issues including problems of immigration along the southern border of the United States, emigration of Jews from the Soviet Union, plans for modernization of the Mexican Navy, weather reports, sports, and a *corrida* provide excellent listening practice for students at the intermediate-high through the advanced and superior levels on the ACTFL scale. Documentaries on such topics as the Spanish fortifications and ports in the Americas and excerpts from speeches such as that of President Alan García on his political philosophy for leading Perú are best suited for the advanced and superior levels. The speech in these telecasts is rehearsed, albeit with moments of spontaneous utterances, and delivered at a relatively fast pace. The discourse, however, contains few instances of regional or social dialect and is an appropriate example of a stable linguistic environment for teaching standard Spanish.

In each program a strong relationship between the video and the audio content helps the learner grasp the topic and understand the gist of the message more quickly and easily. While the newscaster is reporting on the maneuvers of the Mexican navy, for example, a video clip displays the ships involved in the exercise. In the weather report, when the temperatures of certain cities are given, a chart with their names and their temperature is flashed simultaneously on the TV screen. Thus, the visual cues reinforce the oral message, creating a stronger and more complete comprehension environment.

Use of the Computer

The information-processing capabilities of the computer have been added to mediate use of the videodisc materials at the Academy. The computer, in conjunction with sophisticated hardware and software systems, allows students to receive instruction on a personalized basis and to perform tasks that will aid them in acquiring or refining listening and reading comprehension and, to a lesser extent, the other skills. The computer is programmed to control the way in which materials are presented and manipulated so that they become effective tools for instruction and learning. Students (and teachers) are able to access any segment of an IAV lesson in two and a half seconds or less and to hold them "freeze frame" as needed, or to replay them at will. The computer also permits immediate access to help options, such as transcriptions, definitions of words and phrases, explanations of items or concepts, comprehension checks with hints that guide them to complete understanding (or in the case of questions from the text, to the correct response). This computer-controlled interactivity between student and IAV materials thus creates a structured environment that can be repeated until the knowledge and skills targeted for mastery are acquired.

Integration of IAV Lessons into the Spanish Curriculum

A common cause of reported failures in computer-aided instruction is a lack of integration of the CAI materials with course content and objectives. Few students are willing to work with programs that do not improve their performance in courses they are taking. This problem has been addressed at the Naval Academy by analyzing the language and content of the video sequences to determine which, in turn, are appropriate for each unit of a particular course. Designed around one or more of these sequences, each IAV lesson contains specific learning objectives that relate directly to the unit it is meant to serve. For example, two video sequences chosen for lesson 1 in the Beginning Spanish course at the Academy include three Latin Americans who identify themselves and their professions. The lesson content thus matches the goal for Unit 1: to learn to understand and use the Spanish system of names in personal identification.

Students work on each week's IAV lesson in the Academy's language laboratory. Contact time with the materials varies between twenty and forty minutes depending on the individual. The completion of each IAV assignment is counted in place of the customary required listening assignment on audiocassette. The linguistic and cultural knowledge students acquire through the use of IAV programs to develop their receptive skills is further reinforced through speaking and writing activities inside and outside the classroom. These activities and projects require students to use in diverse and creative ways the facts, ideas, and general concepts gained from the IAV experience. The integration of these lessons with the first-year Spanish syllabus has been completed; efforts are underway to accomplish the same for the second-year Spanish curriculum.

Design for Evaluation

Starting in 1987, acquisition and retention of listening comprehension among students enrolled in the IAV-based Beginning Spanish course will be compared with students not using IAV. Experimental (IAV) and control (traditional) groups have been established for comparison purposes. Each group will be tested and tracked for two years from the beginning of its first year to the end of its second year in the spring of 1989. In the fall of 1988 another tracking cycle will begin with a new group of first-year students, who will also be tracked for two years through the spring of 1990. The study is designed to reveal the differences between the two treatment groups as well as to test for possible cumulative effects of exposure to this type of interactivity. In short, the comparison will attempt to answer the question: How effective is interactive video using found text and computer mediation in improving the listening-comprehension and reading skills of Academy students?

Individuals interested in receiving a fact sheet on this project may write to: Director, Annapolis Interactive Video Project, Language Studies Department, U.S. Naval Academy, Annapolis, MD 21402-5030.

10

SSI:
Survival Spanish Interactive©

Alfred W. Jensen
University of Idaho

Mary Ann Lyman
Five Colleges Language Resource Center
Amherst, Massachusetts

Introduction

Technology promises to lighten faculty workloads and increase the efficiency of student learning by offering students immediate feedback and correction of errors. Students appear to enjoy learning a language via technology (Hope, 2), and learn at least as effectively with the computer as without (Lyman, 3). Many studies have examined the use of computers in second-language learning and laboratory settings (Hart, 1), but few have considered the effectiveness of interactive video. The implementation of Survival Spanish Interactive (SSI), a new course at the University of Idaho, demonstrates the versatility and promise of one type of interactive video as another adjunct to the emerging technology for language teaching.

In 1984, the University of Idaho received a grant from the U.S. Department of Education to develop an interactive video approach to beginning language teaching. The grant involved creating a computer program to be joined with a video program tailoring instruction to individual learner's needs. The delivery mode was to be videotape rather than videodisc. The program that was developed lends itself to videodisc applications, however, and the availability of that format is being considered.

Background

Designed to offer individualized help to learners needing tutorials or extra practice with the language, SSI was conceived as the laboratory component or as a stand-alone Spanish course that would correspond to the typical first-year curriculum at the university level. Funds allotted to the project, however, were not sufficient to create the videotaped materials for the year-long course; thus, *Survival Spanish,* a commercial video language course produced by Miami-Dade Community College (4) was chosen and the University of Idaho negotiated the rights to use this preexisting video series in a CALL/IAV-mediated program for the teaching of Spanish.

Videotaped Material

The 1984 version of *Survival Spanish* included thirty video and audio cassettes, a text-workbook for the student, and a teacher's manual. Six additional lessons were added in 1986. The title of the series is justified by the following topics offered in modular design and reflecting functional/notional concepts: retail sales; food, medical and travel services; domestic needs; and personal associations. Each color videotape runs thirty minutes and is available in VHS and Beta formats. The grammar content is equivalent to that of a first-year text, excluding the subjunctive (now incorporated in the 1986 supplement).

Each lesson holds dialogs and communicative activities to nurture beginning conversational Spanish and allows the student to hear clear pronunciation, answer questions, and repeat new sounds and words, comparing his or her speech to the native speaker. Graphic overlays (subscripts) on the video screen allow the student to view given words, phrases, grammatical summaries, or verb conjugations at the same time that these structures are voiced or explained. These visual cues also appear while the native speaker reiterates the expected response, a strategy that allows the learner who processes speech more effectively via the written word to associate verbal and visual stimuli.

The situational dialogs, acted and spoken by native speakers of Spanish, are followed by a more detailed explanation in English of underlying structural and lexical concepts and constitute a pool from which new vocabulary and topics are drawn for instruction. A review of phrases from previous dialogs provides an additional link to past lessons. Each lesson tape holds between four and five concepts or activities; each in turn contains five to seven minutes of video.

Implementation

The technology for the computer interactive component of SSI requires few equipment purchases: (1) Apple II, II-Plus, or IIe microcomputer with at least a single disk drive, (2) an interactive video interface card, BCD Model 450 (BCD Associates), (3) a compatible videotape recorder or player (most Panasonic U-MATIC or Industrial VHS VTRs with a 34-pin edit control connector, and Sony U-Matic or Industrial Beta VTRs with a 20-pin edit control connector will interface properly with the BCD 450), and (4) a color TV monitor with separate audio and video input jacks.

The computer "controls" the videotape player by calling up certain predetermined frame codes of the video program. Depending upon the learner's needs, certain portions of the video program can be played on command. The computer thus serves as a "monitor," reacting to responses, offering immediate feedback, and guiding the student to remedial video sections of the lesson(s) as needed. In this way, a student may repeat difficult sections or proceed beyond others, while the computer in turn "reads" student responses to exercises and invites or leads the learner to an appropriate continuation. As a result, no two students will view the program in exactly the same manner, nor will the same quiz items appear for any given student repeating the same lesson.

Survival Spanish Becomes Interactive

The creation of SSI was accomplished through a team approach to software development. The director of media services at the University of Idaho was responsible for technical advice, preparing the video programs with frame codes, acquiring and maintaining the equipment, and as project director in charge of writing the grant, disseminating results and communicating with funding agencies. A professor of Spanish served as the content expert. A professor of French trained in CAI developed the instructional design and programming sequences. Computer scientists and experts in instructional design were also consulted throughout the project.

Using SUPERPILOT, a Pascal-based authoring language, a "stamp" approach to handling errors, feedback, and basic lesson structure was developed that greatly aided in the completion of the sixty-diskette software component. The "stamp" served as a template. Consisting of a single modifiable stock pattern, the template was transferred onto each initialized blank diskette. This process defined a unified and consistent system of treating the lesson material for each unit. For example, the student unable to perform well on a given communicative exercise quickly became familiar with the various possibilities of assistance (video, related content activities, help screens, etc.), and with what to expect from an error message. The result for the course writers was a unified approach to creating and updating the lessons as the product developed. This "stamp approach" also provided a foundation for the construction of new variables for each succeeding lesson, as well as offering a familiar pattern to the student who had to master a variety of operational procedures in order to use the materials efficiently.

The combination of these numerous possibilities, in turn, defined a truly individualized approach to language learning.

Computer-based exercises developed at the University of Idaho originally followed a pattern designed to adhere to a cadre of elements that researchers felt were essential interrelated components—new and old vocabulary and underlying grammatical principles related to topical functions. The subject-matter experts working on the team were challenged to mesh these elements into the video program in a truly interactive format. In the resulting computer programs, the answers (or variables selected for interaction) became the very words and phrases in Spanish voiced in the video materials; that is, the linguistic protocols voiced in *Survival Spanish* became the vertebrae on which the programs were constructed.

Courseware

Two diskettes accompany each video lesson in SSI. The first offers a menu of exercises based on the topical segments of the videotape. For example, a student working on lesson 9 on eating could choose among the following topics: (1) review of a conversation in a restaurant, (2) dialog study related to the same topic, (3) review of the verb *estar*, (4) use of the verb *ser*, (5) conversation using possession in Spanish, (6) telling time, and (7) vocabulary enrichment. Within each of these topics, the student may choose among watching the video segment, participating in exercises (multiple-choice, question-answer, fill-in-the-blank, and short sentence or phrase translation from English to Spanish), and obtaining a variety of study helps.

The second diskette consists of a chapter review that incorporates sample exercises from each segment of the menu and a chapter exam of the same format mediated by a random number generator that creates a unique test each time the chapter exam is taken. Both the chapter review and the chapter exam are scored and appropriate feedback given to the learner.

In summary, the courseware for SSI was developed to meet the needs of a varying learner population. Because of its modular design, any or all of the lessons may be used on demand and the courses can be tailored to fit the needs of junior high to postsecondary learners.

Evaluation

SSI has occupied a place as one section of beginning Spanish at the University of Idaho since the 1985-86 school year. Limitations in laboratory space and equipment restrict the expansion of this ratio for the moment; nevertheless, continuous informal evaluation of the effectiveness of the course has been established.

During the first year of the study, the interactive component was used in place of two periods of fifty minutes each in a beginning class meeting four times each week. Students in the four-hour course (N=30) were assigned to either the regular class (meeting four times each week) or to the CAI/IAV group. The latter (N=16) met twice weekly in the laboratory and twice weekly with the other students (N=14) in the traditional classroom.

Comparisons between the two groups (Table 1) show that after controlling for experience (number of semesters of previous study of Spanish) and scholastic ability (as measured by the Scholastic Aptitude Test), the regular class members surprisingly performed better than the CAI/IAV students on the course-final examination ($p > .02$). Although the regular class members had significantly more experience in Spanish, previous language training was not the main factor that affected performance on the final exam. Rather, although the SSI materials demonstrate high content validity with respect to the scope and content of a typical beginning Spanish course, the ratio of media-guided versus teacher-guided instruction apparently worked against achievement, at least as measured by the final examination. Whatever the case, these data, based on a small sample, are but a preliminary indication that further work is needed to identify the most efficient frequency of use with interactive instructional materials before offering them to a larger number of classes.

Table 1. Group differences for experience, SAT scores, and final exam scores

	Noncomputer Group Mean	Computer Group Mean	Sign. of F
Experience	4.286	3.250	.014*
SAT Score	99.143	103.938	.197
Final Exam	87.214	84.250	.177

Analysis of covariance of final examination scores by treatment group

Source of Variation	F	Sign. of F
Covariates		
Experience	8.72	.001*
SAT Scores	0.18	.678
Main Effects	16.03	.000*
Group Treatment	5.91	.022*

* $p < .02$, two-tailed test of significance

Subsequent use of SSI (1986-87) has focused on a format in which students meet three times a week in the regular classroom and schedule on their own a once-a-week session in the language laboratory where they study SSI materials independently at CAI/IAV work stations. Data collection is underway to evaluate if this ratio of lab-to-class with SSI will have any differential effects on learning. In the meantime, it is clear that the independent scheduling of the fourth day in the laboratory has enabled some students to enroll in Spanish who otherwise would not have been able to fit the course into their schedules.

The original goals of SSI were to increase the efficiency and "individualization" of learning through technology, and to provide a number of options that would allow for greater flexibility between classroom and laboratory in the teaching of Spanish. While the jury on efficiency is still out, it seems clear from this small-scale pilot study that the students appreciated the flexibility of scheduling that the CAI/IAV version of *Survival Spanish* afforded them, and were able to learn from the SSI materials as well as students who followed traditional classroom models.

Readers interested in receiving further information about SSI are invited to contact the authors at the University of Idaho, Department of Foreign Languages and Literatures, Moscow, Idaho 83843 (Jensen), and Five College Foreign Language Resource Center, The University of Massachusetts, 102 Bartlett Hall, Amherst, MA 01003 (Lyman).

References, SSI©

1. Hart, Robert S. "Language Study and the PLATO System." *Studies in Language Learning* 3, 1 (1981): 1-24.

2. Hope, Geoffrey R. "Elementary French Computer-Assisted Instruction." *Foreign Language Annals* 15, 5 (1982) :347-53.

3. Lyman, Mary Ann. "Comparison of Foreign Language Learning with Computer-Assisted and Non-Computer Assisted Study," pp. 296-300 in *ADCIS 28th International Conference Proceedings.* Bellingham, WA: Association for the Development of Computer-Based Instructional Systems, 1986.

4. *Survival Spanish.* Miami: Miami-Dade Community College, 1984.

11

LLD:
The Language Learning Disc

Joan Rubin

Joan Rubin Associates, Berkeley, California

Introduction

The Language Learning Disc is a two-sided (one-hour) level 3 interactive videodisc with five accompanying diskettes, which together provide an average of eight hours of instruction.

The purpose of this instructional material is to help English-speaking adults "learn how to learn" a foreign language. Many adults (high school and above) are "language phobic" owing to a lack of knowledge about language learning or owing previous unsatisfactory experiences. In addition, even relatively good learners often feel they can improve their learning rate. The goal of the Language Learning Disc is to dispel anxiety and to enhance learning skills by helping viewers recognize how to use more effectively the knowledge and learning skills they already have, and by helping them define and develop efficient strategies to learn a foreign language.

Learners bring different kinds of knowledge, experience, and learning styles to each learning task. Thus, knowing how to organize information and experiences so as to maximize their own learning efforts is essential in effectively learning something new. Each learner must accomplish this learning independently according to his or her individual knowledge, experience, and learning style. The same holds true for learning a foreign language. Successful second-language learners need to be independent, skillful, and informed problem solvers who can marshal the appropriate strategies to learn another language efficiently and well when faced with that challenge. The Language Learning Disc offers a wide variety of training and practice for this very purpose.

Background

The LLD is based on fifteen years of research on learner strategies (see Rubin, 3, for a historical perspective) to identify the strategies that successful (expert) learners use to solve their language-learning problems. Other investigators, notably O'Malley (2), have trained novice or less-successful learners to use some of these strategies to improve their language learning. The LLD has also drawn from research on developing higher-order cognitive skills that demonstrates that performance improves with training in using cognitive and metacognitive strategies (Brown and Palinscar, 1). Comparison of students using different kinds of strategies has shown progressive improvement of performance as learners (1) do exercises blind, that is with no coaching, (2) do the same exercises with cognitive coaching (e.g., use the preceding or the following word to help in filling in the blank) or (3) do the same exercises with metacognitive coaching, in which learners are encouraged to evaluate their learning (e.g., "does attending to the preceding or the following word help more in filling in the blank?").

An important component of learner training is the increase in students' awareness of the knowledge they bring to the task. Wenden (4) has identified three kinds that learners bring to learning languages: knowledge of language and communication, knowledge of the world, and knowledge of their own approach to learning. Many learners fail to realize that they already know a great deal about grammar, vocabulary, and communication. Furthermore, they often do not know how to transfer that knowledge to learning another language. Students may not realize they can use what they know about the world and about human interaction to direct their critical thinking and problem solving. For example, when dealing with particular kinds of texts, whether written or spoken, students can narrow their prediction to probable scope and content by using the rhetorical structure, visual clues, opening sentences or paragraphs, and their knowledge of the world. In reading a narrative, students can learn to anticipate sequences or cause and effect and use these schemata in working through the text. Learners need to be reminded how they filter information through what they already know as well as how this filter can help or hinder as they learn a new communicative system.

The LLD provides opportunities for learners to experiment with a wide range of strategies. Specifically, LLD users can expect to derive the following benefits from this instructional material:
1. Gain insights into their own approach to learning
2. Be able to decide on strategies appropriate to a specific task and to their purpose for learning
3. Be able to use these strategies in classroom self-study or on the job
4. Learn how to use strategies specific to reading, listening, and conversation
5. Be able to define strategies to improve their memory for language learning

6. Learn how to transfer knowledge about language and communication from one language to another
7. Be able to deal with errors more effectively

Disc Design

The LLD is divided into three main sections: (1) introduction, (2) general language-learning strategies (called language orientation and assessment center), and (3) strategies related to conversation, reading, or active listening.

In the introduction, viewers are introduced to the four main characters and to the idea of strategies. The four main characters are: (1) A military attaché assigned to Korea, (2) A plant manager assigned to Argentina, (3) A translator who will be working on Russian texts and television and radio broadcasts, (4) A Japanese sales manager who will promote Japanese pharmaceuticals in the United States. The characters are sensible, rational prototypical adults who will undergo language training in order to perform well on their jobs. They were selected to represent important aspects of successful language learning, such as the higher motivation that comes when there is an immediate need to learn a language and when the purpose of learning is clearly in mind. Each character has a compelling reason to learn the foreign language; each has a very specific language goal to reach, and each represents a carefully researched real-life career that requires second-language skills.

The characters also model how real-life students may react to learning problems that occur in the second-language classroom (or in the real world), and the techniques these learners may use to resolve them. The viewer is drawn into the plot as the actors ask relevant questions and struggle through typical situations.

In the section of the LLD for language orientation and assessment, viewers can elect exercises in one of three language areas—grammar, vocabulary, communication—or can choose a section on memory. Each of the three language areas consists of a review of the knowledge of language and learning strategies that the viewer brings to the learning situation followed by opportunities to extend that knowledge to several foreign languages.

The exercises on communication focus on problems in crosscultural transfer and illustrate how values and underlying meanings are important in understanding (and communicating) what is intended. In a segment on borrowing, for example, viewers first analyze how they vary their communication strategies to accomplish their social purposes. The exercise demonstrates how linguistic differences (formal versus informal register, word choice, information offered) reflect sociocultural appropriateness and success in accomplishing one's purposes. Linguistic switching is used routinely by native speakers according to a number of social parameters. Foreign language learners are made aware of the process in English and then can select exercises that illustrate that effective communication is more than the "transfer" of grammar rules and vocabulary. Viewers thus learn how such transfer can lead to misunderstanding and stereotyping. The goal of this section of the LLD is for students to recognize what is common in communication—variation of language routines to accomplish social purpose—and what is not—the underlying cultural values that define how this variation is to be accomplished.

The subsection on memory in the section of the LLD on orientation and assessment provides six different strategies to enhance retrieval. The goal is to encourage students to consider which of these or other strategies may enhance their ability to organize and store information.

In the third section, learners can choose from exercises that present strategies for improving reading, active listening, or conversation. In the reading and conversation sections, learners can opt for exercises in English or in a foreign language. The English options highlight the strategies viewers may use in effective reading comprehension (e.g., integrate text and pictures, use discourse markers to organize text and predict content, use topic to narrow predictions), or in facilitating listening comprehension in a conversation (e.g., use knowledge of the world to facilitate understanding, listen for familiar names and places, use key words to narrow predictions). The foreign language options allow students to use these strategies with several foreign languages. For example, in the active listening section, learners can choose to do the exercises by listening to Korean weather, a Russian spy story, the news in Russian or Spanish, or to a radio interview in Korean.

Learners can accomplish these purposes using a wide range of topics—reading an instructional manual to connect a VCR, watching a spy story, comparing the elements of crosscultural communication to recognize how values lead to stereotyping and misunderstanding, reading a scuba text to recognize how the reader determines the meaning of new words, or comparing elements used in borrowing money to recognize speech variation. While doing the exercises, students can elect a wide range of languages—as many as twenty. This variety and range of languages in the LLD contstitute one of its unique characteristics and are, in turn, the instruments by which the user gains experience and is led to recognize how to enhance the language-learning process by using strategies effectively.

Production

Project Team

The successful completion of this project was due in large part to the contributions of an enthusiastic and dedicated team[1] supervised by the author.

---

[1]*Instructional design/scriptwriters*/Amy Strage, Nancy Edwards, and Joan Rubin; *programmer*/James Laffey; *artist*/James Balkovek; *video producer*/William Sorensen; *director*/Joe De Francesco; *camera*/Chris Robson; *editor*/Mark Raupach; *pilot testing*/Amy Strage, Lois Harmon, Catherine Davies.

The instructional design and scriptwriting were carried out by subject-matter experts. Storyboarding was executed by an artist, and screen formatting and programming were accomplished by staff and consultants. The video production and premastering was subcontracted to Realtime Video Productions, Inc., of San Francisco.

Supervision of Production

Both the computer presentation and the video production were held to high standards in order to ensure authenticity of language and cultural context. During the video production, native language consultants ensured that the text was followed exactly—something not demanded in normal video productions. These consultants also provided guidance on props, settings, and costumes. Native speakers of Korean, Russian, and Spanish translated all textual materials and then were present during the fourteen days of shooting to ensure accuracy and authenticity; consultants for the remaining seventeen languages represented were also native speakers and/or trained linguists in those languages.

The video interpretation was similarly guided by close supervision in order to ensure that the video matched the intent of the exercises. Furthermore, every attempt was made to ensure that the many ethnic groups represented in the materials were portrayed in a positive fashion.

The video production was a major undertaking, since the LLD contains thirteen major dramatic scenarios incorporating 48 locations (all in and around San Francisco), and some 60 actors. Since this one-hour video required the recreation of authentic scenes from the USSR, Korea, Argentina, and Japan among others, the production team faced a major challenge in identifying locations, props, and costumes. Selection of actors required both natives and Americans who could speak fluent Korean, Russian, or Spanish.

Implementation

Several factors were found of great utility in the course of developing this product.

First, since the video production was done under subcontract, the work of a number of production houses with experience in interactive video was reviewed and several whose work showed high production values were identified. A request for proposal (RFP), which included a sample segment, was developed and presented to the production houses for elaboration. The responses provided important information that guided decision-making. In addition, other issues that would affect production came to light: (1) use of a studio versus on-location shoots, (2) type of tools used to keep track of the interrelationship between video, slides, animation, and computer, and (3) division of labor (for example, the use of independent producer/director/

camera operator versus a fully staffed production and postproduction house). The RFP also allowed the production houses to identify any shortfalls in design and to demonstrate their organizational abilities and attention to detail. Further, by using an RFP, the subcontractor was required to address the specific needs of this production in a detailed fashion. The lessons learned from the RFP make the use of one a *sine qua non* for teachers, researchers, or authors who might undertake a similar videodisc project.

Next, there was considerable discussion concerning the use of storyboards (sketches of the action with the appropriate audio text beside it). Some production houses indicated that storyboards were unnecessary while others judged them essential; nevertheless, a decision was made to use them and it proved to be very helpful. This circumstance required specifying to the artist in writing what kind of shot each picture should be. Since the design procedure included starting with an instructional goal and then writing script and exercises to match (rather than use existing video), tracking the interactive nature of the script, instruction, and video became critical. Constructing the storyboards was a valuable but timeconsuming endeavor. Preparing the directives for each shot enabled the instructional design team to identify flaws in the design and to communicate clearly with the production staff.

Screen design became a major consideration in the reading exercises as well as in the display of other information coming from the computer. In both instances, it was important to identify a set place for each kind of information—materials to be worked on, the question, instructions for how to respond, location of the answer, evaluation (right or wrong), and feedback. Then it was necessary to identify ways to present this information so that the task and answer evaluation were displayed in a clear and uncluttered manner while at the same time allowing the presentation of a relevant portion of language. Much of this problem was clarified by the use of windowing and color coding. The process of preparing screens required indicating the design of each screen to the programmer.

One of the most important steps in the production process was the procedure followed for formative evaluation of the material. The complexity of the instructional package made it essential to determine whether (1) the program worked well under all possible branches, (2) the instructions were easy to follow, and (3) the answer feedback was useful. In order to track all of this, an outline of all possible responses with spaces for comments was developed.

Twenty-six students at the Defense Language Institute (DLI) in San Francisco volunteered to pilot-test the program. As the students interacted with the LLD, a member of the author's staff monitored them and noted on an outline of the script any comments or problems they encountered. The results of this evaluation were extremely useful in revising the program. In addition, after completing the instructional exercise, the DLI students were asked to indicate what they thought they had learned from the LLD and to give their effective judgment of the program. In all instances, the responses proved extremely favorable.

Transportability

The Language Learning Disc is a level 3 videodisc programmed in Turbo-Pascal to run on a Pioneer LDV-1000 player, a Sony PVM 1271Q Monitor, and an IBM PC with a Microkey 1000 series interface card. Input is via a keyboard. With a Microkey 1125 card, other equipment can be made compatible with an IBM PC. Plans are underway to transport the LLD to the Sony View System and the IBM InfoWindow.

Readers who would like further information about the LLD are invited to contact the author at Joan Rubin Associates, Suite C, Berkeley, CA 94702 (415-527-7037).

References, LLD

1. Brown, A. L., and A. S. Palinscar. "Inducing Strategic Learning from Texts by Means of Informed Self-Control Training." *Topics in Learning and Learning Disabilities* 2 (1982) :1-17.

2. O'Malley, J. Michael. "The Effects of Training in the Use of Learning Strategies on Learning English as a Second Language," pp. 145-58 in Anita Wenden and Joan Rubin, eds. *Learner Strategies in Language Learning.* Herefordshire, Eng.: Prentice-Hall (UK), 1987.

3. Rubin, Joan. "Learner Strategies: Theoretical Assumptions, Research History and Typology," pp. 17-34 in Anita Wenden and Joan Rubin, eds. *Learner Strategies in Language Learning.* Herefordshire, Eng.: Prentice-Hall (UK), 1987.

4. Wenden, Anita. "Perspectives on Promoting Learner Autonomy." Plenary address to Fourth Annual Conference on Learner Strategies, La Guardia (NY) Community College, May 1986.

12

S-CAPE:
A Spanish Computerized
Adaptive Placement Exam

Jerry W. Larson
Brigham Young University

Introduction

Each semester language departments are faced with the task of advising and placing students into appropriate courses. This decision is often based primarily upon the number of classes the student has previously taken in the language. However, placement on this basis does not take into account several important factors, such as the effectiveness of the student's past teacher(s), the specific information covered, extracurricular or other out-of-class exposure to the language, and, in general, the student's actual facility with the language. Recognizing the rather imprecise nature of placements on this basis, the need for a more exact and objective—yet convenient—measure is desired.

Administering a formal placement exam to each student before placement decisions are made has been difficult, since an adequate placement test traditionally has required a significant amount of time (ranging from about an hour and a half to two and a half hours for a fairly thorough placement exam) and a lot of coordination effort, i.e., arranging testing times and places, administering tests, scoring answer sheets, recording and reporting the results, and, finally, counseling the students. Particularly if a department faces a large number of new students to be placed, the logistical considerations alone tend to discourage appropriate placement testing procedures.

The author thought that a solution to this problem might be found in the area of computer-assisted testing, given the potential for flexibility, precision, and individualization of computer-delivered tests. Further research into computer-assisted testing techniques uncovered a relatively new, yet potentially superior, testing procedure: computerized adaptive testing.

Computerized adaptive tests have been developed in the field of mental and verbal ability testing (see McBride, 10; Lord, 7; Olsen, 11; Weiss and Betz, 14), but the suitability of this testing procedure to language testing had not yet been pursued. In order to determine the applicability of this approach, development of a computerized adaptive language test (CALT) began in 1984. An initial prototype version of a CALT Spanish placement test was completed under a research grant from the U.S. Department of Education. A subsequent version was produced through support from Brigham Young University in 1986.

Computer Adaptive Testing

The function of an adaptive test is to present test items to an examinee according to the correctness of his or her previous responses. If a student answers an item correctly, a more difficult item is presented; and, conversely, if an item is answered incorrectly, an easier item is given. In short, the test "adapts" to the examinee's level of ability. The computer's role is to evaluate the student's response, select an appropriate succeeding item and display it on the screen. The computer also notifies the examinee of the end of the test and his or her level of performance.

The underlying theory of adaptive testing is the assumption that there is a latent distribution for any ability and that the competence of any individual taking a test of that ability lies somewhere along that ability continuum. This assumption leads to the testing theory known as Item Response Theory (IRT). For further explanation and discussion of Item Response Theory, see Henning (4), Lord (8), Wainer (12), and Woods and Baker (15). An adaptive test operates on IRT and is designed to locate an examinee's ability along the continuum. The purpose of this report is not to discuss in detail the statistical theory and background of adaptive testing. For further understanding of this reasoning, see Green (3), Larson and Madsen (6), Wainer (12), and Weiss (13).

Additionally, computer adaptive tests offer benefits over more conventional paper-and-pencil tests, among them:

1. *Reduction in testing time.* Computer adaptive tests require only a fraction of the time to complete that conventional tests do, since fewer items are necessary.
2. *Decrease in test boredom and frustration.* Since the adaptive test is tailored to the ability level of the examinee, he or she does not have to spend "wasted" time answering items that are far too easy or much too difficult.
3. *Immediate feedback.* Upon completion of the exam, examinees are informed via the computer of their performance score. They do not have to wait for answer sheets to be processed and the results to be filtered back through "the system."

4. *Self-pacing.* Computer adaptive tests are not timed; therefore, the students are able to work at their own pace.
5. *Fewer test administrators required.* Generally, only one test proctor is needed to load the tests into the computers. The computers handle the instructions, branching, scoring, and reporting. Also, the time and expense of handling and processing test forms and answer sheets are eliminated.
6. *Improved test security.* Since each examinee's test is virtually unique, cheating is not a threat.

Development of a Spanish Computerized Adaptive Placement Exam (S-CAPE)

Because of the large number of incoming students each year that enroll in lower-division Spanish courses at Brigham Young University, a definite need for an efficient and effective placement test exists. Advising students on a timely basis regarding appropriate course selection requires having a placement measure that can provide an almost instantaneous assessment of the student's facility with the language. Given these requirements and recognizing the potential and benefits of computerized adaptive tests, the author developed a Spanish computerized adaptive placement exam (S-CAPE).

The S-CAPE Item Bank

Since the focus of the S-CAPE was to be on the lower-division courses (i.e., Spanish 101, 102, and 201), items were written to reflect the curricula of these courses. The item types included grammar, reading, and vocabulary. Several graduate and upper-division Spanish students recommended by the faculty of the Department of Spanish and Portuguese were interviewed to determine their qualifications for assisting with the task of item writing. Four assistants, two native Spanish speakers and two nonnatives, were selected.

During the fall semster of 1984 and the winter semester of 1985, 1443 multiple-choice test items were written. The items were given to members of the Spanish Department faculty for preliminary proofing and screening. These reviewers were asked specifically to judge the quality (i.e., appropriateness of expression, clarity, no misleading distractions, etc.) and appropriate difficulty level of each of the questions. Approximately 1250 items were judged acceptable. These items were then assembled into five separate test forms (A-E) of 250 items each. (Each test form was divided into two parts because the machine-readable answer sheets would accommodate only 150 items.) Of the 250 items, 30 were common to all test forms in order to "link" the forms during the item calibration phase.

The test forms were administered to 199 students from the four courses in question and from the next upper-division course. After testing, Hoyt and KR-21 reliability and point biserial discrimination coefficients were calculated for the data (Table 1). Test results were also analyzed using the Rasch one-parameter model. (The Rasch analysis was run using Microscale Plus ™, a program written specifically for calculating Rasch one-parameter fit statistics. [1]

Table 1. Reliability and point biserial coefficients of test forms A-E

Test Form	Part	Hoyt	KR-21	Max. PBIS
A	1	.95	.93	.79
	2	.94	.92	.82
B	1	.96	.95	.74
	2	.95	.94	.82
C	1	.97	.96	.82
	2	.97	.96	.82
D	1	.96	.95	.79
	2	.95	.94	.83
E	1	.93	.91	.77
	2	.87	.83	.85
n=199				

The Rasch analysis is designed to calibrate and locate each of the test items along a common difficulty/ability continuum or scale. This analysis also identifies "misfitting" items, items that for some reason cannot be properly located on the scale. Misfitting items, because of their potentially problematic nature, were eliminated from further use in the test.

After difficulty indices for each of the items were obtained, the test items from each of the separate test forms were linked together and located along the difficulty scale. (For detailed information regarding the Rasch analysis, item calibration, and linking, see Wright and Stone, 16.) Knowing the difficulty index of each item is critical to the success of an adaptive test, since item selection by the program during the test is based upon this information. (Item selection and display are discussed below in more detail.) The difficulty range of the items ultimately selected for the S-CAPE item bank was from minus 3.6 to plus 6.0 logits, a logit being a Rasch unit of measure along the difficulty scale. Within this range were 96 different ability/difficulty levels. However, only levels zero to fifty were needed in the test-item bank, since these items sufficiently covered the ability range of students in the lower-division Spanish courses.

Once the items had been calibrated, they were again proofread by members of the Spanish faculty, checking for undetected spelling errors, inaccuracies, or any other possible problems. The final item pool contained about 1100 items. Each of these items was coded according to question identification number, item type (i.e., grammar, vocabulary, or reading), difficulty index, and the letter of the correct response choice. From this item pool, nine items at each difficulty level were selected and placed into a random-access item file for use with the placement test itself.

---

[1]. For information regarding Microscale ™, contact Mediax Interactive Technologies, Inc., 3029 Fairfield Avenue, Black Rock, Connecticut 067605.

The S-CAPE Computer Configuration

The final version of the Spanish computerized adaptive placement test is designed to operate on a standard IBM PC or compatible microcomputer with 256K of memory. Either a monochrome or color monitor may be used. If a color monitor is available, the test proctor can select preferred colors for the background, for the text of the items, and for the command lines or prompts to the examinee. The test requires either two floppy disks or one hard disk. When using two floppy disks, one contains the test program and the other stores the students' test performance data, or individual test records. (A floppy disk in drive B will hold approximately 200 student test records.) If a printer is available, the performance record and results of any or all students completing the test can be printed on hard copy or displayed on the computer screen if no printer is available. The floppy-disk format of the S-CAPE makes it portable and versatile. Several copies of the master disk can be reproduced so that testing can be done on several computers simultaneously.

The S-CAPE Software

Before an examinee sits down to the computer, a test proctor will boot up the test, indicate whether a two-drive system or hard disk is being used, select color options if applicable, and indicate which printer port is active (if any). After the program control options have been selected by the proctor, the student then types in his or her name and Social Security (student ID) number. (The program uses the first four letters of the student's last name and the last four digits of the ID number to open a test record file for that student.) The program then asks the examinee to indicate how much previous exposure he or she has had to the Spanish language. Response to this inquiry is made simply by typing the letter(s) of the statements in the list on the screen that correspond to the person's experience with Spanish. For example, students type "A" if they have had "No previous Spanish instruction," or "D" if they had "Three years in secondary school," and/ or "J" if "Spanish is often used in [their] home," etc. They type as many letters as apply and press RETURN. This information is recorded on the individual's test record file and is available for the placement counselor if needed.

Once the record identification information is entered, the computer prepares the student for the test. The first screen explains briefly that the examinee is to respond to the test questions by typing the letter of the best answer choice, A, B, C, D, or E, and to confirm that choice by pressing RETURN. To ensure that the examinee has understood the instructions, a sample test item is given, in addition to an explanation of how to answer the item. After this screen the actual test begins.

The S-CAPE was designed to be an individualized test. As the examinee proceeds through the test, the computer selects and displays items based upon the student's responses to previous items. The testing methodology prescribes that a student be given a series of questions at his or her estimated ability level. Placement into a particular course is determined by performance on these items.

The adaptive testing algorithm has been written so that the first six questions serve as "level checkers," similar to the level-checking procedure used in the ACTFL oral proficiency interview. During the level-check phase, the computer will increase the difficulty level by 6 for correct responses or decrease the level by 5 for incorrect responses. When a student begins the test, the first question presented is from difficulty level 20. (This is a moderately easy item for most beginning students.) If the question is answered correctly, the computer presents a subsequent item at difficulty level 26; if the answer is wrong, the next item will be at difficulty level 15. This procedure allows the test to advance quickly to the examinee's approximate ability level.

After the first six items the tests begin to "probe" in order to fine-tune the measure by increasing or decreasing the difficulty by one level after each response. The test terminates if (1) the examinee answers incorrectly four questions at the same difficulty level, or (2) the examinee answers five questions at the highest difficulty level, i.e., level 50. By requiring at least four misses at a given level, the test makes allowances for lucky guesses or inadvertent errors due to lack of concentration, nervousness, or other distractions.

To avoid an examinee's being presented the same question twice during his or her test, a sequential file is created that contains a key for each question in the item bank. This file is read into an array in memory at the beginning of each individual's test. The array entry for a question is flagged to indicate whether that question has been used. If the question has appeared previously during the test in progress, it will not be selected again. After a student completes the test, the flags are removed and the testing program is ready for the next person.

At the conclusion of the test, the computer displays on the screen the performance level of the student. The student then consults a placement chart that lists the ranges of performance levels that pertain to the various lower-division Spanish courses. Thus, the student is immediately advised of the Spanish class that appears most suited to his or her ability level. These norms or cut-off scores as guidelines for placement were obtained from students enrolled in the courses in question. Students who score at the top of the range of scores for a given course are strongly encouraged to consider enrolling in the next higher course and to challenge themselves a little more than would be the case in the lower class.

Evaluation of the S-CAPE

Preliminary indications from pilot administrations of the S-CAPE indicated that the test did, indeed, reduce the testing time dramatically. But before using it on a large-scale basis, placement guideline scores, reliability, validity, and accuracy of the S-CAPE needed to be established. Also, it was desirable to know the attitudes of students toward this type of test.

Placement Guideline Scores

Three separate testing sessions were conducted in order to determine more accurately the placement guideline scores for the test. First, in the summer of 1985 seventy-four students—ranging from only a very brief encounter with Spanish in high school or junior high school in students completing Spanish 302 at Brigham Young University—took the test. Then, during the last week of the fall semester of 1985, students who had been judged by their teachers as being "definitely qualified" to advance to the next course level were asked to take the S-CAPE. While the intention was to use the scores of these students to establish firmer guideline scores, some students who were not ready for the next higher course inadvertently also took the test. So it was necessary to review and sort through the resulting data from this testing session before being able to determine the guideline criteria.

At the end of the winter semester of 1986, the test was administered to an additional 305 students completing Spanish 101, 102, and 201. Placement guideline scores have now been determined for the Spanish lower-division curriculum at Brigham Young University.

Reliability and Validity

A study was conducted at the end of the summer term of 1986 at Brigham Young University to determine the reliability and validity of the S-CAPE. Data were also collected to compare the amount of time required to complete the S-CAPE with that required for a conventional paper-and-pencil placement test. Forty-three students from Spanish 101, 102, 201, and 302 were randomly divided into two groups, A and B. The students in both groups were given both the S-CAPE and the paper-and-pencil placement test on day one. (The paper-and-pencil placement test used in the study was the College Board *Spanish Reading Test*, Form M-K-RAC2, a test from the Multiple Assessment Programs and Services (MAPS) of the Educational Testing Service, Princeton, New Jersey.) Students in Group A were given the S-CAPE first, then the paper-and-pencil placement test. Those in Group B took the paper-and-pencil version first, then the S-CAPE.

Since the comparative data on the MAPS test is based on a one-hour testing session, the students were told to indicate on their answer sheet which question they were answering when an hour had expired. They then continued with the test until they finished and noted on their answer sheet how much time had elapsed since starting the test. This information provided data for both student performance within the prescribed hour and how long it would take to complete the entire test.

On day two of the study, all the students took only the S-CAPE a second time. An alternate forms reliability coefficient on the student scores from the two administrations of the S-CAPE was calculated using the Pearson Product Moment Correlation formula. The reliability coefficient was .86. The correlation of the S-CAPE and the ETS/MAPS paper-and-pencil placement test was .91. A summary of the comparisons of time and items required for the two tests is found in Tables 2 and 3. T-tests were run on the means to determine the level of significance. It is noteworthy that the S-CAPE required significantly fewer items and significantly less time to complete than the paper-and-pencil test at all class levels.

Table 2. Comparison of mean time in minutes to complete the S-CAPE and MAPS tests

Course	N	S-CAPE	MAPS	t	Significance Level
101	13	19.00	56.23	9.43	.000
102	7	24.57	66.43	7.33	.000
201	11	18.18	63.36	7.98	.000
302	12	15.92	47.33	12.75	.000
Total	43	18.84	57.23	16.90	.000

Table 3. Comparison of mean number of items taken to complete the S-CAPE and MAPS tests

Course	N	S-CAPE	MAPS	t	Significance Level
101	13	30.62	82.62	12.46	.000
102	7	34.14	77.29	9.00	.000
201	11	34.09	81.09	11.35	.000
302	12	32.83	87.00	14.55	.000
Total	43	32.70	82.58	23.55	.000

Placement Accuracy of the S-CAPE

In order to determine how well placements can be made from the S-CAPE scores, another investigation was conducted during the fall semester of 1986. One hundred and seventy-nine students from Spanish 101, 102, 201, and 302 were given the S-CAPE at the beginning of the semester. Midway through the semester the teachers of each student were interviewed and asked to rate on a six-point scale (0-5) how appropriately their student(s) had been placed. A rating of 0-12 represented a "bad to poor" placement and a marking of 3-5 indicated "good to excellent" placement. One hundred and forty-three of the 179 teachers (79.9 percent) indicated that their students had been placed appropriately, i.e., 3, 4, or 5 on the scale. A summary of teachers' ratings is found in Table 4. Only three of the teachers interviewed reported that their student(s) had been placed too high. The majority of those who indicated their student(s) had been poorly placed said the placement should have been one course higher, meaning that, for the most part, the errors in placement seemed to be conservative.

Table 4: Teacher Ratings of Placement Accuracy Using the S-CAPE*

Course	Students	0		1		2		Composite		3		4		5		Composite	
		N	%	N	%	N	%	N	%	N	%	N	%	N	%	N	%
101	132	12	9.1	6	4.5	6	4.5	24	18.2	19	14.4	12	9.1	77	58.3	108	81.8
102	18	4	22.2	0	0.0	2	11.1	6	33.3	1	5.5	2	11.1	9	50.0	12	66.7
201	20	2	10.0	2	10.0	0	0.0	4	20.0	4	20.0	5	25.0	7	35.0	16	80.0
302	9	0	0.0	1	11.1	1	11.1	2	22.2	0	0.0	0	0.0	7	77.8	7	77.8
Total	179	18	10.1	9	5.0	9	5.0	36	20.1	24	13.4	19	10.6	100	55.9	143	79.9

*Ratings of 0, 1, and 2 indicate bad to poor placement; ratings of 3, 4, and 5 indicate good to excellent placement.

Student Attitudes toward the S-CAPE

The forty-three students who took the MAPS paper-and-pencil test and both administrations of the S-CAPE were asked to complete an affect/attitude questionnaire. The questionnaire was designed to reveal how the students felt about various aspects of both types of tests. Students were asked to register their reactions to several statements by circling a number along a Likert-type scale from 1 (strongly disagree) to 7 (strongly agree). The data were analyzed using analysis of variance and t-test routines so that dissimilarities in attitudes of students from different course levels or having different degrees of computer experience could be detected. The items on the questionnaire in order are as follows:

1. The instructions on the paper-and-pencil test were easy to follow.
2. The instructions on the computer test were easy to follow.
3. The questions on the computer test were as easy to read as those on the paper-and-pencil test.
4. Having to take the test on the computer did *not* make me more nervous than taking a paper-and-pencil type test.
5. I prefer taking the computer version of the test over taking the paper-and-pencil version.
6. Of the two types of tests, the computer test seemed easier.
7. Of the two types of tests, the paper-and-pencil test seemed easier.
8. The paper-and-pencil test seemed to test my full range of ability.
9. The computer test seemed to test my full range of ability.

(Item 10 was answered only by students who had very little or no previous computer experience.)

10. I don't think my limited experience with computers had any effect on my performance on the computer test.

Table 5 lists the responses of students by amount of previous computer experience. Table 6 shows the mean responses to the items by course level. (Nine of the students in the study did not return their questionnaires. Three of the questionnaires returned did not indicate course level, hence the discrepancy in the total N between Tables 5 and 6.)

The results of the questionnaire were very approving of the computer adaptive test. Analysis of the data with respect to amount of prior computer

Table 5. Mean responses of students by previous computer experience to attitude questionnaire

Question	Total	None	Self-Taught	One Class	Two or more Classes	F	Significance Level
1	5.41	5.91	5.38	4.67	5.56	1.160	.340
2	6.41	6.36	6.88	6.22	6.22	1.279	.297
3	5.05	4.82	5.75	4.00	5.78	1.980	.135
4	6.46	6.64	6.88	6.22	6.11	1.312	.286
5	6.16	6.36	6.75	6.56	5.00	2.482	.077[1]
6	5.81	6.27	6.38	5.00	5.56	1.330	.281
7	2.46	2.27	1.50	2.89	3.11	1.300	.290
8	3.97	4.27	3.25	3.33	4.89	1.830	.160
9	4.68	4.18	5.38	4.44	4.89	1.454	.244
10*	6.50						

No experience N = 11; Self-taught N = 8; One class N = 9; Two or more classes N = 9
*Item 10 answered only by students with very little or no previous computer experience.
[1]T-tests between group means showed the responses of students having taken two or more computer classes differed significantly from those of students having had only one class or those who were self-taught.

Table 6. Mean responses of students by course level to attitude questionnaire

Question	Total	101	102	Course Level 201	302	F	Significance Level
1	5.41	5.13	5.20	6.00	5.00	0.827	.508
2	6.41	6.25	6.20	6.70	6.18	0.863	.526
3	5.05	4.00	3.60	6.10	5.55	3.639	.023[1]
4	6.46	6.50	6.40	6.40	6.36	0.030	.992
5	6.16	6.63	6.60	5.60	5.91	0.771	.522
6	5.81	6.75	6.80	6.00	4.36	5.277	.005[2]
7	2.46	1.25	1.20	2.10	4.55	13.183	.000[2]
8	3.97	2.88	4.00	4.60	4.55	1.992	.135[3]
9	4.68	4.38	5.20	4.70	4.64	0.346	.795
10*	6.50						

101 N = 8; 102 N = 5; 201 N = 10; 302 N = 11
*Item 10 was directed solely at the issue of computer experience versus nonexperience.
1. T-tests between group means showed that 201 student responses differed significantly from those of 101 and 102 students.
2. T-tests between group means showed that 302 student responses differed significantly from those of the other three course levels.
3. T-tests between group means showed that 101 student responses differed significantly from those of 201 and 302 students.

experience showed no significant difference between persons with computer experience and persons without on any of the items of the questionnaire. Of particular interest is the fact that the computer did not seem to cause the inexperienced students to be more nervous than their counterparts (Item 5). Also of note is that students with no computer experience were apparently just as eager to take the computer test as were students with previous computer experience (Item 6). And, finally, students with little or no computer experience agreed rather strongly that having had limited experience with the computer had little or no effect on their performance on the computer test (Item 10).

Four statistically significant differences were found in the analysis by course level. Students in Spanish 201 were significantly more in agreement than students from the other courses that the questions on the computer test were as easy to read as the questions on the paper-and-pencil test (Item 3). More predictably, however, the upper-level students differed significantly from the other students in disagreeing that the computer adaptive test seemed easier (Item 6). This is understandable, since the upper-ability students were easily able to answer nearly all of the items on the paper-and-pencil test, but the S-CAPE adjusted to their ability level and challenged them, or probed, with further questions of increased difficulty. The significant difference found on Item 7 further supports the outcome of Item 6. The t-test analysis between individual groups on Item 8 revealed that 101 students differed significantly from 201 and 302 students in disagreeing that the paper-and-pencil exam tested their full range of ability.

Application of the S-CAPE

At the beginning of the fall semester of 1986, the S-CAPE was used for the first time as the primary means of determining student placement into lower-division Spanish courses at Brigham Young University. Students were required to take the placement test at their convenience in the Humanities Learning Resource Center (HLRC) either the day before the semester began or during the first two days of the semester. Approximately 350 students were placed that semester using the S-CAPE.

Since the S-CAPE examines students individually, a student may take the test virtually at any time during the year in preparation for a subsequent semester. The test is therefore made available in the HLRC, and students may take it when needed. This kind of flexible administration arrangement greatly reduces the testing load at the beginning of a semester and provides students with placement information well in advance of registration deadlines.

Recommendations and Further CALT-Test Development

While initial observations and evaluations of the S-CAPE have been very positive, further research directed toward improving the test and the testing process is being done. Current collaboration with other CALT-test researchers to develop a more accurate and reliable test is promising. Alternative procedures and algorithms for selecting items and terminating the test are being investigated as well as the possibility of adding items to test the listening modality.

Additionally, research related to test-taking strategies and test anxiety is necessary and would provide insights needed to produce tests that yield a more accurate assessment of knowledge and ability.

Efforts to develop a useful, effective, and efficient computer-adaptive language placement test have been satisfying and rewarding. Evaluations of the S-CAPE have shown that it is possible to use CALT procedures to test languages for placement purposes. The experience and insights gained in developing the S-CAPE are currently being applied to the development of similar tests for French and German at BYU. It should also be noted that other researchers are making significant progress in using CALT procedures for testing language proficiency (see Clark and Thain, 1; Dandonoli, 2; Kaya-Carton and Carton, 5; Madsen and Strong-Krause, 9 and pp. 277-86, this volume).

In summary, the feasibility of using computer-adaptive testing techniques for language testing is very promising. The S-CAPE has greatly reduced many of the administrative headaches associated with placement testing in addition to providing a respectably reliable and accurate measure of a student's ability to function in one of the lower-division Spanish courses at Brigham Young University. Given the limitations of the S-CAPE, this format appears to be an acceptable alternative to paper-and-pencil placements tests both to faculty and administrators in the Department of Spanish and Portuguese as well as to the students themselves.

Readers interested in further information about S-CAPE are invited to contact the author at the Humanities Research Center, 3060 JKHB, Brigham Young University, Provo, UT 84602. For further information about the exam, contact the Humanities Research Center, 3060 JKHB, Brigham Young University, Provo, UT 84602.

References, S-CAPE

1. Clark, John L. D., and John Thain. "Computer-Adaptive Testing at the Defense Language Institute." Paper presented at the Ninth Annual Language Testing Research Colloquium, Hollywood, Florida, April 28, 1987.

2. Dandonoli, Patricia. "ACTFL in Action: Recent Activities of the American Council on the Teaching of Foreign Languages." *Northeast Conference Newsletter* 20 (September, 1986): 26-32.

3. Green, Bert F. "The Promise of Tailored Tests," pp. 69-80 in H. Wainer and S. A. Messick, eds., *Principles of Modern Psychological Measurement. A Festschrift in Honor of Frederic Lord.* Hillsdale, NJ: Erlbaum, 1983.

4. Henning, Grant. "Advantages of Latent Trait Measurement in Language Testing." *Language Testing* 1, 2 (1984): 123-33.

5. Kaya-Carton, Esin, and Aaron Carton. "Multidimensionality of Foreign Language Reading Proficiency: Preliminary Considerations in Assessment." *Foreign Language Annals* 19, 2 (1986):95-102.

6. Larson, Jerry W. and Harold S. Madsen. "Computerized-Adaptive Language Testing: Moving beyond Computer-Assisted Testing." *CALICO Journal* 3, 2 (1985):32-36,43.

7. Lord, Frederic M. "A Broad-Range Tailored Test of Verbal Ability." *Applied Psychological Measurement* 1 (1977):95-100.

8. _____*Applications of Item Response Theory to Practical Testing Problems.* Hillsdale, NJ: Erlbaum, 1980.

9. Madsen, Harold S., and Diane Strong-Krause. "Development of a Multi-Modality ESL Computer-Adaptive Test." Paper presented at the Ninth Annual Language Testing Research Colloquium, Hollywood, Florida, April 28, 1987.

10. McBride, James R. "Adaptive Mental Testing: The State of the Art." Technical Report 423. Alexandria, VA: U.S. Army Research Institute for the Behavioral and Social Sciences, November 1979.

11. Olsen, James B. "Psychometric Recommendations for Computerized Adaptive Testing." Orem, UT: WICAT Systems, 1982.

12. Wainer, Howard. "On Item Response Theory and Computerized Adaptive Tests." *The Journal of College Admissions* 28, 4 (1983):9-16.

13. Weiss, David J., ed. *New Horizons in Testing: Latent Trait Test Theory and Computerized Adaptive Testing.* New York: Academic Press, 1983.

14. _____, and Nancy E. Betz. "Ability Measurement: Conventional or Adaptive." Research Report 73-1, Psychometric Methods Program. Department of Psychology, University of Minnesota, February 1973.

15. Woods, Anthony, and Rosemary Baker. "Item Response Theory." *Language Testing* 2, 2 (1985): 117-40.

16. Wright, Benjamin D., and Mark H. Stone. *Best Test Design.* Chicago: Mesa Press, 1979.

13

The ACTFL Computerized Adaptive Test of Foreign Language Reading Proficiency

Patricia Dandonoli
American Council on the Teaching of Foreign Languages

Introduction

Under a contract with the U.S. Department of Defense, ACTFL has been working on the development of a prototype computerized-adaptive test of foreign language proficiency for reading.[1] The purpose of the test is to provide a means for any foreign language user to obtain an ILR/ACTFL[2] reading-proficiency rating at the conclusion of a test of approximately one hour in length. By means of sophisticated and relatively new statistical and testing techniques—see Henning (4) for a discussion of the foundations of computer-adaptive testing in item-response theory (IRT) and latent trait theory—each test taker will receive only those items, selected from a pool of items of varying difficulty, that are calculated to be closest to his or her ability level. In this way, the adaptive test can more accurately and efficiently arrive at a score for each individual.

Efficient administration and accurate scoring were not the primary reasons that ACTFL undertook this test development project; rather, for several years ACTFL has pursued the adaptation of a technique for testing foreign language oral proficiency that originated within the federal government—

---

[1] ACTFL has been fortunate to have the services of Dr. Esin Kaya-Carton and Dr. Aaron S. Carton as project codirectors. The project advisory committee consists of Michael Canale, James R. Child, David V. Hiple, Judith E. Liskin-Gasparro, June K. Phillips, Renee Meyer, and C. Edward Scebold.

[2] ILR refers to the Interagency Language Roundtable, an unofficial colloquium of over 30 federal agencies involved in foreign language teaching and testing.

the Oral Proficiency Interview (Liskin-Gasparro, 6)—and has disseminated information and training in academia on how to use the methodology. The scoring of the Oral Proficiency Interview (OPI) is based on the *ACTFL Proficiency Guidelines* (1), which, in turn, had their origins in the ILR skill-level descriptions (see Liskin-Gasparro, 6). ACTFL conducts several programs each year on the techniques for administering and rating the OPI, reaching several thousand educators either through one- or two-day familiarization workshops or through five-day intensive workshops. Once workshop participants become enthusiastic about testing oral proficiency, they are especially eager to have instruments that test functional listening, reading, and writing in a similar way. ACTFL believed that developing prototype tests of language proficiency in these skills could be especially timely and useful as models for other individuals interested in applying the concepts in the *Guidelines* to test development. Moreover, since ACTFL continues to refine the *Guidelines,* data are needed from a variety of sources that can be incorporated into future revisions; test data from the OPI and from other proficiency tests will be useful in this process. As a result, the computerized adaptive test project has been viewed less as an effort to produce an instrument in final form than as part of a professionwide research effort on proficiency testing in general.

Overall Description of the Test

Several features of the OPI and assumptions that govern the *ACTFL Proficiency Guidelines* are incorporated in this reading test project:

PURPOSE: The test is designed to evaluate global functional language ability. It is not designed to be tied to a particular curriculum or course and, thus, will be useful in evaluating the language ability of individuals who have acquired language skills in any context.

PASSAGES: The reading materials chosen as test passages are authentic complete texts or extracts. No specially written or edited texts are included. Passages have been selected to reflect a range of expected difficulty that corresponds to the descriptions in the ACTFL/ILR system. For the purposes of this prototype test, content has been restricted to a general nature, avoiding highly job-specific or technical material. Diagrams, photographs, or charts may be integral to some passages; thus the test has the capability to present them as needed. Furthermore, some passages may be of considerable length, so that independently scrollable windows for passages and items are to be incorporated into the test delivery system.

CONTENT: The adaptive format of the test also provides for flexibility in content; thus, the test allows the examinee some options for selection at certain points during the test. This flexibility may increase the interest and motivation of the test taker and give the reader some cognitive preparation in approaching each passage. This thematic unity also helps to avoid what Canale (2) has called the "eye-exam" type of test, where the test taker jumps randomly from topic to topic. The ACTFL test assumes that a reader's orientation or frame of reference is important in understanding a text, and that a certain coherence of content should improve performance. For example, one set of test questions at a relatively low difficulty level might include a table of contents. Following completion of these items, the examinee could be asked to select the next passage to read from the stories listed therein. While the ACTFL computerized test does not give examinees complete control over the testing situation (in fact, the ability to comprehend material with an increasingly wide range of content is related to scoring criteria as noted in the *Guidelines*), content and thematic unity are issues that must be kept in mind.

SCORING: This is a criterion-referenced test. Scores are directly interpretable in terms of specified performance standards, in this case the *ACTFL Proficiency Guidelines* and the ILR Skill Level Descriptions. Individuals wishing to understand or interpret a particular test taker's score need only read the definition associated with that score in these descriptions.

STRUCTURE: The test parallels the ACTFL/ILR Oral Proficiency Interview (OPI) in structure and includes (1) a warmup, designed to reacquaint examinees with the language, put them at ease, and provide the tester with an initial estimate of their speaking ability, (2) level check/probes stages, in which the tester establishes the "floor" and "ceiling" of the examinee's ability, i.e., the level of sustained performance in the language and the level at which performance cannot be maintained, and (3) a wind-down stage, in which examinees are returned to a comfortable level of functioning, so as to leave the test with a positive feeling. In the ACTFL computerized adaptive test of reading, an initial subtest is presented that parallels the OPI warmup. During this phase, an initial estimate of reading ability can be made. Next, the computer selects passages that confirm the level of sustained performance as well as the level of "language breakdown," or the inability to sustain performance.

DIAGNOSTIC INFORMATION: Another important feature of the computerized test is the ability to collect and interpret some type of diagnostic information. As part of the test development and item analysis, ACTFL has kept track of the various features of the language that each item/passage combination addresses. A multidimensional scaling procedure planned prior to running the item calibrations (i.e., calculating item-response theory parameters for each item) can also provide some information about each item. By keeping track of items answered correctly and incorrectly, some limited diagnostic information can be obtained about each examinee, while retaining the possibility of building additional diagnostic features into the test at a later date.

COMPUTER DELIVERY: One of the most unique aspects of this prototype test is its presentation and scoring via computer. When the project was conceived, few operational tests in any content area existed that relied on computers for both delivery and, through item-response theory, branching and scoring. Since that time, several new tests have emerged, although they are dissimilar in many respects from the ACTFL model.

Project Development

Several initial decisions guided the development of the test. First was a commitment to the IBM standard. Compatibility with the funder's equipment was an important factor. Although a variety of other equipment was considered, it was decided that the power and speed necessary for the real-time calculations required to support the branching protocols in the test required hardware at least as powerful as the IBM PC/XT.

Once the basic hardware decision had been made, options for software were considered next. Software was needed that could provided for item banking, item analysis, presentation of items to the examinee (including relatively high resolution graphics and passages of considerable length, i.e., more than one screen), calculate the ability estimates needed for branching, score the test, and store some history data for each test taker.

Several options were considered: programming the entire test from the ground up, adapting a commercial or privately developed authoring system (such as Ten-Core) to do adaptive testing, and when they became available, using commercial authoring systems for computerized adaptive tests. ACTFL's choice was the MicroCAT Testing System from Assessment Systems Corporation of St. Paul, Minnesota, a microcomputer—based system for developing, administering, scoring, and analyzing computerized tests. While not all components of the package are necessary for or entirely suited to ACTFL requirements, Assessment Systems Corporation agreed to work with ACTFL to customize and adapt MicroCAT as needed.

MicroCAT contains several stand-alone subsystems for development, examination, assessment, management, and conventional testing. The development subsystem includes the capability to create and edit items and generate special character fonts (including those reading from right to left) while developing tests using predefined templates and creating customized tests with the Minnesota Computerized Adaptive Testing Language.

The examination subsystem administers the tests to examinees either singly or through a local area network. The assessment subsystem is used to analyze test items using conventional statistics as well as by estimating IRT parameters (using either the one- or three-parameter model—see Henning, 3). The management subsystem allows monitoring of tests when used as part of a local area network; the conventional testing subsystem governs the creation and analysis of conventional (i.e., nonadapative) paper-and-pencil or computer-administered tests. Several custom features have been added by Assessment Systems to MicroCAT for ACTFL's needs. One new feature is the ability to branch by item cluster rather than by individual item alone. Typically, an adaptive test proceeds from item to item, selected on the basis of each item's difficulty index. Since each passage in the test may have several items associated with it, and these items may not be of precisely equal difficulty, the computer is asked to select passages for administration rather than individual items.

Enhanced graphics capability is another added feature. In its current form,

MicroCAT supports only the IBM Color Graphics Adapter. Assessment Systems will extend the graphics capability of the system to allow higher-resolution graphics (such as those available in the new IBM Model 30 personal computer—the VGA standard or the IBM Extended Graphics Adapter) to enable ACTFL to display those passages accompanied by illustrations or photographs.

In order to enter passages with illustrations into the item bank, however, an addtional capability is necessary—a screen-capture facility. Thus, Assessment Systems has added to MicroCAT the capability as well to capture a screen image and store it as an item. Rudimentary editing capability is to be added for this item type. ACTFL has also asked that a new item type be added to MicroCAT that allows items to hold multiple screens of text and/or graphics that can be "paged" by keystroke. Currently, MicroCAT has a scrollable item format for text-based items only.

Current Status

The development of the ACTFL computerized adaptive reading test has involved several complex and interrelated steps. Described briefly below are the activities already undertaken and an assessment of work yet to be done.

The first stage in the development of the test was the creation of a set of specifications from which passages could be selected and items written (see Kaya-Carton and Carton, 5). Early in the project, a committee of experts was named to assist in passage selection. As noted above, only authentic passages are included in the test. Passages were selected and then judged by the committee for their difficulty level vis à vis the *ACTFL Proficiency Guidelines.* The process of obtaining and evaluating these judgments is described elsewhere (Kaya-Carton and Carton, 4). The judgments will be used in conjunction with pilot test data for validity studies. Approximately 350 passages were selected initially and included in the pilot study. Examples of the types of passages selected at various levels are shown in Figures 1, 2, and 3.

Based on the test specifications, several test questions were written in a variety of item types for each passage, including various types of multiple-choice questions, cloze, cloze-elide, jumbled order, etc. In general, these items address global language ability and avoid discrete-point testing. Altogether, more than 700 individual items were written. In no case is an examinee asked for a direct translation of any passage.

Paper-and-pencil versions of the test were pilot-tested using approximately 3000 subjects. Such a large sample was necessary due to the large number of items to be analyzed and for purposes of equating the several paper-and-pencil forms of the test. Pilot tests were administered to high school and college students of French in the United States and Canada as well as to students in France.

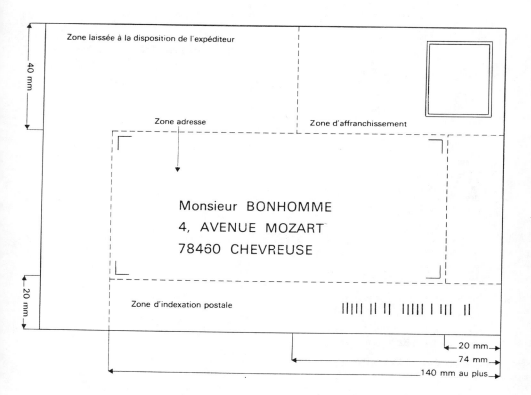

COMMENT DISPOSER VOS ADRESSES

Zone laissée à la disposition de l'expéditeur

40 mm

Zone adresse

Zone d'affranchissement

Monsieur BONHOMME

4, AVENUE MOZART

78460 CHEVREUSE

20 mm

Zone d'indexation postale

20 mm
74 mm
140 mm au plus

Désormais pour vos envois de moins de 20 grammes, n'utilisez que des enveloppes normalisées : longueur égale ou supérieure à 1,4 fois la largeur, compte tenu des dimensions maximales et minimales ci-après :

Dimensions { minimales . . . .   90 mm × 140 mm *
{ maximales   . . . .   120 mm × 235 mm

*   N'utilisez plus d'enveloppes d'un format inférieur à ce minimum.

Figure 1. A sample visual

Tradition française

● LE GRAND CAFÉ
4 bd des Capucines.
Tél.: 742.75.77
Ouvert jour et nuit (170)
L'événement Parisien: époustouflant décor spectacle 1900. Le restaurant de la mer de l'Opéra.

● CHARLOT «ROI DES COQUILLAGES»
12, Place Clichy, 75009 PARIS.
Tél.: 874.49.64
Goûtez l'air du large toute l'année dans ce restaurant voué à toutes les spécialités de la mer.
Jusqu'à 2 h du matin.

● VERDI
36, bd des Italiens, 75009 PARIS.
Tél.: 523.09.34
Fruits de mer - Coquillages - Poissons - Grillades - Spécialités Périgord.

● HIPPOCAMPUS
81, bd Raspail, 75006 PARIS.
Tél.: 548.10.03.
Bar - Restaurant 11 h - 23 h.
Dîner Piano Jazz J.V.S. à partir 21 h.

● MANOIR NORMAND
77, bd de Courcelles 75008 PARIS
Tél.: 227.38.97.
Spécialités poissons - Terrasse
19 h - 22 h tous les jours sauf dimanche.

● LANGOUSTE AMOUREUSE
1, av. des Ternes, 75017 PARIS.
Tél.: 380.15.83.
Poissons - Fruits de mer. Menu à 107 F
Tous les jours jusqu'à minuit.

● CHEZ ROBERT VATTIER
14, rue Coquillère, 75001 PARIS.
Tél.: 236.51.60.
Bar-Restaurant ouvert JOUR et NUIT.
Le cadre, c'est le Bistro des Vieilles Halles.

Spécialités

● BAUMANN
15, rue Matteut, 75008 PARIS.
Tél.: 720.11.11.
C'est le paradis des amateurs de viandes. C'est les 5 célèbres Choucroutes «B» C'est ouvert très tard tous les jours même le dimanche.

● DOMINIQUE
19, rue Bréa, 75006 PARIS.
Tél.:327.08.80.
Spécialités Russes depuis 1/2 siècle.
Ouvert tous les jours 12h 15 à 14h 15 - 19h 15 à 22h 15.

● L'ALSACE
39, avenue des Champs-Elysées, 75008 PARIS.
Tél.:359.44.24.
Ouvert 24 h sur 24.
Splendide terrasse animée jour et nuit où vous dégusterez des fruits de mer de toute première fraîcheur. La Brasserie du Tout Paris.

● TAVERNE KRONENBOURG
24, bd des Italiens, 75009 PARIS.
Tél.:770.16.64
Ouvert tous les jours de 11h à 2h. *Toutes les spécialités alsaciennes mais aussi des huîtres toute l'année. Orchestre tous les soirs LA FÊTE!*

● LE SANTAL
8, rue Halévy, 75009 PARIS.
Tél.:742.24.69.
Spécialités Vietnamiennes - Grillades parfumées - Fruits de mer - Salle climatisée.

● LOUISIANNE (LA)
176, rue Montmartre, 75002 PARIS.
Tél.:236.58.98.
Pour changer un peu: spécialités, cadre, orchestre NEW ORLEANS. Déjeuners DINERS JAZZ.

Figure 2. A sample visual

Figure 3. A sample visual

While a complete treatment of the nature of the item calibration is beyond the scope of this report, the analysis involved equating the several forms of the paper-and-pencil test, running a multidimensional scaling analysis, and developing the IRT item parameter estimates.

The initial programming to modify MicroCAT to accommodate ACTFL's specifications for test administration and scoring is underway at this writing. Once the initial adaptations are complete, ACTFL will bank the items selected for final inclusion and begin computer-based pilot testing. Later programming will allow for the incorporation of graphics-based items.

In time, ACTFL hopes to undertake other additional related research with the test data. As discussed above, the addition of a diagnostic module to the test is planned, as is the ability to develop new item types that take more full advantage of the computer's capabilities.

Readers interested in further information about this project are invited to write to the author, Computer-Adaptive Test Project, ACTFL, P.O. Box 408, 579 Broadway, Hastings-on-Hudson, NY 10706.

References, The ACTFL Computerized Adaptive Test of Foreign Language Reading Proficiency.

1. *ACTFL Proficiency Guidelines.* Hastings-on-Hudson, NY: American Council on the Teaching of Foreign Languages, 1986.

2. Canale, Michael, Personal communication, 1985.

3. Henning, Grant. *A Guide to Language Testing: Development, Evaluation and Research.* New York: Newbury House, 1987.

4. Kaya-Carton, Esin, and Aaron S. Carton. "Issues of Validity in Judging Passages for Testing Reading Proficiency." Paper presented at the Ninth Annual Language Testing Research Colloquium, Hollywood, Florida, April 28, 1987.

5. _____, _____. "Multidimensionality of Foreign Language Reading Proficiency: Preliminary Considerations in Assessment." *Foreign Language Annals* 19, 2 (1986): 95-102.

6. Liskin-Gasparro, Judith E. "The ACTFL Proficiency Guidelines," pp. 11-42 in Theodore V. Higgs, ed., *Teaching for Proficiency, the Organizing Principle.* The ACTFL Foreign Language Education Series, vol. 15. Lincolnwood, IL: National Textbook Company, 1984.

14

CALLIOPE:
An Outreach Project for Computer-Based Foreign Language Instruction in Illinois Schools

Robert S. Hart
University of Illinois

Project Background and Scope

In 1985 the Computer Assisted Language Learning and Instruction Outreach Project for Education (CALLIOPE) was established by the Language Learning Laboratory (LLL) of the University of Illinois at Urbana-Champaign. CALLIOPE is administered by LLL and shares the laboratory's facilities, including a 30-station microcomputer laboratory, a fully equipped video studio, and an 80-terminal PLATO site. Staffing presently consists of one full-time and one half-time visiting lecturer, both with extensive experience in computer-assisted language learning (CALL, which in this paper refers specifically to the computer-assisted learning of foreign languages), and a part-time project coordinator; other LLL personnel also work with the project. Funding is provided by the university as one aspect of its outreach responsibilities.

The ultimate aim of CALLIOPE is to strengthen the quality of foreign language education in Illinois by aiding elementary and high school teachers to use computer technology wherever appropriate. CALLIOPE's immediate purpose is to provide information and technical aid for foreign language teachers who wish to explore the use of CALL and related technologies such as micro/video interface.

The impetus for the project was a general perception that foreign languages have been rather left out of the movement to computerize Illinois schools. In fact, the typical foreign language teacher wishing to experiment with CALL faces a formidable obstacle course. To begin with, access to hardware is often limited, since many schools have only a few microcomputers, and those are often reserved for science or commercial courses. Money to buy courseware is extremely limited. Foreign language software is crude—much commercial courseware is of the "electronic workbook" variety and much of that is poorly done. Lack of comprehensive information sources makes courseware review and evaluation difficult and time-consuming. Creating one's own materials is difficult because few authoring facilities are tailored for foreign language work. Even when hardware and software are available, school routine leaves little time for students to use them. The training of most foreign language teachers does not include the use of CALL or even computer basics. Finally, transcending these specific problems, the fact that many school administrators perceive no connection between computers and foreign language teaching often results in foreign language teachers being ignored, first when plans are made for computer resources, and later when usage priorities are set.

CALLIOPE is intended as a resource, albeit a limited one, that teachers can access in facing these difficulties. The equipment and technical expertise of the LLL provide CALLIOPE with the means to educate teachers about CALL, to disseminate information about courseware and technology, to aid in the development and implementation of materials, and even to develop new software when appropriate.

Project Activities

Since Illinois's computer-oriented language teachers presently lack an organizational umbrella, an immediate priority was to identify potentially interested teachers and make them aware of the services CALLIOPE has to offer. Professional organizations such as the Illinois State Board of Education and the Illinois Foreign Language Teachers' Association aided the project by sharing mailing lists for mass mailings and making available newsletter space. Illinois's regional Educational Service Centers also helped to inform language teachers about CALLIOPE. These organizations, created as resource centers for Illinois schools, do not include foreign languages among their primary curricular responsibilities, but take an interest in CALL and cooperate with CALLIOPE. Project staff members are acting to build still stronger working relationships with these various organizations; one step in this direction was the LLL Roundtable Conference on Resources and Innovations in Foreign Language Education held in Urbana in May 1987, which provided a forum for discussion of many issues relevant to the future of CALLIOPE.

Another important task has been to build an extensive library of microcomputer courseware, covering a wide range of languages, computer hardware, and teaching functions. Also included are instructional management packages, word processors, and courseware authoring facilities—in fact, anything language teachers might find interesting or useful as a teaching tool. Some items have been purchased, but the collection has been largely built from publishers' donations. Keeping the library up to date requires considerable time and effort, but is well worthwhile, since it has proved invaluable for virtually every CALLIOPE activity.

The main function of CALLIOPE, information dissemination, is organized into three distinct activities: workshops, the intensive Summer Institute, and an internship program. Roughly speaking, these programs represent a graded progression. Workshops offer an introduction to CALL, the Summer Institute allows in-depth exploration and development of expertise, and an internship provides time and resources for serious materials development or curriculum formation.

Workshops

During 1986-87 CALLIOPE delivered 14 workshops to language teachers throughout the state. These workshops are generally sponsored by the Educational Service Centers, school districts, or individual schools, often as part of an inservice day, occasionally in association with a conference or professional meeting. They are conducted by one to three staff members and vary in length from a few hours to several days. If the client has computers, they are utilized in order to allow individual hands-on activities. If not, CALLIOPE provides the equipment.

Audiences range in size from half a dozen up to a hundred, and are usually dominated by teachers who have had little or no experience with computers. To provide flexibility in meeting the needs of different audiences, workshop content is built by selecting, in consultation with the client, appropriate units from among a set of modules. Some representative module topics are

- Commercial courseware options
- Evaluating foreign language courseware
- Error diagnosis and feedback
- Foreign language word processing
- Micro/video interface
- Authoring systems
- Speech synthesis and recognition

The objective of any given workshop depends, of course, on the audience, but is usually a general orientation and survey of CALL. The commercial courseware options module is almost always included since teachers, whether sophisticated or naïve about computers, want to inspect commercially available courseware and see what kinds of lessons are available. This hands-on experience is supplemented by a listing of CALLIOPE holdings and publishers' catalogs. Eventually the project hopes to provide systematic courseware reviews in order to facilitate selection and purchase of software.

The workshops are, however, intended to function as something more than a windowshopping spree. Teachers new to CALL are frequently a bit daunted by courseware evaluation and appreciate some discussion of how to go about it. Often they request advice on how to fit computer use into their classroom practice. Normally, there is also some discussion of authoring facilities and what is involved in the authoring process. This information is useful because many teachers do not have enough knowledge to make an informed choice between developing their own materials and buying someone else's. And because intelligent planning requires some anticipation of upcoming technology, the workshop is a useful arena to demonstrate, for example, videodisc, random-access audio, and voice synthesis.

Summer Institute

The second program, the CALLIOPE Summer Institute, is intended for teachers who want to approach CALL in more depth than is possible in a workshop format. The objective is to learn enough to start serious lesson development, or at least to become a CALL resource person for other foreign language teachers. Participation can (optionally) earn graduate credit in humanities or secondary education. About twenty applicants are chosen on the basis of a statement about their background, their particular interests in CALL, and their proposal for a tentative project, which may involve either programming or curriculum development. Those selected receive a stipend that includes costs of residence. Sessions are held in LLL's microcomputer laboratory. The 1986 Institute was organized as two four-week sessions; in 1987 this was replaced by one six-week session to avoid overlap with teaching schedules. The Institute syllabus, which is quite intensive, divides each day into a morning session concerned with instructional design and an afternoon session occupied with programming.

Members of the Institute's instructional staff have had extensive experience with programming, foreign language lesson design, and the practical aspects of foreign language lesson development, reflecting the belief that this high level of expertise is essential to the success of the program. It also allows each instructor to contribute to both design and programming sessions, an arrangement that facilitates integration of the two areas.

In the design sessions, participants see demonstrations of courseware and software, hear lectures, and discuss lesson design and pedagogical issues. Topics include a survey of current courseware, courseware evaluation, word processing, error analysis and feedback, collection of data on learning history, use of authoring systems, interactive audio and video, advanced technologies, and computer-managed instruction. Teachers who have used CALL with their own classes come as guest lecturers to discuss their experiences. As much as possible, however, lecture is avoided in favor of hands-on activities. Participants undertake written and oral evaluation of courseware, try out authoring languages or systems and report on their success, turn out printed materials using word processors, and experiment with instructional management packages.

In the programming component, participants are currently offered a choice of Applesoft BASIC enhanced with EnBASIC (an extension package that adds many of the display and input features required for foreign language work) or IBM BASICA. Reasons for preferring BASIC to instructionally oriented langauges such as PILOT are, first, the greater generality of its programming constructs, and, second, its great portability. The goal of the programming component is to give teachers sufficient expertise so that they can program moderately complex exercise formats. All of the instructional materials and programming examples are specifically designed for language programming. Numerical programming concepts are glossed over and string processing stressed. Graphics are deemphasized as requiring more learning time than is merited by their limited utility. The participants learn how to diagnose specific errors, save items for review, implement program- and file-based language content—in short, how to program most of the instructional design features needed in elementary-level language instruction. Later in the session, participants implement a courseware project of their own design. When finished, they are prepared to do serious development work and should be able to discuss the technical aspects of CALL with ease and confidence.

As judged by the participants' anonymous evaluations, the 1986 Summer Institute was a demanding but satisfying experience. This is corroborated by the fact that all but one individual (who had prior plans) elected to return for the second four weeks, which covered programming and more technical aspects of CALL. During this second session, one team of participants completed an ambitious video project that required recording a set of Spanish games, stories, and songs for grade school students of Spanish; another teacher developed micro/video courseware for presenting French culture and grammar through French TV commercials. Several continued work as interns during summer 1987.

Internships

CALLIOPE's "topmost" component, the internship program, is intended for teachers somewhat experienced in CALL (possibly with a project already under way), capable of working independently, but requiring some free time and technical help to make progress. Prospective interns submit a project proposal and, if accepted, receive a stipend to come to LLL for some period of time and work with the CALLIOPE staff. Most teachers opt to schedule internships for the summer. Some, however, find it preferable to carry on the bulk of the work at home during the year, with periodic short visits to LLL for consultation. The exact terms of an internship are negotiable so that the CALLIOPE staff can accommodate these varying needs. Projects are selected if they might serve as demonstration or model projects, and particularly if they seem likely to form the nucleus of an ongoing program in the teacher's school. CALLIOPE interns have so far developed elementary Spanish lessons and video/micro interface materials. The internship program is expected to grow as workshop participants choose this means of continuing their work.

Lessons Learned and Future Plans

Experience has revealed that workshops alone are not a good format for presenting certain kinds of information. Many questions teachers ask have complex answers that require a background of technical exposition: How shall I choose a word processor for French? Which elementary German package is best? What authoring system is most appropriate for writing foreign language lessons? Those who want to do serious work need something appropriate to keep with them for study and reference. Technical references and computer magazines, if they have the pertinent information at all, do not present it in a way that seems comprehensible or relevant to most language teachers. CALLIOPE is therefore developing a series of publications that will organize reference information in a form specifically designed for CALL. These documents will deal with both technical topics and instructional design issues. A few projected titles are "Critiquing and Evaluating Courseware for Foreign Language Teaching," "Foreign Language Word Processing," "Micro/video Technology," "Answer Judging and Response Analysis."

Lack of finances constitutes a continuing problem. A teacher who comes back enthusiastic from a CALLIOPE workshop only to be told that his or her school cannot afford a few dollars needed to purchase a piece of trial software may simply elect to forget about the whole thing. Even in wealthier schools, systematic use of courseware is often precluded by the need for multiple copies. While CALLIOPE cannot address budget problems directly, it can help teachers to investigate licensing arrangements and to identify existent sources of funding for hardware and software and develop new ones.

Some statewide organizations of teachers interested in CALL would greatly facilitate the work CALLIOPE is doing. Communication with like-minded people is an effecient way to disseminate information and generates enthusiasm. Furthermore, many issues relating to the introduction of CALL into language teaching (for example, methodological and curricular implications) can best be addressed by language teachers themselves, acting in concert. CALLIOPE should foster communication and organization by providing a means through which computer-involved teachers in various parts of the state can become aware of one another. As a starting point, project mailings might incorporate a newsletter.

Concentration of CALLIOPE resources is an issue. Two years of experience indicate that CALLIOPE should focus its programs more selectively: ideally, by concentrating effort on districts or regions where interest is particularly strong. Project staff might, for instance, cooperate with a regional Educational Service Center to devise a staff development program lasting for a number of semesters. Teachers who opt to participate could then count on the project for continuing support of their professional development. Only through intensive, sustained work with groups of such committed individuals will CALLIOPE have a lasting impact. Furthermore, all involved with CALLIOPE would profit from closer involvement of the teachers' home schools. If a participant's work begins and ends at LLL, it cannot serve as a pilot or showcase project, nor is it likely to have any important consequences beyond the classroom of the teacher who did it. An important priority as CALLIOPE progresses is to devise arrangements that assure projects of more local support and greater exposure. Related to this is the issue of conducting CALLIOPE activities at remote locations: since it is often difficult for teachers to leave home for a long period, there have been many requests that classes or Institute sessions be held locally. CALLIOPE is exploring all of these possibilities.

Finally, it is gratifying to note that the flow of information has not been all one way. The CALLIOPE staff have learned a great deal from interacting with teachers, particularly during the Summer Institute, and this has influenced subsequent LLL software and development projects. It became clear, for instance, that many workshop participants wanted to use the computer as a sort of "electronic ditto machine" for quick, simple on-line exercises that related directly to current classroom activities. However, they found most commercial authoring packages difficult to learn and to use and lacking an adequate selection of language-specific functions. This need has stimulated LLL development of the Language Lesson Authoring System (see Cheng, 1, for a preliminary description), a word-processor authoring environment that incorporates many language-specific functions. Hopefully its convenience will encourage teachers to become involved in lesson writing. The video and error analysis development described in Hart (2) has also profited from teacher/researcher interaction. More such software development, perhaps in the form of joint projects, will surely emerge from the internship program. These efforts will, in turn, aid foreign language teachers in their classroom computer use.

CALLIOPE is administered by Professor C.C. Cheng, Director, Language Learning Laboratory, and Professor Robert Hart, Associate Director, Language Learning Laboratory. The project is coordinated by Dr. Nina Garrett, Research Associate, and is staffed by Mr. Ulric Chung and Mr. Rick Treece, Visiting Lecturers. Professor Richard Dennis, Department of Secondary Education, and Ms. Karen Troupe-Phillips, Visiting Lecturer, served on the CALLIOPE staff in 1985-86. Inquiries concerning any aspect of the CALLIOPE project are welcome. Address correspondence to: Language Learning Laboratory, G70 Foreign Languages Building, University of Illinois, 707 S. Mathews Street, Urbana, IL 61801. Phone (217) 333-9776.

References, CALLIOPE

1. Cheng, Chin-Chuan. "An Authoring System for Computer-Assisted Instruction in Chinese," pp. 40-46 in *Proceedings of the 1986 International Conference on Chinese Computing.* Singapore: Institute of Systems Science, 1986.

2. Hart, Robert S. "Current Trends in Computer-Based Language Instruction," pp. 63-74 in Lyle Bachman and Molly Mack, eds., *Computers in Language Research and Language Learning.* (Special issue of *Issues and Developments in Applied Linguistics.*) Urbana, IL: Division of English as an International Language and the Intensive English Institute, University of Illinois, 1987.

15

WestCenter:
Software Programs Developed
at Western Washington
University

Robert S. Balas

Western Washington University

Introduction

For the past three years, a team of researchers[1] at Western Washington University have been developing software programs for foreign language instruction. The first effort was a drill program in a game format called Le Métro. Later efforts tended toward broader, multidimensional problem-solving formats and sought to integrate the programs into the classwork demanded in foreign language study in accordance with specific objectives (listed later in this report). The programs were created through attention to specific pedagogical goals in order to avoid the trap that Ofiesh (1) described when he wrote "Narrow concentration on the specific features of a newly developed technique, to the exclusion of its underlying concepts, can focus attention on the tool rather than on the problems it is meant to solve" (p. 166). In short, Ofiesh counseled that educators must avoid overlooking the programming process in favor of a fascination with the machine.

Software development at WWU is a tripartite exercise consisting of (1) the design of the overall program, (2) the actual programming of the software, and (3) the use of editing units to create the lessons that the student can use effectively. Once a program has been made operational, its true measure

---

[1] The team is composed of the author, a French language teacher; Kriston Bruland, a WWU student computer programmer; and Robert Burke, presently employed as a programmer and systems representative at Host Interface International, Inc., Bellevue, Washington.

of worth is whether it can accomplish its goals—that is, whether the student is better able to comprehend and verbalize the contextualized experience for having used it.

All but one of the programs (Le Métro) described below have been developed in the PILOT authoring language by the author and several creative programmers at Western Washington University as part of the WestCenter Project under an IBM grant for instructional programs.

Nine goals and principles have guided program development and reflect as well their pedagogical orientation.

1. To create editing systems that permit the instructor to enter, edit, and tailor lessons to suit course demands, the texts being used, or personal requirements.
2. To provide for possible future interaction with videodisc, CD-I, and CD-ROM.
3. To make the programs visually interesting through layout and design as well as relatively open-ended and pedagogically sound.
4. To place in the computer laboratory as many text-oriented skills as possible to free the classroom for communicative language instruction in order to enhance the students' exposure to spoken forms of the target language.
5. To create "breadth" in programs by seeking a combination of sound and graphics and writing as stimuli while minimizing the use of English.
6. To design programs that can integrate with classroom activities or can extend classroom activities directly to lab activities.
7. To concentrate on context rather than text as a necessary guide for the development of software programming for all foreign language instructional material.
8. To emphasize "coarse" or general structures rather than discrete information, but to incorporate enough latitude in the programs so that students should be able to do their own fine tuning.
9. To use graphics as an integral part of the language acquisition process rather than simply to use them to "enhance" the programs in which they are used.

The WWU programs are divided into two categories: graphics or audio based (A travers l'image, Images, Vocab, Mandarin, Image Bank) and text based (Métro, Lecture, Form & Function, Kanji).

The remainder of this report describes for each category of software the purpose, user options, operational protocols, error display, and other unique aspects including information on authorship and specific language.

Graphics and Audio Based Centered Software Programs ___

A travers l'image (Robert Balas, Robert Burke) [French only]
Purposes:

1. To develop French syntax
2. To develop grammar/spelling/writing

3. To develop listening/comprehension skills
4. To develop vocabulary
5. To associate sounds with images
6. To develop "chunked" vocabulary in association with single images
7. To access the target language directly with no interference from the native language

Hardware: IBM-PC (128k minimum), interfaced to a Sony CDP-620ES CD player (Programming *A Travers l'image* for a CD-ROM should be finished by the time this information appears in print.)

Options:
1. Listen, view graphics, repeat, write
2. Listen, view graphics, repeat
3. Listen to question, view graphics, record spoken answer
4. Listen to question, view graphics, write answer

Operation: The program permits students to choose a desired area of study. All presentations are introduced by questions and answered in complete sentences that require common syntactic patterns (but students need not be aware of this fact).

a. Nouns
   1. Simple
   2. Grouping (chunked)
b. Verbs (choice of tenses will vary and can be selected)
c. Prepositions
d. Idiomatic expressions
e. Simple sentences (short or long) that contain one conjugated verb and use simple nouns
f. Complex sentences
   1. Conjunctions
   2. Relative pronouns
   3. Complementary

Once the program is loaded, the student selects the area to be practiced and can choose to access sound or simply use the images. (The latter exercise would be elected only once the lesson is mastered as a vocabulary, writing, recording, or syntax exercise.)

1. The student hears an appropriate question and an answer.
2. The student is asked to repeat the response.
3. The student is asked to write the response.
4. The student responds to error markup:
   a. A wrong accented letter changes from white to blue and the student must type in the correct accented letter to proceed.
   b. A primary error is indicated in magenta. Students are then asked to correct the error and the model for the sentence is heard again.
   c. A second major error and the correct sentence is provided.
   d. Students may repeat the pronounced sentence on the diskette as many times as desired.

Figure 1. Title page screen for *A travers l'image* showing a range of icons used in the program

Figure 2. *A travers l'image* program reinforcement for a correct answer that required the following syntactical structure: Subject noun + verb in the past + direct object noun + indirect object noun

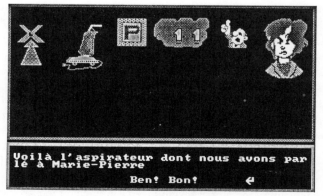

Figure 3. *A travers l'image* picture sequence for relative clause sentences. A correct sentence has just been typed in and verified.

Figure 4. *A travers l'image*. A sentence in the relative clause sequence has just been corrected for a spelling error, signaled after the first entry. The word "tenue" had been spelled without an "e." The error was indicated by the letters turning magenta.

Figure 5. *A travers l'image* signaling of an accent error on a typed answer: omission of the accent on "jeté." The word turned blue.

Figure 6. *A travers l'image* has just made a correction of an incorrect accent mark: the "é" on "jeté." To indicate an accent error the word turns blue.

Unique Aspects: Since the compact disk (CD) holds 70 minutes of spoken French and sound can be accessed on the diskette within 1/7 of a second, pieces of sentences can be captured and recombined with other pieces of sentences. Thus, the 70-minute disk can be expanded at will. Where it is significant for the student to learn intonation, the diskette can be recorded with the greatest latitude of intonation in mind by arranging items categorically in word groups.

The program allows the teacher four editing functions:
1. To select the sequence of graphics displayed
2. To enter the correct sentence matches
3. To access and file sound segments in three-digit codes (AA1, AB4, C2C, etc.)
4. To synthesize the preceding files into a single lesson. (A lesson can hold up to 180 sentences, which are randomized by the program.)

The clarity of the compact disc provides an excellent listening environment for students.

Images (Robert Balas, Kriston Bruland) [French, Spanish, German, Italian, English]

Purposes:
1. To develop vocabulary through a program built around an image
2. To provide syntactic diversity
3. To promote direct contact with the target language
4. To identify sound with an image
5. To establish a high rate of interaction

Hardware: IBM-PC (128K minimum), color monitor, 1 drive for student program (2 drives for Editor), optional cassette player or Tanberg cassette interfaced to computer

Options: Students may listen to questions, see cues, and type in answers or may view questions and cues presented on the screen and then type answers.

Operation: Lessons are categorized by subject area and semantic field. The student selects the desired lesson and then chooses the speed (fast, medium, slow) at which the presentations are to be displayed on the screen. Each picture has 4-10 associated questions and uses vocabulary appropriate to the subject chosen.

Unique Aspects: No native language is necessary unless used for hints/cues to act as "hooks" to aid in recall. Pictures can be used for several questions providing an integration of story, vocabulary, and grammar; for example, one can choose sequences to reflect daily routine, etc. The context requires additional vocabulary. Questions can be asked in past, present, or future tense.

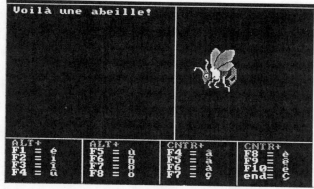

Figure 7. Screen 1 of *Images*. Student sees image plus vocabulary to assist in answering a question to be asked on the next screen.

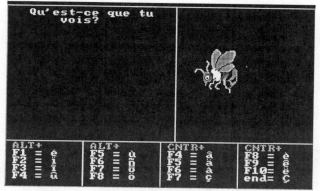

Figure 8. *Images* now asks a question. Student must give a complete sentence response and attempt to give an appropriate answer to the question.

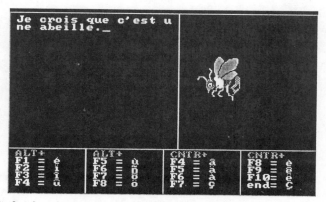

Figure 9. Student has given a complete sentence and an appropriate answer which will be accepted as correct by the *Images* program.

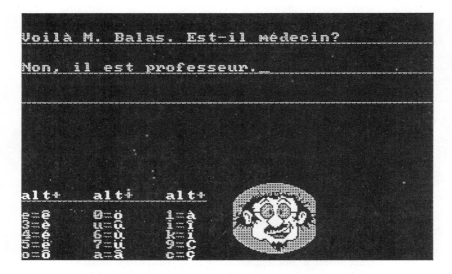

Figure 10. *Vocab* question screen. Student has just typed in answer to question in first line. A complete sentence was not necessary. The word "professeur" correctly spelled would have been sufficient.

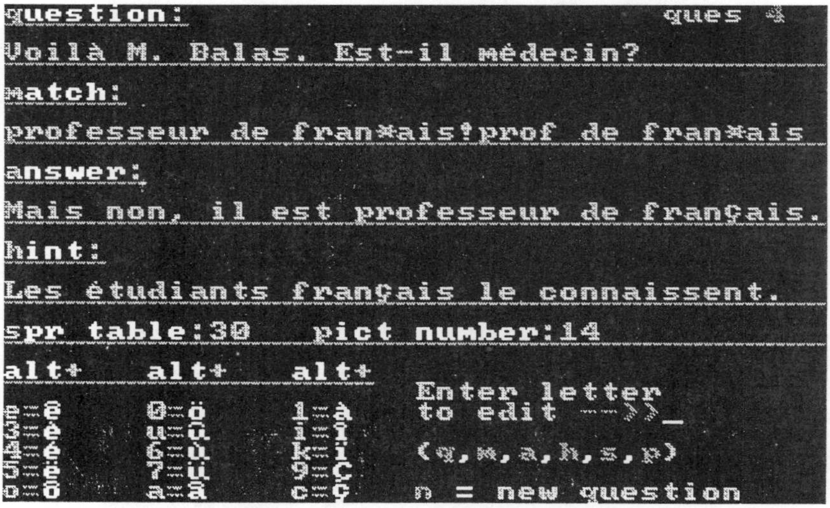

Figure 11. *Vocab* editing screen for lesson creation or correction. Note that match will now require "professeur de français" or "prof de français" for a correct answer. The "*" in the word "français" means the program will not require the accented letter. The entire question, match, answer, hint, and image is contained on this single screen.

Vocab (Robert Balas, Kriston Bruland) [French, Spanish, German, English, Italian]

Purposes:
1. To provide a quick vocabulary-development exercise in a game format using the Image Bank graphics
2. To achieve easy editing for rapid lesson creation
3. To provide flexibility for short answers, verb usage, adjectives, grouped vocabulary, etc.

The program can do many things that can be accomplished with *Images*, but answers must be much more restricted in length.

Hardware: IBM PC, color monitor

Software: DOS must be 3.20 or above

Operation: Students select a lesson. Each lesson contains 50 image-based examples presented chronologically. Usually from 1 to 3 questions are asked about each image. Answers may be up to one line in length; however, the game was designed for short answers. Hints are provided. Students are advised to preview a lesson to familiarize themselves with the vocabulary before doing the lesson.

Unique Aspects: The editing system is a one-screen unit so that all aspects of the program can be entered using the field of one screen. The program is simple and straightforward, and provides an excellent vehicle to get started for authors not accustomed to creating programs.

Mandarin (Edward Kaplan, Charles A. Balas, Qiao Jin) [Uses graphics from Image Bank]

Purpose: To identify Chinese characters with pictures and to answer questions

Hardware: IBM-PC with mouse

Operation: Students identify characters by selecting one of six pictures on a screen. Questions are also asked to cause students to practice character recognition. A supplemental quiz also helps students review characters.

Image Bank (Robert Balas) All languages

Developing the IBM grant program, A travers l'image, led the author to create an extensive number of cartoon/graphic icons to generate vocabulary through visualization. This bank of images (which can be expanded indefinitely) can be used by others for any program requiring graphics (although about 10 percent of the images are directly oriented to French and would necessitate some change in cultural authenticity for other languages).

Text-Centered Software Programs ————————————

Metro (Robert Balas, Robert Urso) [French]

Purposes:
1. To provide a wide range of exercises, from discrete grammar to question/answer
2. To permit controlled drill as well as flexible short sentence writing (two lines maximum)

Hardware: IBM PC (128K minimum), color monitor, 1 drive for both Métro and Editor

Options:
1. Students may play Métro game with exercises.
2. Students may simply do exercises without game.

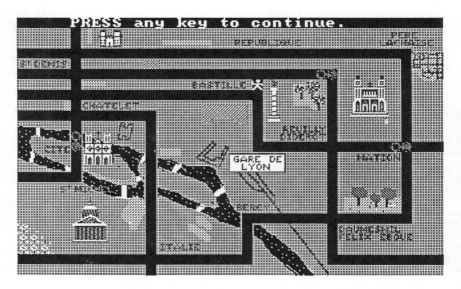

Figure 12. Métro. One-half of central Métro system. Shows passenger ready at Bastille. Cars at Notre Dame and Nation.

3. Instructor may use Editor program to:
   a. Create new 50-question lessons
   b. Edit previously created lessons
   c. Print out student records and clear records file
   d. Print out quiz (One can randomly choose a desired number of questions from selected lessons and send them to the printer)
   e. Copy existing lessons onto new diskettes in a desired order and add new lessons to shape lesson presentations to course demands

Game Play: Students choose the lesson to be played. An instruction screen presents the problem for the lesson and the basic knowledge necessary to accomplish the exercise. For example, from a random starting point on the Métro system in Paris, a random destination is chosen (Tour Eiffel, Arc de Triomphe, Le Louvre, Notre Dame), which the student must reach to have a score recorded on the student record.

If the student gives a correct answer, there are three choices to control movement:
1. Board arriving train
2. Wait while a train passes
3. Get off the train one has already boarded

If a student makes an error, the player must get off the train he/she is riding or board an incoming train whether the player wants to or not. Play continues as the 50 randomized questions are completed. If the player does not reach the destination, the questions are rerandomized and play continues until the destination is reached and the score recorded.

Unique Aspects: As a drill program Le Métro is unique because of the breadth of exercises that can be programmed into the game. Questions may be up to four full lines in length and answers up to two lines. Le Métro also invites the use of graphics, which can easily be created to suggest the game aspect of the program. For example, a picture story presented orally can be supported by a question/answer drill that presents to students the same material in written form. In this fashion, Le Métro can be tailored readily to any text or classroom project.

Lecture (Robert Balas, Kriston Bruland) [French, Spanish, German, English]

Purposes:
1. To develop reading skills
2. To provide contextual question/answer practice and language drill
3. To enrich listening skills
4. To enrich vocabulary

```
NARRATEUR:  Une salade niçoise, préparée
            par Georgette Zunino,
Roussillon.  Nous voici chez Georgette.
Tout le monde a faim.  La vinaigrette
pour accompagner une salade niçoise
consiste d'huile d'olive, de vinaigre,
de moutarde, d'ail, de sel, et de
poivre.

GEORGETTE ZUNINO: Ça, c'est la vinai-
                 grette.
N: Voici comment on compose la salade.

GZ: Alors, on commence par une superbe
salade verte. Voila. Alors la, j'ai
coupé des concombres que j'ai mis au
sel pour les faire dégorger.(con't)....
```

```
C = Continuer.
V = Voir le vocabulaire.
S. = Sauter en arrière.
R = Retourner au menu.
```

Figure 13. Screen 1 of *Lecture*. The text is from a video created by Bernard Petit and produced by Heinle & Heinle, entitled *France from Within*. By pressing "V" students may view screen 2, vocabulary, then return to the text screen. This operation may be repeated as many times as one wishes. Pressing "C" forwards the student to three questions based upon this text screen. If a wrong answer is entered, students may return to the text screen but may no longer access the vocabulary screen. A second chance is then given to answer the question correctly.

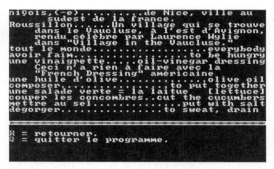

```
niçois,(-e)...........de Nice, ville au
      sudest de la france.
Roussillon......Un village qui se trouve
      dans le Vaucluse, à l'est d'Avignon,
      rendu célèbre par Laurence Wylie
      dans "Village in the Vaucluse."
tout le monde..................everybody
avoir faim................to be hungry
une vinaigrette.....oil-vinegar dressing
Ceci n'a rien à faire avec la
      "French Dressing" américaine
une huile d'olive............olive oil
composer............to put together
une salade verte = la laitue  [lettuce]
couper les concombres..cut the cucumbers
mettre au sel............put with salt
dégorger..............to sweat, drain
```

```
R = retourner.
Q = quitter le programme.
```

Figure 14. *Lecture* vocabulary screen. The vocabulary screen can contain vocabulary or grammatical or cultural information. There is one vocabulary screen available for each text screen. The editing program permits easy access to the screens. Thus it would take about 20 seconds to enter the editor program and correct the small letter on "france" in the second line.

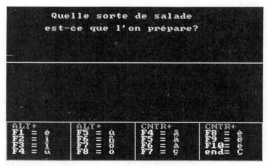

Figure 15. *Lecture* question screen. The student has just pushed "C" and is presented with the first of three questions. The answers can be short or complete sentences according to the desire of the instructor. The 50-question quiz has the same format.

Hardware: IBM PC (128K minimum), color monitor 1 drive for Lecture, 2 drives for Editor, optional cassette recorder or interfaced Tanberg cassette player.

Options:
1. Students may read each screen, access useful vocabulary and linguistic or cultural information, answer three questions after each screen, reread the entire lesson, and then answer up to 50 additional questions.
2. Students may simply read the text without questions.
3. Students will be able to listen to prerecorded text while viewing the screen.
4. Students may go directly to final 50 questions.

Operation: Students select a lesson and have the option to listen to a prerecorded tape of the text. Each screen has a supplemental screen of vocabulary or pertinent linguistic information to assist comprehension of the passage. Students may go back and forth between these screens as many times as desired. Upon completion of a screen, there are three questions asked about the information presented in the reading or about the vocabulary, etc. Answers can be brief or in complete sentences.

Upon completion of a reading lesson (maximum number is set at 15 screens of text), the student has the option of answering up to 50 additional questions, which may be informational, grammatical, or lexical. The student has one chance to answer the question correctly. If an error is made, the option is given to return to the text screen to view the entire context in which the answer is found. There is subsequently a second opportunity to provide an appropriate answer. If a second error occurs, a correct answer is provided. Note the program may seek either a precise answer or an approximate answer according to the instructor's preference when entering the match.

Unique Aspects: Any text may be entered into Lecture. Thus the program can serve very specific situations. Some formats thus far used are: (1) using reading selections for given textbooks, (2) entering dialog for commercially produced language videos (by using the possible backup questions, a total of 50 plus 3 questions per screen are available for each video sequence), (3) making résumés of movies shown and discussed in class so that students can follow up oral exercises at a later time in textual format.

Form and Function (Robert Balas, Kriston Bruland)
[French, English, Spanish)

Purposes:
1. To permit students to explore the parts of speech and their functions in order to learn how sentences are structured
2. To provide an individualized, problem-solving approach to teach grammar outside of the classroom
3. To permit students to work on specific grammatical difficulties

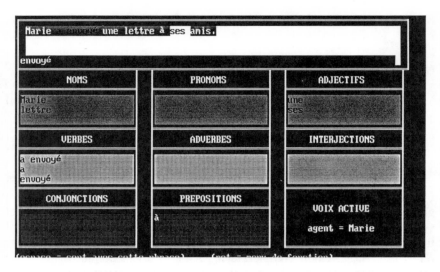

Figure 16. *Form and Function* screen 1 (form). Students select grammatical forms of words in sentences at the top of the screen. Note that "a envoyé" can be broken down into its constitutent parts. Students must choose a form. If it is wrong, the student is alerted and the correct form is given. The box in the lower right corner provides supplemental information. This exercise deals with the passive voice, the active voice, and the French pronominal voice.

Figure 17. *Form and Function* screen 2 (form and function). Same sentence as in screen 1. This time the student must select both the grammatical form and the function of the form in the sentence. Here "une" has been selected as an adjective, then as a determinant. Now the student will make a choice of the definite article or the indefinite article or the partitive or the possessive adjective or the demonstrative adjective or a numerical adjective.

Hardware: IBM PC (128K minimum), color monitor

Operation: This grammar and syntax parsing program allows students to see sentences broken down into parts of speech (noun, pronoun, verb, adjective, adverb, preposition, conjunction, and interjection) as well as to see clauses designated according to function. As the student moves the cursor from word to word, each is categorized below in a series of boxes for each part of speech. Next the screen changes and the same words are categorized by function (i.e., nouns and pronouns are categorized as subject, direct object, indirect object, object of a preposition, etc.; verbs as active, passive, infinitive, present participle/gerund, past participle; clauses as adjectival or adverbial function, etc.).

Students also have the option to choose the proper part of speech for the first screen, then on the second screen again choose the part of speech followed by the function of the part of speech in a sentence. Since there is a secondary menu, it is possible to have students select *fatigués* in the sentence "Ils sont fatigués" first as a predicate adjective, then as the past participle of the verb "fatiguer" functioning as an adjective.

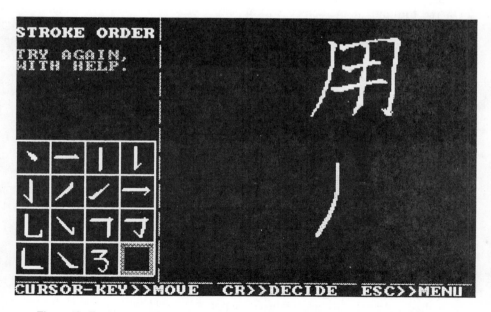

Figure 18. *Kanji* screen. The student is trying to select the proper stroke order and proper stroke for the kanji above. Upon completion of the proper stroke and order, the screen will show a brief story to help the student remember the kanji.

Unique Aspects: The program seems very well adapted to helping students practice problem solving in grammar and syntax so that class time may be used for more practical communication exercises. The editing system is very easy to use, yet the complexity of structures and grammatical forms it can accommodate are quite impressive. The program can be used at almost any level of language study.

Kanji (Charles A. Balas and Qiao Jin with Robert Balas and Edward Kaplan)

Hardware: IBM PC with mouse

Purpose: To instruct students in the proper stroke order for learning Japanese kanji. Additional text information is used as a means of developing a system of recall. The program is built around the book *Remembering the Kanji* published by J. W. Heisig, who has given his permission to use his method.

In Preparation

Raconteur (Robert Balas, Kriston Bruland, Robert Burke) [French]

The screen is divided into three parts: a large section on the top half and a large section on the bottom half, divided by a two-line central window. On the top half of the screen will appear a developing story in pictures, which the student will write in words on the bottom half of the screen. As the student enters his/her story, the bottom window will scroll. To assist the student, three two-line inserts of vocabulary may be called up in the central window. If the student needs further help, three sets of questions may also be called up in the central window. When the student has completed the story, the instructor will be able to call it up on a full screen, double- or triple-spacing the text. Then, by moving the cursor to a word and pressing a specified key, the instructor will color-code errors, poor phrasing, or any other correction. In the space below, the instructor will be able to type in the correct form or offer remediation. There will be an option to print out the text once corrected.

Conclusion

Exploration of the new technology at Western Washington University is now entering the arena of more complicated interactive programs. The programs thus far designed should easily fit into interactive video formats and then hold the promise of broad support for such videos at relatively little cost for hardware. The concentration upon context has aided in the creation of programs combining sound, graphics, and text that seek to center language instruction upon comprehension and speaking, while not sacrificing the reading and writing or grammar skills.

For further information, interested individuals are invited to contact Robert S. Balas, Professor of French, Department of Foreign Languages, Western Washington University, Bellingham, Washington 98225.

Reference, WestCenter

1. Ofiesh, Gabriel D., "Interactive Information Technologies and Their Potential in Education," pp. 166 in S. Lambert and J. Salis, eds., *CD-I and Interactive Videodisc Technology.* Indianapolis, IN: Howard W. Sams and Comp., 1987.

16

Spanish MicroTutor

Frank A. Domínguez
The University of North Carolina at Chapel Hill

Introduction

In 1981 a small group of University of North Carolina faculty members met informally with the associate dean for general education to discuss the need to introduce computing across the undergraduate curriculum. The group was aware of the educational potential of computer-based instructional materials, but realized that the cost of development and the lack of faculty incentives had kept the quality of available materials low and production local. Furthermore, the University of North Carolina College of Arts and Sciences did not yet have a coherent computer policy. Indeed, there was not much knowledge about how to use computers in the undergraduate curriculum nor of how a state institution traditionally strapped for resources could acquire the large number of machines needed for undergraduate instruction. Initially, the solution to both problems was to seek help from outside sources.

The IBM Corporation was the most receptive of the companies approached by the University of North Carolina for funding. Negotiations between the University and IBM began in November of 1982. The resulting three-year contract, signed one year later, provided money and machines to the General College of the University of North Carolina College of Arts and Sciences in exchange for a pledge to put forth "best efforts" to produce computer-based educational materials in the humanities and sciences. Foreign languages was one of the targeted areas.

What Is Spanish MicroTutor?

Spanish MicroTutor was among the first ten instructional software projects undertaken at the University of North Carolina under the IBM grant.

Additional support was provided by the DOE Office of International Studies and Research, the Lindau Foundation, and the University of North Carolina.

Spanish MicroTutor is an interactive computer-assisted language-learning program for students enrolled in the first and second semesters of beginning Spanish. Presently, Spanish MicroTutor consists of ten lesson diskettes containing twenty-seven grammar tutorials (see Figure 1), forty-five exercises, and fifty-four tests, plus a student diskette and a user's manual.

The student diskette has all the registration and recordkeeping routines, and is necessary to access the tutorial features. It includes a concise reference grammar.

Figure 1. Spanish MicroTutor lessons

Syllables	Present Indicative
Accents	Preterite Indicative
Definite and Indefinite Articles	Future Indicative
Nouns	Perfect Tenses
Descriptive Adjectives	Progressive Tenses
Demonstrative Adjectives	Imperfect Indicative
Possessive Adjectives	Imperative
Numbers	Conditional
por y para	Present Subjunctive
Subject Pronouns	Past Subjunctive
Indirect Object Pronouns	*gustar*
Direct Object Pronouns	*tener, tener que*
Reflexive Pronouns	*saber y conocer*
	ser y estar

The average lesson requires from 30 to 45 minutes to complete. Spanish MicroTutor is presently implemented for the IBM PC, XT, AT, or compatibles with a color monitor and 320k. The program is written in PC PILOT with subroutines in Pascal and Assembler.

Program Objectives

The sacrifice of grammatical accuracy in favor of output can establish communication patterns that are later difficult and sometimes impossible to break. However, it is inherently difficult to teach grammar within a limited time to students with very different skill levels in classes oriented toward communicative performance. The logistics of mass instruction, and the desirability of using class time to improve performance and understanding are such that students receive little individual help in learning grammar. Spanish MicroTutor seeks to solve that problem by using the computer to tutor students in grammar outside of class, thereby allowing the teacher to concentrate on the development of communicative skills. Spanish MicroTutor allows the student to strive for mastery at his or her own pace while the teacher uses classroom time for other activities and needs less time to correct exercises.

Spanish MicroTutor is thorough yet flexible in its application to a course of study. Although the lesson modules contain more grammatical information than the usual Spanish language textbook, the program is not meant to teach advanced grammar. Nevertheless, the scope of the program content means that the software can be used with profit as a review tool at any stage. The tutorial lessons are not dependent on a particular textbook; rather the program makes use of high-frequency vocabulary and contains a glossary the student can call up to find the meanings of unfamiliar Spanish words.

User Interface

Spanish MicroTutor is always under the user's control. The student registers for the program in his/her first session. In subsequent sessions the only information the student must enter before advancing to a directory listing of the lessons in the disk is the current date.

Lesson options are selected by moving a highlight bar with the arrow keys and pressing *Enter* or by selecting a highlighted letter. For example, diskette 6 contains lessons on idiomatic verbs. The student's choices are *Gustar, Tener, Saber y conocer*, and *Ser y estar.* A lesson menu appears immediately on the screen, displaying the following choices: Pre-Test, Tutorial, Exercises, Post-Test, Directory, Index, Quit.

All lesson menus display the same choices. The student must determine what segment of the lesson to attempt by again moving a highlight bar with the arrow keys or by a selected keystroke.

Within each lesson segment (Pre-Test, Tutorial, Exercises, Post-Test, etc.) the student can call up a command menu window at the bottom of the screen by pressing the F1 key. The command menu allows the student to manage the program and obtain additional information as needed. The student can skip to other lessons or lesson segments, go to specific pages or exercises, exit the program, or call up a variety of help screens, a glossary, or an index of the lessons on the disk. The index allows the user to skip to any tutorial lesson on that disk from within any other lesson and return to the point of origin. On the XT and the AT, where the lessons can reside on the hard disk, the directory lists all of the lessons in Spanish MicroTutor and the index analyzes all of the tutorials. The student therefore can easily move between all program lessons.

Lesson Structure

In order to provide teachers and students with a flexible tool, all of the Spanish MicroTutor lessons have four segments: Pre-Test, Tutorial, Tutorial Exercises, and Post-Test. The Pre-Test consists of at least ten questions, which the program grades to ascertain the student's understanding of the material. After answering the questions, the student is given a chance to review all the answers and change any that seem incorrect. The program then scores the test and, depending on the score, suggests that the student (1) proceed to another lesson, (2) take the tutorial for the lesson tested, or in some cases (3) go to a review of the basic points of the tutorial.

The heart of the lesson is the *Tutorial*, which introduces the student to the concepts under study. Text screens hold minimal information, but when more information would be advantageous, the student is able to control the rate at which it is added. The program uses color coding to relate grammar explanations and examples, thus attracting the student's attention unobtrusively to the basic material. Movement and flashing of text are also used, but only for very speific purposes—for example, to indicate placement of direct and indirect object pronouns, or to indicate possible sentence structures. Where appropriate within the Tutorial, the student is asked questions about the grammar or is tested to determine understanding of the material.

The *Exercises* follow and allow the student to put into practice what has been learned. The student answers questions (multiple choice, fill-in-the-blank, cloze, etc.) based on the grammar learned in the Tutorial. Depending on the nature of the exercise, the program normally allows the student three chances to enter a correct answer. To each incorrect response there is instant feedback in the form of a hint or, where the program anticipates the incorrect response, an explanation of the error committed. The student can also request the answer by typing *?* and pressing *ENTER*, whereupon the answer is provided with some grammar review information. Help screens and a glossary are available through the Command Menu.

Finally, the student moves on to the *Post-Test*. The Post-Test determines the student's achievement level and, like the Pre-Test, consists of a series of multiple-choice, yes-no, or fill-in-the-blank questions. At the end, the student can change the answers before the program scores the exam. The program then compares Pre- and Post-Test scores and advises the student if further review of the material is needed, after which the program shows the incorrect responses followed by the expected answer.

Special Characters

Alt + a, e, i, o, u generate their accented counterparts as do function keys F2 (á), F4 (é) F6 (í), F8 (ó), and F10 (ú). Alt + !, Alt + ?, and Alt + n generate inverted question and exclamation marks and the ñ. All special characters can also be obtained by entering the extended ASCII code for the accented characters.

Records

The program captures every answer entered by the student and maintains a user file with the date, lesson name, time spent on each lesson segment, Pre- and Post-Test scores, and the percentage of improvement between the two.

User Strategies

The structure of the materials allows the teacher to use the program in three principal modes:

1. Spanish MicroTutor can be the main source of grammar instruction, in which case the student would bypass the diagnostic Pre-Test and go directly to the Tutorial.
2. Spanish MicroTutor can be used with any textbook to reinforce grammar explanations and can add to or substitute for the student workbook. Under this option, the student studies the grammar assignment in the textbook or in class, then takes the Pre-Test to determine his/her command of the material. If the score received is low, the program tells the student to proceed to the grammar Tutorial and the Tutorial exercises. At the end, the Post-Test determines his or her understanding of the material.
3. Spanish MicroTutor can be used as an adjunct to classroom instruction to remediate student grammar deficiencies at any level of language learning.

Evaluation

Spanish MicroTutor has undergone several evaluation cycles at the hands of the educational courseware design staff of the Microcomputer Support Center at the University of North Carolina and the Instructional Design Services of the Media Center. These evaluations assessed the user interface for ease of use and suitability to the tutorial task. The recommendations of both evaluations were incorporated into the program. MicroTutor has also been in use with pilot classes at the University of North Carolina and at Meredith College. Teachers at both institutions praise the clarity with which the grammar is presented. They also appreciate not having to correct student exercises. Student response to the program has been very positive, particularly among low achievers. Students like to pace their learning and strive for mastery. Most students show a marked improvement between Pre- and Post-Test scores. The sample, however, is not yet large enough to determine the impact of the program on the overall language-learning process. Beginning in the fall of 1987, Virginia Polytechnic and Duke University may serve as additional beta test sites. Spanish MicroTutor should be available for purchase from Harcourt Brace Jovanovich in the spring of 1988.

Readers interested in further information may write the author at the Department of Romance Languages, The University of North Carolina, Dey 014-A, Chapel Hill, NC 27514.

17

CLEF: Computer-Assisted Learning Exercises for French

Dana M. Paramskas

University of Guelph

Introduction

CLEF was begun in 1978, inspired by the need to give students in beginning French classes more practice and feedback on grammar skills than could be done with the traditional workbook. The participation of three universities in the design team[1] (Calgary, Guelph, Western Ontario) ensured that the program would be adaptable to a broad range of texts and methods, be user-friendly yet sophisticated in terms of error correction and computer response, and be flexible enough for students with a broad range of skills to profit equally from using it (Holmes et al., 5).

The project, which included versions for both IBM hardware (with color and graphics) and Commodore (monochrome with graphics), was finished in 1986, although some debugging continues for the last part of the series. Outside of Canada, CLEF is distributed by Gessler Publishing (address in Appendix).

Program Description

CLEF is a program that both tutors the student on French grammar and offers immediate application of the grammar points in the form of exercises. The sixty-two lessons (see Figure 1) cover all of French grammar from

---

1. A. Boyd, R. Harley, G. Holmes, M. Kidd, P. Watts (U. of Western Ontario); L. Laidman, M. Milhausen, G. Neno (London Board of Education); D. Mydlarski (U. of Calgary); D. Paramskas (U. of Guelph).

the beginning to the intermediate levels. Color and graphics are used to illustrate theory and add to the enjoyment of the applications for the student (Holmes and Kidd, 4).

Lessons are self-contained and each concentrates on one grammatical point. Instructors are therefore able to shuffle the order of the lessons to suit whatever text or method they are using. The exercises are completely text-independent, and can be used in any course where grammatical knowledge is considered important (Holmes and Kidd, 2).

Each lesson is structured in the following fashion:

A. Grammar presentation
B. From 3 to 5 exercises per lesson. For each exercise:
   1. A presentation of new vocabulary; an optional drill on the new words
   2. Instructions and a reminder of Help options
   3. The exercise
   4. A reversion, which brings back those parts of the exercise that the student did not complete correctly after two tries

Grammar Review

The first part of each lesson is an optional review of the grammar point. The explanations are concise; no attempt has been made to provide the type of comprehensive coverage of rules and exceptions that would be found in many textbooks.

The CLEF grammar review is intended to convey grammatical information in a way that is not duplicated by any other medium. Information is presented in a visualized manner by which the microcomputer's special features are exploited: color coding for pattern presentation and for emphasis, simulated movement, independent manipulation of different areas of the screen, timing, blinking, reverse video, and graphics.

The aim of the CLEF explanations is not only to present information in a unique way; CLEF assists learners who may have difficulty assimilating information conveyed through the more tradiitonal media that involve the spoken or written word (Holmes and Kidd, 3).

Exercises

The drill-and-practice sections of the CLEF lessons comprise between three and five exercises. Students may choose to do any or all of the exercises and in any order. Each exercise is prefaced by the presentation of all the major lexical items that the student will meet in the exercise. First, the items are presented individually. Masculine nouns appear in blue, feminine nouns in red, and the learner can request a translation of any of the items at any time. When all the vocabulary has been presented, those items for which the learner requested a translation appear on the screen, listed according

1. The definite article
2. Subject pronouns
3. *-er* verbs
4. The imperative of *-er* verbs
5. The interrogative with *est-ce que*
6. The indefinite article
7. The negative (*ne ... pas*)
8. *être*
9. *-re* verbs
10. The agreement of adjectives
11. The position of adjectives
12. *-ir* verbs
13. *avoir*
14. Expressions with *avoir* and *être*
15. Contractions with *à* and *de*
16. The possessive construction
17. Possessive adjectives
18. Numbers 1-100 and dates
19. *aller* and the *futur proche*
20. *venir*
21. Prepositions
22. Stress pronouns
23. *faire* and expressions with *faire*
24. The partitive
25. *prendre, comprendre, apprendre*
26. *pouvoir, vouloir*
27. The interrogative and demonstrative adjectives
28. Time
29. *dire, écrire, lire*
30. Interrogative inversion, interrogative adverbs
31. The past indefinite with *avoir* and agreement
32. *partir, sortir, dormir, sentir, servir*
33. The past indefinite with *être* and agreement

34. The direct object pronouns
35. *savoir, connaître*
36. The indirect object pronouns
37. *mettre, remettre, permettre, promettre*
38. Verbs with prepositions
39. *y, en*
40. *devoir, recevoir*
41. *Qui est-ce qui/que, qu'est-ce qui/que*
42. *voir, boire, croire*
43. Relative pronouns: *qui, que, dont*
44. Adverbs
45. Reflexive verbs and agreement
46. Negatives: *jamais, rien, personne,* etc.
47. *conduire, rire, courir*
48. The future
49. Verbs with irregular stems (*envoyer,* etc.)
50. The comparison of adjectives and adverbs
51. The imperfect tense
52. *venir de; depuis* + present/imperfect
53. *souffrir, ouvrir, offrir, couvrir*
54. The conditional
55. *naître, mourir*
56. The demonstrative pronouns
57. The present subjunctive: form
58. The present subjunctive: uses
59. Impersonal expressions (*falloir, valoir* etc)
60. The pluperfect and the past conditional
61. *faire* causatif
62. The passive voice

Figure 1: CLEF lesson contents

to grammatical category. Finally, the student has the option of being drilled on all items for which a translation was requested. Insofar as it is feasible, the vocabulary in any given lesson has been made to relate to a theme; in this way the lessons can also serve as a vehicle for the acquisition of vocabulary. For example, lessons 1 through 4 relate to education; later lessons relate to the house, clothing, sports, etc.

Lesson Design _____

The lesson design incorporates a number of principles the authors believed would produce pedagogically sound courseware that is also well adapted to the microcomputer medium (Holmes and Kidd, 2).

First, in each lesson the exercises follow a progression, from those intended to develop mechanical skills to those that test their mastery in semantically and grammatically meaningful contexts. In some initial exercises, the student is faced with no greater linguistic task than matching nouns and definite articles or subject pronouns with verb forms. The subsequent exercises offer greater challenges. The student is faced with a series of sentences that must be understood fully before the answer can be supplied. In the lesson on the formation of adjectives, for example, "La neige n'est pas noire, elle est..." The exercise formats are varied and show a progression from multiple-choice types requiring passive recognition of a grammatical point to more complex structured-response types demanding active mastery of the structure involved. In some exercises, all of the stimulus sentences are related to a specific theme or situation so as to provide continuity.

A consistent effort is made to motivate the learner by the adoption of a number of different design strategies. For example, in addition to varying the number of items in a multiple-choice format, the list of possible answers is positioned in different locations on the screen. The constructed-response stimulus may sometimes consist of a single sentence, sometimes a dialog format, sometimes a dialog format with graphics. Occasionally, as in the lesson on numbers, the answer to one question will reposition itself on the screen to form part of the stimulus for the next question.

Messages for correct answers are varied, random, and two-tiered, ranging from Gallic excess for a correct answer at first try ("Fantastique!") to a subdued "OK" on the second.

In some cases, as in exercises matching articles and nouns, users may change the article displayed before choosing a noun. Whenever possible, alternate answers are accepted as correct. For example, in a lesson on time, 6:15 is acceptably stated as "six heures et quart," "six heures quinze," "dix-huit heures et quart," or "dix-huit heures quinze" (Paramskas, 6).

Error Analysis

One component of the CLEF lessons that has consumed a large proportion of the time of both course writers and programmers has been the analysis of student input. Without error analysis and meaningful feedback the effectiveness of CALL is seriously curtailed (Harley et al., 1). The CLEF lessons contain a variety of analysis routines. The simplest involves the anticipation of specific errors; for example "ma" for "mon", etc. With longer anticipated incorrect answers, there is a tolerance for spelling errors, which are usually defined as up to two incorrect characters. Routines have been created to handle small, specific errors such as missing capitals, accents, and typing errors such as incorrect spacing.

Error-trapping routines have been designed in a hierarchical fashion. If the correct answer is not there, a check will first be made for the grammatical point being drilled; for example, in the exercise on the position of adjectives, the program first checks to see if the adjective is in the correct place. If it is, further checks are made for form, spelling, etc. If it is not, any other errors are ignored for the time being, and the student is not bombarded by multiple simultaneous error messages that may discourage him or her. The routines continue to check answers until even the smallest typographical error is signaled when there is nothing else wrong with the answer (Paramskas, 6).

Another example of such routines are those used in an exercise on expressions with *avoir*, where the student must distinguish between *a chaud* and *est chaud*. The principal grammar point here is the choice of the correct verb. CLEF routines therefore check the verb first, and only after it is analyzed is the complement looked at.

Students are given two tries for each answer. If they do not succeed after the second try, a consoling message is given, and the answer appears on the screen. The same sentence will then reappear for another try at the end of the exercise, the part titled "Revision."

Help

Another major feature of CLEF is the series of help features intended to make the lessons more "user-friendly." An explanation of all the help features appears in every CLEF lesson immediately after the student has been asked to type in his or her name, and a summary of the features is repeated at the beginning of each exercise.

Students can become frustrated if they are locked into a lesson or exercise. Exercises in CLEF may be chosen from the menu listing in any order or may be repeated or skipped. A "quit" feature is incorporated to allow students to return to the lesson menu (list of exercises) at any time. Should a student need a quick review of the grammar point while in the middle of an exercise, a one-frame grammar summary is available (Paramskas, 6).

Vocabulary

Since CLEF is completely textbook-independent, its vocabulary relies on cognates and sets of words typically found in beginning textbooks. When other kinds of words occur, they are first presented in an introductory vocabulary drill. As a fail-safe, and to deal with a user population other than an anglophone one (for whom cognates are not particularly helpful), there is a dictionary function within each exercise. Users may at any point type "?" plus the word they do not understand. The translation appears at the bottom left of the screen. An expression can be called up by typing any part of the expression. For example, "tout de suite" can be accessed if the student types either "tout" or "suite"; the translation is given as "tout de suite = immediately."

Certain pedagogical decisions had of necessity to be made as the CLEF lessons were being written. Many decisions had methodological implications relating to the approach used in the teaching of French.

Grammar

The CLEF series is based in the premise that its principal use will be in French courses where the acquisition of explicit grammatical knowledge is considered a useful learning activity.

A second consideration is brought out in the grammar explanations themselves. All explanations are given in English. Since one of the major aims of these explanations is the conveyance of information, English is the most effective langauge to help achieve that goal. It would have been feasible to use French in the later lessons of the series, but it was decided to continue with the same format throughout. On the other hand, the instructions in the exercises are given in English from lessons 1 through 19, but French is used thereafter. In addition, all feedback on student answers is given in French in all lessons.

A contrastive approach has been adopted in appropriate sections of some grammar explanations. This will be evident in two ways. First, a grammatical term or concept may be explained with reference to English in order to ensure that the learner understands what is involved. Second, points of French grammar that are particularly troublesome to anglophone learners are treated with this fact in mind. For example, the English possessive construction in "the teacher's book" has a nominal word order that is the opposite to the one required in French. This reversal of word order is visually demonstrated on the screen in CLEF (Holmes and Kidd, 2).

In CLEF a great deal of stress has been placed on the use of context in language learning. This is apparent in two ways. First, many of the exercises revolve around specific everyday themes; second, the later exercises in each lesson require that the student understand the linguistic context provided in the stimulus in order to provide a satisfactory answer.

Conclusion

Although many drill/tutorial programs for French are now available, CLEF remains very useful because of its unique features: the use of graphics (and/or color) to present grammatical concepts; the extended and sophisticated error analysis, which can distinguish between superficial errors and meaningful errors as well as pick up a long list of anticipated errors with appropriate comments to the learner. Being textbook-independent, and including its own dictionary, CLEF can be used in a wide range of learning situations.

CLEF has been purchased by a number of universities, colleges, and school boards in Canada and the United States. It has been reviewed favorably in the *Canadian Modern Language Review, The Northeast Conference Newsletter,* and *PC Magazine* and has been purchased by the National Center for Computer Assisted Language Learning (NCCALL) in Britain for conversion to the Acorn computer. Readers interested in further information about CLEF for the IBM are invited to write to the author at French Studies, Department of Languages, University of Guelph, Guelph, Ontario, Canada N1G 2W1. Similar information on CLEF for the Commodore may be obtained from Professor Glyn Holmes, Department of French, University of Western Ontario, London, Ontario, Canada N6A 3K7.

References, CLEF

1. Harley, Rick E., Helen Heller, and Glyn Holmes. "Input Analysis and Feedback in a CAI System for Languages," pp. 158-61 in *Computer Based Instruction: Frontiers of Thought.* Bellingham, WA: Western Washington University Computer Center, 1981.

2. Holmes, Glyn, and Marilyn Kidd. "Computer Assisted Learning: Design and Implementation." *SPEAQ Journal* 4, 3-4 (1980) :83-96.

3. Holmes, Glyn, and Marilyn Kidd. "The Evolving Case for Computers in the Study of Modern Languages." *ALLC* [Association for Literary and Linguistic Computing] *Journal,* 1, 1 (1982) :7-11.

4. Holmes, Glyn, and Marilyn Kidd. "The CLEF Project: Learning French on Color Micros," pp. 245-51 in *Conference Proceedings, ADCIS.* Bellingham, WA: Western Washington University Computer Center, 1982.

5. Holmes, Glyn, Donna Mydlarski, and Dana M. Paramskas. "Cooperative Courseware Production: A Solution to the Problems of CAI?" pp. 252-58 in *Conference Proceedings, ADCIS.* Bellingham, WA: Western Washington University Computing Center, 1982.

6. Paramskas, Dana M. "Courseware-Software Interfaces: Some Designs and Some Problems." *CALICO Journal* 1, 3 (1983) :4-6.

18

LITLAB:
Computer-Assisted
Investigation of Literature

Stephen Harroff
Indiana University-Purdue University at Fort Wayne

Introduction

This project report describes an approach to teaching literature in a modified laboratory setting in which the computer program is used simultaneously as a mentor for tracing the process of literary analysis and as a tool for gathering and ordering data from a literary text. The project was developed for undergraduate students of French, German, and Spanish enrolled in a course entitled "Methods of Research and Criticism in a Foreign Literature" taught by the author at Indiana University-Purdue University at Fort Wayne.

The investigation of literature is central to an understanding of the role of scholar and humanist; the use of the computer to facilitate such investigation is not—at least for the majority of students. Why then might a microcomputer be an appropriate, even desirable, medium to acquaint beginning students of literature with literary theory and analysis, rather than some other more traditional means? The three pedagogical objectives that have guided the LITLAB project described in this report provide an answer to that question:

1. The computer should allow the teacher to portray the activity of an

The author wishes to express his profound gratitude to Susan R. Harroff, without whose expertise in computer programming, in literature, and in pedagogical aspects of teaching composition this project surely would have taken another, less-satisfying form.

The computer screens represented in Figures 1-10 were printed directly from LITLAB during an actual working session. These illustrations do not clearly show what part of the text was printed by the program and what was entered by the student, nor can they recreate the effect of a system that is interactive and that employs color.

expert in literary analysis using a medium that helps students to grasp ideas more easily because of its appeal to their senses: visual (through use of color highlighting) and kinesthetic (through development of interactive, learner-centered learning units).

2. The tutorial capabilities of the computer should be used to lead students (a) to follow the same type of rudimentary process as might be conducted intuitively by an expert in analyzing a work and (b) to repeat the process often enough and in sufficient contexts so that it becomes natural and commonplace.

3. The computer programs should provide analytic tools that are easy to use and make the analysis challenging and interesting.

The analytic process that serves as a model for this investigation of literature is the experimentation protocol used by scientists in the laboratory. This protocol involves three principles:

1. To be openly inquisitive and willing to disassemble, attempting to uncover all the properties of the object under investigation
2. To follow a systematic, logical procedure
3. To document one's findings rigorously as one works:
   a. describing in a log all objects observed
   b. comparing and contrasting elements in this log with one another
   c. comparing and contrasting elements in the log with known materials using tests and proofs as analytic tools

The use of the experimentation protocol to analyze literature helps students to realize they must get beyond viewing the work as a massive, impenetrable whole in order to examine its component features carefully and individually, and to trace their internal links to one another. The technique used in the course for which the programs described below were designed asks students to follow the procedure that would be used intuitively by the expert in the field, the literary scholar. Students are asked to develop a habitual method of operation in which they practice the following five steps:

1. Uncover the component parts of the literary work by maintaining a log of key words for each feature of
   a. plot
   b. setting—time and place
   c. character
   d. striking image
2. Compare and contrast each of these four with one another looking for patterns of repetition
3. Examine the structure of the work, specifically:
   a. the title
   b. text divisions
   c. beginning/middle/end of the work
   d. beginning/middle end of each division
4. Compare and contrast these observations with characteristics of major themes in world literature

5. Link these observations in turn to the author's world view and to important human issues the work addresses

By following this process rigorously, students learn to act like a literary scholar; at the same time they gain enough data about both the content and the form of the work that they can begin to analyze and interpret the work actively either in a classroom setting or for a short paper. In concert with this—admittedly behaviorist—learning objective, the computer-mediated system described below helps students to emulate the work of the experienced scholar and to keep adequate documentation of their findings.

The Courseware

Reproduced below in figure 1 is the Table of Contents from an opening session for LITLAB from which the students may select the individual programs. The division of the courseware into tutorials and utilities reflects two major premises of this project—that students should be able to observe an expert at work parsing a literary text; they should be able to obtain significant help as they begin to interpret a work of their own choice.

Figure 1. LITLAB Table of Contents

TABLE OF CONTENTS
Tutorials for Analysis and Interpretation
Analysis and Interpretation of Excerpted Passages
1. from Faulkner's *The Hamlet*
2. from Carpentier's *The Lost Steps*

Analysis and Interpretation of a Complete Work
3. Kafka's *The Metamorphosis*

Utilities for Analysis and Interpretation
4. Literary Processor
5. Bibliography and Annotation Processor
6. Essay Processor

7. QUIT

Which number do you select?

The Tutorials

At present the tutorial sections of LITLAB offer students the opportunity to observe the building toward an interpretation using two excerpted passages and one complete short story. The final version is to include treatment of an additional three excerpts and several more complete works, including a drama and a poem. All passages included in the tutorial section are discussed in translation since the method is applicable to literature written in any Western language and all of the works treated are acknowledged masterpieces.

Excerpted Passages. The analysis of excerpted passages involves three steps: (1) color highlighting of key words as the excerpt is displayed on the screen, (2) listing all the key words in a chart, and (3) building an outline for an essay or discussion based upon an analysis of these key words from the excerpt. Once students have selected one of the excerpted passages, they are asked whether they would like a printed copy. Next, they select by simple keystroke one of the traditional elements of prose fiction (plot, setting, characterization, and imagery) for color highlighting on screen of key words in the passage itself. Students may choose to view the color highlighting additively (first plot-related words, then setting, etc.) or by individual element.

Once the student has chosen which element of prose fiction is to be high-lighted, all words in the passage that relate to this key concept are highlighted on screen in the color chosen to represent that element of prose fiction. Keywords of plot are highlighted in red; setting is assigned the color blue, characterization is green, and imagery is boldfaced. (Figure 2 shows a composite list of key words highlighted in an excerpt from Faulkner's *The Hamlet.*) This color markup of the text often allows students to readily "see" for the first time the significant benefit that accrues from a close reading and careful marking of a text.

The next step is to view a file that lists the significant key words by category of element as a stimulus for comparative and contrastive analysis of the concepts. Students are again asked whether they wish to make a printed copy of the screen. There are two reasons students are encouraged to do so. First, having a permanent copy of the data allows them to work independently, emulating the process followed by the excerpt; and second, they may wish to keep the data sheet for future reference either as a guide for the development of their own log, or as a stimulus to future interpretation of the work itself. In either case, students are encouraged to use an unabridged and an etymological dictionary to research any unusual words. Once we have highlighted the text, our next step is to make a file (or list) of the key words by category. For this passage, we have the following data:

Figure 2. Key words highlighted in an excerpt from Faulkner

Plot	Setting	Character	Image
	hamlet	thirteen	Dionysiac
		baby	honey in sunlight
		breasts	bursting grapes
		fiercely-pointed	writhen bleeding
		cones	crushed fecundated vine
		puberty	hard repacious trampling
		maidenhood	goat-hoof
		sullen bemusement	not a living integer
		weary wisdom	teeming vacuum
		enlarging of her	sound-proof glass
		organs	mammalian maturity

Next, we must be certain that we have fully researched any terms which are unusual. I suggest that you rely on a dictionary used for advanced composition courses and on an etymological dictionary. In this passage, we should look up words such as <Dionysiac> <writhen> <fecundated> and <rapacious>.

When you wish to continue, press any key.

(Figure 2 shows in brackets the items the expert might have referenced. A later screen gives the results of that research.)

Based upon this list of key words from the passage, the expert then completes a comparative/contrastive analysis, looking for patterns of repetition and relating them in turn to important examples of the human condition and to major thematic emphases in literature.

Figure 3. Final expert outline

Characterization and the Development of Theme in Faulkner's
<The Hamlet>:
Eula's Introduction, the Fertility Motif and the Love/Death Theme

INTRO: Violent sexual imagery in passage and concentration on physical and emotional descriptors prejudice the reader to associate Eula with erotic sexuality and with an unanticipated and destructive encounter.

I. Elements of Prose Fiction as Expressions of Fertility Motif
  A. Key Aspects of Characterization (Physical)
    1. <breasts> <no longer fiercely-pointed cones>
    2. <enlarging of her organs>
  B. Key Aspects of Characterization (Emotional)
    1. <baby> <thirteen>
    2. <puberty> <maidenhood> <mammalian maturity>
    3. <sullen bemusement> <weary wisdom>
  C. Imagery of Sexual Readiness
    1. <honey in sunlight>
    2. <bursting grapes>
II. Elements of Prose Fiction as Expressions of the Love/Death Theme
  A. Imagery of Isolation
    1. <not a living integer>
    2. <teeming vacuum>
    3. <sound-proof glass>
  B. Imagery of Violent, Destructive Sexuality
    1. <Dionysiac times>
    2. <writhen bleeding>
    3. <crushed fedundated vine>
    4. <hard rapacious trampling goat-hoof>

CONCL: The first love act entails a death of innocence and of the self alone. This work discusses, among other issues, the nature of acquiescence and of 'calling' in an isolated community through the character, Eula.
When you wish to continue, press any key.

The final step in the tutorial on how to deal with excerpted passages allows students to watch an outline developed progressively based upon the information gathered about the passage. The computer's ability to display information in an additive fashion is exploited in order to help the student to develop a point-by-point outline reflecting the student's own analysis prior to the appearance on the screen of the outline developed by the literary expert. The outline proceeds from the title, through the introduction, through each of the major sections and its various subsections, to the conclusion. (Figure 3 displays the final screen of the outline.) Tracing this process as a process helps beginning students of literature become oriented in some of the various steps experts follow in textual analysis while demonstrating that the reader of literature can come to significant conclusions about the artistic beauty of a work and the deeper relevance of its message to human life even in an excerpted passage if (1) the text is analyzed closely, (2) accurate records are kept of one's findings, and (3) a logical process of information gathering is followed. The excerpted-passage portion of the tutorial is recommended to students as being a valuable preparation for the essay examinations they will be required to write on selected passages from literature at regular intervals throughout the term.

Complete Works. The text chosen for computer display of the process of interpreting and writing about a complete work of literature is Kafka's *Metamorphosis.* The tutorial on how to analyze complete works proceeds through a series of steps that differ from those used for excerpted passages because the nature of information about the work has changed and, more importantly, because the goal now includes an anlaysis of the entire work rather than a focus on a brief passage.

The five steps involved in the analysis of a complete work are (1) examination of the title, (2) disclosure of the work's structure and of the interplay of the elements of prose fiction within that structure, (3) consideration of major themes suggested in the work, (4) contemplation of human issues the work addresses, and (5) outlining of a paper or discussion that focuses on some significant aspect of the work. The program again relies on the ability of the computer to present information in an interactive fashion about the process used by the expert; students are encouraged to anticipate both the questions (and the answers) the expert might ask before they are displayed.

The process begins with an exhaustive examination of the title and with the concepts it may suggest in the reader. (Figure 4 shows the completed analysis of the title.) Next, the program steps through an investigation of the structure of the work, first examining the elements of prose fiction relevant at the beginning, middle, and end of the entire work, then determining the external textual divisions, and finally conducting an analysis of the elements of prose fiction for each division (see Figure 5 for a representative screen). At this point, the expert makes an interpretive judgment based upon information gleaned from the text on each of the four traditional elements— plot, setting, characterization, imagery—which will direct the ensuing investigation (see Figure 6). Then the data is linked to major themes in literature. The final step before helping students to develop an outline is to determine what moments or deep issues of the human condition are addressed by the work (see Figure 7). Finally, the complete outline of a paper is built for the user, additively, from title and introduction to conclusion in the same manner as in the tutorial on excerpted passages. Every attempt is made to include analysis of both content and form, to relate the interpretation to significant (in this case, contemporary) human questions, and to maintain a rigorous focus throughout.

Figure 4. Completed title analysis

THE METAMORPHOSIS (Kafka)

Step 1: Consider the significance of the TITLE.

METAMORPHOSIS (physical world) = transformation

FROM	TO
caterpillar	butterfly
crawling	free flight
ugly	beautiful

with interim step of cocoon (closed off from world). Accordingly, we will look for such transformations in:

plot   setting   characterization   images

CONCLUSIONS:

	FROM	TO
Plot	no job	jobs (family)
Setting	Gregor's room	open country
Character	GREgor	GREte
Images	beetle stretching	Grete's stretching

Do you wish to print a copy of this screen?

Figure 5. Prose element analysis in development

Plot	Setting	Character	Image
B E G I N N I N G			
Gregor awakens as dung beetle	Gregor's room Winter	Gregor	Gregor's awkward stretching
Grete (family) awakens to new possibilities	Spring open country	Grete	Grete's graceful stretching
E N D O F W O R K			

To print: Shift   Prt Sc

Figure 6. Interpretive judgment

To date, we have found:

PLOT	Gregor dies in middle of Part Three, thus symmetry of structure is broken, as is his life.
SETTING	The setting is consistently reduced [room > sofa > sheet> exoskeleton] until end, which opens out.
CHARACTER	Gregor decides to die when Grete calls him 'it', thus robbing him of his essential humanity [music].
IMAGERY	Gregor's exoskeleton preserves the exterior even when he is dead. No one knows what is happening to him inside.

When you wish to continue, press any key.

Figure 7. Universal themes

Step 7: Discuss the Poet's Vision.

Now we will focus our attention on how Kafka draws on the themes of love/death, freedom/bondage, and seeming/being in making a specific statement about the quality of human life.

As we do so, we should use the elements of prose fiction as a guide. The most striking aspect of this work—one that no student ever forgets—is Gregor's ludicrous, fantastic, unbelievable, utterly unreal BODY. But is it so unreal?

How might you answer this question if you were:

7 feet 3 inches tall (with size 20 feet)?
3 feet 6 inches tall?
afflicted with elephantiasis?
a paraplegic?

or perhaps were carrying something HIDDEN, like VD or AIDS?

When you wish to continue, press any key.

The Utilities

The second goal of the LITLAB courseware is to provide students with tools that reiterate expert analytical processes and at the same time allow them to easily maintain a permanent record of their findings about any text they may choose to interpret. The special-purpose notetaking processors described below are programs to help students perform the three most basic tasks associated with discussing literature:

1. To analyze and interpret
2. To maintain a bibliography
3. To develop a working outline for a paper or presentation

These utilities are not constructed tutorials, like those already described, that focus on a specific literary work or excerpt and that portray the actual conclusions reached by an expert. Instead, they are much more open-ended. These processors make no intuitive judgments and reach no conclusions; rather, they lead a student through the process of gathering and ordering information about a work of individual choice. They further serve as note-taking media that prompt the student to consider aspects of interpretation and writing students are prone to forget.

The Literary Processor. The literary processor assumes that the student already has completed a careful reading and markup of the literary text. This program serves as a reiteration of the analytic process and as a note-taking facility. The utility processor proceeds through a series of queries that the student answers by keystroke or typed response and may print out at any time. (Yet to be included is a mechanism for storing the data in files that can be updated and expanded.)

The first question addresses the title of the work and its significance for subsequent interpretation of the elements of prose fiction. (Figure 8 shows the results of a sample working session.) Next, the processor directs the student through a numerical charting of the external structure of the work. (Figure 9 holds a sample of the data collected about a work comprising three chapters.) Following documentation of the structure of the text, the student is prompted to type in significant aspects of the elements of prose fiction for each textual division, as suggested by Figure 10. Next, the student is shown a list of the most common literary themes and is asked to specify which one or more is addressed by the work, and which one seems to predominate. Finally, positing with Solzhenitsyn that all great literature has a special conscience, the program asks the student to declare what issues of the human condition this work discusses. This final question is meant to help students begin to achieve a focus for their interpretive writing assignment (which may follow).

The literary processor is not an intelligent system that evaluates students' answers, nor is it an expert system for literature—both concepts beyond the present capabilities of both the programmers and currently popular microcomputers, yet plausible goals for future development. Instead, the program serves as an interactive note-taking medium, designed by a scholar who attempts to direct the work of the student (in the instructor's absence) toward documenting significant ideas about the form and the content of a given work.

This literary processor is pedagogically useful primarily because it directs beginning students through a series of interpretive steps that many heretofore

Figure 8. Sample literary processor results

Give the title of the work:

La casa de Bernarda Alba

Part A is: La casa
Part B is: Bernarda Alba

Which element of prose fiction does La casa suggest?
setting

What other settings might be compared to or contrasted with La casa?
1. rooms in house
2. village
3. outer world

Which element of prose fiction does Bernarda Alba suggest?
character

What other characters might be compared to or contrasted with Bernarda Alba?
1. grandmother
2. Adela
3. Angustias

To print: [CTRL   PRT SC   ]

Figure 9. External structure of a work

To this point, you have the following numeric data:

	Section 1	Section 2	Section 3	Section	Section
Beginning	157	177	196		
Middle	166	186	203		
End	176	195	211		

Now go to the middle of each section, and make lists of plot features, of setting, of characters, and of imagery, for each of the 3 text divisions.

To print: [CTRL   PRT SC   ]

Figure 10. Prompts for literary elements

On what page in your edition does La casa de Bernarda Alba begin?
    Page: 156

On what page does it end?
    Page: 211

The exact middle would be: Page 183

Check the text between page 178 and page 189. Jot down any interesting elements of:

PLOT

SETTING

CHARACTER

IMAGERY

To print: [CTRL   PRT SC   ]

have often simply overlooked. To internalize a process is to repeat it in a variety of contexts, some controlled (as in the tutorials), others open-ended (as in the literary processor). Once students have internalized the process, they can move on to the next plateau of interpretive acumen: discarding this by now too-rigorous system in favor of an intuitive approach that is more pleasing aesthetically because it links the vision and understanding of the poet more directly with that of a skilled interpreter of literature.

The Bibliography and Annotation Processor. This program does not attempt to reproduce the excellent formats for such work found in most of the more expensive word processors. Instead, its intent is to provide students with a tool that helps them learn the standard form of the *MLA Handbook* while they make a record both of the bibliographic entry and the ideas they may wish to use from a given source and that require documentation.

The bibliography and annotation processor prompts the student to enter bibliographic information, which is then stored in a series of files for subsequent modification, for key-word searches, and for eventual printing either as an annotated bibliography or as a list of works cited. The bibliography processor also includes a utility for making brief annotations and for citing brief passages from the work.

The Essay Processor. This program currently exists only as a flowchart that must be coded before it can be used by students and modified for distribution. Current plans involve using the query system employed in the literary processor to develop a systematic method of work so that students can avoid writing essays that are too impressionistic, or do not begin from a truly significant focus or fail to maintain it rigorously. In its current form, the essay processor helps students (1) find an appropriate title, (2) develop a significant focus that shows the interplay between content and form and addresses an equally significant issue of the human passage, (3) reiterate and modify that focus as they proceed through the body of the essay or brief paper, and (4) conclude the essay in an artistic, to-the-point, yet satisfying manner.

Conclusion

The computer disk for LITLAB described above is intended to be distributed as part of a handbook of literary method, a version of which is currently being used for the course on research and criticism involving a foreign literature.

Readers interested in further information on LITLAB or the materials for the handbook and accompanying software should address inquiries to the author at the Department of Modern Foreign Languages, Indiana University-Purdue University at Fort Wayne, 2101 Coliseum Blvd. East, Fort Wayne, Indiana 46805.

APPENDIX

Addresses of Software and Equipment Vendors

(Where the text refers to a specific product, the name of the product appears in parentheses after the vendor name.)

Acornsoft, Ltd.
Betjemar House
104 Hills Road
Cambridge CB2 1LQ England

AIMTECH Corporation
(IconAuthor)
77 Northeastern Boulevard
Nashua, NH 03062

Allen Communication
(Quest)
5225 Wiley Post Way
Salt Lake City, UT 84116

Apple Computer, Inc.
20525 Mariani Ave.
Cupertino, CA 95014

Applied Computer Systems
3060 Johnstown-Utica Rd.
Johnstown, OH 43031

BCD Associates
5809 S.W. 5th Street, Suite 101
Oklahoma City, OK 73128

Broderbund Software, Inc.
17 Paul Street
San Rafael, CA 94903

Cambridge University Press
(Cambridge Micro Software)
The Edinburgh Building
Shaftesbury Rd.
Cambridge CB2 2RU England

Camsoft
10 Wheatfield Close
Miadenhead, Berkshire SL6 3PS
England

Centaur Systems, Ltd.
P. O. Box 3220
Madison, WI 53704

COMPress
P. O. Box 102
Wentworth, NH 03282

CONDUIT
M310 Oakdale Hall
The University of Iowa
Iowa City, IA 52242

Corvus Systems, Inc.
2100 Corvus Drive
San Jose, CA 95124

D.C. Heath and Co.
125 Spring Street
Lexington, MA 02173

Dialogic Corporation
(Dialog 1)
129 Little Rd.
Parsippany, NJ 07054

Digital Equipment Corporation
(DECtalk)
146 Main St.
Maynard, MA 0175

Duke University Humanities Comput-
ing Facility
(CALIS)
104 Languages Building
Duke University
Durham, NC 27706

Ealing College of Higher Education
(Callboard)
School of Language Studies, Grove
House
1 The Grove
London W5 5DX England

Ealing College of Higher Education
School of Business Administration
St. Mary's Rd.
London W5 5RF England

Educational & Information Systems,
Inc.
(Instavox RA-12)
804 North Neil Street
P.O. Box 1774
Champaign, IL 61820

Educational Electronic Corporation
(SONY AV Products)
213 North Cedar Ave.
Inglewood, CA 90301

EMC Publishing, Inc.
300 York Ave.
St. Paul, MN 55101

Films, Inc.
5547 N. Ravenswood Ave.
Chicago, IL 60640

Forlan Software
12 Stanley Street
Luton, Bedfordshire, LU1 5AN

Gamma Productions, Inc.
710 Wilshire Blvd., Suite 609
Los Angeles, CA 90401

George Earl, Inc.
1302 S. General McMullen
San Antonio, TX 78237

Gessler Publishing Co.
900 Broadway
New York, NY 10003-1291

Gutenberg Software, Ltd.
47 Lewiston Rd.
Scarborough, Ontario M1P 1X8
Canada

Heinle and Heinle Publishing, Inc.
20 Park Plaza
Boston, MA 02116

Infocom
55 Wheeler Street
Cambridge, MA 02138

Inner London Educational Computing
Centre
John Ruskin Street
London SE5 OPQ England

Interactive Technologies Corporation
(Genesis)
9625 Black Mountain Road, Suite 315
San Diego, CA 92126

Interkom
(Schoolhouse Software)
290 Brighton Road
Elk Grove Village, IL 60007

International Business Machines
(IBM Voice Option Card)
Contact your local IBM representative.

International Film Bureau, Inc.
332 S. Michigan Ave.
Chicago, IL 60604

International Software
(Lingofun)
P.O. Box 486
Westerville, OH 43081

Langenscheidt Publishing
46-35 54 Rd.
Maspeth, NY 11378

Longman Group, Ltd.
Burnt Mill
Harlow, Essex CM20 2JE

Macmillan Education, Ltd.
Houndmills, Basingstoke
Hands RG1 2XS England

McGraw-Hill Book Co. (UK), Ltd.
Shoppenhangers Rd.
Maidenhead, Berkshire SL6 2QL
England

McLean Company
7112 Benjamin Street
McLean, VA 22101

Microcomputer Workshops
225 Westchester Ave.
Port Chester, NY 10573

Mindscape, Inc.
3444 Dundee Rd.
Northbrook, IL 60062

Mountain Computers, Inc.
(Supertalker II)
3000 El Pueblo Rd.
Scotts Valley, CA 95066

Newbury House Publishers, Inc.
54 Church Street
Cambridge, MA 02138

NNELEC
110 bis, Avénue de Général Leclerc
93506 Pantin, France

Online Product Corporation
(DSA-120 Digital Voice Card)
20251 Century Blvd.
Germantown, MD 20874

P/H Electronics
(P/H IC-2000 Language Laboratory)
117 E. Helena St.
Dayton, OH 45404

The Professor, Inc.
4913 N.W. 2nd Terrace
Pompano Beach, FL 33064

Sensible Software, Inc.
210 S. Woodward, Suite 229
Birmingham, MI 48011

Sharp Electronic Corporation
Sharp Plaza
Mahwah, NJ 07430-1215

Sierra-on-Line, Inc.
36575 Mudge Ranch Road
Coarsegold, CA 93614

Sliwa Enterprises, Inc.
2360-J George Washington Highway
Yorktown, PA 23692

Sony Corporation of America
9 W. 59th St.
New York, NY 10019

Speech, Ltd.
(ProTalker)
3790 El Camino Real, Suite 213
Palo Alto, CA 94366

Springboard Software, Inc.
7808 Creekbridge Cir.
Minneapolis, MN 55435

Street Electronics
1140 Mark Ave.
Carpinteria, CA 93013

Street Electronics
(ECHO IIb)
P.O. Box 50220
Santa Barbara, CA 93150

Styleware, Inc.
5250 Gulfton, Suite 2E
Houston, TX 77081

Tandberg of America
(Learning System 500, TCCR 530,
TAL 812, TAL 822)
1 Labriola Ct.
P.O. Box 58
Armonk, NY 10507

Techmar, Inc.
(Speech Master)
6625 Cochran Road
Solon, OH 44139

3M
(Optical Recording Project)
Building 225-45, 3M Center
St. Paul, MN 55419-1000

The Times Network Systems, Ltd.
P.O. Box 7
200 Gray's Inn Road
London WC1X 8EZ England

Twenty-First Century Software, Inc.
3020 Abraham Dr.
Cedar Falls, IA 50613

Unison World, Inc.
2150 Shattuck Ave., Suite 907
Berkeley, CA 94704

University of Aberdeen
(Language Laboratory)
Regent's Walk
King's College
Aberdeen AB9 2UB Scotland

University of Pennsylvania
Language Analysis Project
(Delta)
440 Williams Hall
Philadelphia, PA 19104-6301

Victor Technologies, Inc.
(Audio Tool for Victor 9000)
380 El Pueblo Drive
Scotts Valley, CA 95066

Votrax, Inc.
(Personal Speech Synthesizer)
1394 Rankin
Troy, MI 48089

Webster/McGraw-Hill
Computer Marketing, 28th Floor
1221 Avenue of the Americas
New York, NY 10124-0025

Wicat Systems
1875 S. State St.
Orem, UT 84057

Wida Software, Ltd.
2 Nicholas Gardens
London W5 5HY England

Index to
Persons Cited

Index to
Topics and Programs Cited

NTC PROFESSIONAL MATERIALS

ACTFL Review

Published annually in conjunction with the American Council on the Teaching of Foreign Languages

Professional Resources

For further information or a current catalog, write:
National Textbook Company
a division of NTC Publishing Group